Action against child labour

Action against child labour

Edited by Nelien Haspels and Michele Jankanish

International Labour Office Geneva

Haspels, N.; Jankanish, M. (eds.)
Action against child labour
Geneva, International Labour Office, 2000

Child labour, role of ILO, IPEC, plan of action, government policy, developing country. 14.02.2
ISBN 92-2-110868-6

ILO Cataloguing-in-Publication Data

For more information contact:

Labour Protection Department
4 route des Morillons
CH-1211 Geneva 22
Switzerland
Tel.:   (+41 22) 799-6486
Fax: (+41-22) 799-6349
E-mail: travail@ilo.org

International Programme on the Elimination of Child Labour (IPEC)
4 route des Morillons
CH-1211 Geneva 22
Switzerland
(+41-22)799-8181
(+41-22)799-8771
ipec@ilo.org

Child labour website:http://www.ilo.org/childlabour
(French and Spanish versions also available)

Graphic design and printing by the International Training Centre of the ILO, Turin Italy

PREFACE

This book is a response to the need for comprehensive and practical information on planning and carrying out action against child labour. It is based primarily on ILO experience, particularly its International Programme on the Elimination of Child Labour (IPEC). It is designed to assist governments, employers' and workers' organizations, non-governmental organizations, and all those who wish to contribute to the elimination of child labour.

The book addresses the strategies, instruments, methodologies and information necessary to plan and carry out effective action. It also highlights particular kinds of exploitation, such as child slavery, and suggests strategies for preventing and eliminating them. It makes it clear that comprehensive approaches are required for sustained success. Unilateral and uncoordinated efforts in the past have sometimes worsened the situation of the very children who were meant to be helped.

This publication is particularly timely as the member States of the ILO adopted a new Convention and Recommendation concerning the prohibition and immediate action for the elimination of the worst forms of child labour in June 1999. The Convention requires States to design and implement programmes of action to remove children from intolerable situations and provide for their rehabilitation and reintegration. It is hoped that this book will guide and inspire such action.

I would like to acknowledge and express my appreciation to the authors of each of the chapters of this book, who brought a range of knowledge and experience to the task. Nelien Haspels, Michele Jankanish and Victoria Rialp oversaw the entire project. Peter Tallon provided editorial assistance. I thank them all.

It is my sincere wish that the ideas in this book will lead to wider and more effective action in the fight against child labour.

Kari Tapiola,
Executive Director,
Standards and Fundamental Principles
and Rights at Work Sector,
International Labour Office

CONTENTS

1   National policies and programmes
Guy Thijs

2   Towards improved legislation
Michele Jankanish

3

Improving the knowledge base on child labour

Kebebew Ashagrie

4   Alternatives to child labour

Nelien Haspels, Feny de los Angeles-Bautista and Victoria Rialp

7   Trade unions against child labour
Satoru Tabusa

8   Awareness-raising
Sherin Khan

9 Action by community groups and NGOs

Pin Boonpala

10 Resources on child labour

List of boxes

List of charts

National policies and programmes

1

Guy Thijs

INTRODUCTION

The issue of child labour has long been viewed with a mixture of indifference and scepticism, but in the last decade the situation has changed dramatically. Child labour has been attracting growing attention both within countries and at the international level, and has emerged as the single most important source of child exploitation and abuse in the world today. As a result of growing awareness of the issue and the recognition that the use of child labour is not conducive to promoting long-term economic development, a large number of countries are attempting to eliminate it. The 1990s have witnessed an unprecedented number of countries adopting national policies and programmes on child labour.

What is the best response to child labour? Should actions focus on improving and enforcing child labour laws, on promoting compulsory education, or both? Are there other methods which might be as effective? Too often the problem of child labour is confronted in a piecemeal and scattered fashion, as a series of separate issues rather than as a whole. It cannot be repeated enough that child labour needs to be tackled in a multi-pronged fashion on all fronts: economic, educational, social and cultural. Moreover, as financial and human resource constraints exist, it is of utmost importance to make optimal use of them. Coherent national policies and programmes of action against the exploitation of children, clearly establishing objectives, setting priorities and providing the necessary resources to ensure implementation, are therefore a crucial starting-point for any meaningful action.

This chapter highlights effective strategies against child labour to facilitate the development of comprehensive national policies and programmes and to provide guidance on their formulation and implementation. Section 1.1 gives an overview of strategies which have proved effective. Section 1.2 introduces the topic of policies, programmes and projects and discusses the process leading to their adoption. Section 1.3 looks into the key features of national policies, programmes and projects and gives examples of how to set priorities for action. Finally, section 1.4 considers a number of questions related to implementing policies and programmes on child labour, in particular the role of society in ensuring that policy commitments are being met, as well as coordinating and accountability mechanisms. Appendices are included on terms of reference for a report on child labour, group work in national planning workshops, and project design.

1.1 STRATEGIC ACTION AGAINST CHILD LABOUR

Many of the ILO's member States have taken up the challenge to combat child labour because the future of young people and hence of society itself is at stake.

The problem

Many children in almost all societies work in one way or another, although the types of work they do and the forms and conditions of their involvement vary among societies and over time. Children's participation in certain types of light work, such as helping parents care for the home and family for short periods in the day, or teenagers working for a few hours before or after school or during holidays to earn pocket money, is considered to be part of growing up for boys and girls and a means of acquiring basic survival and practical skills. This increases their self-worth and confidence and enables them to contribute to the well-being both of themselves and their families. But this is not child labour.

Child labour includes both paid and unpaid work and activities that are mentally, physically, socially or morally dangerous and harmful to children. It is work that deprives them of opportunities for schooling or that requires them to assume the multiple burdens of schooling and work at home and in other workplaces; and work that enslaves them and separates them from their family. This is what is meant by child labour – work carried out to the detriment and endangerment of the child, in violation of international law and national legislation.

Prevention, removal and rehabilitation

If the problem of child labour is to be resolved, governments must not limit their interventions – as most of them have done so far – to the enactment of protective legislation and timid monitoring of its enforcement. What is required is a well-planned and well-integrated series of *complementary measures which will be short-term, medium-term or long-term in nature*, depending on the urgency and magnitude of the problem in each country.

The complex problem of child labour can only be solved through concerted action in society aimed at:

◆ preventing child labour; and

◆ withdrawing children from exploitative and hazardous work, and providing alternatives to them and their families.

Prevention is the most cost-effective measure in the fight against child labour. The results of preventive measures are in many cases not immediately visible, making them less attractive in political terms. Moreover, to be more than superficial they should deal with the root causes of the problem. This may require a scrutiny of the social fabric of society and an exposure of inequalities and vested interests.

In addition, removal and rehabilitation measures are needed, aimed at withdrawing the greatest possible number of children from hazardous work situations, and providing them and their families with viable alternatives. Given that many countries do not have the infrastructure and resources to immediately undertake large-scale rescue and rehabilitation programmes for all child labourers and to enhance income generation for parents, the priorities should be the immediate abolition of the worst forms of child labour and a step-by-step time-bound national programme of action to eliminate all child labour.

As a first step, it may be necessary to start with the removal of children from hazardous and exploitative work and with the protection of working children in order to help attitudes evolve from the acceptance of child labour – as an inevitable fate for the poor – to a commitment to action against it. However, temporary measures to protect working children must be linked to concrete measures to remove them from hazardous work. Otherwise, protective measures tend to perpetuate the practice.

Priority target groups

Although the immediate elimination of all child labour is beyond the reach of many countries, experience shows that significant progress can be achieved provided that there is the will, both at the political level and in society itself, to combat it with determination. Clear priorities must be set for national action. What should these priorities be? First and foremost, action needs to be taken against the worst forms of child labour, that is, those which constitute an infringement of human rights, such as forced labour, debt bondage and prostitution, and those which are especially prejudicial to children's safety or health. National action should be geared to the immediate prevention of such abuses and the withdrawal of children from such work.

Phased and multi-sectoral strategy

While there is a growing consensus on the goal of the total elimination of child labour, and many countries are taking steps in this direction, changes do not come about easily or quickly because child labour problems are engrained in the socio-cultural and economic structure of society. A shift of attitudes is needed among those directly concerned with the problem – children, parents and employers – and society as a whole. Policy reforms, and changes in programmes and institutional structures in key areas such as legislation, education, labour market policies, social security, health, welfare and social development are essential.

Working towards a change in societal attitudes to combat child labour and policy reform should take place simultaneously because the two are intricately related. Extensive awareness-raising and social mobilization lead to changes in attitudes about child labour, which in turn create public demand for the necessary changes in policy.

Among the types of reform, education is universally recognized as a key solution to the elimination of child labour. Improvements in educational systems are not enough, however, because the worst child labour abuses take place among the children of the poorest adults, migrants, lower classes and castes, single-headed households, indigenous people, in sum, among the most vulnerable socio-economic groups in society. These population groups can seldom afford education for their children, even if it were to be more available, relevant and less costly. Their children are sent to work because their contribution and earnings are essential for family survival. Children will continue to be put to work as long as their parents are not earning enough to take care of the family's basic needs. Therefore, interventions in education need to be accompanied by interventions in the labour market and by social protection measures, such as family support services, if programmes are to be effective and successful.

Interventions should aim at empowering the poor and abolishing social discrimination. They can include adequate child labour legislation; a strong and efficient labour inspectorate; an independent and competent judicial system; the provision of incentives to employers to refrain from utilizing child labour; assistance to workers' organizations; action by local councils and non-governmental organizations (NGOs) to fight for the replacement of child workers by adult workers, and to assume a child-watch role in workplaces and communities; the provision of income-earning opportunities to the poor through employment creation and poverty alleviation schemes; small enterprise development; minimum wage systems; credit systems and social safety nets for the most needy. These measures should address both the need for income for adults and the need for schooling for children at the design and implementation stages, so that they do not inadvertently encourage the employment of children along with or instead of adults.

It is therefore necessary to mainstream the needs of working children within broader social and economic development policies that affect children and families. It is often assumed that their needs will be addressed automatically where child or family-focused policies and programmes exist; or that where economic policies are designed to improve the economic conditions in a country, there will be a trickle-down effect that improves the lives of child labourers. But these assumptions have proved invalid in most instances. In the short term, the living conditions of child labourers may actually deteriorate when isolated interventions are implemented, such as premature or arbitrary withdrawal of children from dangerous work without appropriate support systems in place. In the long term the damage to their development is irreversible, and the vicious cycle of poverty will continue from one generation to the next. Thus, a conscious and systematic effort must be made to draw attention to their needs, and to develop appropriate and supportive policies and programmes that benefit them both in the short and the longer term.

Another important pointer in developing responses and approaches to child labour is that *they should never be formulated in isolation without regard for other related policies.* In certain countries, the objective of eliminating child labour in hazardous work has been included in a larger policy framework, for example, a National Plan of Action for Children. In other countries, considering the close links of the problem with education, poverty and unemployment, child labour has been included as an important element in national development plans (e.g. Indonesia, the Philippines and Thailand).

Experience has shown that a phased and multi-sectoral strategy is needed, consisting of the following steps:

◆ *motivating* a broad alliance of partners to acknowledge and act against child labour;

◆ carrying out a *situation analysis* to find out about child labour problems in a country;

◆ helping develop and implement national *policies* on child labour problems;

◆ *strengthening* existing organizations and setting up *institutional mechanisms*;

◆ creating *awareness* on the problem nationwide, in communities and workplaces;

◆ promoting the *development* and *application* of *protective legislation*;

◆ supporting *direct action* with (potential) child workers by providing alternatives to children and their parents;

◆ *replicating* and *expanding* successful projects in the programmes of partners; and

◆ *mainstreaming* child labour issues in socio-economic policies, programmes and budgets.

1.2 DEVELOPING POLICIES AND PROGRAMMES ON CHILD LABOUR

Why a policy on child labour?

A clear national policy against the exploitation of children is the fundamental basis and point of departure for action against child labour. The special merit of a national policy lies in the fact that it articulates societal objectives and commitments and provides a coherent framework for an associated programme of action. A national policy and programme of action on child labour should be placed in the context of national, social and economic development policies that address the larger issues of poverty, education and development.

Policies, programmes and projects

There is often a *tendency to mix the concepts of "policies", "programmes" and "projects"*. In practice the linkages between these three are not always so logical or clearly spelled out. They are, and should be, of course, closely linked. Policies, programmes and projects can be defined as follows:

◆ A **policy** on child labour is a *public commitment to work towards the elimination of child labour*, setting out objectives and priorities and identifying implementing agencies, coupled with resource provisions. The very existence of a policy commitment indicates that political leaders and civil society as a whole are committed to tackling the child labour issue with determination.

◆ Policies have to be carried out through concrete **programmes**. A comprehensive and coherent set of interventions in the field of child labour could involve programmes in areas such as:

Box 1.1. A national policy on child labour

This contains as a minimum the following elements:

◆ A definition of national objectives regarding child labour

◆ A description of the nature and context of the problem

◆ The identification and description of the priority target groups

◆ A description of the main programme areas and type of interventions to be used

◆ The designation of the institutional actors to be involved

❖ collection of information for developing priorities and monitoring progress;

❖ legislation and enforcement;

❖ education and training;

❖ health, welfare and social protection;

❖ advocacy, public-awareness raising and social mobilization; and

❖ poverty alleviation, income generation and social protection.

◆ **Projects** are the building-blocks of programmes. A project is a planned undertaking of related and coordinated activities designed to achieve certain specific objectives within a given budget and period of time. A project may often work with one target group, in a particular sector, using one or a limited range of interventions, over a short period of time. In principle, projects should never be carried out in isolation if long-lasting results are to be obtained. They should always be part of a broader programme and policy to which they make a contribution.

In some countries action against child labour starts with the development of a policy which is carried out through programmes and projects. However, small-scale projects can also be a starting point. Often, a few committed individ-uals start activities on child labour out of indignation over extreme cases of exploitation – sometimes as a reaction to the lack of action by the concerned authorities. In such cases, projects occur long before policies and programmes on child labour are in place.

National polices and programmes are usually subject to political change, and external interventions and changes in government infrastructure may lead to a wavering of the national commitment to eliminating child labour. Individual and sometimes isolated initiatives therefore remain important. Thus, *the strategic process of eliminating child labour is not straightforward. Positive trends need to be constantly reinforced and individual interventions restarted or repeated.*

ILO standards and action through IPEC

International labour standards provide a set of internationally agreed policy guidelines on the protection of children and young workers which are pragmatic and straightforward. The ILO has always stood for the effective abolition of child labour and the protection of working children. This objective is enshrined in a number of instruments, chiefly the Minimum Age Convention (No. 138) and Recommendation (No. 146), adopted in 1973. They set minimum ages for admission to work in general and to specific kinds of work in particular; and they call for and provide guidance for a national policy designed to ensure the effective abolition of child labour. Chapter 2, section 2.3, covers these instruments in detail.

For many years the ILO has been advocating the development of a national policy on child labour as a prerequisite for a successful campaign against child labour. Convention No. 138, the ILO's comprehensive instrument on the problem, explicitly calls upon countries to pursue a national policy designed to ensure the effective abolition of child labour.

Box 1.2. IPEC at a glance

The ILO's technical cooperation programme on child labour – IPEC – works towards the elimination of child labour by strengthening national capacities to address child labour problems, and by contributing to the worldwide movement to combat them.

The priority target groups are bonded child labourers, children in hazardous working conditions and occupations, and children who are particularly vulnerable, that is, very young working children (below 12 years of age) and working girls.

The political will and commitment of individual governments to address child labour in cooperation with employers' and workers' organizations, other NGOs and relevant parties in society such as universities and the media, is the starting point for all IPEC action. Sustainability is built in from the start through an emphasis on in-country "ownership". Support is given to partner organizations to develop and implement measures which aim at *preventing* child labour, *withdrawing* children from hazardous work and providing *alternatives* to them and their families.

Since its inception in 1992, the Programme has expanded tremendously. A total of 37 governments have signed a Memorandum of Understanding with the ILO committing themselves to the elimination of child labour. Preparatory activities are being carried out in 31 more countries and IPEC is supported by 23 donor agencies.

The ILO has always held the position that there are certain absolutes arising from the inherent dignity of the human person which make certain forms of child labour unacceptable. This call was vigorously reiterated at the June 1999 session of the International Labour Conference, where ILO constituents adopted new labour standards which place priority on immediate action towards eradicating the worst forms of child labour (see section 2.4). In addition, in 1998 the Conference adopted the ILO Declaration on Fundamental Principles and Rights at Work in which the abolition of child labour and the elimination of all forms of forced or compulsory labour figure prominently.

Alongside the policy guidance provided in ILO instruments on child labour, the ILO has over the years assisted various countries in developing and implementing national policies and specific programmes of action on child labour. With the advent of ILO's International Programme on the Elimination of Child Labour (IPEC), technical cooperation efforts have been stepped up.

Box 1.3. Ideas for the content of national reports on child labour

1. **Introduction**

2. **Nature and extent of child labour**

    ◆ Macro-level statistics concerning age groups in the population, enrolment in schools, those active in the labour force (estimate) and other economic activity, provincial concentrations, and so on (see Chapter 3).

    ◆ Where and in what sectors are children working, why are they working and under what conditions?

3. **National policies and institutional framework**

    ◆ Past and current policies and statements in relation to child labour – What national policies have been introduced to make school attendance compulsory, enforce labour legislation and combat child labour?

    ◆ Legal framework regulating the employment of children – Are they protected by the law? Are children working illegally? What is the gap between law and practice? Are the law and the infrastructure for its enforcement adequate to combat child labour?

    ◆ How is child labour dealt with institutionally? Who is responsible? What kind of coordination and cooperation exist?

The first steps in policy and programme formulation

Child labour problems cannot be eliminated overnight. Priorities therefore need to be established to ensure that the worst forms are dealt with first (see Chapter 2, section 2.4). Both long-term preventive measures which address the root causes of the problem, and short-term measures have to be identified to remove or protect children from unacceptable forms of child labour and to prevent other children from having to work under such conditions. This is where a policy framework on child labour becomes important. While most countries have similar problems and common concerns, there are no blueprints available that can be transposed "ready-made" from one country to another. To be effective, policies and programmes on child labour must take account of the socio-economic situation of each country: *they must be country specific and be based on a genuine commitment from within the country* to address the problem.

Policies, programmes and projects addressing child labour problems – as any other development problem – are best formulated within the framework of the programming cycle, which has four distinct interrelated phases:

◆ defining and understanding the problem;

◆ planning a course of action;

◆ **Education – What are the strengths and weaknesses of the education system and how does it relate to child labour?**

◆ **How do the social partners contribute to enforcing legislation and combating child labour?**

4. **Programmes for working children**

◆ **What governmental and non-governmental programmes are providing services and assistance to working children and how effective are they?**

◆ **What are the views and perceptions of working children on their situation and what action do they think is required to improve it?**

◆ **Are there overlaps and gaps?**

5. **Conclusions and recommendations**

◆ **National policy on child labour.**

◆ **Review of legislation.**

◆ **Education and child labour.**

◆ **Programmes of action on behalf of working children.**

◆ **Mobilization.**

More detailed terms of reference are provided in Appendix 1.1.

◆ carrying out the activities and making sure they stay on track; and

◆ assessing the effects and impact of the activities and drawing lessons for existing and future activities.

The paucity of data on child labour has contributed to a sometimes emotional debate on the subject in which some tend to downplay the magnitude of the problem, while others exaggerate it. Lack of reliable data obscures the problem and can be counterproductive when it comes to setting national priorities for action. (This topic is discussed in detail in Chapter 3.)

Therefore, one of the first steps is the preparation of a national report on child labour and the organization of one or more planning workshops. A comprehensive report on child labour provides an overall description and assessment of the child labour situation in the country. A complete law and practice review, and an overview of existing policies and programmes that directly or indirectly bear on child labour and the measures already taken to deal with the problem, are prerequisites for a successful planning workshop on child labour. The report stimulates an exchange of views among potential partners on the core problems and facilitates the development of a national policy and plan of action.

Broad consultation on the report

In preparing the overview, it is important that all relevant parties in the combat against child labour – including potential ones – are involved from the very start in the preparation and analysis of the report, to ensure that the end product includes the views of all stakeholders. Key partners are the government agencies in the labour, education, social and economic development fields, workers' and employers' organizations, and non-governmental organizations. As such the preparation of the report on child labour and the development of priorities for action during the planning workshop are a *first step in mobilizing a broad social alliance against child labour.*

In many countries, National Steering Committees or a special task force have been set up to overlook the preparation of the report. Their composition usually reflects the wide range of potential actors mentioned above.

Often, countries also organize "expert" meetings prior to the planning workshop to critically review the report and identify the major lessons that can be drawn from it. Such meetings enhance the quality and credibility of the report, and make the task of the planning workshop easier since the major issues to be discussed have been identified beforehand. The composition of the "expert" group is extremely important. The persons who make it up should be selected based on their widely recognized expertise and should not simply be representatives of a few ministries or other agencies.

Experience shows that a participatory approach to formulating a policy framework, based on sound information and involving all concerned parties, can build consensus on the real problems and priorities for action, and can be a good start for mobilizing broad public support. Over the years, the ILO has supported many countries in organizing national planning workshops on child labour. Experience also shows that a competent situation analysis, followed by the organization of one or more discussion forums or planning workshops where priority target groups of children are determined and broad fields and forms of action are outlined, can be a good start in addressing the problem systematically. The consultative forums serve as venues for formulating the policy framework and a programme of action as a collective and collaborative effort among the different sectors involved.

Box 1.4. The right number of participants

IPEC experience shows that there is in fact no binding formula as far as the number of participants is concerned. In some countries national conferences attended by over 150 participants turned out to be effective forums to develop national programmes of action (Indonesia). Yet in other countries the programme of action was developed by a core group of experts and only later on presented to, and endorsed by, a larger, more representative audience (Thailand). There are also examples where the development of a national programme of action is a consensus-building process starting at community level, followed by provincial consultations and finally leading to a national consensus (Brazil).

Organization of multi-sectoral forums for discussion

After collecting and compiling sound information, multi-sectoral forums are conducted to discuss the national report, and to reflect on the strengths and weaknesses of existing policies and programmes in addressing child labour. Meticulous preparations are made for these meetings. A wide array of participants are invited, with careful thought given to what represents the optimal number, as meetings that are too large are not always productive. The appropriate level of the participants and adequate representation of the different regions in the country should be seriously considered. Appropriate facilities, for example, concerning meeting-room sizes for plenary as well as group work, facilitate productive interaction. Appendix 1.2 provides practical tools and ideas for group work in planning workshops on child labour aimed at identifying priority target groups, core problems and strategies for action.

1.3 SETTING PRIORITIES FOR ACTION

Especially vulnerable groups

Although a policy on child labour should aim at the abolition of all child labour, *flagrant cases of child abuse require priority attention.* That is why IPEC participating countries have started to place priority on children that are particularly vulnerable.

In the June 1999 session of the International Labour Conference, ILO member States adopted a new Convention concerning immediate action for the elimination of the worst forms of child labour (see Chapter 2, section 2.4). The worst forms of child labour which should be eliminated as a priority, are:

◆ all forms of slavery or practices similar to slavery, such as the sale and trafficking of children, debt bondage and serfdom and forced or compulsory labour, including the forced recruitment of children for use in armed conflict;

◆ the use, procuring or offering of a child for prostitution, for the production of pornography or for pornographic performances;

◆ the use, procuring or offering of a child for illicit activities, in particular for the production and trafficking of drugs; and

◆ work which, by its nature or the circumstances in which it is carried out, is likely to harm the health, safety or morals of children.

The difficulties in identifying and locating the children in such situations needs to be recognized: often they are deliberately held captive, isolated and with no access to information and services. In addition, there remain many ambiguities in defining hazardous work. While it is fairly easy to agree on child labour which constitutes a serious violation of human rights, it may be more difficult to define the particularly dangerous occupations and industries. There are, in fact, countless work situations that are liable to seriously harm the physical integrity of children (underground work in mines, work in the construction industry, handling pesticides and so on). In other instances, the work is not intrinsically hazardous but becomes so as a result of the poor conditions under which it is carried out (intense heat or cold, dust and fumes, long working hours, and sexual or other harassment).

Box 1.5. The Philippines – ILO action against the most exploitative and hazardous forms of child labour

During a national planning workshop in the Philippines in 1994, it was recognized that priorities should be set within sectors or occupations which pose a direct danger of physical or emotional injury to the children employed. Within a time frame of two to five years, the following groups were identified for priority action:

◆ children who are the victims of trafficking;

◆ children employed in mining and quarrying;

◆ children in home-based industries, especially under subcontracting arrangements; and

◆ children trapped in prostitution.

Main policy and programme directions

Effective policies on child labour go beyond mere statements. A strong declaration – in which child labour is denounced and a firm commitment made to address the problem – creates the facilitating policy environment for the implementation of *concrete programmes*. For a concrete example of a recently formulated national programme of action, see Appendix 1.3.

Major programme areas

In general, there are four major programme areas that can be distinguished:

❶ Finding out about child labour

The ILO Bureau of Statistics has developed a statistical survey methodology to assist countries in improving their knowledge base on child labour (see Chapter 3). Statistical, sample-based surveys can be very useful in providing a broad picture of the situation in the country, and in highlighting provincial or sectoral variations and gender differences in the child labour situation of a given country. More in-depth studies are useful to identify children in dangerous, exploitative and often clandestine work. Assistance has also been provided for research on specific groups of problems, for example, to the international NGO, Anti-Slavery International, concerning child domestic workers, a group of children especially difficult to reach.[1]

---

[1] Anti-Slavery International (ASI): *Child domestic workers, A handbook for research and action.* (London, 1997).

② Awareness-raising and social mobilization

The overall objective of awareness-raising is a broad social movement against child labour. Indifference towards the suffering of working children needs to change. With such efforts, countries are beginning to see putting an end to child labour not simply as a problem but a solution to poverty and underdevelopment. The importance of awareness-raising as a vital component of any national programme on child labour is now widely recognized (see Chapter 8).

Campaigns against child labour using traditional media (television, newspapers, etc.) can be very useful in reaching the urban upper and middle class and policy-makers, but other innovative or traditional communication channels are also effective to reach children, parents, employers and communities directly involved. Teachers in particular can play key roles, as has been demonstrated in many countries. In others, religious leaders have been instrumental in changing attitudes and opinions on child labour. One of the spin-offs of awareness-raising campaigns, at the national and international levels, is that they have mobilized new partners. Children and their families are, of course, the first line of defence, and fostering greater awareness of the issues among them, as well as better organization and increased participation in efforts to address the problem, are crucial.

③ Protective legislation

Although insufficient on its own, legislation remains a powerful instrument for governments to combat child labour. Child labour legislation can serve as a deterrent when the penalties for offenders are severe and enforcement rigorous. Although the situation has improved in recent years, there are still many countries where penalties are too mild and ineffective considering the gravity of the crimes involved, and few offenders have been convicted under the laws.

From the perspective of prevention there are a number of simple cost-effective measures that can go a long way. Children, parents, communities and even small-scale employers are not always aware of the relevant laws and regulations. Simple, targeted campaigns at the community level, where parents and children are made aware of their legal rights, can have a substantial impact. The translation of relevant Acts and regulations into local languages or dialects has proved useful. Labour inspectors can also play an important role by providing advice and guidance to employers on how to comply with the law.

Chapter 2 deals in detail with national legislation on child labour.

④ Prevention and removal of children from work and provision of alternatives to families

Children at risk of being engaged in child labour need to be prevented from entering work and children already working under exploitative and hazardous conditions need to be withdrawn from work. Both groups need to be provided with viable alternatives (see Chapter 4, section 4.3). As regards removal programmes, care needs to be taken, however, that such measures do not drive the children into clandestine jobs or result in their taking up other demeaning or dangerous work. Prevention and removal programmes usually consist of three interrelated components:

◆ providing education and training to children combined with rehabilitation services if they are traumatized because of the work situation;

◆ developing integrated programmes for disadvantaged population groups who resort to or are prone to utilizing child labour, combining education for children with functional literacy training and education, income-earning opportunities and social safety nets for their families; and

◆ providing information and establishing a workplace or community child-watch or monitoring system to ensure that other children do not enter the vacated jobs.

Education and training

Children at school are less likely to be in full-time employment. On the other hand, children with no access to education have little alternative but to enter the labour market and often perform work that is dangerous and exploitative. Education, as well as skills training, clearly helps prevent and reduce child labour as:

◆ children with basic education and skills have better chances in the labour market; they are aware of their rights and are less likely to accept hazardous work and exploitative working conditions; and

◆ educational opportunities could wean working children away from hazardous and exploitative work, and help them find better alternatives.

Countries that are serious about eliminating child labour make major efforts to provide quality education that is relevant, accessible and free for all children. However, ILO experience shows that even in countries where substantial progress has been made and average school enrolment ratios are high, there are still children from poor population groups who do not benefit from this progress. This suggests that, apart from general improvements in the education system, special measures are often necessary to increase the access to education for children who are especially vulnerable, such as children at risk of working who are not able to continue formal education and training, so that they do not re-enter the labour market as unskilled workers. The younger children may require skills that are useful in improving the quality of life and can be developed further, while the older children generally require vocational counselling and practical training that can lead to income generation either through wage labour or self-employment in a broad array of employable skills.

Rehabilitation

Children who stop working often need assistance in various areas. Some children have been hurt because they were bonded, have been prostituted, or are living and working on the streets without their families or any stable social environment. They might, for example, be suffering from emotional and psychological trauma, occupational diseases, sexually transmitted diseases or malnutrition, or they may be completely illiterate. They therefore require special assistance from social workers, paediatricians and psychologists, and they need lawyers who can give intensive follow-up, counselling and often legal aid. Although the cost of rehabilitation programmes is very high – and many countries lack the infrastructure – they are vital if former child workers are to be satisfactorily reintegrated into society and the school system.

Integrated programmes for children and parents

The impact of programmes which may not specifically address children but bear on the causes of poverty and inequality can have a significant impact on the incidence and extent of child labour. In general, efforts made by governments to *promote economic growth* and, even more importantly, growth that focuses on the most disadvantaged population groups by facilitating their access to productive and adequately paid employment, and/or by affording a minimum of social protection, reduce the economic need for child labour.

As stated earlier, national programmes on child labour should be directly linked to specific programmes on poverty alleviation and other socio-economic development. Surprisingly, many programmes with tremendous potential for reducing child labour have been implemented without such links, thus diminishing their potential impact. Much more could be achieved if the concern to tackle child labour, in particular its more extreme forms, had been built in from the start. Therefore, child labour concerns need to be built into major development efforts in the field of poverty alleviation, health, nutrition, welfare and social protection. Much can also be achieved by ensuring that these development efforts target those local communities and groups in society which rely heavily on child labour for survival.

Chapter 4 covers strategies for education, training and rehabilitation for child workers and their families.

Box 1.6. Poverty alleviation and child labour in Indonesia

In December 1993, the Government of Indonesia launched a nationwide poverty alleviation programme in the so-called backward villages. The programme covered close to 30 villages and each of them received working capital of about US$25,000 as a revolving fund to generate productive economic activities. It was assumed that since poverty was the greatest force driving children into employment for their own survival, all measures to alleviate poverty would solve also the problem of child labour. The case was, however, not that straightforward. A study undertaken by IPEC showed that instead of withdrawing children from work, the programme in some cases led to their withdrawal from school into all sorts of activities to support enterprises developed by the families. A programme component was subsequently developed to integrate child labour concerns into the poverty-alleviation programme. Motivators that have been appointed to facilitate the implementation of the programme are being trained on child labour issues. They identify working children of families participating in the programme that qualify for various governmental and non-governmental educational support schemes or mobilize local resources for that purpose.

Workplace and community monitoring system

When children are withdrawn from work, systematic efforts need to be made to ensure that workplaces and communities remain child labour free. This means first of all that awareness-raising activities should not be limited to the children and parents, but extended to all groups involved: employers, managers and adult workers in workplaces, community leaders and service providers. In a second stage, monitoring mechanisms need to be set up to ensure that the children withdrawn from work remain and complete school and that new children do not enter work. This can be done by establishing a monitoring system in the schools or educational centres, in the workplaces and in the communities where children live (see section 4.4).

Box 1.7. Workplace monitoring

The commitment to eliminate child labour in a few selected industries can be a useful starting point to address child labour practice in other sectors. Successful measures in tackling child labour in certain occupations can have a multiplier effect that will benefit children working in other dangerous work. This is because as soon as population groups – and eventually whole societies – start focusing on the dangers of premature work of children in one sector or geographical area, broad discussion of the acceptability and unacceptability of different forms of child labour in general will follow.

IPEC has devised and implemented comprehensive and effective monitoring and verification systems in a number of countries to ensure that factories and their subcontractors do not employ children under the age of 14. Child labour monitors under the Programme inspect the factories regularly through surprise visits. IPEC's core strategy has proved valid and valuable in workplace monitoring programmes both in the formal sector (for example, the garment industry in Bangladesh) and in the rural informal sector (for example, the football industry in Sialkot, Pakistan).

Direct action and capacity building

Experience indicates that while it may be relatively easy to achieve the initial task of formulating a national policy and programme of action, the next step of ensuring that intentions are translated into practice is more difficult. Projects working directly with children, families, employers and communities, or those that aim at strengthening the capacity of organizations to improve their service delivery to children and families, can provide that link. Action against child labour is relatively recent, and experimental smaller-scale projects are needed to demonstrate in practice that the situation of children can be improved and that they can be removed from hazardous work. Thus, projects provide a basis for wider application and adjustments in programmes and policies dealing with the problem. This type of intervention – whether it is called pilot projects, action programmes, or sub-projects – should, however, never be carried out in isolation. It should always be part of a broader programme to which it makes a contribution. Since projects have an important demonstration and learning function, their design, relevance and feasibility are extremely important. Pointers on project formulation and design are given in Appendix 1.4.

Organizing action against child labour and coordinating measures between the various bodies require the development of expertise and the establishment of institutional mechanisms with the necessary powers to promote and increase public initiatives, both at the national and local levels. Creating institutional capacity to cope with child labour problems is a long-term task.

IPEC experience in this regard is worth noting. It has encouraged the setting up of National Steering Committees on child labour to identify appropriate measures and the organizations responsible for implementing them. These Committees, usually chaired by the minister responsible for labour affairs, include representatives from other concerned ministries, national employers' and workers' organizations and NGOs with expertise in advocacy on children's rights. They are often the stepping-stones towards an institutional mechanism allowing high-level authorities from various backgrounds to collectively examine the issue of child labour. These committees have done much to promote the exchange of experience, eliminate bottlenecks, share successes and forge bonds among the members. Another strategy by key partner organizations is setting up focal points or coordinating units to ensure the smooth implementation of work.

Another positive development has been the increased involvement at provincial and community level of provincial authorities, local community leaders, parents, teachers, and also the working children themselves. In some cases this has brought about the organization of local mechanisms that can undertake action and provide resources and services in the fight against child labour. These councils or committees perform community-watch functions. They also provide vital information on working children, for example the incidence of trafficking and active recruitment of working children.

1.4 CREATING A BROAD SOCIAL ALLIANCE

The need for a broad consultation prior to and during the planning process has been underlined. The importance of raising the level of social concern cannot be overstated, for experience over many years and from around the world clearly demonstrates that significant public pressure is often required to make progress on the child labour issue (see Chapter 9). Strong domestic pressure to ensure that policies and programmes on child labour do not remain merely good intentions is crucial to success. In addition, there is a distinct need for organization and coordination. Indeed, child labour seems to be a matter for everyone and no one. In the public sector, the measures taken by a small number of ministries or other institutions seem few and far between and rarely connected. In the private sector, organizations frequently work in a dispersed way and sometimes in competition with each other.

Box 1.8. Social mobilization in Brazil

An important step in eliminating child labour was taken with the establishment in Brazil of the National Forum for the Prevention and Eradication of Child Labour. The Forum, coordinated by the Ministry of Labour, is composed of 36 institutions, representing the federal government, employers' and workers' organizations and NGOs. The Forum's mandate is to exchange views and experiences, creating a broad social alliance and securing the base of support for policy and programme implementation. The Forum plays an important role in synthesizing actions and mobilizing various social forces capable of intervening in risky situations, by allocating technical and financial resources to implement projects in the areas of education, health, social assistance, income generation, and so on.

The Forum sets priorities for action in geographical areas and in economic sectors (charcoal, sisal, sugarcane), where child labour is rampant, and promotes the development and implementation of multi-sectoral programmes. It coordinates policy and programme efforts at the federal, state and municipal levels. Integrated Action Programmes are implemented by both the government and civil society, and state, regional and municipal commissions are responsible for coordinating and monitoring these programmes.

The importance of *government commitment* and active involvement in efforts to address the problem cannot be overemphasized. The attitude of governments to the needs and rights of children is decisive for the protection and the promotion of children's welfare. A positive trend in this respect is the wide range of governmental agencies that are now actively involved in concerted efforts to deal with the problem. No longer is child labour seen as the sole responsibility of labour and/or social welfare ministries. Others, especially the ministries of education, ministries and departments dealing with youth, the family, media and health, and central coordinating units, such as national planning commissions and Prime Ministers' Offices, are becoming increasingly involved. A very positive trend has also been the increased involvement of government institutions at the provincial and municipal levels.

Workers' and employers' organizations are also among the key players in combating child labour. Workers' organizations are increasingly involved (see Chapter 7). They are especially well placed to advocate the rights of children to adequate education while at the same time asserting the rights of adult workers to adequate remuneration, thereby reducing the dependence of poor families on child labour. *Employers' organizations* have not remained silent in the emerging movement against child labour (see Chapter 6). Dozens of companies in industrialized countries have adopted codes of conduct to demonstrate their commitment against the use of child workers. *Non-governmental organizations* have long played an important role in addressing the problem and pressuring governments to pay attention to it. The attitude of many of these organizations used to be confrontational, exposing what they considered to be inaction by government. The situation, however, has changed tremendously in recent years, with foes often becoming allies. In several countries, partnerships have emerged between governmental and non-governmental organizations, including employers' and workers' organizations, in addressing the problem. While each partner has its own strengths and weaknesses, the secret of success is to arrive at a formula which builds on each other's work and achievements. Much of the increased pressure for action on child labour can be attributed to this growing social movement.

Box 1.9. From community action to the provincial plan in the north of Thailand

In the northern provinces of Thailand, the prevention of child labour and children in prostitution is no longer an action taken by one or two small NGOs, but a joint effort by all concerned. Children, parents, teachers, local government bodies and NGOs all join hands in a concerted effort against the recruitment of young girls for prostitution and other forms of child labour, a situation which has resulted in many children becoming victims of slave-like practices in recent years. Preventive action is as follows:

Action by NGOs

Because NGOs play an important role in monitoring the problem at community level, IPEC supports them in carrying out campaigns and educational and vocational training programmes aimed at preventing children from being lured into prostitution.

The role of youth

Over the years the beneficiaries have been trained to become defenders of their own rights. They have travelled through villages with puppet shows, drama performances and exhibitions which disseminate information against child trafficking, prostitution and other exploitative forms of child labour. Communities, parents and children are informed about dangers and risks, as well as alternatives to exploitative labour. The entire village is thus mobilized to fight prostitution and to seek better opportunities for their children.

Teachers and schools

Primary school teachers and school authorities are mobilized to function as campaign centres against the problem, and teachers are trained to identify girls at high risk of being trafficked.

Coordinating and networking

While promoting the roles of the various key actors, the programme also calls for greater cooperation between them. A working group was set up, including representatives of provincial academic institutions, schools, provincial labour and welfare offices, and NGOs. The working group met on a regular basis to review progress, examine the obstacles and devise strategies to overcome them. In addition, through this coordination mechanism, a study on child labour, child trafficking and children in prostitution at the provincial level was conducted.

Appendix 1.1   Terms of reference for a comprehensive report on child labour

Extent and nature of the problem

◆ **Trends in the extent and distribution of child labour**

❖ general overview and context;

❖ macro-level statistics on the number, proportion and gender composition of children in the labour force, including a critical review of the comprehensiveness and quality of the data and information available (e.g. especially who and what is excluded);

❖ geographical distribution of working children, especially urban and rural;

❖ distribution of working children by economic sector (e.g. large-scale agriculture, small family holdings, mines, industries, manufacturing, services) and by formal and informal sectors;

❖ trends: changes in the number, proportion, composition and distribution of child workers; and

❖ evidence from other economic and social information.

◆ **Characteristics of child labour**

❖ occupations or activities carried out by children, including important differences by age and gender;

❖ context in which work is carried out (e.g. employed, independent, paid or unpaid family helper);

❖ nature of work (e.g. skilled, unskilled, monotonous, strenuous, hazardous);

❖ conditions under which work is carried out (e.g. hours of work; remuneration; type and nature of contract such as temporary, casual or permanent, apprenticeship);

❖ working environment (home, family, factory, fields, bars, streets, etc.); and

❖ dangers to which children are exposed while working, for example: dangers to health and physical development; risk of injury or accidents (workshops, construction, household, city streets); dangers to mental development (isolation, as in cattle herding and domestic services); interference with schooling (monotonous, repetitive, unskilled work); and dangers to moral development (work in bars and night clubs; prostitution; drug trade); violence on the streets (physical and sexual abuse).

Report the results, if any, of the implications of work on the child's health, and physical and mental development. However, programmes of action cannot attempt to deal with all aspects of the problem at the same time and priorities have to be set. Some types of work have more damaging effects than others. The analysis, in this section, of the consequences of child labour practices would help determine where to begin and which children should be the priority target groups.

◆ **Causes of child labour**

❖ economic and labour market trends (e.g. recent developments that may have increased the demand for child labour in certain occupations or sectors, retrenchment due to structural adjustment, precarious employment, piece-rates);

❖ importance of income earned by children (e.g. to support self or family, finance schooling);

❖ schooling unavailable or inadequate (no access to schooling, poor quality of education, family values – see below);

❖ traditions, culture and social beliefs; and

❖ criminal inducement.

Government policies

Policies may be stated through, for example:

❖ legislation;

❖ public commitment to adhere to guidelines established in international conventions (ILO child labour Conventions, United Nations Convention on the Rights of the Child, World Charter on Education for All, etc.);

❖ official statements made in Parliament (bills debated) or as reflected in the press;

❖ relevant policy objectives specified in national and provincial development plans, and the like; and

❖ specific child labour policies.

Have these policies been translated into action? If so, what are the results?

◆ Ratification of international conventions and regional legal instruments

List the international conventions ratified by the government which have a bearing on child labour and have implications for national legislation (e.g. ILO Conventions and the United Nations Convention on the Rights of the Child). It might be useful to refer to any regional charters adopted which include provisions on child labour.

◆ National legislation

Provisions in the Constitution, legislation, government decrees, administrative rules and regulations, legal interpretations and customary law relevant to child labour, to determine the following:

❖ the age of admission to employment or work, including light work and hazardous work; scope of application; exceptions; definition of light work and hazardous work, etc.;

❖ the age of completion of compulsory education;

❖ special provisions to protect children's health and safety (e.g. limits on working hours, prohibition of heavy work, limits on exposure to hazardous substances, etc.); and

❖ inadequacies and gaps in existing legislation (ambiguities, sectors or occupations not covered, e.g. in domestic service, informal sector activities, etc.). The ILO standards on child labour, in particular the Minimum Age Convention, 1973 (No. 138), and the Worst Forms of Child Labour Convention, 1999 (No. 182), will provide a good basis for such an assessment.

◆ Enforcement of legislation

Institutional framework for the implementation and administration of legislation, in particular the following:

❖ the gap between legislation and practice;

❖ the role of the labour inspectorate and law enforcement in reporting on child labour practices and violations of the law, and of administrative and judicial systems in applying penalties and remedies in cases of reported violations;

❖ the role of employers' and workers' organizations in enforcing legislation concerning working children;

❖ institutional structures for tripartite (government, employers' and workers' organizations), community and NGO consultation and participation in enforcing child labour legislation; and

❖ gaps and shortcomings in the existing infrastructure (e.g. adequacy of the labour inspectorate in terms of available resources, trained personnel, etc.).

◆ **Educational achievements**

Describe, and if possible support with statistics, the following:

❖ enrolment figures and ratios distinguishing, if possible, between urban and rural, boys and girls, and indicating the number of hours per day children spend in class and the number of weeks per year that schools function;

❖ drop-out rates of children (if possible, by gender and urban-rural differences), and reasons for dropping out of school;

❖ availability of schools and teachers, distinguishing, if possible, between urban and rural, and indications of relative quality; and

❖ the role and efficacy of the school inspection system in controlling enrolment, attendance and quality of education.

◆ **Cost of education**

The real cost of education:

❖ tuition, if any, for primary and secondary education, whether formally or informally charged;

❖ other costs of schooling (e.g. levies, meals, uniforms, transport, books);

❖ government assistance schemes, if any, that help poor families meet or offset the cost of schooling (e.g. scholarships, school meals, subsidies for uniforms); and

❖ coverage and effectiveness of such schemes, especially in regions where child labour is prevalent.

◆ **Educational policies**

Evaluate the progress towards free universal basic education:

❖ expanding free primary education and targeting underdeveloped regions;

❖ improving the quality of education;

❖ promoting alternative or supplementary schooling for underprivileged or working children and for school drop-outs; and

❖ promoting non-formal education and training schemes for school drop-outs and child workers.

Targeted programmes

This section should review programmes of action by government or by NGOs that have an impact on working children. Some of these may be aimed especially at preventing child labour or removing children from hazardous occupations, and providing them and their families with alternatives in the form of training, complementary or non-formal education, shelter, nutrition, and/or income-earning opportunities. Others may aim to mobilize public opinion, organize community support or take an advocacy role on behalf of working children, including street children. In other cases, child labour may not be explicitly mentioned, but the programmes may have a (potential) impact on child labour, for example, those dealing with poverty alleviation, employment promotion or social protection.

◆ **Government programmes**

Description and assessment of programmes, as well as the institutional arrangements for coordination.

◆ **Programmes of NGOs, and employers' and workers' organizations**

❖ background (how and why the programme started, by whom and when, and what major changes have been made over time?);

❖ structure (how the programme is set up, how many centres/offices does it have and where?);

❖ target group (whom do they reach, how many benefit?);

❖ main objectives, strategies and activities;

❖ support (who supports the programme technically and financially, how much use is made of volunteers?) and links to the government; and

❖ results (how effective it is in reaching its goals and the impact, if any, it has on the children who participate or are otherwise to benefit).

Where possible, provide an evaluation of the overall impact of these programmes on the child labour problem.

◆ **Awareness-raising and community mobilization**

❖ level of awareness among the public about the incidence of child labour, legislation on child labour, the plight of working children, the dangers they are exposed to and the need to combat it; and

❖ activities undertaken to mobilize public opinion and community action in favour of working children.

Conclusions and recommendations

On the basis of the main findings of the report, an attempt should be made to present recommendations as to how the situation could be improved. The views of knowledgeable people or of a reference group should be taken into consideration. These recommendations would be used to facilitate the discussion at the national planning workshop (see Appendix 1.2).

The following questions could be considered:

1. Is the knowledge base concerning the nature and extent of child labour in the country sufficient to understand the problems and causes of the phenomenon? If not, what should be done to improve the information available on the subject? Are "hidden" child workers (e.g. domestics, farm and informal sector workers) identified and their situation understood? Which children are most at risk and deserve priority attention?

2. Do past and present public policies show a strong commitment on the part of the government, and of society in general, to reducing the incidence of child labour? How can the measures adopted so far be made more effective? What should be the priorities and which government ministries, departments or institutions should be responsible for implementing such policies? Are there any income-generating, training and welfare programmes for families and communities aimed at relieving the pressure for children to work?

3. Is the legal framework sufficiently clear and comprehensive to effectively combat child labour practices and protect the rights of children to healthy physical and mental development? If not, what measures should be taken to improve clarity and coverage? What needs to be done to make the enforcement machinery more effective and to narrow the gap between legislation and practice, especially for children not easily reached (e.g. in agriculture, domestic service, the informal sector)? How can employer and worker, and community involvement be improved?

4.   How effective is the education system in providing all children with access to good-quality schooling? What can be done to expand the system and encourage working children to attend school or alternatively to provide them with the education and training they need to improve their income-earning opportunities in the future? How can out-of-school working children who have not completed their basic education best be reached through educational services?

5.   Which ministry or government department should take the lead and coordinate child labour activities? Which other ministries should be involved? How can NGO programmes on behalf of working children be strengthened? How can cooperation and collaboration between government and NGOs be improved? What should be done to increase awareness of the public at large and to mobilize community support for action aiming at the elimination of child labour and the protection of working children?

Appendix 1.2 Ideas for group work in national planning workshops on child labour

Experience shows that a "participatory approach" in formulating a policy framework, based on sound information and involving all concerned parties, can be a good consensus-building exercise to determine the priority target groups, the real nature of the problem and appropriate interventions. Participatory workshops focus on work in small groups, rather than long presentations of speakers, to enable all participants to share their experience and give their input.

The workshop agenda usually consists of a number of panel presentations, plenary discussions on key topics related to child labour, and more detailed discussions in small groups on the priority target groups, the core problems and the main strategies to address child labour, for example, in the main programme areas: 1) policy, legislation and law enforcement; 2) education; 3) advocacy and awareness-raising; and 4) social welfare and protection. Each group formulates a set of recommendations on the main programme area assigned to it. The results of the group work are subsequently discussed in plenary and provide the basis for the National Plan of Action on Child Labour.

Some ideas for leading the discussions in each work group are given below.[2]

Group work 1:

Priority target groups – analysis of the target groups and all other persons and agencies participating and involved in the problem.

- ✓ ask workshop participants to discuss all interest groups and organizations that are involved or may be affected by the problem (working children, parents of working children, employers, government agencies, NGOs, etc.);

- ✓ classify all groups involved and determine: 1) the priority target groups, i.e. children engaged or prone to be involved in hazardous and/or exploitative work and working conditions; 2) the intermediate partner groups, such as parents, employers and community leaders; 3) organizations who are or might be mobilized in combating child labour; 4) the strengths and weaknesses of these organizations; and 5) potential supporters and opponents; and

- ✓ discuss with the participants whose interests and views are to be given priority and determine priority target groups for action. This should lead to the second step and the question: "What are the core problems?".

Group work 2:

Problem analysis – identification of core problems, their causes and effects

- ✓ ask all participants to identify one problem which they deem to be the core problem in the main programme area assigned to the group;

- ✓ participants explain their choice and in the subsequent discussions try to agree on a single core problem, its main causes and effects (chart A1.1).

---

[2] There are, of course, various methods that can be used to facilitate the process of developing a plan of action. In many of the planning workshops on child labour supported by ILO-IPEC, variations of the ZOPP (Goal Oriented Planning for Projects) method were used. ZOPP was originally developed by the national aid agency, Deutsche Gesellschaft für Technische Zusammenarbeit (GTZ), Germany.

Chart A1.1. Problem analysis

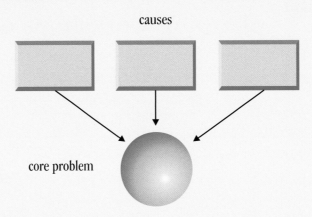

The main causes for the core problem are placed in a parallel line above the core problem.

The main effects of the core problem are placed in a parallel line below the core problem.

✓ The problem analysis can be concluded when the participants are convinced that all the essential information necessary to explain the problem has been included in the problem tree (an example is provided in chart A.1.2).

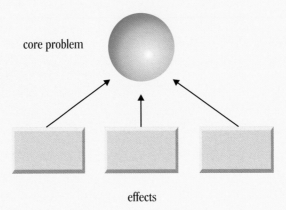

Group work 3:

Identification of strategies – formulation of recommendations for action

✓ recall the main strategies against child labour: prevention of child labour, withdrawal of children from work and provision of alternatives to them and their families;

✓ review the problem tree and identify measures to address the problem in the main programme area assigned to the group;

✓ discuss alternative solutions to a specific problem and make choices based on whether the proposed measures are expedient and realistic; and

✓ identify the agencies responsible for action and the time frame of the proposed strategies.

◆ **The national plan of action**

Based on the results of the group work and the plenary discussions, a National Plan of Action is formulated for endorsement by the Government. An example of the National Plan for Cambodia is given in Appendix 1.3.

Chart A1.2. Example of a problem tree on child labour and education, Dhaka, Bangladesh, 1993

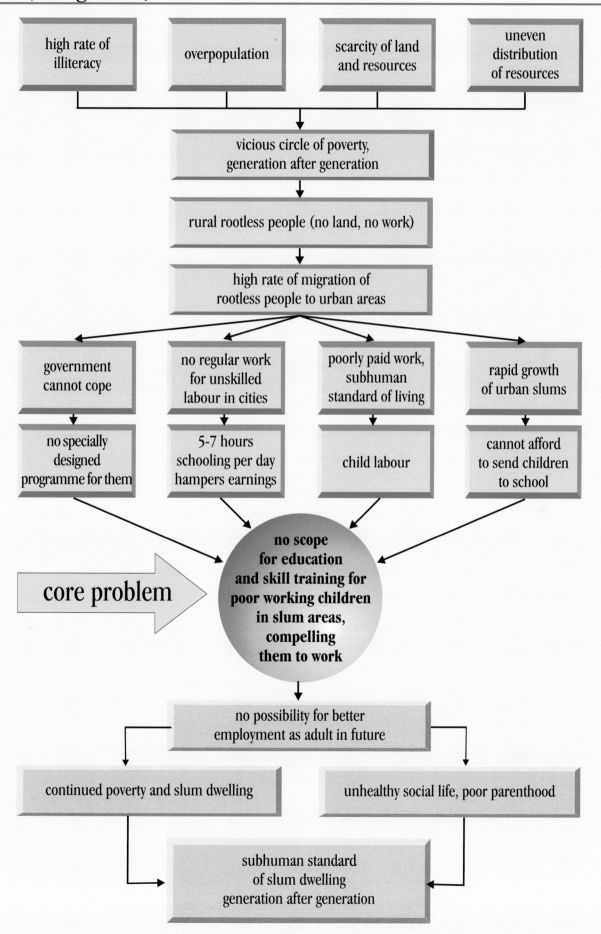

Appendix 1.3   Example of a national plan of action on child labour, Cambodia, 1997

◆ **Target groups for priority action**

During the workshop the following target groups were identified as priorities for action:

✓ children in prostitution;

✓ children trafficked;

✓ children working in forced labour situations;

✓ child domestic workers;

✓ children in bondage;

✓ children carrying heavy loads;

✓ children working in the hazardous agriculture sector of rural areas;

✓ children working in hazardous establishments and risky services;

✓ children working along the border; and

✓ child scavengers.

◆ **National policy development on child labour**

Objectives	Programme activities	Agencies	Time frame
❶ **To develop comprehensive national policies and programmes to effectively prevent, decrease and eliminate child labour**	① Develop a national mechanism on child labour and/or strengthen the existing national mechanisms ② Research and compile existing child labour related legislation.	• Government • NGO and IO • Workers' and employers' organizations	Short term
❷ **To ensure and improve the accessibility of education for all, in line with the constitutional mandate for nine years of free education**	① Expand education, especially universal primary education, and promote access to education of girls and rural children ② Improve the effectiveness of provision of skills-oriented training based on the needs of society ③ Improve the understanding of parents and children of the value of education ④ Increase national education budget	• Government • NGO and IO • Community • Parents and children	Medium term

IO = international organization;   NGO = non-governmental organization.

Objectives	Programme activities	Agencies	Time frame
③ **To improve the effectiveness and ensure enforcement of legislation related to the protection of working children and other forms of child exploitation**	① Review, ratify and effectively implement ILO Convention No. 138 on minimum age of employment and other relevant international conventions	• Government • NGO and IO	Short term
	② Review and prepare other legislation or decrees to protect working children in the informal sector and from forced labour	• Government • NGO and IO	Short term
	③ Increase the number of labour inspectors, and enhance their capacity and capability through further training	• Government • NGO and IO	Short term
	④ Expand the participation of other partners in the alleviation of child labour, including social organizations, employers' and workers' organizations and others	• Government • Employers' and workers' organizations • NGO and IO	Short term
④ **To enhance national public awareness of child labour and its consequences for society**	① Improve the understanding of child labour among children, parents and communities through awareness-raising programmes ② Mobilize groups to take action	• Government • NGO and IO • Community • Parents and children • Teachers • Employers' and workers' organizations	Medium term
⑤ **To promote international assistance in the elimination of child labour in Cambodia**	① Identify need for international support ② Request the assistance of multilateral and bilateral donors and technical agencies, particularly that of ILO-IPEC, in developing and implementing programmes to alleviate child labour in Cambodia	• Government • NGO and IO • International community • Community	Long term

◆ Education and child labour

Objectives	Programme activities	Agencies	Time frame
① **To expand education, especially universal primary education**	① Educate and improve the understanding of parents, children and communities about the value of education	• Children and parents • Community • Government • NGO and IO	Medium term
	② Provide non-formal education and vocational skills training	• Government • NGO and IO • Children and parents	Short term
	③ Develop training curricula and programmes for out-of-school children, in particular working children	• Government • NGO and IO	Short term
	④ Improve the living standard of rural families to enable them to send their children, in particular girls, to school	• Government • NGO and IO • Children and parents	Medium term
② **To encourage school drop-outs to continue education**	① Develop a policy and procedure on reintegrating drop-outs so that they continue their education ② Improve the living standard of poor families who wish to send their children back to school	• Government • NGO and IO • Children, parents and community	Medium term

IO = international organization;   NGO = non-governmental organization.

Objectives	Programme activities	Agencies	Time frame
❸ **To prevent school children from dropping out or looking for hazardous occupations**	① Disseminate information or build awareness on the consequences of school drop-out and seeking jobs at an early age ② Provide assistance for staying in school to extremely poor schoolchildren who wish to drop out ③ Provide skills and vocational training in communities to children who wish to seek employment	• Government • NGO and IO • Community • Children and parents	Medium term
❹ **To encourage and provide education to children of ethnic minorities**	① Develop training curricula and programmes for working children of ethnic minorities ② Educate and improve the understanding of parents and children of ethnic minorities on the value of education ③ Organize classes and training programmes for ethnic minority children	• Government • NGO and IO • Community • Children and parents	Long term

◆ Legislation and enforcement

Objectives	Programme activities	Agencies	Time frame
❶ **To improve existing legislation related to the protection of working children and child welfare by:** **a) enforcement of labour law and the law on suppression of kidnapping and trafficking/sale of and exploitation of persons;** **b) making recommendations for improving law enforcement**	① Gather and review documents relating to employment of children ② Draft a declaration on the employment of children based on existing documents and legislation ③ Update or reform existing legislation in accordance with society and local reality ④ Develop additional law or legislation, if necessary	• Government • NGO and IO	Medium term
❷ **To raise awareness of child labour related legislation and responsibilities of key actors**	① Inform and educate families, employers and working children about labour law and the impact of work on children ② Improve the understanding and expand the responsibilities of labour inspectors, in particular with regard to enforcement of labour law ③ Disseminate legislation on the employment of children	• Government • Workers' and employers' organizations • NGO and IO	Short term
❸ **To improve the effectiveness of existing mechanisms in enforcing legislation on employment of children**	① Provide training to labour inspectors on how to carry out child labour inspection and interventions ② Improve the effectiveness of child labour inspection and intervention by labour inspectors and social workers ③ Strengthen the capacity of labour inspectors and social workers to intervene through reporting by NGOs, children and families ④ Establish child labour networks throughout the country	• Government • Workers' and employers' organizations • NGO and IO • Community	Short term

IO = international organization;   NGO = non-governmental organization.

◆ Social welfare and protection

Objectives	Programme activities	Agencies	Time frame
1 To prevent and protect children from prostitution and trafficking	① Disseminate information to improve the understanding of parents and children on the negative impact of child labour on health and development of children through: - posters - TV/radio on practices of child deception and coercion into prostitution - mobilizing child victims to raise awareness among other children at risk, in communities, schools and urban areas	• Government • NGO and IO • Community • Children and parents	Short term
	② Enhance existing legislation such as legislation on suppression of kidnapping and trafficking/sale of and exploitation of persons, and other legislation on the protection of children's welfare	• Government • Community • NGO and IO	Medium term
	③ Provide education and vocational training to female children in rural areas and high-risk areas by: - encouraging and assisting them in getting an education - organizing mobile classes in remote rural areas - providing vocational skills training	• Government • Community • NGO and IO	Medium term
	④ Set up credit schemes and small businesses	• Government • Community • NGO and IO • Private sector	Short term
2 To rescue and rehabilitate child prostitutes	① Educate and raise awareness of brothel owners on child prostitution and withdraw children from forced labour ② Provide alternatives to prostitution	• Government • NGO and IO • Community	Medium term
3 To reduce the incidence of child domestic work and children carrying heavy loads	① Educate and improve the understanding of children, families and communities of the effects on them and society of such types of child labour ② Provide skills and vocational training to children and their families ③ Provide non-formal education to children ④ Provide credit programme to working children and their families ⑤ Encourage and assist in providing educational opportunities to children	• Government • NGO and IO • Employers' and workers' organizations • Community • Children and parents	Medium term
4 To protect working children in hazardous occupations	① Enhance the capability and capacity of labour inspectors in: - labour law - labour law enforcement - improving the effectiveness of child labour inspection and intervention ② Improve the understanding of working children and their employers by: - publishing posters on hazardous occupations for children - publishing posters for parents and employers on the rights and basic protection of working children - telling stories of working child victims to other working children and their parents - providing medical check-ups and sharing information on primary health care protection among children	• Government • NGO and IO • Employers' and workers' organizations • Working children and their parents • Community	Medium term

IO = international organization;   NGO = non-governmental organization.

Objectives	Programme activities	Agencies	Time frame
5 To remove children from their hazardous working environment or bonded labour, forced labour, prostitution and other types of hazardous occupations	① Improve working conditions of children ② Eliminate bonded labour and forced labour ③ Undertake surveys and other assessments of the most intolerable or worst forms of child labour ④ Provide skills and vocational training, and offer credit to families of working children	• Government • NGO and IO • Community • Employers' and workers' organizations • Research institutes	Medium term
6 To rehabilitate child victims of hazardous occupations	① Rescue and educate victims ② Provide necessary services to victims ③ Reintegrate victims with their families and communities	• Government • NGO and IO • Community	Short term

IO = international organization;   NGO = non-governmental organization.

Appendix 1.4 Pointers to project design

In the text below reference is made to projects only for the sake of brevity. However, the pointers are valid for both programmes and projects, and for many other types of operations, such as subprojects, subprogrammes, action programmes, umbrella projects, and major programmes.

The programming cycle

Projects have four main phases (chart A1.3), which are interrelated:

◆ problem analysis: defining and understanding the problem;

◆ project design: planning a course of action;

◆ implementation and monitoring: carrying out the project and making sure it stays on track; and

◆ evaluation: assessing effects and impact and drawing lessons for existing and future projects.

Chart A1.3. The programming cycle

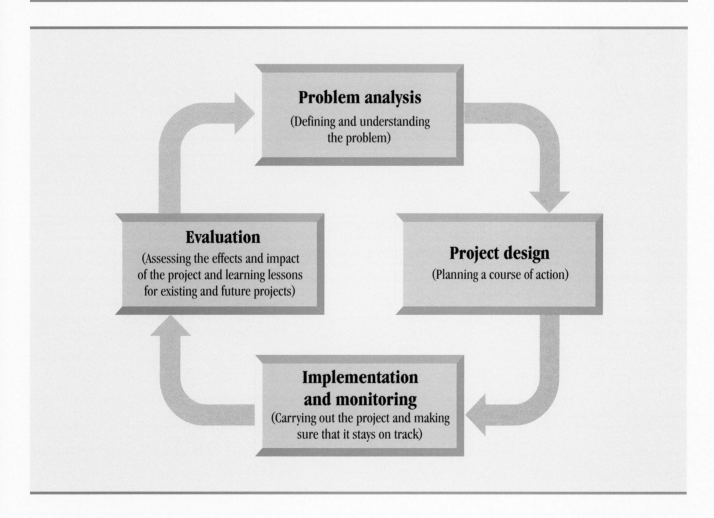

Effective project design facilitates implementation and monitoring and enables high-level evaluation, which in turn should lead to improved project design and implementation. As a result, the cycle becomes an upward spiral.

What makes an effective project?

◆ *Relevance.* A project may be both feasible and cost-effective but still may not be relevant because it fails to tackle the problem it sets out to address.

◆ *Feasibility.* How realistic is it? What risks does the project face and what are the nature and extent of its resources?

◆ *Cost-effectiveness.* When comparing different strategies for the same project or different projects, the best alternative is the one which achieves the expected objectives at a lower cost.

◆ *Sustainability.* The final test of an effective project is whether it can go on delivering benefits after external assistance has been withdrawn. It is not projects which should be sustained but their achievements.

The logical framework

The logical framework was developed in the 1970s and has been used widely in development work since then. It is a tool to set out the main project components in a systematic way and to show the relation between components.

Basic components

Problem analysis and strategy	• The justification of the project analysis, and who will do what, where and when
Target groups, partner organizations and the institutional framework	• The groups who are supposed to benefit • The groups who carry out the project • The division of duties among all concerned
Objectives and indicators	• The aims and ways of measuring success
Outputs, activities, and inputs	• The products and concrete results • The work to be undertaken • The material and human resources needed
Assumptions and preconditions	• The external factors which may form a risk to the project's success and the conditions needed to enable success
Planning, monitoring and evaluation	• Planning of work, supervising the project's progress and plans for evaluation
Budget (estimate)	• The price tag of the project broken down by item

Writing up a project within the logical framework helps to structure and formulate ideas and results in a project document with a clear standardized format. After the start of a project, the project document becomes the tool for managing each phase in the programming cycle and forms the basis for developing other tools such as workplans and progress reports.

Well-written project documents or workplans are useful tools, but cannot alone guarantee successful results. This also depends on the sincerity and the know-how of the people using them. A logical framework is not a static blueprint. Every logical framework is the fruit of an analysis made at a certain moment in the programming cycle, and reflects the knowledge and concerns of the people and organizations involved. If the situation changes, the tools have to be adapted accordingly.

Problem analysis

As already noted, child labour is a many-sided problem. Therefore sound problem or situation analysis is important not only at the level of developing polices and programmes but also at the level of project design. Since projects often work with one target group, in a particular sector or location, it is important that those who design them have a solid understanding of the specific needs and problems associated with that target group, sector or location. Problem analysis identifies the needs and characteristics of a target group and stimulates new forms of response. It typically incorporates three elements: the definition and description of a situation or a problem; an analysis of existing responses to the problem; and an assessment of the needs not met.

Undertaking problem analysis can best be done through a partnership with all concerned – government, voluntary organizations, municipal authorities, academic institutions, community leaders, the children and their families. Besides contacting key informants it is also useful to review existing documentation such as censuses, surveys, policy statements, and so on. Key information includes education statistics, particularly the figures on school enrolment and drop-out rates, as most children not at school can be presumed to be actual or potential workers.

Project strategy

The project strategy must make clear what the project seeks to do, for whom, with whom and how. This section is the most important part of a project document as it outlines responses to the problems. It sets out the target groups, the project partners, the project approach and the types of interventions. It is important to **define the target group** precisely if the activities of the project are to be properly focused. Wherever practical, children themselves, their parents, employers and key informants in the community should be consulted on the project design. Do they want the project? Does it meet their needs? By involving them at the preparatory stage serious design pitfalls are avoided and chances of success are increased by developing a sense of project ownership.

A very important aspect of the project strategy is **choosing partners** through which the project will work. Usually one organization becomes the implementing agency with the main responsibility for designing and carrying out a project. But projects should not be conceived, nor do they operate in, a vacuum. In the case of child labour projects the specialized expertise of different agencies at the governmental and non-governmental level is required to take concerted action on a specific child labour problem.

The types of intervention will vary depending on whether the project aims to prevent child labour, and/or withdraw children from work, and provide them and their families with viable alternatives, and/or improve working conditions as a first step towards the elimination of child labour. Projects that work directly with children and their families are called "direct support action projects". Those that aim at strengthening the capacity of organizations to deliver services, coordinate activities or improve enforcement are called "institutional development projects". In many cases, projects combine both approaches.

As child labour is often due to ignorance about the harmful effects of premature work on children, all action programmes should always contain **an awareness-raising component, for advocacy purposes.** In addition, all direct action programmes should contain an awareness-raising and advocacy component to ensure that employers, managers and adult workers refrain from resorting to child labour, otherwise children withdrawn from work will be replaced immediately with other children. In the case of self-employed children, efforts should be made to reach their clients with messages on child labour. Awareness-raising and advocacy can be combined or followed up with **a monitoring component** to ensure that geographical areas or specific occupations stay child labour free.

It is essential to **address sustainability concerns** from the start of the action programme to increase the chance that its benefits will be long-lasting, and that its results and output will continue to be used and become the responsibility of the target groups and partner organizations after termination of the project.

From objectives to output

After the description of the strategy, target groups and partners, projects always contain the following four elements:

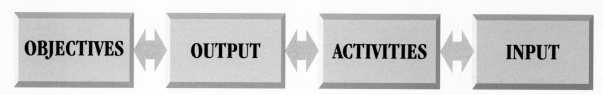

These elements are interrelated, and if the linkages between them are clear enough this will enable the project designers to predict that:

◆ if the input is available, then the activities will take place;

◆ if the activities take place, then the output will be produced; and

◆ if the output is produced, then the objective(s) will be achieved.

An **objective** is a simple expression of a desired end. If the problem is clearly stated, the solution to it will be the objective. **Outputs** are the products which result from the project activities. The key words are "to produce". Examples might be material, curricula, reports, or people trained. **Activities** then are the actions undertaken to produce the desired outputs, i.e. what will be done, not the results themselves. The key words are "to do". Outputs are produced by a certain date, while activities describe the project process. And finally **inputs** are the funds, equipment, expertise, human resources, and so on, necessary for carrying out the activities. The project designer must decide realistically what are the minimum resources needed to carry out the project and who will provide them.

Indicators

Indicators are precise, measurable factors, which help both to explain the stated objectives and allow for project evaluation because they provide evidence as to whether output has led to the achievements of the objectives.

Some examples of indicators include: the adoption of key legislation; major investments in the provision of education and socio-economic development programmes for disadvantaged groups prone to resorting to child labour; a decrease in the number of children involved in certain economic sectors (this indicator is relatively easy to use in programmes which aim to withdraw a number of children from work, but more difficult in the case of measures geared towards prevention); an increase in the number of child/forced/hazardous labour cases reported, and so on.

Monitoring and evaluation

Monitoring and evaluation are the final elements of the programming cycle. It is important to determine at the very beginning how the project will provide progress reports, and how it will be evaluated. **Monitoring** is concerned largely with ensuring that input leads to output. It is essential for the project management to make regular progress reports on project implementation – that input is being made available as planned, that activities are taking place in line with the workplan and that output is produced on schedule. Project management must always be in a position to adapt the project to the needs and conditions which could not have been foreseen at the project design stage. **Evaluation** is the act of discovering whether objectives are being achieved or likely to be achieved. It must be distinguished both from project appraisal, which is an assessment prior to deciding whether to undertake a project, and monitoring, which is the continuous overview of the implementation of a project, involving the regular reporting of basic information. Evaluation is thus a key tool for improving the management of ongoing projects, improving the preparation of new projects, and providing inputs into programme evaluation.

Evaluation issues

◆ **effectiveness;**

◆ **efficiency;**

◆ **relevance;**

◆ **validity of design;**

◆ **unanticipated effects;**

◆ **alternative strategies;**

◆ **causality; and**

◆ **sustainability.**

Towards improved legislation

2

Michele Jankanish

INTRODUCTION

Legislation has been the single most important response of governments to the problem of child labour. Although insufficient on its own, legislation can be a powerful instrument in combating child labour. It can serve as a deterrent to the economic exploitation of children, being the basis for both preventive measures and punitive action against violators.

Assistance in revising and developing national legislation and drafting rules to facilitate its implementation has been a major and traditional aspect of the ILO's work. This has been reinforced in recent years with assistance from the International Programme on the Elimination of Child Labour (IPEC) to governments, focused on legislative reform and on improving the enforcement of laws on child labour. For example, assistance has been provided in consolidating and harmonizing disparate laws affecting children, and in expanding the coverage of laws and increasing penalties for offenders, such as for those exploiting children in prostitution and trafficking. In several countries, there are discussions about enlarging the scope of laws to cover the informal sector, strengthen law enforcement, and set up specific judicial bodies to hear cases on child abuse, including child labour.

This chapter outlines the framework for developing or revising national legislation on child labour.[1] It can be used to raise awareness on the basic legal protection to be given to children in relation to work, as a reference for conducting reviews of the adequacy of legislation, and to advocate for legislative change. It contains information on international legal standards on child labour, including the new ILO standards on the worst forms of child labour. It gives a number of examples from national legislation and of initiatives to improve national legislation on child labour. Checklists are given on basic considerations for national legislation, for improving national legislation on child and bonded labour, and for involving employers' and workers' organizations. Several appendices provide further information on the ratification of relevant ILO Conventions and minimum ages established in ratifying countries. Excerpts from texts of relevant ILO standards are provided in Appendix 2.5.

2.1 LEGISLATION AND THE FIGHT AGAINST CHILD LABOUR

> *"Although the fight against child labour will not be won through legislation, it certainly cannot be won without it. Child labour laws can play a catalytic and supportive role in efforts to establish a more humane order and in prodding society to give the child the best it has to offer."* [2]

---

[1] For a recent overview of national law and practice on child labour, see ILO: *Child labour: Targeting the intolerable*, Report VI (1), International Labour Conference, 86th Session, 1998 (Geneva, 1996), including legislation applicable to minimum age, forced labour, prostitution, pornography, and the sale and trafficking of children.

[2] ILO: "Child labour: Law and practice", in *Conditions of Work Digest* (Geneva, ILO), Vol. 1, 1991.

The first questions to ask when faced with a working child are: Does the law allow the child at his or her age to engage in the activity and, if so, under what conditions? Is the authority of the State brought to bear on behalf of protecting the child? Through legislation, the broad aspects of national policy towards the elimination of child labour can be defined. The law alone can provide legal sanctions, where appropriate, for violators of the law and can create legal avenues of redress for victims. It can also point the way to and enable practical action to be taken to eliminate child labour.

Almost all countries have enacted legislation to deal with some aspects of child labour, such as setting minimum ages for work or, where children are legally permitted to work, specifying the conditions under which they may work. Many countries have set higher minimum ages for hazardous work. There are still shortcomings, however, especially in the coverage of many of the laws, which often exclude work in which children are engaged, such as in agriculture, domestic service, family undertakings and work in the informal sector. Legislative provisions might not meet international standards, which is a particular problem for countries that have ratified international treaties. Serious gaps in the application of laws also persist. Legislative commitments often lie dormant, sometimes due to lack of resources for effective monitoring and enforcement, sometimes due to lack of political will, but often simply because the authorities do not know how to tackle the problem of eliminating child labour, given the invisibility of many child workers and the fact that poverty, discrimination and cultural attitudes that foster it are so deeply entrenched in society.

There are also problems of another kind. Sometimes relevant legal provisions are so numerous and in different parts of the law that even those responsible for their enforcement can be confused. Legal provisions might be inconsistent with one

Box 2.1. The role of legislation

Legislation plays a fundamental role in a national policy on child labour. It can:

- set the principles, objectives and priorities of such policy and provide a conducive environment for the development of national institutional capacities to combat child labour;

- place the authority of the State behind the protection of children;

- clarify society's values and commitments towards children;

- provide a yardstick for evaluating performance;

- move towards ensuring the observance of universal standards established in international instruments to protect children;

- create specific legal duties and responsibilities;

- identify and focus attention on hazards to children;

- provide a basis and procedure for complaints and investigations;

- provide legal redress for victims; and

- provide sanctions for violators.

another; for example, the age for compulsory education and the minimum age for work might not be in harmony. Finally, there might not be sufficient publicity given to information about the laws, especially to families, children and employers.

2.2 SOURCES OF LAW ON CHILD LABOUR

The Constitutions of many countries have provisions on the protection of children, or more specifically on child labour and bonded labour.

Legislative provisions on child labour – those which set minimum ages, prohibit certain types of work and regulate conditions of work – may be found in a special section of the general labour code, in separate Acts, or in various laws on contracts of employment, conditions of work (hours of work, days of rest, night work, vacations), safety and health, social security, and so forth. Civil codes can also contain generally applicable principles.

Separate provisions may also cover the apprenticeship, training and vocational education of young people. Not to be overlooked are laws which affect child labour indirectly, such as compulsory education laws. Some laws specifically link the age of work with the age of completing school. Some countries, particularly as a result of the ratification of the United Nations Convention on the Rights of the Child, are taking the approach of adopting comprehensive child protection laws which consolidate a wide range of provisions to protect children, including those on child labour.

Criminal law is also relevant, especially concerning the commercial sexual exploitation of children and the sale and trafficking of children. Some countries have enacted specific statutes on bonded labour, child prostitution, child pornography and the sale and trafficking of children.

2.3 INTERNATIONAL LABOUR STANDARDS AND NATIONAL LEGISLATION

Introduction

One of the most important tools available to the ILO for improving the legislation and practice of its member States in the fight against child labour is the adoption and supervision of international labour Conventions and Recommendations.[3] These international instruments are elaborated through a tripartite process which

---

[3] For a detailed technical explanation of the procedures for adoption and implementation of international labour Conventions and Recommendations, see ILO: *Handbook of procedures relating to international labour Conventions and Recommendations,* International Labour Standards Department (Geneva, Rev.1/1995).

Box 2.2. ILO Conventions and Recommendations

◆ International labour Conventions are open to ratification by ILO member States. A country that ratifies a Convention has legal obligations to apply the provisions of the Convention in law and practice.

◆ ILO Recommendations do not create binding obligations and are not open to ratification. Rather, Recommendations give guidance as to policy, legislation and practice. They often supplement Conventions.

involves governments, employers' and workers' organizations. They are debated and adopted by the ILO's International Labour Conference, which is composed of government, employer and worker delegates from the 174 member States.

After they are adopted, Conventions become open to ratification by the member States. States which ratify ILO Conventions subject themselves to supervisory machinery which involves regular reporting to the ILO on the application of ratified Conventions; examination and public comment by ILO supervisory bodies (Committee of Experts and Conference Committee)[4] on the extent of compliance; and a complaints procedure for investigating and acting upon complaints alleging non-compliance made by governments of other ratifying States or by employers' or workers' organizations. Member States may seek technical assistance from the ILO in preparing for ratifying Conventions and in applying them.

Even if a country has not ratified a Convention, Conventions and Recommendations provide guidance and are statements of international consensus on issues.

From time to time, ILO member States are asked to submit reports on the status of their law and practice concerning matters dealt with in selected Conventions, even if they have not ratified them, and in Recommendations. These surveys, along with reports from countries which have ratified the particular Convention, provide a good overview of the situation on the subject matter of the instruments and the extent to which the principles of international labour standards are applied.

---

[4] The supervisory bodies referred to in this book are the Committee of Experts on the Application of Conventions and Recommendations (referred to as the Committee of Experts) and the tripartite Committee on the Application of Standards of the International Labour Conference (referred to as the Conference Committee). The Committee of Experts is a body of independent experts entrusted with the technical examination of reports supplied by governments to the ILO, as well as other relevant information, concerning the application of ILO standards. The report of the Committee of Experts is discussed by the Conference Committee which reports to the International Labour Conference.

The concern for the safety, health and development of children underlies the ILO instruments on child labour. Interference with the growth and development of children affects not only their health, but their long-term prospects. Placing priority on the healthy growth and development of children, including their education, means limiting access to work and, depending upon age and type of work, prohibiting it altogether.

The ILO adopted its first Convention on child labour in 1919, the year of its formation: the Minimum Age (Industry) Convention, 1919 (No. 5), prohibits the work of children under the age of 14 in industrial establishments. Subsequently, nine sectoral Conventions on the minimum age of admission to employment were adopted applying to industry, agriculture, trimmers and stokers, maritime work, non-industrial employment, fishing and underground work (see Appendix 2.1).

Finally, as the above instruments cover specific economic sectors and occupations only, the ILO decided to adopt one comprehensive instrument towards the total abolition of child labour, the Minimum Age Convention, 1973 (No. 138). It applies to all sectors of economic activity and whether or not children are employed for wages. It covers work done by children both for another person and on their own behalf (self-employment). This book sets out the provisions of Convention No. 138 and its accompanying Recommendation, the Minimum Age Recommendation, 1973 (No. 146), as they provide a comprehensive guide to drafting national legislation. Even though the Convention is broad in scope and coverage, some flexibility is provided. This flexibility is expressed in provisions which allow for exclusions or exceptions under certain circumstances; some of these provisions apply to all countries, while others are designed specifically for developing countries.

Box 2.3. ILO Declaration on Fundamental Principles and Rights at Work (excerpt)

The International Labour Conference "declares that all Members, even if they have not ratified the Conventions in question, have an obligation arising from the very fact of membership in the Organization, to respect, to promote and to realize, in good faith and in accordance with the Constitution, the principles concerning the fundamental rights which are the subject of those Conventions, namely:

(a)   freedom of association and the effective recognition of the right to collective bargaining;

(b)   the elimination of all forms of forced or compulsory labour;

(c)   *the effective abolition of child labour*; and

(d)   the elimination of discrimination in respect of employment and occupation."

Box 2.4. The Minimum Age Convention, 1973 (No. 138)

National policy

◆ Ratifying States undertake "to pursue a national policy designed to ensure the effective abolition of child labour and to raise progressively the minimum age for admission to employment or work to a level consistent with the fullest physical and mental development of young persons".

◆ Recommendation No. 146 provides guidance on necessary policy and enforcement measures.

Coverage

◆ The Convention applies to all sectors of economic activity, whether or not the children are employed for wages.

◆ Certain sectors may initially be excluded from application of the Convention by developing countries.

◆ Limited categories of work can be excluded for special and substantial problems of application.

◆ Exclusions and exceptions are provided for education and training and artistic performances.

Basic minimum age

◆ The Convention establishes that the minimum age should not be less than the age of completing compulsory schooling and in no event less than 15 years of age.

◆ It allows a developing country to specify initially a general minimum age of 14 years instead of 15.

Minimum age for hazardous work

◆ A higher minimum age of at least 18 must be set for hazardous work – "employment or work which by its nature or the circumstances in which it is carried out is likely to jeopardize the health, safety or morals of young persons."

◆ A lower age of 16 is allowed where the health, safety and morals of young persons are fully protected and where they have received adequate specific instruction or vocational training in the relevant branch of activity. Both conditions must be fulfilled to allow such a lower age, along with a requirement that the organizations of employers and workers be consulted beforehand.

Minimum age for light work

◆ The Convention allows a lower age for light work from 13 to 15 years of age, provided that the work is not hazardous to the child's health or development, and does not hinder the child's education.

◆ A minimum age for light work at 12 instead of 13 can be set in countries where the basic minimum age of 14 is allowed, after consultation with the employers' and workers' organizations.

Enforcement

The Convention calls for:

◆ all necessary measures to ensure effective enforcement;

◆ appropriate penalties;

◆ definition of persons responsible for compliance; and

◆ record keeping.

The table below gives a summary of the minimum age provisions of Convention No. 138.

General minimum age (Article 2)	Light work (Article 7)	Hazardous work (Article 3)
In normal circumstances:		
15 years or more (not less than compulsory school age)	13 years	18 years (16 years conditionally)
Where economy and educational facilities are insufficiently developed:		
14 years	12 years	18 years (16 years conditionally)

If a country has not ratified Convention No. 138, check which other ILO child labour or related Conventions might be ratified, including the Forced Labour Convention, 1930 (No. 29), and the Labour Inspection Convention, 1947 (No. 81).

A recent important development is the adoption by the International Labour Conference, in June 1998, of the Declaration on Fundamental Principles and Rights at Work and its Follow-up. The adoption of the Declaration is expected to contribute significantly to the fight against child labour in all member States, even if they have not ratified child labour Conventions.

National policy

Convention No. 138 and Recommendation No. 146

The principal commitments of a State which ratifies Convention No. 138 are to:
- *pursue a national policy designed to ensure the effective abolition of child labour; and*
- *raise progressively the minimum age for admission to employment or work to a level consistent with the fullest physical and mental development of young persons.*

Convention No. 138 is not a static instrument prescribing a fixed minimum standard, but a dynamic one aimed at encouraging the progressive improvement of standards and promoting sustained action to attain the objective of eliminating child labour.

Recommendation No. 146 contains the broad policy framework and measures for the prevention and elimination of child labour. To ensure the success of the national policy provided for in the Convention, the Recommendation states that:

high priority should be given to planning for and meeting the needs of children and youth in national development policies and programmes and to the progressive extension of the inter-related measures necessary to provide the best possible conditions of physical and mental growth for children and young persons.

The Recommendation provides that special attention should be given to developing policies in the fields of:

◆ employment promotion;

◆ income generation and alleviation of poverty;

◆ social security and family welfare; and

◆ education and training.

Box 2.5. Policy in national legislation, Portugal

The Government of Portugal makes specific reference to the Minimum Age Convention, 1973 (No. 138), in its law, with a cross-reference to the Law on the Education System which establishes nine years of compulsory basic education, thus establishing a direct link between the minimum age for admission to employment or work and the age of compulsory education. It also has taken up suggestions from Recommendation No. 146. For example, it establishes the minimum age for admission to work at 16 years and refers to the following measures as being adopted in the light of Recommendation No. 146: policies to promote employment, including financial incentives to promote employment of young persons above age 18 and vocational training; measures on professional schools and training; and measures to combat poverty.

Particular attention should be given to the needs of children without families and migrant workers. Full-time compulsory education or training is also called for, at least up to the minimum age for employment or work.

Adopting national policies

The special merit of a national policy is that it articulates societal objectives and commitment and, if pursued faithfully, provides a coherent framework for an associated programme of action. A complete and implementable national policy and programme of action will contain at least the following elements:

◆ a definition of national objectives regarding child labour;

◆ a description of the nature and context of the problem;

◆ identification and description of the priority target groups;

◆ description of the main programme areas and types of interventions; and

◆ designation of the institutional actors to be involved.

While some countries rely on the legislative process as the main means of developing a national policy on child labour, many are developing broader policy frameworks including programmes of action.[5] The following steps are often taken by countries in adopting a national policy:

STEP 1: Collection of reliable information through surveys and other methods of assessing the child labour problem.

STEP 2: A forum for governments, employers' and workers' organizations, and NGOs to reflect on the strengths and weaknesses of existing policies and programmes.

In countries such as Bangladesh, Indonesia, Kenya, the Philippines, Thailand and Turkey national seminars or conferences led to the adoption of national programmes of action, which go beyond a statement of intent and set out strategies to combat child labour.

---

[5] For example, Bangladesh, India, Indonesia, Nepal, the Philippines, the United Republic of Tanzania, Thailand and Turkey.

Box 2.6. Comments by the ILO Committee of Experts

The ILO Committee of Experts examines a broad range of measures as evidence of a national policy to eliminate child labour. The policy could be one piece of legislation or a body of law which serves as a comprehensive policy on child labour. Such a policy, for example, could include legislation on minimum age, compulsory education, broad implementing legislation which establishes institutional structures, and a combination of provisions which address some of the root causes of child labour.

Examples are given below from recent comments by the Committee of Experts related to application of Article 1 of the Convention on the pursuance of a national policy to abolish child labour.[6]

Togo

In assessing whether a national policy for the abolition of child labour was being pursued, the Committee noted the role played by the Ministry of Technical Education and Vocational Training with a view to matching training and employment and improving skills, and the role of the Ministry of Social Affairs to ensure the protection and well-being of children and young persons. At the same time, the Committee wished to know whether coordination and consultation mechanisms had been established or envisaged in the application of a national policy designed to ensure the effective abolition of child labour.

Romania

The Committee noted with interest that the payment of the child allowance for children of school age, established by the Act on social aid, is made by schools in order to enforce school attendance during compulsory education. Concerning the reported increase in the number of children who live and work in the street, the Committee asked what measures the Government was pursuing in this regard as part of the national policy to ensure the effective abolition of child labour in accordance with Article 1 of Convention No. 138.

Guatemala

The Committee noted that the Code of Childhood and Adolescence contains several provisions aiming at the protection of young workers; it sets forth the right of children and young people to be protected from economic exploitation, and engagement in whatever work that may be dangerous to their physical and mental health or which hinders their education (section 53 (1)), and declares that childhood should be dedicated to education, sports, culture, and recreation suitable to their age (section 53 (2)).

Furthermore, the Committee noted that the Plan of Social Development (PLADES 1996-2000) contains policies focused on child labour, with a view to progressively raising the minimum age for admission to employment; that the Unit of Young Workers of the Ministry of Labour and

---

[6] ILO: *Report of the Committee of Experts*, Report III (Part 1A), International Labour Conference, 85th Session, Geneva, 1997, pp. 384, 386, 387; ibid., 86th Session, 1998, pp. 432-433, 435-436.

Social Providence has been instituting awareness campaigns for employers, parents and children concerning their rights under labour law and their right to formal education; and that the Memorandum of Understanding was signed in June 1996 with the ILO regarding IPEC.

The Committee requests the Government to continue to supply information on developments concerning the national policy for the elimination of child labour, concrete measures taken accordingly, and progress made in the application of the Convention in practice.

Venezuela

The Committee noted with interest the ample information submitted with the Government's report concerning the national policy aiming at the abolition of child labour, and the wide variety of economic and social measures taken in relation to this policy. For instance, the IXth National Plan includes provisions on promoting participation of civil society in the protection and socialization of childhood and adolescence, on special programmes aimed at the reinsertion of those excluded from the education system, on the creation of a Social Network for Protection of Childhood and Adolescence, and on the widening and diversification of services offered by the National Institution of Minors (INAM) for children and adolescents in especially difficult circumstances.

The problem of child labour is also addressed in the Intersectoral Plan of Attention to Childhood and Adolescence, including the introduction of a system of registering children and young persons who are working, and the eradication in seven years of work by children under 12 years of age. Decree No. 1366 of 12 June 1996 establishes a programme of family subsidy, beneficiaries of which include low-income families with children receiving basic education (1st to 6th grades). Documents called "Agenda Venezuela" also contain various social measures to mitigate the effects of the macroeconomic adjustment programme.

The Committee requests the Government to continue to supply information on measures relevant to the effective abolition of child labour, and also to include statistics and extracts from inspection reports which would help the appreciation of the application of the Convention in practice.

STEP 3: Identification of priority target groups in the programmes of action.

Examples are provided in box 2.7.

Box 2.7. Identifying priority target groups in national programmes of action

Benin

Children who are:

◆ apprentices in the informal sector;

◆ young girls in urban areas (domestic service, servants, sales girls); and

◆ workers in agriculture.

India

Children who are:

◆ working in hazardous employment such as in the production of glass, brass, locks, gems, matches, fireworks, slates, tiles, carpets and *bidis* (cigarettes).

Indonesia

Children who are:

◆ scavengers in dump sites;

◆ working in sea-fishing;

◆ working on *jermals* (offshore fishing);

◆ working in deep-sea pearl diving; and

◆ working as street hawkers.

Kenya

Children who are:

◆ in domestic service;

◆ working in the service sector;

◆ working in commercial agriculture;

◆ working in quarrying and mining;

◆ working in the tourist sector; and

◆ working in the informal sector.

Nepal

Children who are:

◆ working in hazardous and abusive work;

◆ in prostitution;

◆ in bonded labour; and

◆ girls.

Philippines

Children who are:

◆ victims of trafficking;

◆ working in mining and quarrying;

◆ working in home-based industries, especially under subcontracting arrangements;

◆ trapped in prostitution;

◆ working on sugar-cane plantations;

◆ working on vegetable farms;

◆ engaged in pyrotechnics production; and

◆ engaged in deep-sea diving.

Thailand

Children who are:

◆ under 13 years old;

◆ working in hazardous working conditions;

◆ working in illegal establishments;

◆ under confinement; and

◆ in work which is physically and/or sexually abusive.

STEP 4: Identification of main programme areas and types of interventions in the programmes of action.

Main programme areas usually include review and revision of legislation, enforcement, awareness-raising, improvement of education and training, capacity building of organizations in combating child labour and the development of specific rehabilitation programmes. Concerning legislation, the first step is to review the legal situation, determine if there are inconsistencies, confusion and insufficiencies in the law, and identify priority areas for legislative change. Even though action can be taken in areas to which the law has not been extended, it is preferable to extend the coverage of the law as widely as possible, in particular to the priority areas which have been identified.

Box 2.8. Reviewing legislation in Nepal

As part of its strategy toward the elimination of child labour, the Government of Nepal held a national workshop on policy and programming on child labour. The preparatory work included an analysis of the national legislative framework and recommendations for change.[7] It identified relevant national legislation which included The Children's Act 1992, the Labour Act 1992 and Labour Rules 1993, the Common Law Code 1963, the Foreign Employment Act 1985, the Flesh Trafficking (Control) Act 1986, Citizen Rights Act 1955, Begging (Prohibition) Act 1962, and the Prison Act 1963. Thus, numerous laws contained provisions on the employment or work of children. In the process, the Government identified anomalies in the law, areas where harmonization was needed, for example concerning ages and definitions, and areas for strengthening the law.

It was concluded that the legislative scheme needed further review and improvement by, for example, consolidating into one Act, as far as possible, the provisions on employment and self-employment of children, and work done by children in domestic service and work in family undertakings; by applying the provisions to all work, including self-employment; by progressively extending labour inspection to cover all kinds of workplaces; by raising the minimum ages as the economy and educational facilities develop; and by making the penal provisions more stringent to act as a deterrent. In addition, it was recommended that legislation should be adopted to implement the constitutional provisions on bonded labour, including establishing an effective agency for enforcing the law and providing for the rehabilitation of the bonded labourers. To facilitate enforcement of child labour provisions, it was also recommended that the implementation of the Birth, Death and Other Personal Incidents (Registration) Act 1976 be strengthened so that an authentic record of the age of a child would be available.

[7] ILO-IPEC: *Child labour in Nepal*, Volume II, *An overview and proposed plan of action*, prepared for the National Workshop on Policy and Programming on Child Labour, Kathmandu, 22-25 August 1995.

STEP 5: Adoption of a national policy and programme of action geared towards the immediate elimination of the worst forms of child labour.

An example of a targeted policy is given in box 2.9.

Box 2.9. National policy and plan of action for the prevention and eradication of the commercial sexual exploitation of children, Thailand

Within its overall strategy to combat child labour, the Government of Thailand adopted a national policy and plan of action for the prevention and eradication of the commercial sexual exploitation of children in Thailand in 1996. Legislation is an integral part of the policy.[8]

The aims of the National Policy in combating the commercial sexual exploitation of children are:

◆ preventing and eliminating entry by children under 18;

◆ prohibiting luring, threats, exploitation, and acts of violence in operating a commercial sex business; and

◆ punishing those who bring children into the business and officials who fail in their duty to enforce relevant policies, laws, rules and regulations.

Five major plans have been adopted as part of the Policy (1997-2006) which are geared towards:

◆ prevention;

◆ suppression;

◆ assistance and protection;

◆ rehabilitation and adjustment to normal life; and

◆ establishment of structures, mechanisms and systems for supervising, controlling, following up and speeding up implementation.

Legislative measures taken were:

◆ adoption of the Prostitution Prevention and Suppression Act; and

◆ the Rape and Child Pornography amendment to the Penal Code Amendment Act.

---

[8] *National Policy and Plan of Action for the Prevention and Eradication of the Commercial Sexual Exploitation of Children, Thailand*, National Committee for the Eradication of Commercial Sex, National Commission on Women's Affairs, Office of the Prime Minister, Thailand, 1996.

Coverage of the law (scope of application)

The law should state to which industries, occupations and type of activity it applies, or provide broad coverage by providing no exclusions. The broadest coverage possible is desirable.

Convention No. 138 and Recommendation No. 146

Convention No. 138 covers **all economic sectors and all employment or work.** This means that a child's work can be prohibited or restricted whether or not there is a formal employment relationship.

Box 2.10. Coverage of the law

The Committee of Experts has noted recently its satisfaction with changes in law that provide broader coverage. For example, the Committee referenced the adoption of the Work Place (Protection of Young Persons) Regulations 1996, by Malta, and noted with satisfaction that section 3 (2) prohibits not only employment under a contract of service or otherwise, but also prohibits providing work which includes service as a homeworker or as a self-employed person to a young person of compulsory school age (i.e. a person 5 years or older who has not reached age 16).

Exclusion for problems of application

The Convention provides for several flexibility provisions. The first one relates to the exclusion of **limited categories of employment or work** for which **special and substantial problems of application** arise, after consultation with organizations of employers and workers. However, work that is likely to jeopardize the health, safety or morals of young persons may not be excluded under this provision (Article 4). States must review excluded categories on an on-going basis and make progress towards eliminating the special and substantial problems which make broad application difficult.

The limited categories are not listed in the Convention. However, during the preparatory work, some ILO constituents indicated that it would be difficult to cover child labour in family undertakings, domestic service in private households and some types of work carried out without the employer's supervision, for example, home work[9], because of practical difficulties of enforcing laws in the categories in question – not because of the absence of possible exploitation or abuse in these situations. Coverage in these sectors is encouraged because they are the source of most child labour.

---

[9] The Home Work Convention (No. 177), adopted in 1996, calls for the promotion of equal treatment between homeworkers and other wage earners in relation to minimum age, among other things; the Home Work Recommendation (No. 184) suggests programmes to eliminate child labour in home work.

Box 2.11. Extension of coverage in Sweden

An example of a country having recourse to this provision is Sweden, which had excluded domestic work under Article 4 in its first report to the ILO after ratification of the Convention. The Committee of Experts has recently noted with satisfaction that Sweden has now changed its law so that work done by employees under the age of 18 in the employer's household is covered by the Work Environment Act, which fixes the minimum age for admission to employment. As a consequence, the exclusion of domestic work in the employer's household from the application of the Convention is no longer necessary.

Limiting the scope of application

This flexibility provision applies to developing countries. A country whose economy and administrative facilities are insufficiently developed may **initially limit the scope of application of the Convention to certain branches of economic activity or types of enterprise** (Article 5) following consultation with organizations of employers and workers. The following sectors, however, **must be covered as a minimum**:

◆ mining and quarrying;

◆ manufacturing;

◆ construction;

◆ electricity, gas and water;

◆ sanitary services;

◆ transport, storage and communication; and

◆ plantations and other agricultural undertakings mainly producing for commercial purposes. (This, however, allows exclusion of family and small-scale holdings producing for local consumption and not regularly employing hired workers.)

Countries limiting application initially are still to report on child work in excluded categories and on their progress towards achieving broader coverage of the law. This clause can only be used at the time of ratification. Thus a country will commit itself at the beginning to broad coverage or to progressive coverage of branches of economic activity or types of enterprise.

Recommendation No. 146 suggests that where a minimum age is not immediately fixed for certain branches of economic activity or types of undertaking, appropriate minimum age provisions should be made applicable to types of employment or work which present hazards for young persons. The Recommendation also provides that where it is not immediately feasible to establish a minimum age for all employment in agriculture and in related activities in rural areas, a minimum age should be fixed at least for employment on plantations and in other agricultural undertakings (paragraphs 8 and 11).

Without general coverage of the law the objective of the elimination of child labour cannot be achieved.

Exclusion for work as part of education and training

Work for **general, vocational or technical education or other training institutions**, and work in undertakings performed by those at least 14 years old, is not covered by the Convention if:

◆ it is performed according to conditions prescribed by the competent authority;

◆ there has been consultation with the organizations of employers and workers concerned; and

◆ it is part of authorized training.

To come under this exclusion, the education or training must be an integral part of:

◆ an education or training course for which a school or training institution is primarily responsible;

◆ a programme of training (apprenticeship) mainly or entirely in an enterprise where the programme has been approved by the competent authority; and

◆ a programme of guidance or orientation designed to facilitate the choice of an occupation or of a line of training.

Countries should pay special attention to how education, training and apprenticeship programmes are conducted. The assumptions often are that:

● *work in educational and training institutions is well controlled and that there is a small risk that young persons will be exposed to detrimental effects normally associated with employment; and*

● *apprenticeships are carried out under a form of contract of employment, usually within a formalized programme under the supervision of national education authorities, and, thus, are subject to extensive and detailed regulation.*

This, however, is often an area of abuse. Laws applicable to vocational education, training and apprenticeship programmes should ensure protection of young persons from hazardous work. Training should meet the criteria of the Convention and should not be a subterfuge to avoid child labour provisions. Therefore, Recommendation No. 146 speaks of the importance of measures to "safeguard and supervise the conditions in which children and young persons undergo vocational orientation and training" (paragraph 12 (2)).

Exceptions for artistic performances

Exceptions from the basic minimum age can be granted:

◆ after consultation with the organizations of employers and workers concerned; and

◆ by permits in individual cases which must:

❖ limit the number of hours that can be worked, and

❖ specify the conditions of work.

Box 2.12. Comments by the ILO Committee of Experts on artistic performances

Recent comments in the ILO's Committee of Experts on the Application of Conventions and Recommendations have been addressed to legislative developments in some countries concerning the process for granting exemptions for artistic performances. In Belgium, for example, a 1992 law provides that, through an individual authorization from the competent Minister, work by children may be authorized in specific cases such as theatrical roles, fashion shows or participation in fashion photographic sessions. The application to obtain an individual derogation from the prohibition of child labour can only be made personally by the organizer, who must be resident in Belgium, and not by impresarios or agencies. The competent official who issues the derogation may establish a whole series of specific measures according to the activity and may interview the child.

The Committee of Experts also noted with satisfaction an amendment to Swedish law which changes the exemption for artist performances. Previous law provided a general exclusion of artistic performances and similar work as long as it was not hazardous and did not entail excessive strain. The new provision permits the employment of a child under the age of 13 only by an individual permission from the Labour Inspectorate, as required by Article 8 (1) of the Convention, and on condition that the work is not hazardous and does not entail excessive physical and psychological strain on the child.

General minimum age for admission to employment or work

Convention No. 138 and Recommendation No. 146

A minimum age for admission to employment or work is to be set. It must not be less than the age of completion of compulsory education and, in any case, not less than 15 years. The general minimum age is to be determined at the time of ratification of the Convention. It could be raised later, but not lowered (Article 2).

> *Countries are to pursue national policies to raise progressively the minimum age for admission to employment or work to a level consistent with the fullest physical and mental development of young persons.*

Recommendation No. 146 provides that the minimum age should be fixed at the same level for all sectors of economic activity and the objective should be to raise progressively to 16 years the minimum age for employment or work.

For countries whose economy and educational facilities are insufficiently developed, the minimum age can be set initially at 14 years. Employers' and workers' organizations must be consulted to fix the age for admission to employment at age 14. Countries which use this provision have to continue to report to the ILO on whether the reason for setting the lower age continues to exist.

Social policy Conventions

Two social policy Conventions[10] require that the school-leaving age and the minimum age for employment be prescribed. Although the ages are not specified in these Conventions, they provide that the employment of school-age children during school hours should be prohibited where educational facilities are available. The underlying principle is that the employment of children must not deprive them of the possibility of receiving an education.

Problems in national legislation

National legislation often falls short of providing complete coverage by either excluding or omitting persons working otherwise than under a contract of employment, excluding categories of work and excluding branches of economic activity. Many countries have not established a single minimum age for **any employment or work**. Commonly excluded categories are agriculture, family undertakings and domestic service. Other excluded categories include enterprises with fewer than a specified number of workers, apprentices, self-employed workers, homeworkers and temporary or casual workers.

Many countries, however, do conform to the spirit of Convention No. 138 concerning a minimum age. Some 45 countries have set the minimum age for admission to employment or work at 15, and another 37 at 14. In 23 countries the basic minimum age is 16. At least 122 countries have legislation prohibiting work for children below the age of 14, at least in some sectors.[11]

---

[10] The Social Policy (Non-Metropolitan Territories) Convention, 1947 (No. 82) and the Social Policy (Basic Aims and Standards) Convention, 1962 (No. 117).

[11] See Appendix 2.2 for the ages set by countries that have ratified Convention No. 138. See also ILO: *Child labour: Targeting the intolerable*, op.cit., table 4, pp. 39-46, for information on minimum age by regions of the world.

Minimum age for light work

Convention No. 138 and Recommendation No. 146

National laws or regulations may permit the employment of young persons on light work from the age of 13 to 15. Light work may be provided for those who are 15 years or older and have not yet finished their compulsory education. The competent authority must determine the activities that will be allowed as light work, as well as the hours and conditions of such work. The age for light work can be set at 12 by countries who have set 14 as the general minimum age because their economy or educational facilities are insufficiently developed (for as long as the situation lasts).

Light work is work which is "not likely to be harmful to the health or development of young persons and not such as to prejudice their attendance at school, their participation in vocational orientation or training programmes approved by the competent authority or their capacity to benefit from the instruction received" (Article 7).

The legislation of some countries contains more precise definitions of light work. It might include:

◆ simple and well-defined tasks;

◆ lack of physical or mental effort that could endanger the child's health or development;

◆ limited number of daily and weekly hours;

◆ regular breaks and weekly rest of at least 48 hours;

◆ no night work; and

◆ permission to work only in a family undertaking or under parental supervision.

Link to school attendance

The importance of safeguarding a child's attendance at school and the ability of the child to benefit from education is underlined. While the method for doing so is left up to the ratifying State, prohibiting work during school hours should be a minimum prerequisite for accomplishing this. In addition, limiting hours outside school hours during term time appears equally important in order to limit fatigue and allow time for study and recreation.

Minimum age for hazardous work

Convention No. 138 and Recommendation No. 146

Convention No. 138 establishes an obligation to set a higher minimum age of 18 for hazardous work (Article 3).

The Convention foresees that there might be work that is not placed in the same category as hazardous work, but still requires more maturity or physical development than at age 15. Thus the age could be set at 16 or 17 for certain kinds of work. The Convention provides that age 16 may be designated on condition that:

◆ the health, safety and morals of the young persons concerned are fully protected; and

◆ the young persons have received adequate specific instruction or vocational training in the relevant branch of activity.

Both these conditions must be fulfilled to allow such a lower age, as well as prior consultation with the employers' and workers' organizations concerned. This means that truly hazardous work is still to be subject to a minimum age of 18.

Though not adopted as a provision in the Convention, there was a feeling among some delegates to the International Labour Conference that adopted Convention No. 138 that any exceptions to age 18 should be on an individual case-by-case basis. Countries may wish to pursue that option to provide maximum protection.

Box 2.13. Flexibility provisions do not undermine the prohibition of hazardous work

Work defined as hazardous should not be excluded from national laws and regulations. While flexibility is allowed to ratifying States under Convention No. 138, protecting children from hazardous work should not be undermined by the flexibility provisions. This can be seen from the following:

◆ work which is likely to jeopardize the health, safety or morals of young persons cannot be excluded because of problems of application;

◆ even where economies and administrative facilities are not well developed, certain sectors must be covered; and

◆ it is suggested that a minimum age for hazardous work in all sectors and types of enterprises be provided (Recommendation 146).

Definition of hazardous work

Age 18 must be set for "any type of employment or work which by its nature or the circumstances in which it is carried out is likely to jeopardize the health, safety or morals of young persons".

63

"any type of employment or work"

This refers to activities and not necessarily occupations as a whole, though entire occupations can be designated. The work does not depend upon a contract of employment or other formal employment relationship.

"by its nature or circumstances in which it is carried out"

Because this provision refers to work "likely" to jeopardize the safety, health or morals of young persons and not only work which is recognized as having that effect, it is necessary to examine both the nature of the work and the circumstances in which it is carried out. The competent authorities are to take into account that certain types of activities which are not in themselves hazardous may become so in certain circumstances, for example, depending upon the hours of work, the place of work and the working conditions and environment.

"likely to jeopardize their health, safety and morals"

"Health and safety" refers not only to physical dangers, but also extends to other factors such as stress and psychological well-being. This provision also relates to work which poses dangers to the morals of young persons. Examples in national law include prohibited work in establishments which sell alcoholic beverages, or more generally in cabarets, night clubs and the like, and in the making, selling or distributing of writings, pictures, videotapes or other items which threaten the morals of young persons.

Methods for determining hazardous work

The Convention also provides that the types of employment or work concerned shall be determined by national laws or regulations or by the competent authority, leaving it to the individual countries to determine the content of these activities. Whatever the method chosen, it is necessary that a determination be made, and for this purpose prior consultations must be held with the concerned organizations of employers and workers, if they exist in the country.

"determined by national laws or regulations or competent authority"

While the exact method is left up to countries, the absence of a determination signifies non-fulfilment of an obligation of the Convention. There are also practical difficulties inherent in not making a definite determination, for example, concerning imposing sanctions for violations, giving notice to employers and providing clear guidelines to inspectors.

"after consultation with the concerned organizations of employers and workers"

Consultation is obligatory before the determination of the types of hazardous work is made. These groups should be good resources with knowledge of the requirements of different kinds of jobs and occupations, but they must also be aware that work affects young people differently than adults. Work which might seem safe for an adult can carry special risks for young people.

Recommendation No. 146 gives further guidance on determining hazardous work:

◆ **take full account of international labour standards**. Examples given are those concerning dangerous substances, agents or processes (including ionizing radiations), the lifting of heavy weights and underground work. There are also other ILO instruments of more general applicability concerning safety and health at work; and

◆ **re-examine the determination periodically and revise as necessary, particularly in the light of advancing scientific and technological knowledge**. As countries develop, it may be appropriate to impose restrictions on work by young persons in activities not previously practised in the country (for example, in connection with the mechanization of agriculture and increasing use of pesticides and other chemicals). There might also be improved safety techniques which replace certain dangerous activities or make an activity less dangerous.

Box 2.14. Special Hazard Review, United States

A Child Labour Working Team was formed in April 1994 by the National Institute for Occupational Safety and Health (NIOSH) of the United States Department of Health and Human Services to identify research, surveillance and intervention actions to prevent injuries and illnesses among working children and adolescents. This was a Special Hazard Review, a strategy of NIOSH to disseminate information that will help protect workers from workplace hazards under the Occupational Safety and Health Act of 1970. The Act emphasizes the need for standards to protect the safety and health of workers. The Team included representatives from federal and state government agencies responsible for labour, health and human services, agriculture and education, and from universities. It received expert presentations from a number of disciplines.

As part of the study, the following were reviewed:

◆ data on youth employment;

◆ occupational injury and illness data for youths;

◆ risk factors unique to children and adolescents;

◆ applicable federal and state laws and regulations;

◆ national objectives for the occupational safety and health of youths, including federal and private sector objectives; and

◆ NIOSH projects focused on children and adolescents (e.g. adverse neuro-behavioural effects in children of farm workers; support from farm safety; promoting safety and health in vocational, technical, and industrial programmes).

Safety and health Conventions

Provisions having relevance to the fixing of a minimum age for employment or work to protect children from particularly hazardous or arduous work are also found in some Conventions usually not considered as child labour Conventions. The following safety and health Conventions contain minimum ages for specific work or work processes:

◆ The **White Lead (Painting) Convention**, 1921 (No. 13), prohibits the employment of males under age 18 (prohibited to all females) in any painting work of an industrial character involving the use of **white lead or sulphate of lead** (Article 3).

◆ The **Radiation Protection Convention**, 1960 (No. 115), prohibits the engagement of persons under age 16 in work involving **ionizing radiation** and requires different levels of permissible doses to be fixed for those under age 18 and for other older workers (Article 7).

◆ The **Benzene Convention**, 1971 (No. 136), prohibits the employment of those under age 18 in work processes involving exposure to **benzene** (Article 11(2)).

◆ The **Maximum Weight Convention**, 1967 (No. 127), provides that the assignment of young workers under age 18 to the **manual transport of loads** should be substantially less than that permitted for adults (Article 7). Similarly, the **Occupational Safety and Health (Dock Work) Convention**, 1979 (No. 152), stipulates that lifting or cargo-handling appliances should be operated by a person of at least 18 years of age with the necessary aptitude and experience or by a person in training under proper supervision (Article 38(2)).

Problems in national legislation

Shortcomings in national legislation are particularly frequent regarding the requirements of a higher minimum age, as well as other protective conditions of work where hazardous work is concerned. Almost all countries have adopted some measures to prohibit or restrict dangerous work by young persons, though a great number of countries fail to cover comprehensively employment or work in hazardous or dangerous work by young persons.

Box 2.15. Top ten hazards to children prohibited in national legislation

◆ **Work in mining, quarries and underground**

◆ **Maritime work**

◆ **Work with machinery in motion and dangerous machinery**

◆ **Work with explosives**

◆ **Work involving heavy weights and loads**

◆ **Work in construction and/or demolition**

◆ **Work involving exposure to noxious and radioactive substances**

◆ **Work with lead/zinc metallurgy**

◆ **Work in transportation, operating vehicles**

◆ **Work in entertainment, alcohol production and sale**

Approaches vary considerably. Several countries have made little or no determination of what specific kinds of work are covered by the prohibition. Where prohibitions exist, the most frequent method is to forbid certain jobs or categories of jobs, for example, working with machinery of various sorts or in specified occupations. Another approach is to set the minimum age for employment or work in certain sectors, most often in factories or on ships, at a higher age than for other employment or work.

In some countries, the definition of hazardous work is limited to a general statement concerning work that is "dangerous, dirty, unhealthy or detrimental to morals", and no further elaboration of activities is provided, or administration authorities are to define it. In other cases, hazardous occupations are listed in some detail, with or without authority given to administrative authorities to update or supplement the lists.

Conditions of employment

Convention No. 138 and Recommendation No. 146

Convention No. 138 refers to conditions of work for children who are of the legal age to work or who are allowed to work under particular exceptions:

◆ **Light work** – the number of hours and the conditions in which light work may be done are to be set by the competent authority (Article 7).

◆ **Artistic performances** – permits that allow children to work in artistic performances must limit the number of hours of work and prescribe the conditions in which the work is allowed (Article 8).

Recommendation No. 146 provides further guidance on conditions of employment:

◆ **Measures** should be taken to ensure that the working conditions for those under the age of 18 are maintained at a satisfactory standard and supervised closely.

◆ **Measures** should also be taken to safeguard and supervise the conditions in which **vocational orientation and training** are provided in enterprises, training institutions and schools for vocational or technical education, and standards should be formulated for the protection and development of the young persons involved.

In setting standards for conditions of work and training, including the conditions applicable to light work, the following should be given special attention:

◆ fair remuneration and its protection, bearing in mind the principle of equal pay for equal work;

◆ strict limits on daily and weekly hours of work, and the prohibition of overtime to allow enough time for education and training, including the time needed for homework, and time for rest during the day and for leisure activities;

◆ a minimum consecutive period of 12 hours of night rest, without exception, unless for a genuine emergency, and weekly rest days;

◆ an annual holiday with pay of at least four weeks and, in no case, shorter than that granted to adults;

◆ coverage by social security schemes, including employment injury, medical care and sickness benefit schemes, whatever the conditions of employment or work; and

◆ maintenance of satisfactory standards of safety and health and appropriate instruction and supervision.

In addition, most international labour standards apply without any distinction being made as to age: they are thus applicable to children on the same basis as to adult workers.

Night work Conventions

Conventions Nos. 6 and 90 regulate the night work of young persons in industry, while **Convention No. 79** covers night work of young persons in non-industrial occupations.[12] Convention No. 6 prohibits the employment of young persons under 18 years of age in any industrial undertaking during the night. Night is defined as a period of at least 11 consecutive hours, including the time between 10 p.m. and 5 a.m. with exceptions for those over the age of 16 in certain continuous work processes such as the manufacture of iron and steel. Recommendation No. 146 calls for a consecutive period of 12 hours of night rest.

Convention No. 90 also prohibits the employment or work of those under age 18 during the night, but prolongs the period beyond that of Convention No. 6 – night is a period of at least 12 consecutive hours. For those under age 16, the night period must include the time between 10 p.m. and 6 a.m., while the competent authority is to prescribe a similar compulsory interval for those who have attained age 16 but are under age 18, within a given margin of flexibility.

Convention No. 79 provides definitions of "night" in relation to age and whether the children are subject to full-time compulsory school attendance.

Medical examination of young persons Conventions

Several Conventions place another condition on the employment of children and young persons – the requirement of medical examinations to prove fitness for employment. These Conventions apply to industry, non-industrial occupations, underground work and employment at sea.[13] They call for a thorough medical examination of children and young persons under 18 years of age (21 years in the case of underground work) before they can be admitted to employment, and continued medical supervision until 18 years of age.

---

[12] Night Work of Young Persons (Industry) Convention, 1919 (No. 6); Night Work of Young Persons (Industry) Convention (Revised), 1948 (No. 90); Night Work of Young Persons (Non-Industrial Occupations) Convention, 1946 (No. 79). The Governing Body of the ILO has decided that these Conventions should be revised, possibly to consolidate provisions on night work of young persons into one instrument. Such revision, however, has not yet been placed on the agenda of the International Labour Conference for action.

[13] Medical Examination of Young Persons (Industry) Convention, 1944 (No. 77); Medical Examination of Young Persons (Non-Industrial Occupations) Convention, 1946 (No. 78); Medical Examination of Young Persons (Underground Work) Convention, 1965 (No. 124); Medical Examination of Young Persons (Sea) Convention, 1921 (No. 16).

Box 2.16. Vigilance committees in India and Pakistan

I ndia and Pakistan have adopted specific laws on bonded labour and call for the setting up of vigilance committees. Such committees are to be set up at the district level and comprise elected representatives of the area, representatives of the district administration, bar associations, press, recognized social services, and labour departments of federal and provincial governments.

The functions of the committees include advising the district administration on matters relating to the effective implementation of the law, helping in the rehabilitation of freed bonded labourers, monitoring application of the law, and providing bonded labourers with necessary assistance to achieve the objectives of the law. However, as pointed out by the Committee of Experts, social monitoring is needed at the local level to make the law work. In addition, the committees need to be strengthened to accomplish the objectives set out in the law.

Forced labour

The Forced Labour Convention (No. 29)

A fundamental ILO Convention that protects children against some of the worst forms of exploitation is the Forced Labour Convention, 1930 (No. 29), which aims at suppressing the use of forced or compulsory labour.

Forced or compulsory labour is defined as "all work or service which is exacted from any person under the menace of any penalty and for which the said person has not offered himself voluntarily".

Convention No. 29 is one of the most widely ratified of the ILO Conventions. Since it applies to everyone, whatever age, it protects children from forced or compulsory labour and is applicable to some of the worst forms of child labour, such as children in bondage and their exploitation in prostitution and pornography.

In 1994 (and again in 1997) the Committee of Experts expressed its grave concern about forced child labour, and particularly the exploitation of children for prostitution and pornography. It has stated on several occasions that forced labour exploitation of children is one of the worst forms of forced labour, which must be fought energetically and punished severely. The Committee has called for action not only by the States in which such exploitation of children occurs, but also by other countries to assist in the eradication of these practices, especially exploitation by tourists and visitors from outside.

Children in prostitution and pornography

Prostitution is most commonly dealt with in penal legislation. Some countries have enacted specific provisions on the use of children in prostitution or on sexual exploitation and abuse which cover prostitution, the enticement of children into sexual acts, the procurement of children for prostitution and/or the drawing of economic benefit from sexual activities involving children.

Child pornography has also received specific references in national legislation or has more generally been included in laws regulating pornography or obscene or indecent publications. It is common practice to make it a crime both to produce and to disseminate child pornography, with generally higher penalties for commercializing it. Possession of pornographic material depicting children has also recently become a criminal offence in some countries. The use of new technologies to construct and disseminate child pornography, and to make it instantly available to a global audience through the Internet, presents a major new challenge to law-makers and law enforcement officials alike, and calls for new forms of international cooperation.

Some examples are provided in box 2.17.

Enforcement

Convention No. 138 and Recommendation No. 146

Convention No. 138 provides that **all necessary measures** must be taken by the government to ensure the effective enforcement of the provisions of the Convention in practice. The political will to provide adequate enforcement is a prerequisite for a coherent and concerted national policy for the elimination of child labour. Measures for effective enforcement include:

◆ appropriate penalties;

◆ specification of the persons responsible for complying with national legislation. This can be done in national legislation and regulations or by the competent authority. (The majority of countries hold the employer responsible for violations of child labour laws, but some national legislation holds parents responsible for certain violations.); and

Box 2.17. National legislation on children in prostitution and pornography

Republic Act No. 7610, the Philippines

The Philippines has adopted legislation specifically on child prostitution. It provides penalties for those who engage in or promote, facilitate or induce child prostitution. The Act aims at stronger deterrence and special protection against child abuse, exploitation and discrimination. Article III, Child prostitution and other sexual abuse, states that:

> *"Children whether male or female, who for money, profit or any other consideration or due to the coercion or influence of any adult, syndicate or group, indulge in sexual intercourse or lascivious conduct, are deemed to be children exploited in prostitution and other sexual abuse."*

Penalties are provided for those who engage in or promote, facilitate or induce child prostitution which includes, but is not limited to, the following:

◆ procuring a child prostitute;

◆ inducing clients of child prostitutes by written or oral advertisements or other similar means;

◆ taking advantage of influence or relationship to procure a child prostitute;

◆ threatening or using violence towards a child to engage the child as a prostitute; and

◆ giving monetary consideration, goods or other pecuniary benefits to a child prostitute.

Child Protection and Adoption Act, Zimbabwe

It is a criminal offence to allow a child to live in or frequent a brothel, to cause a child to be engaged in prostitution or immoral acts, to seduce a child or to allow a child to consort with someone engaged in prostitution.

National legislation on child pornography
Juveniles (Amendment) Act, 1997, Fiji

A recent amendment to the law of Fiji inserts a new section to the Juveniles Act prohibiting the production, distribution or use of pornography featuring juveniles or persons who look like juveniles. The law provides for punishment of up to 14 years imprisonment.

◆ registers or other documents to be kept by the employer with information (names and ages or dates of birth, duly certified where possible) about workers who are less than 18 years old. The national law, regulations or the competent authority is to prescribe the registers or other documents to be kept.

Recommendation No. 146 emphasizes the working of inspection services:

◆ strengthening labour inspection and related services by, for example, providing special training for inspectors on detecting abuses in the employment or work of children and young persons, and on correcting such abuses;

◆ strengthening government services for the improvement and inspection of training offered in enterprises;

◆ placing emphasis on the role which can be played by inspectors in supplying information and advice on effective means of complying with relevant provisions of the law and in securing enforcement of the law;

◆ coordinating labour inspection and inspection of training to provide economic efficiency;

◆ having the labour administration services work in close cooperation with the services responsible for the education, training, welfare and guidance of children and young persons;

and gives special attention to:

◆ the enforcement of provisions concerning hazardous types of employment or work;

◆ the prevention of work during the hours when instruction is available where education or training is compulsory; and

◆ taking measures to facilitate the verification of ages, such as:

Birth registration	maintaining an effective system of birth registration, including issuance of birth certificates;
Lists of young workers	requiring employers to keep and make available to the competent authority registers or other documents which give the names and ages or dates of birth of children and young people who are employed and who receive vocational orientation or training in their enterprises;
Documents for those in the informal sector	issuing licences or other documents to children and young persons who work in the streets, in outside stalls, in public places, in itinerant occupations or in other circumstances which make checking employers' records impracticable and which indicate their eligibility to work.

The Labour Inspection Convention (No. 81)

For countries which have ratified the **Labour Inspection Convention**, 1947 (No. 81), the following provision is particularly relevant:

"The functions of the system of labour inspection shall be: (a) to secure the enforcement of the legal provisions relating to ... the employment of children and young persons...."

The **Labour Inspection Recommendation,** 1947 (No. 81), further suggests that annual reports on the work of inspection services give information on the classification of persons employed, which should include a heading on children and young persons.

National legislation

Most national legislation contains specific measures to facilitate enforcement of minimum age and other child labour provisions, as well as machinery for enforcement. Virtually all countries have some form of labour inspection and, indeed, 120 countries have ratified Convention No. 81. Even so, in practice many encounter serious problems in enforcing child labour laws.[14]

The Forced Labour Convention (No. 29)

A broad policy framework is required to put an end to children in bondage. A comprehensive national policy and programme of action covering legislative reforms, effective enforcement systems, and a system of compulsory and free education are required. Most countries include the principle of the prohibition of forced labour or slavery in their Constitutions or labour legislation. See Checklist 2.3 for guidance on developing legislation on child bondage.

Box 2.18. Types of enforcement provisions in national legislation

◆ **Designation of persons responsible for complying with the law**

◆ **Labour inspection**

◆ **Special child labour units**

◆ **Record keeping**

  ❖ **Registers of young workers**

  ❖ **Evidence of age**

  ❖ **Notification of the competent authority**

  ❖ **Lists displayed at the workplace**

◆ **Work permits**

◆ **Medical examinations for fitness for work**

◆ **Posting information about the law**

◆ **Penalties for violations of the law**

  ❖ **Fines and/or imprisonment**

  ❖ **Revoking licences to operate**

◆ **Penalties for violation of compulsory education laws**

◆ **Complaint and investigative procedures**

◆ **Provision for advisory committees**

---

[14] See ILO: *Child labour: Targeting the intolerable,* op.cit., Chapter 5, for an overview of national law and practice, and problems and progress in enforcement.

2.4 NEW INTERNATIONAL LABOUR STANDARDS ON THE WORST FORMS OF CHILD LABOUR

There has been growing international consensus that more specific attention needs to be given to the worst abuses of child labour. To this end the ILO's Governing Body decided to propose new instruments on child labour. The overriding purpose of the new instruments is to ensure that children in all countries, irrespective of their level of develoment, are protected from the worst forms of child labour. A new Convention and Recommendation were discussed for the first time at the International Labour Conference in June 1998 and adopted unanimously in June 1999.[15] These are the Worst Forms of Child Labour Convention, 1999 (No. 182), and Recommendation, 1999 (No. 190).

The new Convention complements Convention No. 138. The basic obligation of ratifying States is to take immediate and effective measures to secure the prohibition and elimination of the worst forms of child labour as a matter of urgency. The Recommendation gives further guidance for legislative and practical action. The new Convention is the only instrument focused on the worst forms of child labour. Immediate action for the elimination of such forms is the priority for national and international action towards the total abolition of child labour.

The Convention and Recommendation apply to all children under the age of 18 in conformity with the general age stipulated in the United Nations Convention on the Rights of the Child and the minimum age for hazardous work in ILO Convention No. 138. Unlike Convention No. 138, however, the new standards apply to all sectors of activity without the possibility of limiting their scope to certain sectors or branches of activity.

The expression **"the worst forms of child labour"** comprises:

◆ all forms of slavery and practices similar to slavery, such as the sale and trafficking of children, debt bondage and serfdom and forced or compulsory labour, including forced or compulsory recruitment of children for use in armed conflict;

◆ the use, procuring or offering of a child for prostitution, for the production of pornography or for pornographic performances;

◆ the use, procuring or offering of a child for illicit activities, in particular for the production and trafficking of drugs; and

◆ work which, by its nature or the circumstances in which it is carried out, is likely to harm the health, safety or morals of children.

---

[15] Conference reports on the subject: ILO: *Child labour: Targeting the intolerable*, op. cit.; idem: *Child labour*, Report VI(2), International Labour Conference, 86th Session, Geneva, 1998; idem: "Report of the Committee on Child labour", Provisional Record No. 19, International Labour Conference, 86th Session, Geneva, 1998; idem: *Child labour*, Report IV(1), International Labour Conference, 87th Session, Geneva, 1999; idem: *Child labour*, Reports IV(2A) and (2B), International Labour Conference, 87th Session, Geneva 1999; idem: "Report of the Committee on Child Labour", Provisional Record Nos. 19, 19A, 19B and 26, International Labour Conference, 87th Session, Geneva, 1999.

It is difficult to designate specific work at the international level which, by its nature or the conditions in which it is performed, is likely to harm the health, safety or morals of children. Therefore, the Convention provides that governments are to determine which jobs or work are considered to be dangerous and which should be prohibited for children after consultation with the concerned employers and workers, and taking into consideration relevant international standards, in particular paragraphs 3 and 4 of the Recommendation. These paragraphs provide further guidance on which should be considered as hazardous work.

Box 2.19. Highlights of Convention No. 182 and Recommendation No. 190 on the worst forms of child labour

The Convention:

◆ covers children under age 18;

◆ requires immediate and effective measures for the prohibition and elimination of the worst forms of child labour as a matter of urgency;

◆ includes as worst forms of child labour:

❖ slavery, forced labour, sale and trafficking of children; forced recruitment of children for use in armed conflict;

❖ use of children in prostitution, pornography, illicit activities; and

❖ hazardous work;

◆ requires effective enforcement, including penal or other sanctions;

◆ requires measures for prevention, removal, rehabilitation and social integration, and access to free basic education;

◆ requires taking account of the special situation of girls and other children at special risk;

◆ requires monitoring mechanisms and programmes of action; and

◆ provides for international cooperation and/or assistance.

The Recommendation encourages member States to:

◆ adopt national programmes of action which:

❖ identify and denounce the worst forms of child labour;

❖ protect the very young, girls, children in hidden work situations and other especially vulnerable children;

❖ include measures for prevention, removal, rehabilitation and social integration; and

❖ raise awareness and mobilize society;

◆ consider given criteria in determining hazardous work;

◆ establish monitoring mechanisms to ensure effective implementation;

◆ compile data;

◆ provide appropriate penalties and remedies;

◆ designate certain activities as criminal offences;

◆ consider a wide range of measures aimed at eliminating the worst forms of child labour; and

◆ cooperate with international efforts and enhance cooperation and/or assistance among members.

Box 2.20. Recommendation No. 190

In determining work which is likely to harm the health, safety or morals of children, consider:

(a) work which exposes children to physical, psychological or sexual abuse;

(b) work underground, under water, at dangerous heights or in confined spaces;

(c) work with dangerous machinery, equipment and tools, or which involves the manual handling or transport of heavy loads;

(d) work in an unhealthy environment which may, for example, expose children to hazardous substances, agents or processes, or to temperatures, noise levels, or vibrations damaging to their health;

(e) work under particularly difficult conditions such as work for long hours, or during the night or work where the child is unreasonably confined to the premises of the employer.

Work that might otherwise be considered hazardous could be authorized as from the age of 16 if the health, safety and morals of the children concerned are fully protected, and if the children have received adequate, specific instruction or vocational training in the relevant branch of activity.

2.5 OTHER INTERNATIONAL TREATIES

Several other international treaties are relevant to child labour and the protection of children from exploitative and hazardous work. Foremost among these is the United Nations Convention on the Rights of the Child, 1989, which has been almost universally ratified[16]. This Convention is the most comprehensive treaty on the rights of children, whom it defines as persons under the age of 18, unless the age of majority is attained earlier. It seeks to protect a wide range of children's rights, including the right to be protected from economic exploitation and from performing any work that is likely to be hazardous or to interfere with their education, or to be harmful to their health or physical, mental, spiritual, moral or social development.

The Convention requires States parties to take legislative, administrative, social and educational measures to ensure implementation and, in particular, to provide for (a) a minimum age for admission to employment, (b) appropriate regulation of the hours and conditions of employment, and (c) appropriate penalties or other sanctions to ensure the effective enforcement of its provisions, taking into account the relevant

[16] Other instruments include the International Convenant on Economic, Social and Cultural Rights; the International Covenant on Civil and Political Rights; the Supplementary Convention on the Abolition of Slavery, the Slave Trade, and Institutions and Practices Similar to Slavery; and the Convention for the Suppression of the Traffic in Persons and of the Exploitation of the Prostitution of Others.

provisions of other international instruments. The Committee on the Rights of the Child, which oversees implementation of this Convention, has identified ILO Convention No. 138 as being of key importance[17] and urges States parties that have not already ratified it to do so.

The right of the child to education is also recognized under this Convention, which provides that primary education should be compulsory and available free to all. Several other articles have a particular bearing on some of the worst forms of child labour, such as sexual exploitation and sexual abuse, the abduction of, sale of or traffic in children for any purpose or in any form, and all other forms of exploitation prejudicial to any aspects of the child's welfare. It calls on States parties to take all appropriate measures to promote physical and psychological recovery and social reintegration of a child victim of neglect, exploitation or abuse.

Box 2.21. United Nations Convention on the Rights of the Child

Article 32 recognizes the right of the child to be protected from economic exploitation and any work that is likely:

◆ to be hazardous; or

◆ to interfere with the child's education; or

◆ to be harmful to the child's health or physical, mental, spiritual, moral or social development.

Other relevant articles include:

◆ Article 33, requiring States parties to take measures to prevent the use of children in illicit production and trafficking of narcotic drugs;

◆ Article 34, requiring protection against sexual exploitation;

◆ Article 35, prevention of abduction, sale and trafficking of children for any purpose;

◆ Article 36, requiring protection against all other forms of exploitation prejudicial to any aspects of the child's welfare;

◆ Article 28, granting a child's right to education; and

◆ Article 39, providing for measures to promote the physical and psychological recovery and social integration of child victims.

[17] See UNICEF: *Implementation handbook for the Convention on the Rights of the Child* (New York, 1998).

2.6 INITIATIVES TO IMPROVE CHILD LABOUR LEGISLATION

Action towards improving national legislation is being taken in many countries. Initiatives in legislative reform include consolidating and harmonizing disparate laws concerning children, expanding coverage of the law, increasing penalties, providing compensation for child victims of violations of child labour laws and reinforcing enforcement mechanisms. Some examples of these have already been given in this chapter. This section highlights comprehensive legislative approaches to addressing the child labour problem through legislation enabling the establishment of structures to deal with the problem, and through efforts at developing model legislation.

Box 2.22. Legal framework for sharing responsibility between government and civil society, Brazil

The Government of Brazil has adopted enabling legislation for dealing with the protection of children, including provisions on child labour, which sets up a decentralized structure to take action against child labour at all governmental levels in cooperation with civil society.

In addition, the question of child labour and the ratification of Convention No. 138 has been included in the National Human Rights Programme (*Programa Nacional de Direitos Humanos*) launched by the President of the Republic on 13 May 1996.

The legal structure starts with the Constitution, which contains provisions on promoting children's rights, including the right to education, and the protection of children against exploitation, violence, cruelty and oppression, among others. There is also a provision on the minimum age for admission to employment. The provisions are implemented through the Statute of the Child and Adolescent (ECA).

The Statute of the Child and Adolescent (ECA)

The ECA was adopted in 1990 and provides for the promotion and protection of children's and adolescents' rights, including guidelines for combating child labour. Key aspects are decentralization, participation and mobilization, and the consolidation of provisions on child labour.

◆ Decentralization is a cornerstone of the policy and is to be accomplished through legally mandated Councils at the national, state and municipal levels.

2.7	# LESSONS LEARNED

The review and improvement of national legislation are an integral part of a national strategy to eliminate child labour. Effective policies need a solid framework of child labour laws. They provide a basis for advocating improvements in practice and legal avenues to stop the worst abuses.

Making the law known is critical, especially to children, parents and small and informal sector enterprises, as it contributes to a better understanding of the protection afforded to children and can raise awareness of the risks of child labour.

Improved training is needed for those responsible for enforcement, especially where enforcement of child labour laws is only one aspect of an inspector's work. Involvement of employers' and workers' organizations, NGOs, communities and other segments of civil society may be needed in monitoring the law, especially in the urban informal sector and rural areas.

The National Council for the Rights of Children and Adolescents (CONANDA) is an interdisciplinary council composed of governmental and non-governmental representatives. It is responsible for policies regarding children and adolescents under the ECA. Its function is mainly political: formulation of policies, monitoring and evaluation of activities, and mobilizing society. It provides the orientation for the actions of state and municipal councils that have responsibilities for children and adolescents. The Ministry of Justice heads the National Council. The Council has selected child labour, sexual exploitation of children and adolescents, and juvenile delinquency as priority areas for action.

State councils are similar to the National Council. There are 27, one for each state.

Municipal councils are created by municipal laws. The municipal government appoints half the members, while civil society elects the other members, normally in a public assembly attended by relevant NGOs. The Councils supervise all activities concerning children and all projects and programmes must be registered with it.

There are also autonomous tutelary councils at the municipal level composed of five members from civil society. These are charged with ensuring that the rights of children and adolescents are protected.

◆ **Participation and mobilization.** The ECA encourages and provides for the active participation of different segments of society in the implementation of the law and encourages the mobilization of organized groups for the rights of children and adolescents.

◆ **Child labour provisions.** Numerous articles of the ECA are devoted to child labour and the protection of working minors. The minimum age for admission to employment is 14, consistent with the Constitutional provision, with an exception of 12 for apprenticeships.

IPEC supports activities to build the capacity of the state and municipal councils, including activities to train trade unions and others to participate in the councils.

Box 2.23. Special committees on child labour

A number of countries, such as Colombia, Kenya, Thailand and Turkey, have established specialized bodies within government to supervise and implement action on child labour. In Turkey, for example, a Child Labour Unit was established in 1992 in the Ministry of Labour and Social Security to coordinate child labour activities, develop new concepts and strategies, and improve national legislation. In addition to improving enforcement of child labour laws, its programme includes strengthening the capability of the Ministry, local government bodies, employers' and workers' organizations, and NGOs to deal effectively with child labour.

High-level committees consisting of government representatives, employers' and workers' organizations, NGOs and academics have been set up in Colombia, Kenya and Thailand to assist in policy formulation and programme implementation.

The Brazilian Government created the Executive Group on the Eradication of Forced Labour (GERTRAF) in 1995. The Group is interministerial and its principal objective is to combat forced labour, including forced child labour.

In Portugal, the Council of Ministers established a plan in June 1998 for the Elimination of the Exploitation of Child Labour (PEETI). A National Committee to Combat Child Labour was to be formed with the participation of various ministries, associations and municipalities, workers' and employers' organizations, and NGOs.

A proliferation of laws may lead to confusion among those responsible for enforcement. Consolidating provisions on child labour can help in better implementation and enforcement of the law.

Laws are not static. They evolve with time along with changes in economic circumstances, social structures and cultural attitudes. Improvement in educational facilities, for example, should be accompanied by improvement in the law, especially concerning the minimum age for admission to employment or work and restrictions on hours of work.

Including provisions in legislation which call for periodic studies and reports, setting up statutory advisory committees or bodies, and requiring periodic reviews of prohibited types of work – all ensure continued attention to the issue of child labour and can facilitate progressive improvement in national legislation.

The consideration of ratifying Conventions Nos. 138 and 182 can serve as a catalyst for revising and improving legislation. Ratification of these Conventions is a concrete manifestation of the country's political commitment to take affirmative action on child labour. It provides a rallying point for action against child labour and creates a climate of confidence for advocacy and collaborative action. The ratification process raises awareness of Convention No. 138 and the child labour problem. In IPEC-participating countries, technical advisory services, tripartite consultations and advocacy efforts of IPEC programme partners can play an important part in facilitating the ratification process.

Box 2.24. Designing model legislation

The Child Labor Coalition in the United States, concerned with the resurfacing of child labour problems, especially reports of children working illegally and in dangerous occupations, developed a tool for use by the States in strengthening child labour laws. This advocacy tool is in the form of a Model State Child Labor Law published in 1992 to spur legislative thinking and action. The model sets standards for the employment of minors consistent with the Coalition's primary objective of protecting the health, education, and well-being of working minors regardless of their occupation.

The model law, among other provisions:

◆ revises and updates the list of Hazardous Occupation Orders – those occupations, machines, and work sites that are prohibited to minors under the age of 18;

◆ provides equal protection under the law for migrant and seasonal farm worker children and prohibits minors from dangerous agricultural occupations and substances;

◆ establishes a linkage between educational fulfilment and continuation of work;

◆ reasonably restricts employment for all minors under the age of 18;

◆ requires work permits as a means to monitor employment and facilitate investigations; and

◆ requires labour education prior to employment, so that minors are knowledgeable about the laws protecting them in the workplace.

| Checklist 2.1 | # General principles |

☐ Countries should commit themselves to pursue a national policy designed to ensure the effective abolition of child labour.

☐ Policies should call for the immediate suppression of the worst forms of child labour.

☐ At the very least, national legislation should prohibit the employment of children under 12 or 13 in all sectors of activity and in all types of enterprise or employment

☐ National legislation should prohibit hazardous work in all occupations and sectors of activity.

☐ National legislation should prohibit abusive work and activities such as slavery and slave-like conditions, the use of children in prostitution and pornography.

☐ National legislation should provide for effective enforcement measures, including sufficient authority and resources to labour inspectorates and law enforcement.

☐ National legislation should provide the conditions under which children of legal age can work.

☐ Compulsory education laws and provisions on minimum ages for work should be harmonized.

| Checklist 2.2 | # Improving national legislation |

General considerations

☐ Designate a national authority with considerable power and influence having the mandate and responsibility for the elimination of child labour.

☐ Ratify relevant ILO Conventions, especially the Minimum Age Convention, 1973 (No. 138) and the Worst Forms of Child Labour Convention, 1999 (No. 182).

☐ Consider the provisions of ILO Recommendation No. 146, and Recommendation No. 190 concerning the worst forms of child labour, to guide national policy.

☐ Consider obligations under the United Nations Convention on the Rights of the Child.

☐ Identify measures which contribute to a national policy to eliminate child labour.

☐ Review all relevant legislation to identify insufficiencies, duplication or inconsistencies.

☐ Harmonize laws affecting child labour, including those on education and health.

☐ Consult with employers' and workers' organizations, particularly in circumstances provided for in Conventions Nos. 138 and 182.

☐ Create statutory advisory committees with broad representation such as from employers' and workers' organizations, NGOs, child advocates, education and health professionals, safety experts, community and youth groups, and other concerned groups as appropriate.

☐ Make the law known. Disseminate information widely in easily understood language. This could include information and education campaigns on the law and risks of child labour:

  ❖ for children, their parents and communities;

  ❖ for employers and potential employers;

  ❖ for professions who work with children, such as teachers; and

  ❖ for the public.

☐ Post information on the law in places of work, schools and communities.

☐ Adopt provisions in law which require periodic reports on child labour.

Coverage of the law

☐ Extend the law to all areas where child labour occurs, including the agricultural sector, domestic service, the informal sector and family undertakings.

☐ Work with enforcement authorities to identify ways to extend coverage and enforcement of the law to hard-to-reach areas.

☐ Check whether child labour provisions are included in the provisions applicable only to persons working under employment contracts, thus excluding self-employment. Ensure that self-employed child workers are protected.

☐ Set out intended exceptions clearly. If general authority is given to competent authorities to grant exceptions, provide specific guidelines or restrictions.

☐ Ensure that, as a minimum, the sectors identified in Article 5 of Convention No. 138 are covered, and that all hazardous work is covered as provided in Convention No. 182.

☐ Ensure that laws applicable to vocational education, training and apprenticeship programmes protect young persons from hazardous work and specify conditions in consultation with employers' and workers' organizations.

Minimum age

☐ Set minimum ages for admission to employment or work in line with Convention No. 138. The minimum age should be:

❖ no less than the age of compulsory education;

❖ no less than 15, or 14 in developing countries;

❖ no less than 18 for hazardous work; and

❖ no less than 13 for light work, or 12 in developing countries.

☐ Provide in law, regulation or by decision of the competent authority the types of employment or work to which the minimum age of 18 applies.

☐ Provide procedures for reviewing and updating restrictions and prohibitions on hazardous work and activities.

Enforcement

☐ Provide for effective enforcement, and monitoring measures and machinery.

☐ Establish child labour units and provide for coordination among government agencies responsible for enforcing laws affecting child labour.

☐ Specify those responsible for complying with the law.

☐ Provide adequate penalties.

☐ Provide for birth registration and other measures to facilitate the verification of ages.

☐ Target hazardous activities and occupations.

☐ Provide for lists or registers of young persons to be kept by employers.

☐ Address measures for prevention, removal of children from hazardous and unauthorized work, and rehabilitation of victims of child labour.

☐ Recognize links with the education system in child labour laws, for example concerning enforcement measures.

Conditions of work

☐ Determine whether light work is specifically addressed and defined in legislation; designate which activities are allowed and the hours and conditions for such work.

☐ Ensure that light work does not interfere with education and training.

☐ Ensure that any exceptions from minimum age provisions for artistic performances require individual permits specifying hours and conditions of work and prior consultations with organizations of employers and workers.

☐ Provide for measures to ensure that working conditions for those under age 18 are maintained at a satisfactory level and supervised closely.

- ☐ Provide standards for and take measures to safeguard and supervise the conditions of young persons in vocational orientation and training schools or programmes.

- ☐ Prohibit night work.

- ☐ Provide for medical examinations.

Worst forms of child labour

- ☐ Ratify Convention No. 182.

- ☐ Consider the provisions of the Forced Labour Convention, 1930 (No. 29), and the United Nations Supplementary Convention on the Abolition of Slavery, the Slave Trade, and Institutions and Practices Similar to Slavery (1956).

- ☐ Where necessary, improve the law prohibiting bonded labour, including the establishment of monitoring committees.

- ☐ Check the laws applicable to child prostitution and pornography. Consider the necessity and desirability of improving enforcement and extending criminal jurisdiction to acts committed by citizens outside the country.

Checklist 2.3 Legislation on bonded labour

The following checklist is based on a programme of action against child bondage developed during an ILO Asian Regional Seminar on children in bondage.[18]

- ☐ Specify forms of child bondage.

- ☐ Prohibit all forms of bondage.

- ☐ Provide appropriate sanctions.

- ☐ Provide compensation to victims.

- ☐ Provide for liquidation of debts and other obligations.

- ☐ Provide for enforcement and monitoring machinery, including inspection authority and special committees or task forces.

- ☐ Include provisions for the establishment of special courts and for speedy disposal of cases.

- ☐ Give protection to victims from reprisals.

- ☐ Complement the law by giving publicity to the law and violations.

---

[18] ILO: *A programme of action against child bondage*, in collaboration with the United Nations Centre for Human Rights (Geneva, 1992).

Checklist 2.4 Involving employers' and workers' organizations, and others

In implementing the provisions of Convention No. 138, governments can make use of several flexibility provisions. However, advance consultation with employers' and workers' organizations is required.

☐ Have advance consultations with employers' and workers' organizations before setting the general minimum age at 14 instead of 15 (allowed in countries whose economy and educational facilities are insufficiently developed) (Article 2).

☐ Consult employers' and workers' organizations before deciding whether to exclude limited categories of work because there are substantial problems of application (Article 4).

☐ Consult employers' and workers' organizations before exercising the option of limiting the scope of application initially to certain branches of economic activity or types of enterprise (allowed in countries whose economy and administrative facilities are insufficiently developed) (Article 5).

☐ Consult employers' and workers' organizations in determining the types of hazardous work to which the higher minimum age of 18 applies and in deciding whether the exception for authorizing certain work from age 16 is to be used and how it will be applied (Article 3).

☐ After consultation with employers' and workers' organizations, prescribe the conditions for carrying out work which is excluded from coverage of the Convention within the framework of training and education (Article 6).

☐ Consult employers' and workers' organizations before allowing exceptions for participation in artistic performances (Article 8).

Consultations are also required under Convention No. 182:

☐ Consult employers' and workers' organizations before determining types of work likely to harm the health, safety or morals of children, and identifying where such work exists (Article 4).

☐ After consultation with employers' and workers' organizations, designate monitoring mechanisms (Article 5).

☐ Design and implement programmes of action in consultation with employers' and workers' organizations, taking into consideration the views of other concerned groups as appropriate (Article 6).

Appendix 2.1   ILO Conventions on child labour and forced labour (as at 31 July 1999)

Convention		Age
No. 5	**Minimum Age (Industry) Convention, 1919**	14
No. 7	**Minimum Age (Sea) Convention, 1920**	14 on condition of school attendance
No. 10	**Minimum Age (Agriculture) Convention, 1921**	14
No. 15	**Minimum Age (Trimmers and Stokers) Convention, 1921**	18
No. 33	**Minimum Age (Non-Industrial Employment) Convention, 1932**	14
No. 58	**Minimum Age (Sea) Convention (Revised), 1936**	15
No. 59	**Minimum Age (Industry) Convention (Revised), 1937**	15
No. 60	**Minimum Age (Non-Industrial Employment) Convention (Revised), 1937**	15
No. 112	**Minimum Age (Fishermen) Convention, 1959**	15
No. 123	**Minimum Age (Underground Work) Convention, 1965**	16 or higher as specified
No. 138	**Minimum Age Convention, 1973**	15 (14); 18 hazardous work; 13 (12) light work
No. 182	**Worst Forms of Child Labour Convention, 1999**	18

Forced labour		
No. 29	**Forced Labour Convention, 1930**	

Appendix 2.2 | Minimum ages in ILO Conventions

Basic minimum age for admission to employment and work*		Reduced minimum age for light work	Higher minimum age for unhealthy and hazardous work	
14 years	15 years	12-13 years	16 years	18 years
Conventions Nos. 5, 7, 10, 33 and 138 (for countries "whose economy and educational facilities are insufficiently developed")	Conventions Nos. 58, 59, 60, 112 and 138	Two years lower than the basic minimum age set respectively under Conventions Nos. 33, 60 and 138	Convention No.123	Conventions Nos. 15, 112, 138 and the Conventions dealing with night work and other hazardous work

* Under Convention No.138, the basic minimum age "shall not be less than the age of completion of compulsory schooling". Conventions Nos. 33 and 60 (non-industrial employment) prohibit the employment of children who are over the minimum age but "who are still required ... to attend primary school".

Appendix 2.3

Ratification of ILO Conventions on child labour and forced labour

(as at 31 August 1999)

Convention No.	Title of Convention	Total of ratifications (in brackets, total of denunciations following ratification of revising Conventions)
5	**Minimum Age (Industry), 1919**	75 [23]
59	**Minimum Age (Industry) (Revised), 1937**	36 [16]
7	**Minimum Age (Sea), 1920**	54 [23]
58	**Minimum Age (Sea) (Revised), 1936**	52 [20]
10	**Minimum Age (Agriculture), 1921**	55 [23]
15	**Minimum Age (Trimmers and Stokers), 1921**	69 [27]
33	**Minimum Age (Non-Industrial Employment), 1932**	25 [8]
60	**Minimum Age (Non-Industrial Employment) (Revised), 1937**	11 [10]
112	**Minimum Age (Fishermen), 1959**	30 [18]
123	**Minimum Age (Underground Work), 1965**	42 [10]
138	**Minimum Age, 1973**	78
29	**Forced Labour, 1930**	149

Convention No.138 – List of countries with specified minimum age:

14: Argentina, Bolivia, Botswana, Egypt, El Salvador, Equatorial Guinea, Ethiopia, Guatemala, Honduras, Nepal, Nicaragua, Niger, Rwanda, United Republic of Tanzania, Togo, Venezuela (16 countries).

15: Belgium, Bosnia and Herzegovina, Burkina Faso, Chile, Costa Rica, Croatia, Cuba, Cyprus, Denmark, Dominica, Dominican Republic, Finland, Germany, Georgia, Greece, Guyana, Indonesia, Iraq, Israel, Italy, Republic of Korea, Libyan Arab Jamahiriya, Luxembourg, Malaysia, Mauritius, Netherlands, Norway, Philippines, Poland, Slovakia, Slovenia, Spain, Sweden, Switzerland, Turkey, the former Yugoslav Republic of Macedonia, United Arab Emirates, Uruguay, Yugoslavia, Zambia (40 countries).

16: Albania, Algeria, Antigua and Barbuda, Azerbaijan, Belarus, Bulgaria, China, France, Hungary, Ireland, Jordan, Kenya, Kyrgyzstan, Lithuania, Malta, Portugal, Romania, Russian Federation, San Marino, Tajikistan, Tunisia, Ukraine (22 countries).

| Appendix 2.4 | Chart of ratifications of ILO Conventions on child labour and forced labour by country (as at 31 August 1999) |

Country	No. 5	No.7	No.10	No.15	No.33	No.58	No.59	No.60	No.112	No.123	No.138	No.29
Total	73	54	55	69	25	52	36	11	30	42	78	149
Afghanistan												
Albania	X		X			X	X			X	X	X
Algeria			X*			X*					X	X
Angola		X										X
Antigua and Barbuda											X	X
Argentina	X	X	X	X	X	X					X	X
Armenia												
Australia		X	X	X		X			X	X		X
Austria	X		X		X							X
Azerbaijan											X	X
Bahamas	X	X	X									X
Bahrain												X
Bangladesh				X			X					X
Barbados	X	X	X									X
Belarus			X*	X*		X*	X*	X*		X*	X	X
Belgium	X*	X*	X*	X*	X*	X*			X*	X*	X	X
Belize	X	X	X	X		X						X
Benin	X				X							X
Bolivia	X									X	X	
Bosnia and Herzegovina											X	X
Botswana											X	X
Brazil	X	X*				X						X
Bulgaria	X*	X*	X*	X*		X*	X*	X*	X*	X*	X	X
Burkina Faso	X				X						X	X
Burundi							X					X
Cambodia												X
Cameroon	X		X	X	X					X		X
Canada		X		X	X							X
Cape Verde												X
Central African Republic	X		X		X							X
Chad	X				X							X
Chile	X	X	X	X							X	X
China		X		X			X			X		
Colombia	X	X	X	X								X
Comoros	X		X		X							X
Congo	X				X							X

Country	No. 5	No.7	No.10	No.15	No.33	No.58	No.59	No.60	No.112	No.123	No.138	No.29
Costa Rica									X*		X	X
Côte d'Ivoire	X				X							X
Croatia											X	X
Cuba	X*	X*	X*	X*	X*	X*	X*	X*	X*		X	X
Cyprus				X		X				X	X	X
Czech Republic	X		X							X		X
Democratic Republic of the Congo												X
Denmark	X	X		X		X			X		X	X
Djibouti	X		X	X	X	X				X		X
Dominica											X	X
Dominican Republic	X	X	X								X	X
Ecuador									X	X		X
Egypt											X	X
El Salvador											X	X
Equatorial Guinea											X	
Eritrea												
Estonia	X	X	X	X								X
Ethiopia											X	
Fiji	X					X	X					X
Finland		X*		X*							X	X
France	X*		X*	X*	X*	X*			X*	X*	X	X
Gabon	X		X		X					X		X
Gambia												
Georgia											X	X
Germany		X*	X*	X*					X*		X	X
Ghana				X		X	X					X
Greece	X*	X*		X*		X*					X	X
Grenada	X	X	X	X		X						X
Guatemala			X*	X*		X	X		X		X	X
Guinea	X		X		X				X			X
Guinea-Bissau		X										X
Guyana	X	X	X	X							X	X
Haiti	X											X
Honduras											X	X
Hungary		X	X	X						X	X	X
Iceland				X		X*						X
India	X			X						X		X
Indonesia											X	X
Iran, Islamic Republic of												X
Iraq				X*		X*	X*				X	X
Ireland	X*	X*	X*	X*							X	X

Country	No. 5	No.7	No.10	No.15	No.33	No.58	No.59	No.60	No.112	No.123	No.138	No.29
Israel	X*		X*						X*		X	X
Italy		X*	X*	X*		X*	X*	X*	X*	X*	X	X
Jamaica		X		X		X						X
Japan	X	X	X	X		X						X
Jordan										X	X	X
Kazakhstan												
Kenya	X*			X*		X*	X*		X*	X*	X	X
Korea, Rep. of											X	
Kuwait												X
Kyrgyzstan											X	X
Lao PDR												X
Latvia	X	X		X								
Lebanon				X		X	X					X
Lesotho	X											X
Liberia						X				X		X
Libyan Arab Jamahiriya							X*				X	X
Lithuania											X	X
Luxembourg	X*	X*	X*	X*			X*	X*			X	X
Madagascar	X				X					X		X
Malawi												
Malaysia		X¹		X²						X	X	X
Mali	X			X								X
Malta	X*	X*	X*	X*							X	X
Mauritania	X			X	X	X				X		X
Mauritius	X*	X*		X*		X*	X*				X	X
Mexico		X*				X			X	X		X
Moldova, Republic of												
Mongolia						X				X		
Morocco				X								X
Mozambique												
Myanmar				X								X
Namibia												
Nepal											X	
Netherlands	X*	X*	X*	X*	X*	X*			X*	X*	X	X
New Zealand		X	X			X	X	X*				X
Nicaragua	X*	X*	X*	X*							X	X
Niger	X*				X*						X	X
Nigeria				X		X	X			X		X
Norway	X*	X*	X*	X*		X*	X*		X*		X	X

¹ Sarawak.

² Sabah and Sarawak.

Country	No. 5	No.7	No.10	No.15	No.33	No.58	No.59	No.60	No.112	No.123	No.138	No.29
Oman												X
Pakistan				X			X					X
Panama			X	X		X			X	X		X
Papua New Guinea		X	X									X
Paraguay							X	X		X		X
Peru			X			X	X		X			X
Philippines							X				X	
Poland	X*	X*	X*	X*					X*	X	X	X
Portugal		X									X	X
Qatar												X
Romania	X*	X*	X*	X*			X*				X	X
Russian Federation			X*	X*		X*	X*	X*	X*	X*	X	X
Rwanda										X	X	
Saint Kitts and Nevis												
Saint Lucia	X	X		X								X
Saint Vincent and the Grenadines	X	X	X									
San Marino											X	X
Sao Tome and Principe												
Saudi Arabia										X		X
Senegal	X		X		X							X
Seychelles	X	X	X	X		X						X
Sierra Leone	X	X		X		X	X					X
Singapore	X	X		X								X
Slovakia	X		X							X	X	X
Slovenia											X	X
Solomon Islands												X
Somalia												X
South Africa												X
Spain	X*	X*	X*	X*	X*	X*	X*	X*	X*	X	X	X
Sri Lanka	X	X	X	X		X						X
Sudan												X
Suriname										X		X
Swaziland	X						X			X	X	X
Sweden		X*	X*	X*		X*					X	X
Switzerland	X			X		X				X	X	X
Syrian Arab Republic										X		X
Tajikistan											X	X
Tanzania, United Republic of	X³	X³		X		X³	X				X	X
Thailand										X		X

³ Zanzibar.

Country	No. 5	No.7	No.10	No.15	No.33	No.58	No.59	No.60	No.112	No.123	No.138	No.29
The Former Yugoslav Republic of Macedonia											X	X
Togo	X*				X*						X	X
Trinidad and Tobago				X								X
Tunisia						X	X*		X*	X	X	X
Turkey				X		X	X			X	X	X
Turkmenistan												X
Uganda	X									X		X
Ukraine			X*	X*		X*	X*	X*	X*	X*	X	X
United Arab Emirates											X	X
United Kingdom	X	X	X	X								X
United States						X						
Uruguay	X*	X*	X*	X*	X*	X*	X*	X*	X*		X	X
Uzbekistan												X
Venezuela	X*	X*									X	X
Viet Nam	X									X		
Yemen				X		X	X					X
Yugoslavia	X*	X*		X*		X*			X*	X*	X	X
Zambia	X*									X	X	X
Zimbabwe												X

* Convention denounced as a result of the ratification of revising Conventions or Convention No. 138.

Appendix 2.5 Excerpts from selected ILO standards on child labour

The first Convention on child labour was adopted at the first session of the International Labour Conference in 1919. This instrument – the Minimum Age (Industry) Convention, 1919 (No. 5) – fixed at 14 years the minimum age for admission of children to industrial employment. Subsequently, many international labour Conventions and Recommendations were adopted prohibiting the employment of children under a certain age and regulating their conditions of work in particular sectors or occupations. The most recent instruments on the subject are the Worst Forms of Child Labour Convention (No. 182), and Recommendation (No. 190), adopted in 1999. The fundamental and most comprehensive instruments towards the total abolition of child labour are the Minimum Age Convention (No. 138) and Recommendation (No. 146), adopted in 1973. Excerpts from these and other Conventions and Recommendations relating to night work, hazardous employment, the handling of heavy weights and medical examinations are reproduced below.

PROHIBITION AND ELIMINATION OF THE WORST FORMS OF CHILD LABOUR

Worst Forms of Child Labour Convention, 1999 (No. 182)

Excerpts, Articles 1 to 8.

Article 1

Each Member which ratifies this Convention shall take immediate and effective measures to secure the prohibition and elimination of the worst forms of child labour as a matter of urgency.

Article 2

For the purposes of this Convention, the term "child" shall apply to all persons under the age of 18.

Article 3

For the purposes of this Convention, the term "the worst forms of child labour" comprises:

(a) all forms of slavery or practices similar to slavery, such as the sale and trafficking of children, debt bondage and serfdom and forced or compulsory labour, including forced or compulsory recruitment of children for use in armed conflict;

(b) the use, procuring or offering of a child for prostitution, for the production of pornography or for pornographic performances;

(c) the use, procuring or offering of a child for illicit activities, in particular for the production and trafficking of drugs as defined in the relevant international treaties;

(d) work which, by its nature or the circumstances in which it is carried out, is likely to harm the health, safety or morals of children.

Article 4

1. The types of work referred to under Article 3(d) shall be determined by national laws or regulations or by the competent authority, after consultation with the organizations of employers and workers concerned, taking into consideration relevant international standards, in particular Paragraphs 3 and 4 of the Worst Forms of Child Labour Recommendation, 1999.

2. The competent authority, after consultation with the organizations of employers and workers concerned, shall identify where the types of work so determined exist.

3. The list of the types of work determined under paragraph 1 of this Article shall be periodically examined and revised as necessary, in consultation with the organizations of employers and workers concerned.

Article 5

Each Member shall, after consultation with employers' and workers' organizations, establish or designate appropriate mechanisms to monitor the implementation of the provisions giving effect to this Convention.

Article 6

1. Each Member shall design and implement programmes of action to eliminate as a priority the worst forms of child labour.

2. Such programmes of action shall be designed and implemented in consultation with relevant government institutions and employers' and workers' organizations, taking into consideration the views of other concerned groups as appropriate.

Article 7

1. Each Member shall take all necessary measures to ensure the effective implementation and enforcement of the provisions giving effect to this Convention including the provision and application of penal sanctions or, as appropriate, other sanctions.

2. Each Member shall, taking into account the importance of education in eliminating child labour, take effective and time-bound measures to:

(a) prevent the engagement of children in the worst forms of child labour;

(b) provide the necessary and appropriate direct assistance for the removal of children from the worst forms of child labour and for their rehabilitation and social integration;

(c) ensure access to free basic education, and, wherever possible and appropriate, vocational training, for all children removed from the worst forms of child labour;

(d) identify and reach out to children at special risk; and

(e) take account of the special situation of girls.

3. Each Member shall designate the competent authority responsible for the implementation of the provisions giving effect to this Convention.

Article 8

Members shall take appropriate steps to assist one another in giving effect to the provisions of this Convention through enhanced international cooperation and/or assistance including support for social and economic development, poverty eradication programmes and universal education.

Worst Forms of Child Labour Recommendation, 1999 (No. 190)

I. Programmes of action

2. The programmes of action referred to in Article 6 of the Convention should be designed and implemented as a matter of urgency, in consultation with relevant government institutions and employers' and workers' organizations, taking into consideration the views of the children directly affected by the worst forms of child labour, their families and, as appropriate, other concerned groups committed to the aims of the Convention and this Recommendation. Such programmes should aim at, inter alia:

(a) identifying and denouncing the worst forms of child labour;

(b) preventing the engagement of children in or removing them from the worst forms of child labour, protecting them from reprisals and providing for their rehabilitation and social integration through measures which address their educational, physical and psychological needs;

(c) giving special attention to:

    (i) younger children;

    (ii) the girl child;

    (iii) the problem of hidden work situations, in which girls are at special risk;

    (iv) other groups of children with special vulnerabilities or needs;

(d) identifying, reaching out to and working with communities where children are at special risk;

(e) informing, sensitizing and mobilizing public opinion and concerned groups, including children and their families.

II. Hazardous work

3. In determining the types of work referred to under Article 3(d) of the Convention, and in identifying where they exist, consideration should be given, inter alia, to:

(a) work which exposes children to physical, psychological or sexual abuse;

(b) work underground, under water, at dangerous heights or in confined spaces;

(c) work with dangerous machinery, equipment and tools, or which involves the manual handling or transport of heavy loads;

(d) work in an unhealthy environment which may, for example, expose children to hazardous substances, agents or processes, or to temperatures, noise levels, or vibrations damaging to their health;

(e) work under particularly difficult conditions such as work for long hours or during the night or work where the child is unreasonably confined to the premises of the employer.

4. For the types of work referred to under Article 3(d) of the Convention and Paragraph 3 above, national laws or regulations or the competent authority could, after consultation with the workers' and employers' organizations concerned, authorize employment or work as from the age of 16 on condition that the health, safety and morals of the children concerned are fully protected, and that the children have received adequate specific instruction or vocational training in the relevant branch of activity.

III. Implementation

5. (1) Detailed information and statistical data on the nature and extent of child labour should be compiled and kept up to date to serve as a basis for determining priorities for national action for the abolition of child labour, in particular for the prohibition and elimination of its worst forms as a matter of urgency.

(2) As far as possible, such information and statistical data should include data disaggregated by sex, age group, occupation, branch of economic activity, status in employment, school attendance and geographical location. The importance of an effective system of birth registration, including the issuing of birth certificates, should be taken into account.

(3) Relevant data concerning violations of national provisions for the prohibition and elimination of the worst forms of child labour should be compiled and kept up to date.

6. The compilation and processing of the information and data referred to in Paragraph 5 above should be carried out with due regard for the right to privacy.

7. The information compiled under Paragraph 5 above should be communicated to the International Labour Office on a regular basis.

8. Members should establish or designate appropriate national mechanisms to monitor the implementation of national provisions for the prohibition and elimination of the worst forms of child labour, after consultation with employers' and workers' organizations.

9. Members should ensure that the competent authorities which have responsibilities for implementing national provisions for the prohibition and elimination of the worst forms of child labour cooperate with each other and coordinate their activities.

10. National laws or regulations or the competent authority should determine the persons to be held responsible in the event of non-compliance with national provisions for the prohibition and elimination of the worst forms of child labour.

11. Members should, in so far as it is compatible with national law, cooperate with international efforts aimed at the prohibition and elimination of the worst forms of child labour as a matter of urgency by:

(a) gathering and exchanging information concerning criminal offences, including those involving international networks;

(b) detecting and prosecuting those involved in the sale and trafficking of children, or in the use, procuring or offering of children for illicit activities, for prostitution, for the production of pornography or for pornographic performances;

(c) registering perpetrators of such offences.

12. Members should provide that the following worst forms of child labour are criminal offences:

(a) all forms of slavery or practices similar to slavery, such as the sale and trafficking of children, debt bondage and serfdom and forced or compulsory labour, including forced or compulsory recruitment of children for use in armed conflict;

(b) the use, procuring or offering of a child for prostitution, for the production of pornography or for pornographic performances; and

(c) the use, procuring or offering of a child for illicit activities, in particular for the production and trafficking of drugs as defined in the relevant international treaties, or for activities which involve the unlawful carrying or use of firearms or other weapons.

13. Members should ensure that penalties including, where appropriate, criminal penalties are applied for violations of the national provisions for the prohibition and elimination of any type of work referred to in Article 3(d) of the Convention.

14. Members should also provide as a matter of urgency for other criminal, civil or administrative remedies, where appropriate, to ensure the effective enforcement of national provisions for the prohibition and elimination of the worst forms of child labour, such as special supervision of enterprises which have used the worst forms of child labour, and, in cases of persistent violation, consideration of temporary or permanent revoking of permits to operate.

15. Other measures aimed at the prohibition and elimination of the worst forms of child labour might include the following:

(a) informing, sensitizing and mobilizing the general public, including national and local political leaders, parliamentarians and the judiciary;

(b) involving and training employers' and workers' organizations and civic organizations;

(c) providing appropriate training for the government officials concerned, especially inspectors and law enforcement officials, and for other relevant professionals;

(d) providing for the prosecution in their own country of the Member's nationals who commit offences under its national provisions for the prohibition and immediate elimination of the worst forms of child labour even when these offences are committed in another country;

(e) simplifying legal and administrative procedures and ensuring that they are appropriate and prompt;

(f) encouraging the development of policies by undertakings to promote the aims of the Convention;

(g) monitoring and giving publicity to best practices on the elimination of child labour;

(h) giving publicity to legal or other provisions on child labour in the different languages or dialects;

(i) establishing special complaints procedures and making provisions to protect from discrimination and reprisals those who legitimately expose violations of the provisions of the Convention, as well as establishing helplines or points of contact and ombudspersons;

(j) adopting appropriate measures to improve the educational infrastructure and the training of teachers to meet the needs of boys and girls;

(k) as far as possible, taking into account in national programmes of action:

(i) the need for job creation and vocational training for the parents and adults in the families of children working in the conditions covered by the Convention; and

(ii) the need for sensitizing parents to the problem of children working in such conditions.

16. Enhanced international cooperation and/or assistance among Members for the prohibition and effective elimination of the worst forms of child labour should complement national efforts and may, as appropriate, be developed and implemented in consultation with employers' and workers' organizations. Such international cooperation and/or assistance should include:

(a) mobilizing resources for national or international programmes;

(b) mutual legal assistance;

(c) technical assistance including the exchange of information;

(d) support for social and economic development, poverty eradication programmes and universal education.

MINIMUM AGE FOR ADMISSION TO EMPLOYMENT

Minimum Age Convention, 1973 (No. 138)

The General Conference of the ILO adopted Convention No. 138 in 1973 on a minimum age for admission to employment, stating that "the time has come to establish a general instrument on the subject, which would gradually replace the existing ones applicable to limited economic sectors, with a view to achieving the total abolition of child labour". Articles 1 to 9 are quoted in their entirety.

"Article 1

Each Member for which this Convention is in force undertakes to pursue a national policy designed to ensure the effective abolition of child labour and to raise progressively the minimum age for admission to employment or work to a level consistent with the fullest physical and mental development of young persons.

Article 2

1. Each Member which ratifies this Convention shall specify, in a declaration appended to its ratification, a minimum age for admission to employment or work within its territory and on means of transport registered in its territory; subject to Articles 4 to 8 of this Convention, no one under that age shall be admitted to employment or work in any occupation.

2.   Each Member which has ratified this Convention may subsequently notify the Director-General of the International Labour Office, by further declarations, that it specifies a minimum age higher than that previously specified.

3.   The minimum age specified in pursuance of paragraph 1 of this Article shall not be less than the age of completion of compulsory schooling and, in any case, shall not be less than 15 years.

4.   Notwithstanding the provisions of paragraph 3 of this Article, a Member whose economy and educational facilities are insufficiently developed may, after consultation with the organizations of employers and workers concerned, where such exist, initially specify a minimum age of 14 years.

5.   Each Member which has specified a minimum age of 14 years in pursuance of the provisions of the preceding paragraph shall include in its reports on the application of this Convention submitted under article 22 of the Constitution of the International Labour Organization a statement –

(a)   that its reason for doing so subsists; or

(b)   that it renounces its right to avail itself of the provisions in question as from a stated date.

Article 3

1.   The minimum age for admission to any type of employment or work which by its nature or the circumstances in which it is carried out is likely to jeopardize the health, safety or morals of young persons shall not be less than 18 years.

2.   The types of employment or work to which paragraph 1 of this Article applies shall be determined by national laws or regulations or by the competent authority, after consultation with the organizations of employers and workers concerned, where such exist.

3.   Notwithstanding the provisions of paragraph 1 of this Article, national laws or regulations or the competent authority may, after consultation with the organizations of employers and workers concerned, where such exist, authorize employment or work as from the age of 16 years on condition that the health, safety and morals of the young persons concerned are fully protected and that the young persons have received adequate specific instruction or vocational training in the relevant branch of activity.

Article 4

1.   In so far as necessary, the competent authority, after consultation with the organizations of employers and workers concerned, where such exist, may exclude from the application of this Convention limited categories of employment or work in respect of which special and substantial problems of application arise.

2.   Each Member which ratifies this Convention shall list in its first report on the application of the Convention submitted under article 22 of the Constitution of the International Labour Organization any categories which may have been excluded in pursuance of paragraph 1 of this Article, giving the reasons for such exclusion, and shall state in subsequent reports the position of its law and practice in respect of the categories excluded and the extent to which effect has been given or is proposed to be given to the Convention in respect of such categories.

3.   Employment or work covered by Article 3 of this Convention shall not be excluded from the application of the Convention in pursuance of this Article.

Article 5

1.   A Member whose economy and administrative facilities are insufficiently developed may, after consultation with the organizations of employers and workers concerned, where such exist, initially limit the scope of application of this Convention.

2.   Each Member which avails itself of the provisions of paragraph 1 of this Article shall specify, in a declaration appended to its ratification, the branches of economic activity or types of undertakings to which it will apply the provisions of the Convention.

3.   The provisions of the Convention shall be applicable as a minimum to the following: mining and quarrying; manufacturing; construction; electricity, gas and water; sanitary services; transport, storage and communication; and plantations and other agricultural undertakings mainly producing for commercial purposes, but excluding family and small-scale holdings producing for local consumption and not regularly employing hired workers.

4.   Any Member which has limited the scope of application of this Convention in pursuance of this Article –

(a) shall indicate in its reports under article 22 of the Constitution of the International Labour Organization the general position as regards the employment or work of young persons and children in the branches of activity which are excluded from the scope of application of this Convention and any progress which may have been made towards wider application of the provisions of the Convention;

(b) may at any time formally extend the scope of application by a declaration addressed to the Director-General of the International Labour Office.

Article 6

This Convention does not apply to work done by children and young persons in schools for general, vocational or technical education or in other training institutions, or to work done by persons at least 14 years of age in undertakings, where such work is carried out in accordance with conditions prescribed by the competent authority, after consultation with the organizations of employers and workers concerned, where such exist, and is an integral part of –

(a) a course of education or training for which a school or training institution is primarily responsible;

(b) a programme of training mainly or entirely in an undertaking, which programme has been approved by the competent authority; or

(c) a programme of guidance or orientation designed to facilitate the choice of an occupation or of a line of training.

Article 7

1.   National laws or regulations may permit the employment or work of persons 13 to 15 years of age on light work which is –

(a) not likely to be harmful to their health or development; and

(b) not such as to prejudice their attendance at school, their participation in vocational orientation or training programmes approved by the competent authority or their capacity to benefit from the instruction received.

2.   National laws or regulations may also permit the employment or work of persons who are at least 15 years of age but have not yet completed their compulsory schooling on work which meets the requirements set forth in sub-paragraphs (a) and (b) of paragraph 1 of this Article.

3.   The competent authority shall determine the activities in which employment or work may be permitted under paragraphs 1 and 2 of this Article and shall prescribe the number of hours during which and the conditions in which such employment or work may be undertaken.

4.   Notwithstanding the provisions of paragraphs 1 and 2 of this Article, a Member which has availed itself of the provisions of paragraph 4 of Article 2 may, for as long as it continues to do so, substitute the ages 12 and 14 for the ages 13 and 15 in paragraph 1 and the age 14 for the age 15 in paragraph 2 of this Article.

Article 8

1.   After consultation with the organizations of employers and workers concerned, where such exist, the competent authority may, by permits granted in individual cases, allow exceptions to the prohibition of employment or work provided for in Article 2 of this Convention, for such purposes as participation in artistic performances.

2.   Permits so granted shall limit the number of hours during which and prescribe the conditions in which employment or work is allowed.

Article 9

1.   All necessary measures, including the provision of appropriate penalties, shall be taken by the competent authority to ensure the effective enforcement of the provisions of this Convention.

2.   National laws or regulations or the competent authority shall define the persons responsible for compliance with the provisions giving effect to the Convention.

3.   National laws or regulations or the competent authority shall prescribe the registers or other documents which shall be kept and made available by the employer; such registers or documents shall contain the names and ages or dates of birth, duly certified wherever possible, of persons whom he employs or who work for him and who are less than 18 years of age."

Source: ILO: *Official Bulletin*, Volume LVI, Number 1, 1973, pages 21-27.

Minimum Age Recommendation, 1973 (No. 146)

This Recommendation, adopted by the Conference of the ILO in 1973, supplements Convention No. 138. It expresses the desire of the Conference "to define further certain elements of policy which are the concern of the International Labour Organization". These relate to national policy, minimum age, hazardous employment or work, conditions of employment, and enforcement. The text of the operative part of the Recommendation follows.

"I. National policy

1.   To ensure the success of the national policy provided for in Article 1 of the Minimum Age Convention, 1973, high priority should be given to planning for and meeting the needs of children and youth in national development policies and programmes and to the progressive extension of the inter-related measures necessary to provide the best possible conditions of physical and mental growth for children and young persons.

2.   In this connection special attention should be given to such areas of planning and policy as the following:

(a) firm national commitment to full employment, in accordance with the Employment Policy Convention and Recommendation, 1964, and the taking of measures designed to promote employment-oriented development in rural and urban areas;

(b) the progressive extension of other economic and social measures to alleviate poverty wherever it exists and to ensure family living standards and income which are such as to make it unnecessary to have recourse to the economic activity of children;

(c) the development and progressive extension, without any discrimination, of social security and family welfare measures aimed at ensuring child maintenance, including children's allowances;

(d) the development and progressive extension of adequate facilities for education and vocational orientation and training appropriate in form and content to the needs of the children and young persons concerned;

(e) the development and progressive extension of appropriate facilities for the protection and welfare of children and young persons, including employed young persons, and for the promotion of their development.

3. Particular account should as necessary be taken of the needs of children and young persons who do not have families or do not live with their own families and of migrant children and young persons who live and travel with their families. Measures taken to that end should include the provision of fellowships and vocational training.

4. Full-time attendance at school or participation in approved vocational orientation or training programmes should be required and effectively ensured up to an age at least equal to that specified for admission to employment in accordance with Article 2 of the Minimum Age Convention, 1973.

5. (1) Consideration should be given to measures such as preparatory training, not involving hazards, for types of employment or work in respect of which the minimum age prescribed in accordance with Article 3 of the Minimum Age Convention, 1973, is higher than the age of completion of compulsory full-time schooling.

(2) Analogous measures should be envisaged where the professional exigencies of a particular occupation include a minimum age for admission which is higher than the age of completion of compulsory full-time schooling.

II. *Minimum age*

6. The minimum age should be fixed at the same level for all sectors of economic activity.

7. (1) Members should take as their objective the progressive raising to 16 years of the minimum age for admission to employment or work specified in pursuance of Article 2 of the Minimum Age Convention, 1973.

(2) Where the minimum age for employment or work covered by Article 2 of the Minimum Age Convention, 1973, is still below 15 years, urgent steps should be taken to raise it to that level.

8. Where it is not immediately feasible to fix a minimum age for all employment in agriculture and in related activities in rural areas, a minimum age should be fixed at least for employment on plantations and in the other agricultural undertakings referred to in Article 5, paragraph 3, of the Minimum Age Convention, 1973.

III. *Hazardous employment or work*

9. Where the minimum age for admission to types of employment or work which are likely to jeopardize the health, safety or morals of young persons is still below 18 years, immediate steps should be taken to raise it to that level.

10. (1) In determining the types of employment or work to which Article 3 of the Minimum Age Convention, 1973, applies, full account should be taken of relevant international labour standards, such as those concerning dangerous substances, agents or processes (including ionizing radiations), the lifting of heavy weights and underground work.

(2) The list of the types of employment or work in question should be re-examined periodically and revised as necessary, particularly in the light of advancing scientific and technological knowledge.

11. Where, by reference to Article 5 of the Minimum Age Convention, 1973, a minimum age is not immediately fixed for certain branches of the economic activity or types of undertakings, appropriate minimum age provisions should be made applicable therein to types of employment or work presenting hazards for young persons.

IV. Conditions of employment

12. (1) Measures should be taken to ensure that the condition in which children and young persons under the age of 18 years are employed or work reach and are maintained at a satisfactory standard. These conditions should be supervised closely.

(2) Measures should likewise be taken to safeguard and supervise the conditions in which children and young persons undergo vocational orientation and training within undertakings, training institutions and schools for vocational or technical education and to formulate standards for their protection and development.

13. (1) In connection with the application of the preceding Paragraph, as well as in giving effect to Article 7, paragraph 3, of the Minimum Age Convention, 1973, special attention should be given to –

(a) the provision of fair remuneration and its protection, bearing in mind the principle of equal pay for equal work;

(b) the strict limitation of the hours spent at work in a day and in a week, and the prohibition of overtime, so as to allow enough time for education and training (including the time needed for homework related thereto), for rest during the day and for leisure activities;

(c) the granting, without possibility of exception save in genuine emergency, of a minimum consecutive period of 12 hours' night rest, and of customary weekly rest days;

(d) the granting of an annual holiday with pay of at least four weeks and, in any case, not shorter than that granted to adults;

(e) coverage by social security schemes, including employment injury, medical care and sickness benefit schemes, whatever the conditions of employment or work may be;

(f) the maintenance of satisfactory standards of safety and health and appropriate instruction and supervision.

(2) Sub-paragraph (1) of this Paragraph applies to young seafarers in so far as they are not covered in respect of the matters dealt with therein by international labour Conventions or Recommendations specifically concerned with maritime employment.

V. Enforcement

14. (1) Measures to ensure the effective application of the Minimum Age Convention, 1973, and of this Recommendation should include –

(a) the strengthening as necessary of labour inspection and related services, for instance by the special training of inspectors to detect abuses in the employment or work of children and young persons and to correct such abuses; and

(b) the strengthening of services for the improvement and inspection of training in undertakings.

(2) Emphasis should be placed on the role which can be played by inspectors in supplying information and advice on effective means of complying with relevant provisions as well as in securing their enforcement.

(3) Labour inspection and inspection of training in undertakings should be closely coordinated to provide the greatest economic efficiency and, generally, the labour administration services should work in close cooperation with the services responsible for the education, training, welfare and guidance of children and young persons.

15. Special attention should be paid –

(a) to the enforcement of provisions concerning employment in hazardous types of employment or work; and

(b) in so far as education or training is compulsory, to the prevention of the employment or work of children and young persons during the hours when instruction is available.

16. The following measures should be taken to facilitate the verification of ages:

(a) the public authorities should maintain an effective system of birth registration, which should include the issue of birth certificates;

(b) employers should be required to keep and to make available to the competent authority registers or other documents indicating the names and ages or dates of birth, duly certified wherever possible, not only of children and young persons employed by them but also of those receiving vocational orientation or training in their undertakings;

(c) children and young persons working in the streets, in outside stalls, in public places, in itinerant occupations or in other circumstances which make the checking of employers' records impracticable should be issued licences or other documents indicating their eligibility for such work."

Source: ILO: *Official Bulletin*, Volume LVI, Number 1, 1973, pages 34-37.

NIGHT WORK

Night Work of Children and Young Persons (Agriculture) Recommendation, 1921 (No. 14)

"The General Conference of the International Labour Organization recommends:

I. That each Member of the International Labour Organization take steps to regulate the employment of children under the age of fourteen years in agricultural undertakings during the night, in such a way as to ensure to them a period of rest compatible with their physical necessities and consisting of not less than ten consecutive hours.

II. That each Member of the International Labour Organization take steps to regulate the employment of young persons between the ages of fourteen and eighteen years in agricultural undertakings during the night, in such a way as to ensure to them a period of rest compatible with their physical necessities and consisting of not less than nine consecutive hours."

Source: ILO: *Official Bulletin*, Volume IV, Number 22, 30 November 1921, pages 492-493.

Night Work of Young Persons (Non-Industrial Occupations) Convention, 1946 (No. 79)

Excerpts, Articles 1 to 6

"Article 1

1. This Convention applies to children and young persons employed for wages, or working directly or indirectly for gain, in non-industrial occupations.

2. For the purpose of this Convention, the term "non-industrial occupation" includes all occupations other than those recognized by the competent authority as industrial, agricultural or maritime occupations.

3. The competent authority shall define the line of division which separates non-industrial occupations from industrial, agricultural and maritime occupations.

4.   National laws or regulations may exempt from the application of this Convention –

(a)   domestic service in private households; and

(b)   employment on work which is not deemed to be harmful, prejudicial, or dangerous to children or young persons, in family undertakings in which only parents and their children or wards are employed.

Article 2

1.   Children under fourteen years of age who are admissible for full-time or part-time employment and children over fourteen years of age who are still subject to full-time compulsory school attendance shall not be employed nor work at night during a period of at least fourteen consecutive hours, including the interval between eight o'clock in the evening and eight o'clock in the morning.

2.   Provided that national laws or regulations may, where local conditions so require, substitute another interval of twelve hours of which the beginning shall not be fixed later than eight thirty o'clock in the evening nor the termination earlier than six o'clock in the morning.

Article 3

1.   Children over fourteen years of age who are no longer subject to full-time compulsory school attendance and young persons under eighteen years of age shall not be employed nor work at night during a period of at least twelve consecutive hours, including the interval between ten o'clock in the evening and six o'clock in the morning.

2.   Provided that, where there are exceptional circumstances affecting a particular branch of activity or a particular area, the competent authority may, after consultation with the employers' and workers' organizations concerned, decide that in the case of children and young persons employed in that branch of activity or area, the interval between eleven o'clock in the evening and seven o'clock in the morning may be substituted for that between ten o'clock in the evening and six o'clock in the morning.

Article 4

1.   In countries where the climate renders work by day particularly trying, the night period may be shorter than that prescribed in the above articles if compensatory rest is accorded during the day.

2.   The prohibition of night work may be suspended by the Government for young persons of sixteen years of age and over when in case of serious emergency the national interest demands it.

3.   National laws or regulations may empower an appropriate authority to grant temporary individual licences in order to enable young persons of sixteen years of age and over to work at night when the special needs of vocational training so require, subject to the period of rest being not less than eleven consecutive hours in every period of twenty-four hours.

Article 5

1.   National laws or regulations may empower an appropriate authority to grant individual licences in order to enable children or young persons under the age of eighteen years to appear at night as performers in public entertainments or to participate at night as performers in the making of cinematographic films.

2.   The minimum age at which such a licence may be granted shall be prescribed by national laws or regulations.

3.   No such licence may be granted when, because of the nature of the entertainment or the circumstances in which it is carried on, or the nature of the cinematographic film or the conditions under which it is made, participation in the entertainment or in the making of the film may be dangerous to the life, health, or morals of the child or young persons.

4.   The following conditions shall apply to the granting of licences:

(a) the period of employment shall not continue after midnight;

(b) strict safeguards shall be prescribed to protect the health and morals, and to ensure kind treatment of, the child or young person and to avoid interference with his education;

(c) the child or young person shall be allowed a consecutive rest period of at least fourteen hours.

Article 6

1. In order to ensure the due enforcement of the provisions of this Convention, national laws or regulations shall –

(a) provide for a system of public inspection and supervision adequate for the particular needs of the various branches of activity to which the Convention applies;

(b) require every employer to keep a register, or to keep available official records, showing the names and dates of birth of all persons under eighteen years of age employed by him and their hours of work; in the case of children and young persons working in the streets or in places to which the public have access, the register or records shall show the hours of service agreed upon in the contract of employment;

(c) provide suitable means for assuring identification and supervision of persons under eighteen years of age engaged, on account of an employer or on their own account, in employment or occupations carried on in the streets or in places to which the public have access;

(d) provide penalties applicable to employers or other responsible adults for breaches of such laws or regulations.

2. There shall be included in the annual reports to be submitted under Article 22 of the Constitution of the International Labour Organization full information concerning all laws and regulations by which effect is given to the provisions of this Convention and, more particularly, concerning –

(a) any interval which may be substituted for the interval prescribed in paragraph 1 of Article 2 in virtue of the provisions of paragraph 2 of that Article;

(b) the extent to which advantage is taken of the provisions of paragraph 2 of Article 3;

(c) the authorities empowered to grant individual licences in virtue of the provisions of paragraph 1 of Article 5 and the minimum age prescribed for the granting of licences in accordance with the provisions of paragraph 2 of the said Article."

Source: ILO: *Official Bulletin*, Volume XXIX, Number 4, 15 November 1946, pages 274-280.

Night Work of Young Persons (Industry) Convention (Revised), 1948 (No. 90)

Excerpts, Articles 1 to 6.

"Article 1

1. For the purpose of this Convention, the term "industrial undertaking" includes particularly –

(a) mines, quarries, and other works for the extraction of minerals from the earth;

(b) undertakings in which articles are manufactured, altered, cleaned, repaired, ornamented, finished, adapted for sale, broken up or demolished, or in which materials are transformed, including undertakings engaged in shipbuilding or in the generation, transformation or transmission of electricity or motive power of any kind;

(c) undertakings engaged in building and civil engineering work, including constructional, repair, maintenance, alteration and demolition work;

(d) undertakings engaged in the transport of passengers or goods by road or rail, including the handling of goods at docks, quays, wharves, warehouses or airports.

2. The competent authority shall define the line of division which separates industry from agriculture, commerce and other non-industrial occupations.

3. National laws or regulations may exempt from the application of this Convention employment on work which is not deemed to be harmful, prejudicial, or dangerous to young persons in family undertakings in which only parents and their children or wards are employed.

Article 2

1. For the purpose of this Convention the term "night" signifies a period of at least twelve consecutive hours.

2. In the case of young persons under sixteen years of age, this period shall include the interval between ten o'clock in the evening and six o'clock in the morning.

3. In the case of young persons who have attained the age of sixteen years but are under the age of eighteen years, this period shall include an interval prescribed by the competent authority of at least seven consecutive hours falling between ten o'clock in the evening and seven o'clock in the morning; the competent authority may prescribe different intervals for different areas, industries, undertakings or branches of industries or undertakings, but shall consult the employers' and workers' organizations concerned before prescribing an interval beginning after eleven o'clock in the evening.

Article 3

1. Young persons under eighteen years of age shall not be employed or work during the night in any public or private industrial undertaking or in any branch thereof except as hereinafter provide for.

2. For purposes of apprenticeship or vocational training in specified industries or occupations which are required to be carried on continuously, the competent authority may, after consultation with the employers' and workers' organizations concerned, authorize the employment in night work of young persons who have attained the age of sixteen years but are under the age of eighteen years.

3. Young persons employed in night work in virtue of the preceding paragraph shall be granted a rest period of at least thirteen consecutive hours between two working periods.

4. Where night work in the baking industry is prohibited for all workers, the interval between nine o'clock in the evening and four o'clock in the morning may, for purposes of apprenticeship or vocational training of young persons who have attained the age of sixteen years, be substituted by the competent authority for the interval of at least seven consecutive hours falling between ten o'clock in the evening and seven o'clock in the morning prescribed by the authority in virtue of paragraph 3 of Article 2.

Article 4

1. In countries where the climate renders work by day particularly trying, the night period and barred interval may be shorter than that prescribed in the above articles if compensatory rest is accorded during the day.

2. The provisions of Articles 2 and 3 shall not apply to the night work of young persons between the ages of sixteen and eighteen years in case of emergencies which could not have been controlled or foreseen, which are not of a periodical character, and which interfere with the normal working of the industrial undertaking.

Article 5

The prohibition of night work may be suspended by the government, for young persons between the ages of sixteen and eighteen years, when in case of serious emergency the public interest demands it.

Article 6

1.   The laws or regulations giving effect to the provisions of this Convention shall –

(a)   make appropriate provision for ensuring that they are known to the persons concerned;

(b)   define the persons responsible for compliance therewith;

(c)   prescribe adequate penalties for any violation thereof;

(d)   provide for the maintenance of a system of inspection adequate to ensure effective enforcement; and

(e)   require every employer in a public or private industrial undertaking to keep a register, or to keep available official records, showing the names and dates of birth of all persons under eighteen years of age employed by him and such other pertinent information as may be required by the competent authority.

2.   The annual reports submitted by Members under Article 22 of the Constitution of the International Labour Organization shall contain full information concerning such laws and regulations and a general survey of the results of the inspections made in accordance therewith."

Source: ILO: *Official Bulletin*, Volume XXXI, Number 1, 31 August 1948, pages 24-31.

Hazardous employment

Lead Poisoning (Women and Children) Recommendation, 1919 (No. 4)

Excerpts.

"1. The General Conference recommends to the Members of the International Labour Organization that, in view of the danger involved to the function of maternity and to the physical development of children, women and young persons under the age of eighteen years be excluded from employment in the following processes:

(a)   in furnace work in the reduction of zinc or lead ores;

(b)   in the manipulation, treatment, or reduction of ashes containing lead, and the de-silvering of lead;

(c)   in melting lead or old zinc on a large scale;

(d)   in the manufacture of solder or alloys containing more than ten per cent of lead;

(e)   in the manufacture of litharge, massicot, red lead, white lead, orange lead, or sulphate, chromate or silicate (frit) of lead;

(f)   in mixing and pasting in the manufacture or repair of electric accumulators;

(g)   in the cleaning of workrooms where the above processes are carried on.

2.   It is further recommended that the employment of women and young persons under the age of eighteen years in processes involving the use of lead compounds be permitted only subject to the following conditions:

(a)   locally applied exhaust ventilation, so as to remove dust and fumes at the point of origin;

(b)   cleanliness of tools and workrooms;

(c)   notification to Government authorities of all cases of lead poisoning, and compensation therefor;

(d)   periodic medical examination of the persons employed in such processes;

(e) provision of sufficient and suitable cloak-room, washing, and mess-room accommodation, and of special protective clothing;

(f) prohibition of bringing food or drink into workrooms.

3. It is further recommended that in industries where soluble lead compounds can be replaced by non-toxic substances, the use of soluble lead compounds should be strictly regulated.

4. For the purpose of this Recommendation, a lead compound should be considered as soluble if it contains more than five per cent of its weight (estimated as metallic lead) soluble in a quarter of one per cent solution of hydrochloric acid."

Source: ILO: *Official Bulletin*, Volume I, April 1919-August 1920, pages 428-429.

White Lead (Painting) Convention, 1921 (No. 13)

Excerpt.

"Article 3

1. The employment of males under eighteen years of age and of all females shall be prohibited in any painting work of an industrial character involving the use of white lead or sulphate of lead or other products containing these pigments."

Source: ILO: *Official Bulletin*, Supplement to Volume IV, Number 23, 7 December 1921, pages 13-16.

Radiation Protection Convention, 1960 (No. 115)

Excerpts.

"Article 6

1. Maximum permissible doses of ionizing radiations which may be received from sources external to or internal to the body and maximum permissible amounts of radioactive substances which can be taken into the body shall be fixed ... for various categories of workers.

2. Such maximum permissible doses and amounts shall be kept under constant review in the light of current knowledge.

Article 7

1. Appropriate levels shall be fixed in accordance with Article 6 for workers who are directly engaged in radiation work and are –

(a) aged 18 and over;

(b) under the age of 18.

2. No worker under the age of 16 shall be engaged in work involving ionizing radiations."

Source: ILO: *Official Bulletin*, Volume XLIII, Number 2, 1960, pages 41-46.

Benzene Convention, 1971 (No. 136)

Excerpt.

"Article 11

2. Young persons under 18 years of age shall not be employed in work processes involving exposure to benzene or products containing benzene: Provided that this prohibition need not apply to young persons undergoing education or training who are under adequate technical and medical supervision."

Source: ILO: *Official Bulletin*, Volume LIV, Number 3, 1971, pages 246-251.

Benzene Recommendation, 1971 (No. 144)

Excerpt.

"20.   Young persons under 18 years of age should not be employed in work processes involving exposure to benzene or products containing benzene, except where they are undergoing education or training and are under adequate technical and medical supervision."

Source: ILO: *Official Bulletin*, Volume LIV, Number 3, 1971, pages 255-259.

Occupational Safety and Health (Dock Work) Convention, 1979 (No. 152)

Excerpt.

"Article 38

2. A lifting appliance or other cargo-handling appliance shall be operated only by a person who is at least 18 years of age and who possesses the necessary aptitudes and experience or a person under training who is properly supervised."

Source: ILO: *Official Bulletin*, Volume LXII, Number 2, Series A, 1979, pages 70-76.

MAXIMUM WEIGHT

Maximum Weight Convention, 1967 (No. 127)

Excerpts.

"Article 1

For the purpose of this Convention – ... the term "young worker" means a worker under 18 years of age.

Article 7

1. The assignment of women and young workers to manual transport of loads other than light loads shall be limited.

2. Where women and young workers are engaged in the manual transport of loads, the maximum weight of such loads shall be substantially less than that permitted for adult male workers."

Source: ILO: *Official Bulletin*, Volume L, Number 3, Series I, July 1967, pages 1-4.

Maximum Weight Recommendation, 1967 (No. 128)

Excerpts.

"1. For the purpose of this Recommendation ... the term "young worker" means a worker under 18 years of age.

19. Where young workers are engaged in the manual transport of loads, the maximum weight of such loads should be substantially less than that permitted for adult workers of the same sex.

20. As far as possible, young workers should not be assigned to regular manual transport of loads.

21. Where the minimum age for assignment to manual transport of loads is less than 16 years, measures should be taken as speedily as possible to raise it to that level.

22. The minimum age for assignment to regular manual transport of loads should be raised, with a view to attaining a minimum age of 18 years.

23. Where young workers are assigned to regular manual transport of loads, provision should be made –

(a) as appropriate, to reduce the time spent on actual lifting, carrying and putting down of loads by such workers;

(b) to prohibit the assignment of such workers to certain specified jobs, comprised in manual transport of loads, which are especially arduous."

Source: ILO: *Official Bulletin*, Volume L, Number 3, Series I, July 1967, pages 25-29.

MEDICAL EXAMINATIONS

Medical Examination of Young Persons (Sea) Convention, 1921 (No. 16)

Excerpts.

"Article 2

The employment of any child or young person under eighteen years of age on any vessel, other than vessels upon which only members of the same family are employed, shall be conditional on the production of a medical certificate attesting fitness for such work, signed by a doctor who shall be approved by the competent authority.

Article 3

The continued employment at sea of any such child or young person shall be subject to the repetition of such medical examination at intervals of not more than one year, and the production, after each such examination, of a further medical certificate attesting fitness for such work. Should a medical certificate expire in the course of a voyage, it shall remain in force until the end of the said voyage."

Source: ILO: *Official Bulletin*, Supplement to Volume IV, Number 23, 7 December 1921, pages 24-25.

Medical Examination of Young Persons (Industry) Convention, 1946 (No. 77)

Excerpts.

"Article 2

1.   Children and young persons under eighteen years of age shall not be admitted to employment by an industrial undertaking unless they have been found fit for the work on which they are to be employed by a thorough medical examination.

Article 3

1.   The fitness of a child or young person for the employment in which he is engaged shall be subject to medical supervision until he has attained the age of eighteen years.

2.   The continued employment of a child or young person under eighteen years of age shall be subject to the repetition of medical examinations at intervals of not more than one year.

3.   National laws or regulations shall –

(a)   make provision for the special circumstances in which a medical re-examination shall be required in addition to the annual examination or at more frequent intervals in order to ensure effective supervision in respect of the risks involved in the occupation and of the state of health of the child or young person as shown by previous examinations; or

(b)   empower the competent authority to require medical re-examinations in exceptional cases.

Article 4

1.   In occupations which involve high health risks medical examination and re-examinations for fitness for employment shall be required until at least the age of twenty-one years.

2.   National laws or regulations shall either specify, or empower an appropriate authority to specify, the occupations or categories of occupations in which medical examination and re-examinations for fitness for employment shall be required until at least the age of twenty-one years.

Article 5

The medical examination required by the preceding Articles shall not involve the child or young person, or his parents, in any expense.

Article 7

1.   The employer shall be required to file and keep available to labour inspectors either the medical certificate for fitness for employment or the work permit or workbook showing that there are no medical objections to the employment as may be prescribed by national laws or regulations.

2.   National laws or regulations shall determine the other methods of supervision to be adopted for ensuring the strict enforcement of this Convention."

Source: ILO: *Official Bulletin*, Volume XXIX, Number 4, 15 November 1946, pages 254-261.

Medical Examination of Young Persons (Non-Industrial Occupations) Convention, 1946 (No. 78)

Excerpts.

"Article 2

1. Children and young persons under eighteen years of age shall not be admitted to employment or work in non-industrial occupations unless they have been found fit for the work in question by a thorough medical examination.

Article 3

1. The fitness of a child or young person for the employment in which he is engaged shall be subject to medical supervision until he has attained the age of eighteen years.

2. The continued employment of a child or young person under eighteen years of age shall be subject to the repetition of medical examinations at intervals of not more than one year.

3. National laws or regulations shall –

(a) make provision for the special circumstances in which a medical re-examination shall be required in addition to the annual examination or at more frequent intervals in order to ensure effective supervision in respect of the risks involved in the occupation and of the state of health of the child or young person as shown by previous examinations; or

(b) empower the competent authority to require medical re-examinations in exceptional cases.

Article 4

1. In occupations which involve high health risks medical examination and re-examinations for fitness for employment shall be required until at least the age of twenty-one years.

2. National laws or regulations shall either specify, or empower an appropriate authority to specify, the occupations or categories of occupations in which medical examination and re-examination for fitness for employment shall be required until at least the age of twenty-one years.

Article 5

The medical examinations required by the preceding Articles shall not involve the child or young person, or his parents, in any expense.

Article 7

1. The employer shall be required to file and keep available to labour inspectors either the medical certificate for fitness for employment or the work permit or workbook showing that there are no medical objections to the employment as may be prescribed by national laws or regulations.

2. National laws or regulations shall determine –

(a) the measures of identification to be adopted for ensuring the application of the system of medical examination for fitness for employment to children and young persons engaged either on their own account or on account of their parents in itinerant trading or in any other occupation carried on in the streets or in places to which the public have access; and

(b) the other methods of supervision to be adopted for ensuring the strict enforcement of the Convention."

Source: ILO: *Official Bulletin*, Volume XXIX, Number 4, 15 November 1946, pages 261-268.

Improving the knowledge base on child labour

3

Kebebew Ashagrie

INTRODUCTION

Although child labour has long existed and is believed to be increasing and becoming more harmful, the actual level, nature, causes and consequences of the practice have not been fully determined in the past. The main reason for the dearth of data on child labour has been the absence of an appropriate survey methodology to probe into the work of children which, for the most part, is a hidden or invisible phenomenon. In view of the absence of adequate data, little is known about many important aspects of child labour at both the national and global levels. There is, however, a wide variety of guesstimates as to the number of working children under 15 years of age, ranging from 200 to 400 million worldwide. Even if such estimates were to be regarded as realistic, mere global totals do not provide insight into the various forms of the practice and the problems inherent therein. The ILO's Bureau of Statistics now estimates that, in developing countries alone, there are at least 120 million children between the ages of 5 and 14 who are fully at work. If those for whom work is a secondary activity are included, the total working children in this age group is at least twice as many (or more than 250 million).

For several reasons, a paucity of data on child labour has in recent times contributed to an increasingly intensive and sometimes emotional debate on the subject in which some tend to downplay the magnitude of the problem, while others exaggerate it. Lack of reliable data obscures the problem and can be counter productive when it comes to setting national priorities for urgent action. Following experimental work in the early 1990s, the ILO has developed statistical survey methodologies to assist countries in collecting and improving their information base on child labour.

So far child labour surveys based on recently developed methodologies have been carried out nationally or in selected areas of 19 countries or territories. These include Bangladesh, Cambodia, Costa Rica, Georgia, Ghana (selected areas), Indonesia (selected areas), India (one state), Kenya, Namibia, Nepal, Pakistan, the Philippines, Senegal, South Africa, Sri Lanka, Thailand, Turkey, Ukraine, and the West Bank and Gaza. New child labour surveys are either under way or in the process of starting, or are being planned, in the following countries: Angola, Belize, Benin, Brazil, Burkina Faso, Cambodia (second round), Colombia, Costa Rica (second round), Côte d'Ivoire, Dominican Republic, El Salvador, Ethiopia, Ghana (second round), Guatemala, Haiti, Honduras, India, Indonesia (second round), Jamaica, Madagascar, Mali, Mongolia, Morocco, Mozambique, Nepal (second round), Nicaragua, Nigeria, Pakistan (second round), Panama, Peru, the Philippines (second round), Romania, Russian Federation, United Republic of Tanzania, Trinidad and Tobago, Turkey (second round), Uganda, Venezuela, Viet Nam, Zambia and Zimbabwe.

Child labour is a concern not only in the Asian, African, Latin American and Caribbean regions, but also in countries in transition and in developed nations. The ILO is already collaborating with Eastern European countries such as Georgia, Romania and Ukraine in conducting such surveys, to be followed by other countries including Armenia, the Russian Federation and, in the Baltic States, Lithuania. In Western Europe, Portugal has already carried out a household-based survey in close collaboration with the ILO, and the same collaboration is expected with Italy and Spain, which are preparing to investigate the phenomenon of child labour in their respective countries. Child labour surveys will be carried out as far as possible in all IPEC participating countries to optimize the complementary effects of IPEC and the Statistical Information and Monitoring Programme on Child Labour (SIMPOC) – see below.

Given the effectiveness and popularity of the newly developed survey methodologies for quantifying child labour in all its different facets, an externally funded programme (SIMPOC) was formulated and launched at the beginning of 1998. SIMPOC, an interdepartmental programme between the ILO's International Programme on the Elimination of Child Labour (IPEC) and the ILO's Bureau of Statistics, is designed for a five-year period with the major aim of assisting individual countries in generating comprehensive quantitative and qualitative statistical data on child labour at the national level that is comparable among countries, subregions or regions. SIMPOC is also aimed at capacity building of national statistical offices and ministries of labour for the production and use of such data on a regular basis in the future. For this purpose, under the SIMPOC programme, the staff of IPEC and SIMPOC are to be trained to design and carry out child labour surveys and analyse the data collected. The surveys are expected to become an integral part of the regular national statistical programmes, so that statistical information on child labour can be produced and disseminated at regular intervals. A large majority of the countries listed above have undertaken the surveys under the auspices of SIMPOC.

Through SIMPOC, comprehensive child labour information systems consisting of both quantitative and qualitative data will also be developed at national, international and regional levels with a computer programme that facilitates updating the database as new information becomes available. Such a database will provide policy and decision makers with more detailed and better-quality information for the design, implementation, monitoring and evaluation of policies and programmes. The dissemination of this data, through the publication of a regular trend report, is planned under SIMPOC – which will contribute considerably to raising public awareness and enhancing the understanding of the problem of child labour.

This chapter aims to assist countries develop or improve survey programmes on child labour by providing technical and practical guidelines to researchers on designing and conducting the surveys; it also offer insights about obtaining information from children. An appendix lists detailed variables in different types of child labour surveys.

More detailed methodological and related technical guidelines are being prepared for publication under the title: *Surveys of child labour and activities of children: An ILO manual on concepts, methods and procedures.*

3.1 CHILD LABOUR STATISTICS: METHODOLOGICAL CONSIDERATIONS

Data requirements

ILO and IPEC experience has shown that detailed and reliable data are crucial in setting targets and developing and implementing effective programmes on child labour. Since 1992, the ILO has taken the lead in developing methodological child labour sample surveys at national levels.

The *survey methodologies* were developed to enable countries to obtain benchmark statistics on children's work in general or to produce statistics on specific core variables. These methods were first tested in four countries (Ghana, India, Indonesia and Senegal). Following their refinement and recommendations for quantifying child labour, several countries collaborated with the Bureau of Statistics in adopting the methodologies and conducting national surveys for collecting comprehensive data.

Based on detailed results of the experiments and national child labour surveys conducted in several countries using the newly developed methodologies, the ILO was able to:

(i)   produce regional and global estimates;

(ii)   identify and quantify not only the different forms of hazard and risk working children face, but also the extent and nature of the injuries and diseases suffered while working; and

(iii)   acquire much knowledge and experience, thereby enhancing considerably its competence for providing technical assistance to individual countries in designing and undertaking comprehensive child labour surveys, and processing, analysing and using the statistical data obtained for formulating and implementing appropriate action programmes to combat the worst forms of child labour at the national and global levels.

To obtain a complete picture of the child labour situation, the information sought through surveys at the national level involved answers to the following questions, among others:

◆   Who are the working children and how many are there in the various countries?

◆   How old are the children when they start to work for the first time and how do they live?

◆   Why do they work and in which sectors are they engaged?

◆   What are their specific occupations and the conditions of their work?

◆   What types of exploitation and abuse do they face at work?

◆   How safe are they physically and mentally at their workplace or in their occupations?

◆   Do they also go to school? If so, what are the consequences of their work on their schooling? And if they do not go to school, why not?

◆   Who are their employers? Why do they employ them? And how do they treat them in comparison with their adult workers?

◆   How many children are engaged on a full-time basis in housekeeping activities of a domestic nature in their own parents' or guardians' households, thereby sacrificing their education?

◆   Do any children live away from their parents' or guardians' home, and if so, where do they live and what do they do?

◆   What are the perceptions of parents about their working children? What are the perceptions of the children themselves and their employers?

Survey methodologies

Introduction

It is evident that answering all the above questions would require the collection of comprehensive information on working children. Consequently, the ILO Bureau of Statistics designed four survey approaches and tested them in a number of countries together with a supplementary inquiry. Three of the survey approaches were implemented, respectively, at the level of households, employers/establishments/ enterprises, and street children. The fourth method tested was a "time use" approach. The supplementary inquiry was applied at the community level (cities, towns, villages). The main purpose was to determine which survey methodology would yield the best results.

The surveys measured as many variables as possible, particularly in relation to the various non-schooling activities of children in the 5-14 age group, their characteristics and those of their parents or guardians, and so on. The principal variables considered for the investigation related to the following subjects, as expressed in broad terms:

◆ the demographic and socio-economic characteristics of the children, including their schooling and training status, occupations, skill levels, hours of work, earnings and other working and living conditions and the reasons for working, as well as the hardships and risks, especially work-related or environmental injuries and diseases they face at their workplace which are detrimental to their health, education, and physical and mental development;

◆ the socio-economic situation of their parents or guardians, or other relatives with whom the children live, as well as the particulars of their employers;

◆ the migration status of the children and how they live (in particular those on the streets); where the children have been working, for how long and why they are working, their own immediate and future plans and those of employers using child workers; and

◆ the perceptions of the parents or guardians about their working youngsters and those of the children themselves and their employers.

Definitions of child labour

The concepts, definitions, classifications and the like, used for the purposes of the experimental surveys in all the countries, were generally in line with internationally recommended standards concerning such elements as the economically active population, the labour force, classifications of industry, occupation, status in employment, age grouping, households, enterprises and establishments and so on (see Chapter 2), with some variations to reflect the unique circumstance of child work and the peculiarities of the individual countries.

Depending on the availability of basic information or demarcations regarding the general characteristics of the areas covered and the availability of appropriate sampling frames, the different elements considered for the stratifications included development levels of the selected rural and urban areas – for example, poorly developed/well developed, slum/non-slum blocks, income classes (low, middle, high), overall rates of literacy/illiteracy of the general population, school attendance levels and so on. This was because it is known that factors such as these and the incidence of child labour are either positively correlated or vary inversely, depending on the factor being considered.

For the purposes of the experiments, a "child" was defined as a person between five and 14 years of age. In the absence of a universally endorsed definition of "child labour", all activities of children were enumerated and quantified so that the data could be tabulated according to the different characteristics or categories of the variables included in the questionnaires. Depending on the level and nature of the quantified activities or variables, those which were judged or expected to have negative effects or consequences on the health, education and normal development of the working child were considered as falling within the boundaries of "child labour".

The main focus of the surveys in all four countries was on the economic activity of the children, whether paid in cash or in kind, or in unpaid family work, thus respecting the international definition of "economic activity". In this respect, some types of work or production for own household consumption, such as carrying water, fetching firewood, pounding and husking food products, were also considered as falling within the boundaries of economic activity. While the dividing line between economic and non-economic activities for cases such as the above is rather thin and not always obvious, these and many others (for example, preservation of fruit by drying or bottling, weaving cloth, and dressmaking and tailoring), were considered to fall within the margin of economic activity or the "production boundary" as defined by the System of National Accounts (SNA, 1993).

While schooling activities were measured in the majority of cases, in some instances non-schooling activities of a non-economic nature (especially household chores or housekeeping services provided in the child's own parents' or guardians' homes) were also estimated separately. In all the surveys, both the "current" and the "usual" economic activity approaches were applied, the first in reference to activities during a short period such as the week (or seven days) prior to the date of the interview, and the second in reference to a long period such as the 12 months (or 365 days) preceding the inquiry date. The latter reference period takes seasonality into account, which is an important factor since a considerable proportion of children's activities is seasonal, including activities undertaken when schools are closed.

Household-level survey

In all the selected areas the household-based surveys were carried out strictly on a relatively rigorous sample basis using a multi-stage (two- or three-stage) stratified sampling design. Using the household listing as a sampling frame as well as the basic information that was collected during the listing, all the listed households in each unit of the segment were then grouped into three strata as follows:

(i)   households with at least one paid child worker (in the specific age group);

(ii)   households without a paid child worker but with at least one child working as an unpaid family worker (in the same specific age group); and

(iii)   other households (in the same age group).

As a final step in the sample selection procedure, a specified number of households in each of the above three strata were selected by means of systematic sampling which formed the final stage sampling units. Through these sampling procedures or slight variations, between 4,000 and 5,000 households were selected to represent the sample size for the surveys in each of the four countries.

Where suitable statistical software packages were not available in the statistical offices of the countries concerned, a self-weighting systematic sampling design with probability proportional to size (PPS) was adopted. This approach helped by providing a uniform weight for estimating totals. It also facilitated the computation of percentages, means and ratios of the population parameters directly from the sample data.

The questionnaire that was applied at the household level consisted of two parts. The first part was addressed to the head of the household (or a proxy) to obtain information on the demographic and socio-economic composition of the household, including such aspects as housing facilities, household migration status and living standards, and the education level and economic activity status of the household members. The second part was used to collect the required information from the individual children themselves.

As a supplement, a simple questionnaire was used to interview elected and appointed leaders, administrators and the like, in the communities or towns and villages of the selected areas so as to identify the major local socio-economic characteristics, assess development levels and determine the differential in the incidence of child labour. This investigation was also used to list the households which served as a sampling frame.

The details of the variables considered for the household-based survey approach and the community/town/village level, as well as those for establishments or employers, are listed in Appendix 3.1.

During the household listing stage, basic information on a limited number of variables relating to each household and its members was also obtained to facilitate the stratification of the households in each segment and the sample selection of households.

Establishment survey

The employer's (establishment or enterprise) questionnaire was addressed to the owner of the business or a designated respondent, seeking information on the particulars of the ownership, the goods produced and services rendered, the number of children and adults engaged, their working conditions, the reasons for using child workers, facilities and health care at the workplace and so on.

In this approach, probability sampling became prohibitive due to the absence of basic information which could serve as a master frame, such as an exhaustive list or directory of employers in respect of the areas selected for the surveys. In view of this problem, only those employers identified by the children themselves or their parents during the interview at the household level, or those enterprises known or suspected to be using child workers, were located and interviewed on a random basis. In this way, up to a total of 200 entities were identified and enumerated in urban and rural areas selected in each country.

Survey of street children

Due to the special problems of collecting data on children working and living on the streets (i.e. children not residing in a household), an individual questionnaire was formulated and used to assemble information on variables relating to the schooling and non-schooling activities of such children, their living and working conditions, parents, migration status and so on. Given that children working on the streets often live on their own and do not have a usual place of residence or home, they could not be represented in a sample of households.

Therefore, for the children on the streets, a "purposive" or "convenience" approach was applied and, as far as possible, enumerators who were selected and trained for the interviews were those who knew the core areas where such children were found. The children were visited in their localities in the evenings, and in some cases at night if that proved to be more convenient. In the urban core, many children tend to form groups to eat and sleep together.

The time-use approach

The methodological experiments included a "time use" module for interviewing individual children within the households and working and living on the streets. A list of economic and non-economic activities was constructed and used to identify which activities children had been engaged in during the 24 hours preceding the time of the survey and to determine how much time had been devoted to each activity.

3.2 BASIC RESULTS

Variations exist in the results of the surveys conducted in the four countries owing to their differences in terms of social, cultural, political and economic development levels, average family size, household income and expenditure, literacy or illiteracy levels of the adult population, and especially the school enrolment and attendance ratios of young children. The findings are also influenced by the differences in the reference period of the surveys, for example, whether it covers a schooling period, agricultural season, and so on. For the same reasons, the findings also vary between any two areas covered by the survey within each country.

The statistical results from the surveys have proved the existence of a positive correlation – in some instances a strong one – between child labour and such factors as poverty, illiteracy, the level of rural community underdevelopment, urban slum conditions, school truancy or drop-outs, abandoned or runaway children, large family size, female-headed households, the parents' – especially the father's – occupations, and permanent absence or death of the father, among others.

Household survey

The household-based survey has been found to be the most effective means of investigating the child labour phenomenon in all its facets. It does, however, exclude homeless children who live and work on the streets, with no fixed place of usual residence. As a result the data obtained through household surveys did not include information on such children who might have been working on the streets, although the number of such youngsters would be relatively very small in most countries. Nonetheless, since such children are among those who usually encounter the worst situations, a separate survey had to be designed and tested, and is described further in this section.

In the household-based survey, the best time to visit the sample households was found to be late afternoons or early evenings. While finding an adult respondent was relatively easy in the daytime, there was difficulty contacting the children themselves in the households during the daytime and proxy informants tended to be unreliable, especially concerning certain questions or variables.

Establishment survey

In many cases the establishment-based investigation was not particularly successful, notably where it was difficult to identify employers and managers of workplaces. While it was hoped that the information obtained from the household heads and the children themselves would allow a list to be compiled of establishments where the children work, this proved difficult, mainly because many children were not available during the household inquiry and many adults (usually mothers or proxies) were unable to provide the precise address of the children's place of work. Nevertheless, in some countries it was possible to compile lists consisting of a reasonable number of establishments for the purposes of testing the instruments designed for employers using child labourers.

Where a list or directory of establishments does not exist or cannot be compiled on the basis of the information obtained from the household-level survey, a micro-level approach can be taken in which the type of formal sector activities (industries, services) where children may be working are identified and the enterprises engaged in these activities are investigated. In view of the fact that a large majority (90 per cent) of economically active children are unpaid family workers and some others are self-employed or casual labourers, this approach may often suffice. It is to be noted that in a few of the countries where a proper sample survey of establishments proved difficult, small purposive or convenience inquiries were carried out which produced some interesting statistical results, though for the most part these were qualitative and not representative of enterprises as a whole.

Another problem regarding the establishment-based inquiry was the lack of full, or even any, cooperation on the part of the employers, especially where the employment of youngsters under a specified age is illegal. For this reason, the use of the term "child activity" or "child work" instead of "child labour" in the survey instruments, and by field personnel during interviews, may lead to a better response rate at all levels. In addition, conducting a well-formulated campaign, prior to the launching of the survey, in the various localities and at the national level to publicize the importance of the data to be collected for improving children's welfare (schooling, health, and the like, including working conditions if children have to work) could make respondents much more cooperative.

Survey of street children

As stated earlier, homeless children are not represented in household samples since they have no usual place of residence or home. These children, however, face daily risks, hazards and exploitation that are detrimental to their mental and physical development.

A purposive approach was applied using well-trained interviewers who were well acquainted with the inner city where such children usually work or congregate. In one country in particular, a micro-level inquiry was conducted successfully taking as a starting-point the fact that most homeless children are usually found in large urban centres. The interviewers were sent out in the early evening and often at night with a detailed questionnaire to interview at random the children they found. In many cases, the informal sector operators for whom the children work were also interviewed. The exercise resulted in useful statistical data, enabling the survey team to analyse the various characteristics of street children: age; sex; educational background; migration status and reasons for being on the streets; types of economic activity and occupation; earnings; living conditions (food, sleeping place, etc.); difficulties encountered; skills; future plans; activity patterns and background information of their parents; and so on.

The time-use approach

The survey experiment based on a "time use" module was not successful for the purposes of investigating children's activities and the intensity of their work. Even when presented with a long list of economic and non-economic activities, many children could not recall the activities in which they had been engaged during the 24 hours preceding the date of the survey. And even when they were able to identify the activities, they had little recollection of the amount of time spent on each. Most children seem to remember only those activities which they most like, especially those in which they made "good" earnings. In many instances, it was difficult to consult the children themselves, and approaching proxies for this purpose was found to be futile since they could not account for the children's daily activities or their time allocation on each. Consequently, the results obtained from the "time use" exercise were found to be unsatisfactory.

However, better-quality data may be obtained if the investigators or interviewers spend time in the area where the children can be found and interact with them and/or observe them throughout the day. Unfortunately, this approach is neither practical nor feasible where the geographical coverage is wide and the sample size is large in order to make estimates at the national level. It is therefore recommended that, with the exception of a micro-level time allocation exercise, the application of a "time-use" approach to individual children to identify all their activities over a specific period of time (such as 24 hours) and to quantify the time devoted to each should be discouraged.

3.3 RECOMMENDATIONS ON CONDUCTING SURVEYS

In view of the above, **the overall recommendation** is to conduct a household-based sample survey which should be supplemented by surveys of employers (establishments and enterprises) and street children. Below are some details on each of these three survey approaches which could serve as technical guidelines.

Household-based surveys

Justification

The justification for these surveys and their suitability lies in the fact that by definition a household is a unit consisting of either an individual living alone or a group of two or more persons living together with a common provision for food and other essentials necessary for living. Whether they are one-person or multi-person households of related and/or unrelated individuals, such households serve as the ultimate sampling units which best represent any specific population under consideration or study. The only persons who are not represented through household-based sample inquiries are the homeless, nomads, and household members who are absent from the household permanently or for a long period at the time of enumeration. If such persons do not live in another household within the country, they will not be represented in a household-based national sample survey. However, such groups normally only constitute a very small proportion of the total population within any specific age cohort. Even then, much information could be collected on those who are away from the households (such as street children) by addressing various relevant questions to the household head or a proxy. This information could, in turn, be used to design a more appropriate investigation of such persons to find out more details on all aspects of their activities, occupations, living conditions and so on.

The use of households as units of enumeration could permit the gathering of a wealth of statistical information on all or any segment of a country's population, subject to the availability of resources. The ILO methodological experiments carried out in 1992-93, and national surveys undertaken since then concerning child labour in several countries, have proved the household approach to be the most effective means for a profound assessment of the level, nature and determinants of the practice at the national level. During such surveys, information could also be collected on the activity patterns of adults not only because the additional cost involved would be marginal, but because such data are important for studying the interrelationship between the activities of children and the activities of other members of the same household and, in particular, those of their parents or guardians.

Besides providing a national picture, another advantage of a comprehensive household-based survey is that, if implemented through well-designed sampling and stratification procedures, it would permit segregation of the statistical information not only into rural/urban areas and informal/formal sectors, but also, and more importantly, into small geographical areas within any large geographical region or province. The information on small localities would be crucial for formulating and implementing policies and action programmes appropriate for combating child labour in specific geographical areas or communities where the problem may be quite serious.

It should be noted that the household-based survey of child labour could be carried out either as a "free-standing" or "stand-alone" inquiry, or as a module attached to other ongoing household-based surveys. The latter approach is much more efficient in many ways, particularly if the module is implemented as a supplement to an established programme of a labour force survey (LFS) conducted on a sample basis at the national level. This undertaking will not only result in substantial cost savings, but the operation could be achieved in less time. Operationally, it means that the module would be piggybacked onto one of the rounds of the LFS and that the interviews for both the LFS and the module would be carried out at the same time. Since the LFS questionnaire always seeks to enumerate the demographic and socio-economic composition of household members, there would be no need to repeat this part in the module for children. Through empirical studies it has been demonstrated that the incidence of child labour and the demographic and socio-economic characteristics of the "adult" household members are correlated positively or negatively depending on the different variables considered. Therefore, information on other household members has to be collected as well.

The attractiveness of the modular option stems from the fact that there would be no need to list all the households selected in the initial stage of sampling, representing the primary-stage sampling units (PSUs), or to collect the basic information required for the stratification and selections of the second stage sampling units (SSUs). Also, since there would be no repeat questions on the demographic and socio-economic characteristics of the children, the entire module would be considerably shorter. In addition, where the ILO and national statistics offices have collaborated closely in attaching a comprehensive child labour module to ongoing household-based surveys, significant savings have been realized. For example, in Turkey, where the module was attached to one of the two rounds of the national LFS, the cost of the operation amounted to only one-fifth (20 per cent) of the total resources that would have been needed if a stand-alone child labour survey had been conducted. A similar approach was carried out in Cambodia where the cost of the child labour survey component was about one-tenth (10 per cent) of the estimated total resources.

A sample questionnaire which could be used for a child labour modular inquiry attached to a household-based labour force survey can be provided on request by the ILO's Bureau of Statistics.

Coverage and classification of child labour

To avoid limiting the coverage of the incidence of various forms of child work, all types of activities (schooling and non-schooling, economic and non-economic activities) of children within a specified age group would be represented through sampling and enumerated, and the volume or workload of their activities quantified, so that the assembled statistical information could be cross-tabulated by the different characteristics of the variables included in the questionnaire. Depending on the level and nature of the quantified activities or variables, those which are judged or expected to have negative effects or consequences on the health, education and normal development of the working children could be considered as falling within the boundary of "child labour". The data should then be further dissected into various categories of affected children based on the degree of harm caused by the quantified activities.

Since the comprehensive household survey would investigate all the activities of children in the particular age cohort, the data collected would make it possible to identify the specific occupations of the working children, their working conditions, accidents/injuries/illnesses suffered – including their frequency and gravity – problems related to the workplace environment, particulars of employers using children, the specific industries in which children work, the effect of their work on their normal life (including their schooling), and other related matters which would assist in assessing more fully the extent, nature and causes of child labour. Such detailed information would also become instrumental for focused study of a particular category of working children, or occupation, industry and the like, and for formulating and implementing policies and programmes for the immediate elimination of the most harmful of children's activities, as well as for the complete eradication of child labour in the long term.

Given that some international conventions, declarations and resolutions seek to protect all children under 18 years of age from different types of harmful activities, it is strongly recommended that the survey of child labour should cover children from 5 to 17 years of age. One advantage of using this broad age cohort is that it would allow breakdown of the data obtained by different age groups, thereby satisfying the requirements of the various instruments, as well as national needs for respecting compulsory schooling regulations, labour codes and other legal requirements of individual countries. Examples of groupings are: 5-14, 15-17 and 5-17 years, the 5-14 age group broken down further by 5-9 and 10-14 years, all commonly used by most countries. It may be useful to have the results also separately classified for children under 11, 12-13, and 14 years, in view of ILO Convention No. 138 and Recommendation No. 146 concerning Minimum Age for Admission to Employment (both adopted in 1973). Convention No. 138 generally prohibits economic activity of children under the age of 15, while making exceptions for those aged 14 years and for those between 12 and 13 years, depending on different circumstances in individual countries.

It is also recommended that work of a domestic nature (household chores) performed by children in their own parents' or other relatives' homes where they actually reside should be included in the investigation of children's schooling and non-schooling activities. This is to measure the time spent on this type of work to identify those children who are working more than the daily number of hours that may be considered as normal to learn common household chores and related activities. The final data compiled on these children should then be tabulated separately from those relating to children who are economically active (as defined in accordance with international standards). Non-economic work of a domestic nature in the parents' or guardians' household would then be classified and tabulated into various ranges according to the number of hours during which such work was performed. A threshold could then be established beyond which the activity could be deemed as constituting child labour.

The above is based on the argument that many non-schoolgoing children perform housekeeping activities in their parents' or guardians' households for various reasons, one being to make adult household members available for economic activity elsewhere. For many of these children this is a full-time occupation involving preparing and serving meals, washing clothes, cleaning floors, taking care of younger siblings, serving as messengers in and around the household, and so on, all this at the sacrifice of the education and playtime to which each child is entitled under the United Nations Convention on the Rights of the Child. Even those who attend school are found to be spending several hours a day performing such activities which are detrimental to their schooling, health and normal development to adulthood. Such children suffer fatigue which affects their school performance and many are exposed to hazardous situations, for example cooking food over an open fire. Children who are put under the guardianship of relatives or other persons are especially susceptible to much abuse in these areas of work. Behind the guardianship status there are often other arrangements which amount to child labour, including bondage which is among the worst forms of the practice.

The sampling approach to be adopted for surveys on children's activities should in principle be a multi-stage stratified sampling design to capture a good number of working children. In areas where the child labour incidence is suspected to be rare, or where children's activities are highly diversified, an over-sampling is recommended. Conversely, where there is a homogeneity of activities (in rural areas, for example), under-sampling (a smaller sample) could be considered.

Where statistical software packages are not readily available, a self-weighting systematic sampling design with probability proportional to size (PPS) of the population being considered should be adopted, since this will have a uniform weight for estimating totals and will also facilitate the computation of percentages, means and ratios of the population parameters directly from the sample data.

Questionnaire contents

The questionnaire should be designed in two parts.

Part I should be directed *to the head of the household or the adult responsible for the household* and should be concerned with characteristics of each household member, housing particulars, household living standards, and schooling and non-schooling activities of children under 18 years, as follows:

◆ It should include questions on the demographic and socio-economic composition of all household members, including current economic activity as measured in reference to a short period such as one week or seven days preceding the survey date, and usual principal and subsidiary economic activities as measured in reference to a longer period such as 12 months or 365 days preceding the survey date for measuring seasonal activities.

◆ Regarding each household member under 18 years, it should ask the household head (or the proxy) about the child's schooling and non-schooling activities (both current and usual economic and non-economic) and about types of occupation, goods produced or services rendered, and location of the workplace; if working as an employee, the name, address and industry of the employer; whether working as self-employed or for someone else, earnings, hours of work and other benefits and conditions of work, and contributions to the household; the types, frequency and seriousness of work-related injuries and illnesses, and other aspects of health and safety at the workplace; the occupations and earnings of children who work and live elsewhere, and how and why they left, where they live and how often they are in touch with the household; awareness of recruiters to recruit children to work and live elsewhere and on the type of work they are recruited for; the reasons parents and guardians allow children to work and their perceptions about their working child or children. Information on housekeeping services provided by children in their own parents' or guardians' household should also be collected with an indication of the number of hours devoted to such services to identify those children who regularly toil for several hours a day or on a full-time basis.

◆ It should also collect information on housing/dwelling particulars of the household and availability of facilities (including water, electricity, sanitation, and the like), household income and expenditures, recent migration status of the household and if migrated, reasons and other details. All these variables could be used to cross-classify the results on the level of child labour for a more meaningful analysis of the findings.

Part II is related to detailed information on children under 18 years *as provided by the children themselves* for an in-depth study of their activity patterns and the impact on them. Many of the questions addressed to the household head or the parents/guardians are repeated to the children both for comparison and validation. Also, the children can be more specific than their parents on matters such as working conditions, injuries and illnesses, workplace hardships, and relations with the employer. The information to be obtained from the children should include the following:

◆ whether enrolled in a school or training institution, and especially current attendance and difficulties encountered; if never attended or a drop-out, the reasons; participation in economic activities as paid or unpaid workers, and in work of a domestic nature such as housekeeping activities carried out regularly in their own parents'/guardians' households; the types and number of hours devoted to such work on a daily/weekly basis; the hardships of such work and whether the children have any leisure time for playing, studying and the like. If self-employed, the types of goods produced or services rendered;

◆ if combining schooling or training with work (whether economic activity or non-economic work, including housekeeping activities), the effect of such work on schooling or training;

◆ if working for someone else, name, address and industry of the employer; salaries/wages and mode of payment; hours of work and whether working during evenings/nights and weekends or public holidays; details of all other benefits (paid holidays, overtime pay, full or subsidized meals/uniform/training, and the like); social security benefits (including health or unemployment insurance, family benefits, and pension schemes);

◆ if working on a commercial farm, the main commodities;

◆ if working as self-employed or on own account, the working environment and the address of the workplace;

◆ work-related injuries and illnesses; other safety and health aspects sustained at the workplace during the preceding 12 months; types and seriousness of the injuries/illnesses; responsibility for covering costs of medical treatment and hospitalization;

◆ whether or not supervised on the job by adult(s), and the negative consequences of working (e.g. frequency of exhaustion, heavy physical work, stress, risks); if the job or the work environment is hazardous, and type of hazard (e.g. chemical, physical, biological), with details within each category;

◆ whether or not part or all of earnings are saved, and if saved, the reasons for saving; whether part or all of earnings are given to parents/guardians, the regularity of such payments/contributions and how they are made (directly by the working child, or by the employer if working for someone else);

◆ the age when the child started to work for the first time; reasons for working; whether or not satisfied with present job and reasons if not satisfied; own perceptions about working; current choice and future plans;

◆ where relevant, whether or not the child knows recruiters of young persons to work and live elsewhere; if the child is knowledgeable, the types of work the youngsters are recruited for, where they are taken, and other details.

Pilot test of survey instruments

Once the content of the questionnaire is agreed upon, the guide for enumerators and supervisors should be prepared. The questionnaire and the guide need to be tested and finalized on the basis of a pilot survey conducted with a small sample of households.

Sampling and stratification

The sampling and stratification procedures to be adopted depend on the availability of basic information on various factors and at different levels. Up-to-date information or demarcations regarding the general characteristics of the areas to be covered, the composition of the population and/or the households within each area, and so on, would be required to serve as a master frame in designing several phases of sampling and stratification. In the experimental surveys, the various elements or classifications considered for the stratification included: development levels of the selected rural and urban areas (e.g. poorly developed/well developed, slum/non-slum blocks); income classes (low, middle, high); overall rates of literacy/illiteracy of the population; school attendance levels; family size, and so on.

Again, depending on the sample size and the other factors, an over-sampling may be needed to capture adequately the incidence of child labour, which is more rare than finding an adult in the labour force.

Surveys of employers (establishments or enterprises)

Scope

A survey of establishments or enterprises to study child labour can cover only a small part of all child workers, i.e. only those children who are employed for wages. According to ILO-IPEC experimental surveys carried out in Ghana, India, Indonesia and Senegal, the proportion of employed children among total child workers was found to be around 10 per cent. Thus, a survey of employers or establishments can give statistical information about only a small segment of child workers to supplement the results obtained through the household approach. However, these child workers might form the most vulnerable section of all working children; some of them may be exposed to danger, maltreatment by employers, underpayment and environmentally bad working conditions. Such facts may not, however, be revealed through the survey of establishments as most employers will not divulge such information. (This information can be more readily obtained from the child employees themselves who are covered by the household survey.) Nevertheless, a survey of establishments employing child labour may be undertaken as a supplementary effort to find out more about the employers who have recourse to it.

Practical difficulties and operational procedures

The experimental studies revealed many practical difficulties in conducting the survey of establishments. The most important was the difficulty in identifying the establishments that employ child labour. Most developing countries do not have an updated or exhaustive national list or directory of employers. The task of preparing such a list and identifying those employing children in the ultimate areal unit is time-consuming and requires considerable resources, both human and financial. Also, many establishment owners try to hide the fact that they actually engage children, and even if they admit to it, they may provide only partial information. The alternative is to survey the establishments which employ the children belonging to the sample households.

In spite of the problems that may arise, a survey of employers should be attempted. The following alternative operational procedures, which can be modified according to national requirements and circumstances, may be considered:

◆ constructing a list/directory of employers using a child workforce based on the responses provided by the children and their parents during a household-based child labour survey (this approach is strongly recommended);

◆ preparing, through local inquiries, a frame of enterprises employing child labour in the areas known to have a concentration of such units. For each unit, some broad information relating to the type of productive activity and the scale of operation (in terms of employment) may be ascertained;

◆ selecting a sample of enterprises engaged in different activities in which children are known or suspected to be working (if the total number of enterprises in the frame is small, all of them may be surveyed); and

◆ collecting the required information by interviewing all owners or operators of enterprises (this amounts to a census which could be prohibitive in terms of resources and time required to complete the survey operations).

The main difficulty in applying the above operational procedures is the preparation of a proper framework. An alternative could be to list all the enterprises along with the listing of households in the selected areal units, and elicit information as to whether or not they employ child labour. All the enterprises/establishments (employing any child labour) in each geographical unit in the sample for the household survey can be taken up. Such a scheme might also permit estimates of total child workers employed in enterprises. But it may call for a large number of ultimate areal units in the sample to obtain an adequate number of sample enterprises for the survey. Therefore, the strategy may be formulated according to the national circumstances of a country.

The three possible strategies are:

◆ as undertaken in the experimental surveys, a verification of the establishments in which the child workers identified during the household survey are reported to be employed;

◆ a survey of all the establishments (employing child labour) located in the ultimate areal units in the sample for the household survey; and

◆ a survey of establishments selected purposely from a list (prepared through local inquiries) of enterprises employing child workers.

Surveys of street children

Scope

Children who may live and work on the streets with no fixed place of usual residence cannot be covered through a household-based child labour survey. Certain activities of children can prove difficult to quantify through sample surveys; for example, prostitution, trafficking and other illegal activities are not easy to investigate given that, for the most part, such activities are hidden. A purposive or convenience survey approach may have to be used to collect qualitative information. It may be possible to contact a few of the children involved in these activities who are willing to be interviewed. However, much information can be gathered through the "key informants" system – contacting and interviewing knowledgeable persons in the community where the activities are known to exist. The investigators would have to be sociologists, psychologists, and social workers.

Questions addressed to youths in the streets should relate to most of the variables directed at the children aged 15 years mentioned under the household-based survey. Additionally, street children should be asked to provide information on their migration status and reasons for being homeless or for coming to the present place, on living conditions (food, sleeping places and facilities, health and safety), on the background characteristics of their parents/guardians and siblings, on whether or not they are in regular contact with their parents/guardians and/or siblings, on their present difficulties or problems, and on their prospects or plans for the future.

Operational difficulties in collecting data on street children

The actual fieldwork for collecting data from street children may be operationally difficult within the general framework of a survey. The investigators may have to visit the spots or places where the groups gather, perhaps late at night. There may even be some resistance from the group and in some cases it may even be dangerous to visit such spots for survey purposes. If so, help should be sought from local influential persons, social workers and the like, and sometimes even from police personnel.

The first operational step in the survey of street children is to identify the different places in the city (included in the geographical coverage of the survey) where groups of street children usually gather to sleep. This has to be done through local enquiries of social workers, law enforcement officers and so on. After identifying these spots, a sampling of them can be undertaken if they are numerous, but otherwise they should all be surveyed.

If a city has a large number of such places where street children gather, an alternative procedure could be to survey those which fall in the areal units selected for the household survey in the city. But since such places are not generally uniformly spread throughout the city, this scheme may not cover enough sample spots for the survey unless a special stratification is adopted. Therefore, as suggested earlier, an initial identification of such spots and a sampling of them (if necessary) may be more fruitful, particularly when such a survey cannot aim at statistical estimates for a larger geographical area.

In the selected spots, a complete enumeration of all the children can be attempted if their number is small. The children congregating at a particular place may often be homogeneous with respect to their activities and, therefore, if there is a large number of children in a given spot, a sample can be selected. To draw the sample, a list of all the children has first to be drawn up. Each child in the sample can then be interviewed to fill out the questionnaire. However, a survey of street children would have a number of limitations:

◆ the survey may not provide a reliable estimate of total street children by various categories, as the sample selected may not be representative;

◆ children living individually on the streets may not be covered since many of them move from place to place continuously;

◆ it may not be possible to get reliable information on some of the activities (illegal or disreputable) pursued by street children, which they may not want to report to the investigators; and

◆ if there is resistance in some places (or even threats of violence), the investigators may try to avoid collecting data in such places unless security is provided.

As far as possible, interviewers of street children should be those who are reasonably acquainted with the areas and streets where the children are usually found, who may even know some of the children themselves, and who are well trained in putting the children at ease, for example by providing them with soft drinks.

3.4 RECOMMENDATIONS FOR INTERVIEWING CHILDREN

Children are key informants on questions about "terms and conditions" and the "effect(s)" of their working situation on them. They may not be able to judge whether their well-being is damaged or will be damaged, but they can – if willing – give a description of their experiences and feelings.

The obvious way of collecting this information is by interview. A standard context for research interviews is the household-based surveys. But for reasons already explained, it is impossible to conduct in-depth interviews with child workers inside an employer's workplace (or premises). The atmosphere is wrong, the time-frame is wrong, the employer may be obstructive; the child is most unlikely to be forthcoming and – fearing repercussions from the employer – may even give answers which please the employer, especially if the employer is present at the interview. This may also be true even at the household level, which makes it important to interview the child alone, particularly away from his/her parents or so-called "guardians". However, contacting the child when and where he/she is completely alone may not be so easy.

Creating the right setting

In-depth interviews with children should therefore be conducted in a setting outside the place of work, preferably a place where the child feels safe and comfortable. Unless the interviewer has a great deal of experience in interviewing children, it will also be necessary to build up the child's confidence in the person concerned. Training in working with children will also be needed because creativity is needed to elicit correct information.

Box 3.1. Case examples of interviewing children

◆ In Bangladesh, an NGO called Shoishab persuaded employers in certain vicinities of Dhaka – such as a large apartment block or a street network – to permit their young domestic workers to attend an educational class several times a week. During the course of learning to read and write, opportunities were used to encourage the child domestics to talk about their situations. Drawing and story-telling were used for self-expression. When confidence had been built up, in-depth interviews could be conducted.

◆ In Haiti, an NGO called Foyers Maurice Sixto has set up "family centres" for *restavek* children (domestic workers). The children may be sought out by enquiry among the local church congregation, or recommended by their parents. The centre provides a caring environment for the child domestics where they can rediscover their childhood, and develop their talents and self-esteem. This setting is suited to in-depth research into the children's predicament.

◆ In the Philippines, an NGO called Visayan Forum in Manila made contact with young domestic workers in the park where they went on their day off. This led to the establishment of an Association of Household Workers. Visayan Forum conducts interviews to analyse the domestics' situation, and brings together those in the same ethno-linguistic group so that they can share their problems and give each other support.

Thus, interviewing children in depth, as opposed to asking broad questions, is best done over a period of time in a relatively unstructured and informal way. The ideal setting is an existing project in which (ex)-working children are participating, for example, a drop-in centre or an education programme.

If no such project currently exists, it is suggested that any attempt to collect in-depth information from the child workers at the employer's workplace or premises is postponed until it does. Here is a case where "action" should precede "research". However, there is no need to feel that the task is impossible. Some NGOs have set up projects with the twin purposes of action and research in mind, and have trained those who work with the children to collect information from them as part of their job.

Alternatively, researchers might identify – with help from social welfare departments and others – an existing institution such as a children's home where some children (child domestics or ex-domestics) are to be found, and conduct research among them. It cannot be stressed enough that in-depth qualitative research work with children, especially with those whose situation makes them especially vulnerable and predisposed not to trust adults, cannot be conducted by strangers in a cursory manner. The findings will be inaccurate and useless.

The interview process

In interviewing children about the effects of terms and conditions of work on their physical and mental well-being, it would be a good idea to seek advice from professional child care workers, as well as follow the suggestions below.

First, if you ask a child questions in a way which leads to a "yes" or "no", the child will probably answer accordingly. If you say: "Please tell me about....", or "Please describe to me...", you are likely to get more information. Similarly, sometimes a "leading" question such as "What do you think of....?" or "What do you know (or "Do you know") about the difficulties (or other situation) at your school, or where you work, or with your employer, or at your home...?", will result in more information.

Second, much information can only be gained indirectly.

Terms and conditions: A child will not understand these words very well. So ask him or her to describe the whole day's activities, from the moment he/she gets up in the morning, right through until bedtime. Questions can be included about what the employer says and does; and about meals, sleeping space, rest breaks and so on. From the very specific, the child could then be asked more general questions about visits from family members, holidays, outings, pay, and the like.

Effects on well-being: This is more difficult. As far as health is concerned, you could include "before" and "after" questions such as: "How does ...compare to ...at home?" (food, bedtime, getting-up time, aches and pains). For psychological impact, you could ask about "my happiest times", and "my saddest times", and about contact with friends and relations. The most important thing is to create an atmosphere in which the child feels sufficiently comfortable to tell stories about his or her intimate experiences and reveal his or her feelings. There may be some subjects – such as sexual abuse – which are especially hard to bring out. This is why time, trust, and the advice of child specialists are needed.

> *It should be borne in mind that this kind of investigation can be highly stressful for the child. Some researchers have found that an interview can make a child depressed, or cause him or her subsequently to run away. Therefore, they do not undertake in-depth interviewing without being prepared to provide help for the child – from their own NGO or some other childcare source – if help is sought.*

Bearing in mind the delicacy with which interviewing should proceed, work out ahead of time what kind of subjects are relatively easy to open up, and what kind should not be opened without caution. You can then proceed from one to another, depending on the child's reaction. For example, you can start with questions about tasks, pay, and "gifts" such as shelter, clothing, fare home, and medical expenses. Then proceed to working hours, where the child sleeps, food and care, how often he/she has a day off. From these responses you may spot natural openings to questions about the treatment the child receives and how he or she feels about it. If at any time the child becomes distressed, you can stop.

Box 3.2. Case examples – focus groups

In Senegal, ENDA, an NGO, conducted a research project with young women domestics by focus group discussion. Each group discussion was treated as a social event - a "tea debate". Around 50 participants attended. They were mainly girl domestics, but also included some of their "aunties" and some older women domestics.

The ENDA facilitators found that the young girls were constrained and would not speak up. The older women automatically saw it as their role to dominate proceedings and act as a controlling influence. The facilitators therefore divided the groups up, and put the youngest domestics together. In a position of peer solidarity they could bring out their intimate problems, including sexual abuse by employers, and the fact that they felt forced into prostitution because their wages were so low.

As a result of these findings, a programme against sexually transmitted diseases was launched by ENDA. Group solidarity also developed, and many of the young domestics have become members of a movement campaigning on behalf of the rights of young workers.

Growing confidence and capacity for self-expression are the product of a sensitive research process, which is itself part of ongoing action. The ENDA experience illustrates both the action-research-action cycle, and the value of putting the voices of young people at the centre of research on their behalf.

In Dakar, however, only one-third of domestic servants live in employers' houses. This makes external meetings practicable, whereas elsewhere they may only be possible to arrange for older children. There is also a network of urban community organizations based on people's place of origin to provide a "way in". The older women in these organizations, while they may have tried to dominate proceedings, were those whom ENDA originally enlisted to make the tea debate take place. So their contribution was important.

It should be noted that in all the above in-depth research techniques, the results would not provide or depict a complete picture of the child labour situation at the national level since they are only micro-level studies. Repeating such techniques all over a country would require a tremendous amount of resources – both human and financial. It would also be difficult to avoid double-counting of the working children. Nonetheless, the techniques are effective research methods for focused studies of specific categories of child labour in selected areas and communities in a country.

In addition to noting the child's responses to specific questions, you may also want to write down some of your observations: "observation' is a useful research technique. Immediately after the interview is over, write a few paragraphs about the child. If you are working with a colleague, the colleague could write the observation while the interview is going on. But in this case the colleague should be very unobtrusive and sit somewhere off to the side. If the interview is conducted in a separate room with just the child present, there should only be one adult interviewer or the child is bound to feel overwhelmed.

Have your observation headings ready ahead of time. For example: dress, cleanliness, facial expression, willingness to speak up, body language, signs of emotion, personality, ability to express him/herself. You may think you will remember all these things later when you read your interview notes, but very quickly one interviewee blurs into another.

Other in-depth techniques

Drawing, painting, acting out and story-telling are revealing methods of eliciting information. They are especially useful in cultural settings where people are not used to being bombarded with questions.

Many NGOs use these kinds of techniques within non-formal education programmes. In Indonesia, **drama** and **role-playing** are used as a strategy for "breaking the silence" when working with children and young people who are socialized not to speak up in front of adults.

Another technique is the **focus group discussion.** This is normally a semi-structured session with 6 to 12 participants picked for their special knowledge of the subject. Here, the participants could be child and adult domestics – split into two separate groups. Each group should have a facilitator trained in creating the kind of atmosphere which helps people speak up with confidence. A set of questions can be explored in depth.

3.5 FURTHER RESEARCH

Collecting in-depth information from children themselves is needed to obtain a full picture of the practice and its potentially harmful effects. However, interviewing children presents special difficulties. Programme actions which create the right environment may be needed first. Indirect techniques which utilize children's natural forms of expression should be used to the maximum, particularly for thoroughly studying specific child labour categories.

Research is also needed in several areas to complete or highlight parts of the child labour picture. The following research areas are suggested:

Carry out industry studies aimed to:

◆ increase generalizability of information and conclusions;

◆ initiate cooperation with employers;

◆ identify workplace improvements;

◆ design effective industry approaches;

◆ understand non-economic reasons for hiring children; and

◆ complete a technical methodological manual.

Study economic incentive programmes to allow for:

◆ impact assessments of specific ongoing programmes; and

◆ assessment of newly designed experimental programmes.

Measure hazardous work and activities to:

◆ identify the prevalence and types of hazard children face, and their consequences; and

◆ help implement *priorities* aimed at the worst forms of child labour.

Analyse newly available child labour surveys to:

◆ improve understanding of the reasons for the supply of child labour ; and

◆ better understand the nature and extent of child labour.

Investigate the child labour relationship to:

◆ adult employment and education;

◆ school quality and relevance; and

◆ family size, gender and birth order.

Appendix 3.1   List of detailed variables in child labour surveys

Variables to be considered in surveys designed for quantifying child labour in all its forms are indicated below, with those considered as essential followed by an asterisk **. (This list is not exhaustive and the applicability of some of the variables is dependent on the cultural, social and other circumstances of a particular country.)

Particulars at the community/town/village level to be provided mainly by the leaders of the community; some of the information may be readily available:

◆   physical features (area, terrain);

◆   population size* and density\dispersal;

◆   land ownership;

◆   economic profile* (per capita income/poverty level, unemployment rate, main activity or industry, seasonality of agriculture, irrigation system);

◆   education system*, schooling accessibility* and cost*;

◆   existence of by-laws or other legal instruments and of enforcement mechanisms, especially with respect to children;

◆   literacy/illiteracy level*;

◆   health system*, its quality*, accessibility* and cost*;

◆   catastrophes (flood, drought, and their frequency);

◆   availability and cost of water supply*, electricity*, public transport*;

◆   telephone, radio, television;

◆   organized entertainment and availability of recreational facilities* (playgrounds, sports complexes, public parks, social clubs, etc.);

◆   quality of environment (cleanliness of streets, public buildings, etc.); and

◆   proximity/distance to neighbouring community/town/village.

Household/dwelling characteristics, migration status and general living standard of the household on which information is to be provided by the household head (or proxy):

◆   type of dwelling and construction materials, and overall condition of dwelling;

◆   dwelling ownership* and, if rented, amount paid*;

◆   total number of rooms and number of functional/usable rooms;

◆   availability of facilities (kitchen, water system, electricity/natural gas, hot water, heating system and type of fuel used for heating/cooking, bathroom, toilet, etc.);

◆   usual place of residence of the household;

◆   most recent migration of the household and reason(s) for migration;

- average monthly/weekly consumption expenditure of the household* (including approximate imputed value of goods produced and consumed by the household);

- average monthly/weekly income of the household* (including economic and non-economic activity incomes earned in cash and in kind); and

- type of source from which the largest share of the total monthly income earned by the household.

Demographic and broad socio-economic characteristics of household members on which information is to be supplied by the household head (or proxy):

- number of usual members of present household*;

- age*, sex* and marital status* of each household member;

- for those 18 years and over: current/usual economic activity* (working, unemployed, not economically active): if working, status in employment*, earnings* (wages/salaries and other benefits in cash or in kind); actual hours worked* (per day/week) or actual days/weeks/months worked* (per week/per month/per 12 months);

- education level and technical/vocational training of the child*; birthplace*, most recent migration* and reason(s) for migration – whether both parents are alive* or only mother, father; and if both alive, whether living together, separately or divorced; if one alive, whether single or remarried; number* of sisters and brothers under the age of 18, and number living together and currently working, at school or in training*; if father is monogamous or polygamous and number of spouses (where applicable);

- whether* one/both parents are working as paid employee, employer, self-employed/independent/own account worker, farmer, herder, artisan, other (specify); and

- if any child (or children) 5-17 years old living away from present household, total number*, and for each child to indicate name, sex, age, present place of residence and main and secondary activities, working environment* and address of the workplace*; whether or not any contact with parents'/guardians' household, frequency/regularity of contact; if in economic activity, whether sending money or other benefits to parents/guardians, and how regularly this is sent; whether there was any arrangement for living and working away from own parents'/guardians' household – all above with *.

Socio-economic characteristics of children 5-17 years old on which information is to be provided by household heads (or proxies) and the children themselves:

- current/usual economic activity and status (employer, employee/paid worker, self-employed/independent/own-account worker, unpaid family worker, paid/unpaid apprentice)*, working environment* and address of the workplace*, domestic work in own parents'/guardians' or other relatives' household*;

- current occupations (main and secondary)*;

- if had worked previously, main occupations and reason(s) for leaving each job or employment;

- current industries (main and secondary)*;

- sector (formal/informal)*;

- earnings/remuneration/wages/salaries (cash, in kind, other)* and other employment benefits (paid holidays, paid sick leave, pension and other social security insurance, health insurance, unemployment insurance, other (specify));

- employment or occupational injuries*, diseases*, etc.*; type*, duration*, permanent disability*, etc;

◆ whether part or all earnings given to parent(s)/other relatives, and if given, how much regularly (day/week/month) or occasionally*;

◆ whether part of earnings kept in savings regularly (day/week/month) or occasionally, and how much and where;

◆ whether employer provides meals at workplace free or at cost (which is deducted from wages/salary), or other (specify);

◆ actual duration of work (number of hours per day/per week)*;

◆ whether working during weekends/official holidays and if working, how much is paid or earned in cash/in kind (per hour/day);

◆ if working during nights, how many hours of work per night and how much paid or earned in cash/in kind (per hour/night);

◆ nature of employment/work (part time/full time, permanent/temporary/seasonal, regular/casual, contractual (specify))*;

◆ if part time, temporary, or casual work, reason(s) and whether available for additional work and number of hours per day/week of this work;

◆ age when first started to work or became economically active and kinds of work/job occupied previous to current one*;

◆ whether currently looking for work/employment and kind of work/job sought*, and if had worked before; job experience or occupations;

◆ reason(s) for working*, or for not working and seeking work*;

◆ whether likes current work/employment/job* and if not, reason(s) and what kind of work preferred*;

◆ whether still attending school or technical/vocational training on a full- or part-time basis*, and if being trained, what kind of training*; difficulties/problems in attending school*;

◆ if has left school/training, (reason(s))*;

◆ whether employer providing training at workplace or elsewhere, free of charge or paying fee and amount being paid per day/week/month;

◆ whether living with parents/other relatives*, with employer*, or living alone* and responsible for own food and amount being paid* (per day/per week), and if living alone, type of dwelling (concrete, wooden, other (specify), and with running water (or how water is obtained), type of toilet used, type of lighting and whether free as provided by (specify), or owned, rented and amount of rent, or whether living with friends and sharing rent, etc., and amount for which responsible;

◆ whether paying income tax and how much; specify for what period;

◆ whether travelling between residence and workplace on foot, or by private/employer/public transport; free or paying and if paying cost per day/week/month;

◆ relationship with employer (good, or bad and reason(s))*;

◆ whether currently a member of workers' organization/employers' organization, and name of the organization(s); if member and paying fee, amount paid regularly (per week/month) or occasionally;

◆ whether currently registered at employment/manpower office/service;

◆ current difficulties/problems as a worker*;

◆ future prospect(s)/plan(s) (specify);

◆ if providing housekeeping services or engaged in household chores in own parents'/guardians' household on a regular basis, number of hours per day (or week) and type of services*; and

◆ if idle (i.e., not attending school/training institution and not engaged in any economic or non-economic activities, including housekeeping activities or household chores in own parents'/guardians' home), main reason for idleness*.

Particulars of establishments/enterprises/employers (also applicable to a micro-survey approach) on which information is to be supplied by the respective management on:

◆ location of establishment, etc., and type of goods produced or services rendered*;

◆ size/total number of workers/employees by major occupational group and nature of employment, separately for those aged under 10 years, 10-14 years, 15-17 years and 18 years and over*;

◆ actual/usual/normal duration of work (number of hours per day/week), and average wages/salaries, and other benefits (per day/week/month), separately for those aged under 10 years, 10-14 years, 15-17 years and 18 years and over*;

◆ number of workers under 18 years attending school full time/part time, separately for those aged under 10 years, 10-14 years and 15-17 years*;

◆ date business started and since when using/engaging workers aged under 10 years, 10-14 years and 15-17 years*;

◆ reason(s) for using child labour and method(s) used for recruiting this type of labour*;

◆ whether satisfied with work performed by child labour; if not satisfied, the reason(s)*;

◆ provision for training young workers at workplace, at other institutions, and type of training provided: free training (at employer's expense), subsidized (government or other organization(s)), worker and employer sharing cost, worker paying alone for training*;

◆ employer's future plans with respect to the recruitment and use of workers aged under 10 years, 10-14 years and 15-17 years*.

Bibliography on child labour surveys, statistics and related matters

Ashagrie, K. 1993. "Statistics on child labour: A brief report", in *Bulletin of Labour Statistics* (Geneva, ILO Bureau of Statistics), No. 1993-3, Sep.

—. 1994. *Inter-regional Seminar on Methodological Surveys of Child Labour, Bangkok, 1-5 August 1994:* A preliminary report (Geneva, ILO Bureau of Statistics, 1994).

—; Haspels, N. 1995. "Comprehensive and reliable data", in *Children at Work* (Geneva, ILO), No. 1, June.

—. 1997. *Methodological child labour surveys and statistics: ILO's recent work in brief* (Geneva, ILO Bureau of Statistics, June).

—. 1998. *Statistics on working children and hazardous child labour in brief* (Geneva, ILO Bureau of Statistics, Apr.).

—. 1998. "Child labour statistics: Methodological considerations", in *General Report* (Report IV), 16th International Conference of Labour Statisticians, Geneva, Oct. 1998.

Eurostat/IMF/OECD/United Nations/World Bank. 1993. *System of National Accounts 1993*, prepared under the auspices of the Inter-Secretariat Working Group on National Accounts (Brussels/Luxembourg, New York, Paris, Washington, DC).

ILO/IPEC. 1995. *Child labour*, report prepared for the 264th Session of the Governing Body (GB.264/ESP/1), Geneva, Nov. 1995.

—. 1996. *Child labour surveys: Results of methodological experiments in four countries 1992-93* (Geneva, Mar.).

—. 1996. "Children at work: How many and where?", in *World of Work* (Geneva), No. 15, Mar./Apr.

—. 1996. *Child labour: What is to be done?*, document for discussion at the Informal Tripartite Meeting at the Ministerial Level during the International Labour Conference (ITM/1/1996), Geneva, June 1996.

—; Gujarat Institute of Development Research. 1993. *Child labour in India: Results of a methodological survey in Surendranagar and Surat Districts of Gujarat State*, by Pravin Visaria and Paul Jacob (Ahmedabad, Dec.).

—; Direction de la prévision et de la statistique. 1993. *Le travail des enfants au Sénégal: Enquête méthodologique*, by Abdoulaye Sadio (Dakar).

—; Ghana Statistical Service. 1994. *Child labour in Ghana: A methodological sample survey - A survey of child labour in Accra Metropolitan, Sene and Sissala Districts* (Accra, Aug.).

—; Central Bureau of Statistics. 1994. *Working children in Bandung, Indonesia*, by Abuzar Asra (ed.) (Jakarta).

—; State Institute of Statistics. 1995. *Child labour in Turkey*, by Tuncer Bulutay (Ankara, Nov.).

Alternatives to child labour

4

Nelien Haspels,
Feny de los Angeles-Bautista
and Victoria Rialp

INTRODUCTION

Many experimental programmes have been undertaken in the education and socio-economic fields in recent years to prevent child labour, withdraw children from work and ensure that children and parents are provided with realistic and viable alternatives to child labour.

Education is one of the key solutions in the elimination of child labour. Children with no access to education have little alternative but to enter the labour market, often performing work that is dangerous and exploitative. Education and skills training help to prevent and reduce child labour, as:

◆ children with basic education and skills have better chances in the labour market; they are aware of their rights and are less likely to accept hazardous work and exploitative working conditions; and

◆ educational opportunities can wean working children from hazardous and exploitative work and help them find better alternatives.

The ILO and its International Programme on the Elimination of Child Labour (IPEC) has supported action research on many issues related to educational policies and programmes. It has also analysed the impact of action programmes with educational components on child labour, such as those providing non-formal education, (pre-) vocational training and other social support services for (former) working children, and promoting their enrolment in formal schools. There are many examples of effective educational programmes that are successful in preventing and eliminating child labour. The challenge is to mainstream such innovative initiatives into larger formal and/or non-formal education systems[1].

Improvements in education systems are not enough, however. First, children who have been traumatized by work need rehabilitation. Secondly, the worst child labour abuses take place among the most vulnerable socio-economic groups in society. These groups can seldom afford education, even if it is available, relevant and less costly. Their children are sent to work, because the children's contribution and earnings are essential for family survival. It is reasonable to assume that children will continue to be sent to work as long as their parents are not earning enough. Therefore, measures to improve education need to be part and parcel of integrated programmes for disadvantaged population groups, programmes which aim to empower the poor and abolish social discrimination by providing income-earning opportunities. These can be employment creation and poverty alleviation schemes, small enterprise development, minimum wage systems, credit systems and social safety nets for the most needy. The programmes should address both the need for income for adults and schooling for children at the design and implementation stages, so that they do not inadvertently encourage the employment of children along with or instead of the employment of adults.

Finally, given that the supply of child labour is so large, actions to provide alternatives to children need to be combined with intensive awareness-raising in workplaces, among employers, managers and young and adult workers, and in communities. Workplace and community child watch or monitoring systems need to be set up to ensure that new children do not enter the vacated jobs.

---

[1] For more information, see N. Haspels, F. de los Angeles-Bautista, P. Boonpala and C. Bose: *Action against child labour: Strategies in education* (Geneva, ILO-IPEC, forthcoming) and ILO-IPEC: *Alternatives to child labour: A review of action programmes with a skills training component in Asia* (Bangkok, 1998).

Prevention and removal programmes usually consist of three interrelated components:

- *education and training to children, combined with rehabilitation services;*

- *integrated programmes for disadvantaged population groups resorting to or prone to resort to child labour, combining education for children with functional literacy training and education, income-earning opportunities and social safety nets for their parents; and*

- *information and the establishment of a workplace or community child-watch or monitoring system.*

As the examples in this chapter show, initiatives have been taken by a wide range of partners in the public and the private spheres, reflecting the need for multisectoral, multidisciplinary action against child labour.

The primary focus of this chapter is on educational and rehabilitation services for children, with examples of the various types of measures for families; and on monitoring mechanisms to ensure that geographic areas and specific workplaces remain child labour free. Guiding principles for planning action programmes, based on IPEC experience, are presented in a series of checklists.

4.1 STRATEGIES IN EDUCATION

While education is the alternative to child labour, lack of access to education and poor-quality education can contribute to the problem of child labour, often because parents and children prefer work over schooling not only to gain income for the family, but also to learn skills for later life. A whole range of interventions in education is necessary to attract children to school, and to keep them there and out of work.

Investment in a country's human resources is crucial, not only for younger generations, but for socio-economic development as a whole. Therefore, renewed national commitment, policy reform and massive investment in basic education are vital to meet the challenge. A holistic approach to education is required. Children should be provided with access to quality education from early childhood onwards up to at least 15 years of age. In the long term, this will be the most durable solution. However, given that many countries are still far from providing quality education for all, immediate remedial measures are needed.

ILO-IPEC experience shows that even in countries where substantial progress has been made and average school enrolment ratios are high, there are still children from poor population groups who do not benefit from this progress. This suggests that apart from general improvements in the education system, special measures are often necessary to increase access to education for children who are especially vulnerable.

Transitional education has to be provided to prevent such children from taking up hazardous work or to wean them away from it. They need to be equipped with basic education, practical knowledge and skills. Such education should consist of an integrated package of basic education, life skills and practical skills training, and should ideally aim at mainstreaming the children into formal education and vocational training systems. However, options also have to be provided to the children who are unable to continue formal education and training, so they do not re-enter the labour market as unskilled workers.

The younger children may require skills that are useful in improving their quality of life and can be developed further, while the older children generally require vocational counselling and practical training that can lead to income generation either through wage labour or self-employment in a broad array of employable skills.

A measure which can be undertaken relatively quickly and which does not require massive investment is the incorporation into children's and parents' education of explicit messages on the dangers of premature work and the rights of children to education, wherever there is a high risk of child labour.

Educating children about their rights and about child labour issues

Children need to know their rights and the dangers and risks of work to their health, safety, and education. They need to learn to protect themselves and to have information about their rights: which laws exist specifically for their protection, and to whom they can turn for help when they are at risk of being exploited. Education on children's rights can and should be integrated into the curriculum through social studies, health education, literacy and language learning. In this way, children are also in a better position to protect themselves, express themselves, negotiate and assert their rights. Education on rights teaches them about their responsibilities to themselves and to others; it helps them become productive citizens of their own communities while receiving adequate care and protection.

Box 4.1. Awareness-raising about child labour for teachers and children – a joint effort of the Provincial Labour Welfare and Protection Office and the Provincial Primary Education Office of Srisaket Province, Thailand

There is a high incidence of migration among children from Srisaket province to the cities in search of jobs. During 1993-94, the project mobilized teachers and school administrators in preventing child labour. A total of 22 schools with high drop-out rates participated in the campaign among teachers and children to keep them from entering work, and encourage them to stay at school and continue with secondary education.

In Phase I of the project, teachers were trained on child labour. Teaching materials were developed for use by teachers (a handbook) and by children in the classroom. In Phase II, teachers used the suggested methods in the handbook and classroom materials (magazines, newspaper clippings, pamphlets, videos and animation about child labour) to inform and teach children about the effects of child labour on their health and safety, and about existing laws applicable to them. Child labour corners or exhibits were set up in school libraries or other parts of the school. Children engaged in group discussions and were involved in various activities such as art, writing and quizzes on child labour issues.

Teachers also recognized the need to work with parents who decide on whether children go to school or to work. They tried to convince them that in the long term it would be more beneficial to continue their children's education and to postpone their employment. Teachers who participated in the campaign met regularly to follow up on the project's progress and development. The project involved additional work for the teachers who were the main resources in the project, fully committed and creative in developing and implementing strategies for the prevention of child labour.

The outcome was that most of the children in the 22 schools completed their basic education up to the secondary level. As a result, the Thai Ministry of Education has developed a child labour curriculum which is to be integrated into the primary school curriculum, particularly in provinces where there is a high incidence of child labour and school drop-out.

Investment in early childhood development programmes

Integrated early childhood development programmes that address the physical, social, emotional and cognitive development of young children have in recent years received more attention and visibility because of their evident impact. Children who participate in various forms of these programmes are healthier, socially well adjusted and better prepared for learning experiences in later childhood.

Thus, the programmes help prevent school failure, which contributes to children dropping out and being recruited for full-time hazardous work. The more successful children are at school, the more persistent parents tend to be about keeping them there. At the same time, most early childhood development programmes involve a parent education component and are good entry points for educating both parents and children about the detrimental effects of full-time and dangerous work of children.

Box 4.2. Strengthening pre-school education – The Ministry of Education in the United Republic of Tanzania

Many children among farmers and shepherd families in the United Republic of Tanzania start to work during their early childhood years and this is an obstacle to their entry into and completion of primary school. Therefore, the Ministry of Education launched a programme to bring children from poor families into school at an earlier stage and pre-empt their participation in child labour before they enter primary school. The goal was to motivate children to stay at school by preparing them for school and creating an interest for learning through early childhood education.

The project was conducted in five regions where the drop-out rates were high and children's participation in cattle-herding and domestic work clearly affected their school participation. A series of baseline surveys on school enrolment and child labour were conducted. Awareness-raising took place among school committees and ward coordinators about the need to set up early childhood centres and to educate them about child labour issues. Fifty pre-school teachers were trained and a manual for child labour was developed for use by primary school teachers and school committees.

The project succeeded in generating enthusiasm for school among children, parents and teachers. It is now government policy to provide for early childhood education. The Ministry of Education has also prepared a manual on child labour, labour laws and children's rights to be used in the primary school civics curriculum throughout the country.

Increasing access to education

More schools are needed in communities with high concentrations of child labour, especially in rural areas, and these schools need to provide the complete basic education course and the necessary ingredients to meet the basic learning needs.

Box 4.3. The Multi-grade Education Programme – The Bureau of Elementary Education, Department of Education, Culture and Sports, the Philippines

In the remote rural communities of the Philippines, where significant numbers of children often work in agriculture, the challenge of building enough schools to provide basic education to children from highly dispersed families has been formidable. For decades, school administrators in rural provinces resorted to organizing multi-grade classes where children from three different grade levels were taught by one teacher. It was difficult for teachers to implement the national curriculum, designed for homogeneous groups in single-grade classes. In addition, as these schools were located in remote areas, more experienced teachers who could choose their assignments seldom opted to teach in them. There was also a perception among parents and educators in these communities that multi-grade schools were poor alternatives or substitutes for the single-grade classes.

However, given the demographic conditions in these rural communities, it was unlikely that the population of children for each age level would increase to a size that would merit the opening of six-classroom schools with one teacher for every grade level. Therefore, in the process of exploring all available options to achieve the goals of education for all, the Department of Education, Culture and Sports (DECS) decided to develop more fully and upgrade the multi-grade education programme as a viable strategy to address the educational needs of children in these communities.

The programme had a dual focus: expanding access to education and improving the quality of education for children in the poorest and most remote rural communities. There were different stages in the process of improving the multi-grade schools.

Activities included: teacher training; training of trainers and supervisors; development of a re-organized curriculum for multi-grade classes based on the minimum learning competencies used in all public schools; and preparation of sample lesson plans, a teacher's handbook on multi-grade teaching, and multi-level student materials.

One component of the Multi-grade Education Programme by the DECS, initiated in 1995 in cooperation with an NGO, the Community of Learners Foundation, focused on the setting-up of demonstration schools in six of the poorest provinces of the country. The central features of this component were: (i) an innovative multi-stage training programme for teachers and supervisors in the provinces that emphasized active, experiential approaches to teaching and learning; (ii) a focus on parent and community participation so that multi-grade schools became an integral part of the life of the community, with parents more fully involved as partners in their children's education; (iii) the setting-up of demonstration schools as micro-resource centres for collaborative learning among teachers from the clusters of multi-grade schools; and (iv) the organization of monthly workshops for teachers to sustain their continuing professional development and to alleviate the problem of isolation while working in single-teacher schools.

At the end of the first year of the project there was a dramatic increase in the enrolment of children in the primary grades, indicating a change in children's and parents' attitudes towards the multi-grade schools in their community. The working relationship between teachers and their supervisors, and between the teachers and the community members, improved. In most provinces, cooperation was evidenced in improved physical conditions of the school, changes in teaching methods and the atmosphere in the classrooms. While the project is still at an early stage of implementation, it has successfully demonstrated that it is possible to involve teachers, parents and community members in improving the quality of education for their children.

Improving the quality of formal and non-formal education

Both formal and non-formal education systems can be made more responsive to children who are at risk of premature work or who are already working. The structure of educational programmes, the content of the curriculum and the teaching approaches applied in schools should include relevant, useful knowledge and skills, which meet the developmental needs of children and prepare them to earn income later in life and become responsible adults in their communities. Innovative education methods which have been tried out successfully on a small scale in experimental non-formal education programmes should be incorporated and expanded in the formal education system.

Box 4.4. The Prashika Project – Eklavya Bhopal, Madhya Pradesh, India

Eklavya was established by a small group of highly educated people who believe that education is critical for social change and should be available to all. Instead of setting up an alternative system, parallel to the public schools, they chose to work through government schools to help make education more dynamic and meaningful. The programme initially focused on improving the science education programme in middle school classes in urban and rural communities. From 16 classes in one district in 1972 the programme has expanded to 14 districts covering 450 schools and 50,000 students.

Science education was improved through the introduction of more active, experiential learning methods and learning-by-doing techniques such as experiments, field trips and group discussions. Eklavya trained teachers to be facilitators in their work with children, to unlearn teaching methods that emphasize passive rote learning with a heavy reliance on textbooks and to shift to more cooperative forms of working in small groups, encouraging questions and discussion. Children, teachers and other resource persons participated in the development of the curriculum. Eklavya was able to help teachers and children relate the content of science education to the children's own lives and environment.

From the initial focus on science education, Eklavya expanded to other curriculum areas such as the social sciences. An integrated approach was introduced to organize the curriculum by thematic units of study which linked different content areas. Emphasis was given to developing children's self-expression and critical thinking. After-school activities were introduced such as activity centres and libraries, a children's magazine called *Chakmak*, a children's club, children's fairs, contests and exhibitions. These are now considered to be integral parts of the educational programme.

Non-formal education as an entry, a re-entry or alternative for (former) working children

It is often not possible to insert (former) working children directly into formal school, because they are older, have experience and are not used to the school environment. Therefore, many initiatives have been undertaken in recent years to adapt educational programmes and make them more suited to the needs of former child workers. It has been found that quality non-formal education can act as a bridge between work and school and facilitate the entry of children into formal schools. However, the initiatives have been small scale to date and are often isolated from the mainstream educational programmes within the country. Serious efforts still have to be made to further strengthen flexible non-formal remedial education programmes which provide adequate entry points into a country's educational and vocational training system. In some countries, efforts have already been made. Non-formal education programmes have been established alongside the formal education system, and accreditation and equivalency programmes have been developed to allow for an easier transition between formal and non-formal education. In most countries, however, stronger linkages need to be created between the formal and non-formal education streams.

Box 4.5. Non-formal education in Andhra Pradesh, India – The Bhagavatulu Charitable Trust (BCT)

The BCT has been operating as a service organization in integrated rural development since 1976. In 1993, it started addressing child labour problems by setting up non-formal education centres in cooperation with 25 NGOs. A total of 160 centres are now providing classes for children to prepare them for re-entry into formal schools. BCT started with two-hour evening classes for 280 to 300 days a year. The children continued to work while they attended these classes. The BCT curriculum takes two-and-a-half years to complete and is organized in five stages of six months each. Six of the non-formal education centres were converted into full-time schools to ensure that children would not go to work. The curriculum is completed in 18 months to two years. At the end of the programme, children are qualified to join Class 5 of the formal school. By 1996, 160 schools were operational and more children were enrolling in these day schools than in the evening programmes. When children move to the formal school and there are no new participants, BCT moves to another area where there are more children who work and do not attend school.

In cooperation with the Rishi Valley Rural Education Programme, BCT upgraded and redesigned the curriculum. It introduced more active, "learning by doing" approaches which were successful in motivating children to stay at school until their parents became accustomed to not relying on the income that they brought to the family. Ninety per cent of the children have moved on to the formal schools. Village committees have since built more schools and 2,000 children benefit from these.

Box 4.6. Fe y Alegría (Faith and Joy) Integral Popular Education Movement Association – a church-affiliated network of education projects in 12 Latin American countries

Fe y Alegría in Peru consists of a network of 46 education projects implemented in different parts of the country: near Lima, the capital; in a coastal town; in the Andean region and in the Amazonian forest area. A range of flexible education and training opportunities is provided to children from poor families, aged 5 to 16, who are at high risk of school failure or dropping out of school. It also works with older children who enter school for the first time. Fe y Alegría promotes the active participation of students and the communities in their school activities. It also improves material facilities, and provides teaching aids and teacher training.

School No. 43, for example, is located in a squatter settlement in Ventanilla where child labour is rampant. It is home to displaced Quechua highlanders who are refugees from armed conflict. Children attend classes which have been organized in two shifts: children aged 10-16 (secondary-level group) attend the morning shift to pre-empt their full-time employment but allow them to work part-time; young children aged 6 to 10 attend the afternoon sessions. The school provides a wide range of educational activities which emphasize practical life and work skills that help prepare the children for work. Secondary school students have the option to focus on basic vocational skills such as carpentry, electrical work, sewing or preparation for higher education and further technical training. The technical options include nursing, handicrafts, forestry, hydroponics, English, computer education, and shoe repair.

There are several significant features of Fe y Algería. An explicit policy of inclusion is pursued so that children do not feel they are discriminated against. It emphasizes nurturing the self-esteem of students and building solidarity among them. Pregnant girls are encouraged to stay at school and continue with their schooling after they have given birth. Follow-up support is given to students after graduation, e.g. those needing employment while pursuing higher education. Finally, students and teachers are actively involved in planning, decision-making and managing conducive learning environments.

In Guatemala, Fe y Alegría works in five districts with specific groups of children, youth and women from indigenous groups in urban poor communities, covering 6,200 families from 184 communities. Programmes include education for work, formal education, including distance education by radio, teacher training, literacy training and micro-enterprise training. The educational programmes include craft and technical training in fields where there is high demand, such as tailoring, carpentry, shoe-making, woodwork, general and automotive mechanics, dressmaking, baking, welding, electricity, electronics and cosmetics. Fe y Alegría prioritizes the development of practical life skills within the curriculum. It emphasizes the development of a work ethic and commitment to service, participatory management, research-based planning and community-based education.

For some older children, a few years of non-formal education will be the only option. These children need to be provided with an integrated package of general education, along with practical life and work skills so that they can re-enter the labour market at an appropriate age with more knowledge about their rights as workers and skills that will allow them access to better jobs. Ideally, however, this type of education should be a transition to mainstreaming the younger children in particular into regular schools.

Box 4.7. The Alternative Learning System for Continuing Education (ALS-CEP) – Bureau of Non-Formal Education, Department of Education, Culture and Sports, the Philippines

ALS-CEP is classified as an Equivalency Programme which is designed to be parallel to and comparable to the formal school system. It is designed to inculcate self-reliance and self-help among the poor to enable them to participate effectively in productive activities and to improve their life through the attainment of higher levels of functional literacy. Out-of-school youth are among the target groups of the programme. One of the components of the programme is the Placement Test (PEPT) which is administered by regular public schools for out-of-school students who are enrolled in a self-study programme. In this way, over-age children who have been out of school and who wish to re-enter formal school can complete the basic education cycle and qualify for secondary education or vocational training.

Approaches to vocational education

Many non-formal education programmes for (former) working children include practical or vocational skills training components in the curriculum. Vocational training is often very popular among families which are prone to resort to child labour. Short-term vocational training is often combined with or delivered after functional literacy training and can provide immediate economic alternatives.

However, there are issues to resolve in the definition and approaches to vocational education. First, a distinction must be made between more formal vocational training, which is usually longer term and systematically linked to apprenticeship programmes, and less formal training. Most formal vocational programmes require close adult supervision and the available slots for students are limited.

There are also non-formal vocational training programmes linked to both formal and non-formal education programmes which are often short term and deal with specific skills and topics that are not necessarily marketable or highly productive. Non-formal education programmes can teach children skills that will provide immediate economic alternatives as well as psycho-social support. But these should not be viewed as a complete substitute for formal education, rather as transition programmes to facilitate the child's re-entry into the formal school system. In situations where there are no local institutions or schools offering such vocational education programmes, it may be necessary to provide scholarships.

Experience has shown that practical skills training in the form of "learning by doing", experiments and arts and crafts are an integral part of basic education. When (pre-) vocational training is included in non-formal education programmes, care should be taken to ensure that children and youth acquire basic skills which lay a foundation for training in specific trades or occupations. Vocational training should be geared to the provision of marketable skills that can be adapted to the changing needs in the job market. The gender bias in education is even more pronounced in the field of vocational training and specific attention needs to be given to facilitate girls' access. In most countries, better linkages need to be created between education and vocational training, and between non-formal and formal vocational training.

Box 4.8. Vocational training for child workers, Mirpur, Bangladesh

The Bangladesh Jatio Sramik League (BJSL), Metal Workers Union of Bangladesh, a national trade union centre established in 1969 with almost 100,000 members throughout the country, has worked on literacy, human rights and other social issues. The BJSL has also started to address child labour by providing non-formal education and skills training for child workers. At the start, 75 children (60 boys and 15 girls) participated. There are now four instructors who work with 300 children.

The children are involved in several programme activities: general education (for two hours each day, six days a week for six months) which addresses literacy skills; skills training (also for two hours a day) with four choices: sewing or embroidery; welding and lathe machining; production activities involving commissioned work arranged by instructors and linked to skills training which serves as on-the-job training, providing income for the children; and recreation, including board games, cricket and football. The skills chosen were based on the assessment of the programme staff of what would be marketable skills for the children's employment in the future.

Food supplements were part of the programme, but were removed in Phase 2. The programme organizers felt that providing both stipends and food supplements might discourage parents from sending their children to regular government schools which cannot provide for these additional incentives. The stipends were retained but the feeding programme was discontinued.

The programme generated tremendous interest from the parents who brought their children to participate, while the children expressed their enthusiasm for the programme and were optimistic about finding a better job. Some plan to set up their own workshops. There will be more emphasis on life skills and management skills so that the children will learn about costs and earnings, managing their income and being more realistic about their abilities and the possibilities for earning.

Box 4.9. The Sema Life Development Project – Special Project Division, Office of the Permanent Secretary, Ministry of Education, Thailand

The project was launched in August 1994 to address the needs of girls from the northern part of Thailand who were recruited by persuasion or deception into prostitution. Many of them were from the hill tribes, and some were children of illegal migrants and refugees. The main strategy was to involve children, families and communities in preventing child prostitution.

Data collection and analysis were undertaken at the home and village levels, and 5,000 child victims and potential victims of prostitution were identified. An information campaign, including education on HIV/AIDS, was organized, as many parents had encouraged their children to engage in the sex trade to maintain a relatively comfortable lifestyle for the family. Many girls were vulnerable to being recruited into prostitution because they wanted to fulfil their filial responsibility.

During the first phase, 94 primary schools in eight northern provinces were involved. In the project design, primary schools were designated as the campaign centres for the prevention of prostitution. They helped identify girls at high risk and organized prevention activities. Boarding-schools and secondary schools in target areas were expected to provide opportunities for the girls to complete their education beyond the primary level. Vocational training in marketable trades for the local communities and non-formal education services were provided to those unable to join the general education stream in secondary school. Scholarships enabled the girls to enrol in boarding-schools or vocational colleges.

Ban Vieng'pan School is the project centre for 41 schools in a locality which is home to Burmese refugees. Within four months the project managed to start enrolling many girls in schools. In this area, 40 per cent of students dropped out after primary level, and 5 per cent of the students were "southward bound", i.e. recruited for the sex trade in the south. Teachers were actively involved in the campaign against child prostitution and educated children about the laws related to prostitution and the dangers – including sexually transmitted diseases and HIV/AIDS – and about the ways that children are manipulated by agents. The teachers identified alternative occupations in the community and started to organize courses in weaving, sewing, flower-arranging and handicrafts with the participation of community resource persons and social workers. The social welfare offices also provided financial and technical support for vocational training.

A significant initiative of the teachers as advocates for the girls was to intervene when recruiters tried to establish contact with them. The teachers informed the local police and the parents and continued to monitor the girls, especially when parents were consenting to the recruitment of their children. However, they also realized that child prostitution is part of organized crime, which placed understandable limits on the degree to which teachers could take action.

The project has been successful in raising community awareness, preventing the recruitment of more children into prostitution and supporting them through education and training. But the demands on the teachers in time and energy needed were tremendous. Pressing problems related to the lack of funding support, especially for teacher training, mobilization efforts, administrative back-up, and assistance to facilitate work with other government agencies or within the Ministry of Education. However, efforts have been made to strengthen coordination within and among agencies at the local and provincial levels, which will culminate in the adoption of a coordinated Provincial Plan of Action to prevent child labour.

4.2 PREVENTION AND REHABILITATION PROGRAMMES FOR CHILDREN FROM ESPECIALLY VULNERABLE GROUPS

Population groups that are most vulnerable to child labour require special attention. Many of the most abusive types of child labour are hidden and few organizations have the capacity to identify and handle them. Child victims may also have developed various coping mechanisms and often there will be differences in the needs of boys and girls. Thus, special efforts are required to first identify the groups for priority action and then develop a range of appropriate interventions.

It is essential to prevent children from becoming engaged in extreme forms of child labour. This involves intensive awareness-raising, and the provision of viable alternatives. In cases where organizations aim to withdraw children from the worst forms of child labour, the types of intervention need to include identification and rescue of children working under forced labour conditions, legal aid, intensive counselling and other rehabilitation measures for the children and their families.

Child victims of bondage, commercial sexual exploitation and trafficking

Victims of human rights violations such as children in bondage and children forced into prostitution, domestic work or sweatshops in their own or other countries are often damaged and traumatized beyond recovery (see also Chapter 5). It is therefore critical that these types of child labour abuse be prevented through effective law enforcement and large-scale awareness-raising in schools and communities where there is a high incidence or risk. Local community monitoring mechanisms should be activated to identify those at high risk and to monitor the situation of those who have been rescued.

Girls

While progress is being made in many countries to increase the access of girls to education, they continue to have less access worldwide than boys. At the same time, girls and women bear a major share of the burden of poverty. Giving girls access to quality education is a first essential step towards empowering them and enabling them to break through the vicious cycle of poverty.

Box 4.10. Literacy Awareness and Educational Support Programme – Child Workers in Nepal Concerned Centre (CWIN)

CWIN is an organization of human rights activists which has committed itself to promote children's rights and has initiated programmes for children who are victims of human rights violations. These include child labourers from tea estates and carpet factories, street children and children from poor urban and rural communities, many of whom work under bonded labour arrangements.

CWIN aims to eliminate child labour and rehabilitate child victims. Improvement in the situation of abused children goes hand in hand with lobbying for children's rights and creating nationwide awareness. CWIN's strategy is multi-pronged. It raises awareness, educates children and their families and provides a whole range of other support services such as obtaining legal protection for children, lobbying for the amendment of laws and forming pressure groups to lobby for the rights of children. It seeks to rehabilitate destitute families by providing alternative sources of income and shelters to homeless children.

CWIN's educational programmes include a literacy and awareness programme for around 1,400 children in Sundhupalchowk, Ilam, Jhapa and Kathmandu. Classes focus on the three Rs (reading, writing and arithmetic) as well as education on children's rights, for a period of nine months. Teachers are drawn from groups of workers, teachers, women, human rights workers and social workers in the surrounding areas. Facilitators are recruited from the community, the tea estates or the carpet factories, and are trained for ten days. CWIN has developed literacy materials on children's rights and uses these in tandem with materials developed by the Ministry of Education for non-formal education programmes. One objective of the literacy classes is to help child workers understand their rights to fair wages and to be able to determine if they are being paid in full.

CWIN also provides informal education programmes and multi-grade classes in its Common Room and Transit Homes, which are shelters for homeless children, many of whom have never been to school or have had to drop out. After participating in these programmes, the children are assisted through scholarships to attend formal schools. There are various assistance schemes to cover school fees for returning children, and uniforms and supplies, as well as residential care. Some children attend private schools, but more attend the local public schools.

CWIN has recently initiated an experimental education and skills training programme. The first vocational courses were on bicycle repair and electrical wiring. Older children were provided with tool kits and some provision for food and lodging, so that they could start out on their own. The programme still needs strengthening, especially in terms of sustaining contact with the children and ensuring that they are in a safe condition. There is a need to further address the needs of these children and to develop viable alternatives for them.

Successful strategies include intensive awareness-raising in communities where there are social and cultural constraints, provision of schools and childcare facilities near the girls' homes, recruitment of female teachers, promotion of gender fairness and equality at schools, and investment in the education and skill training of mothers. An especially vulnerable target group is pregnant girls and teenage mothers. Prevention through family life education for boys and girls at school is still the most cost-effective measure. Special programmes to allow pregnant girls and young mothers to continue their education are also needed, as these young women are otherwise forced to start working themselves and involve their children from an early age in meeting basic survival needs.

Box 4.11. Cheli-Beti Programme – Education for Rural Development Project, Government of Nepal

The Cheli-Beti programme was launched as a pilot project to address the special needs of girls and women in the region. The situation of girls required special attention because girls were married off early, put to work in the husbands' households or other workplaces at an early age and usually never enrolled in school.

The strategies of the Cheli-Beti (C-B) programme included: (i) intensive awareness-raising in villages on the importance of educating girls; (ii) identifying and training female educators from the area to work as field coordinators and teachers for the programme; (iii) utilizing local schools as resource centres; and (iv) identifying villages where 15-25 girls could be gathered and motivated to attend the classes facilitated by the local C-B teacher.

The curriculum included reading, writing, mathematics, personal hygiene, household management with emphasis on health and sanitation, and practical skills, such as planting and caring for fruit-bearing plants, making kitchen gardens, sewing and solving common health problems such as stopping diarrhoea and de-worming. The teaching methods were interactive and made frequent use of songs, games, problem-solving exercises and field trips. The children who completed the C-B classes were encouraged to enrol in formal schools. They were given equivalency tests and enrolled in the grade levels for which they qualified, usually Grade 3.

Eighty-six per cent of the participants completed the classes, learned both life and learning skills, and were literate by the end of the project. The girls said that they appreciated the value of education and felt that they would be better able to support their own sons and daughters when they went to school. However, while most of the C-B graduates went on to primary school, many of them did not complete the cycle in the formal schools. Some of the C-B teachers are now teaching in the local primary schools. Unfortunately, the innovative methods in the C-B programme were not adopted in the regular primary schools. However, the programme strategy and methods have been adopted by the Basic and Primary Education Project (BPEP) and the Women's Education Project (WEP) as their Out-of-School Programme. This programme is now implemented in 40 of the 75 school districts, and several NGOs also use the C-B curriculum for their literacy programmes.

Children living and working on the streets

The lifestyle of street children has to be taken into account when designing education and rehabilitation programmes. Most successful programmes have a phased and integrated approach. In the first instance, peer or adult street workers reach out to street children to establish contact and gain their trust by involving them in street education activities, motivating them to participate in educational programmes and helping them acquire the basic skills that will enable them to learn in a structured environment. They need help to adjust to adult authority after being used to surviving on their own and developing a variety of defence mechanisms against adults who may have exploited them or who may have violated their rights. They are often hostile or intimidated by adult authority figures in schools, even in child-focused programmes. Street education programmes, which provide an atmosphere of freedom and democratic consultation, and which build up rapport gradually and develop trust, have been more effective than enrolment in formal schools, especially at the initial re-entry stages.

Box 4.12. Rehabilitation and prevention programme for child beggars and street children – De Laas Gul Welfare Programme (DLG), Lahore, Pakistan

DLG is a local NGO working with women through provision of vocational training, literacy and promotion of education. One of its objectives is the mainstreaming of disadvantaged children into regular schools. The organization has established about 30 schools in local communities, providing primary education and non-formal education. The ILO-IPEC programme focuses on beggar families and communities, and on street children. The project provides non-formal education programmes in its centres. It also aims to work with parents and the mullahs or community religious leaders to raise awareness about the hazards facing children who work on the street and about the value of education.

The project works with 45 child beggars and 40 scavengers, through rehabilitation activities, non-formal education, vocational skills training and the provision of health care. Emotional rehabilitation is considered the first step when the children are newly recruited to join the programme. Counsellors work with the children at all times to orient them to the centre, and to encourage their self-expression. Older children who have been programme participants, and who have been trained as peer counsellors, also help the newly recruited children to adjust. The initial activities are designed to motivate children to engage in enjoyable learning actvities such as drawing, listening to stories, and watching videotapes.

The children are categorized into three groups. The first consists of small children. The objective is their complete withdrawal from begging or other street-based work, getting them to study at the centre and ultimately enter formal schools. These children are taught reading, writing and arithmetic and are prepared for the entrance examinations to enter formal school. The project provides books and supplies for those children who go on to formal school.

Non-formal education programmes are usually needed for a smoother transition between life and work on the streets and formal schooling. Special attention has to be paid to matching the learning methodology and process to the learning styles of street children. Hands-on-learning, experimentation and observation, and learning-by-doing are what they have been doing to survive. Many street children may not be "school smart" but they are certainly "street smart". They are adept at problem-solving and assessing situations from the perspective of survival. They have worked, and will assess the relevance of schooling to their immediate future in the world of work. It must be worthwhile for them to decrease their time on the streets and spend it in the classroom learning skills that help them improve their life.

Many street children also need counselling services to cope with traumatic experiences of violence, sexual exploitation or other harassment at home or on the street. Rehabilitation for substance abuse may also be necessary. Such support services should be a priority before the children can be expected to attend school and stay there.

The parents pay for school fees (about 45-50 rupees per year for primary education) and buy the children's uniforms and school bags. The project staff believe that parents are happy and willing to send boys to school, but not girls.

The second group of children consists of those who are older, and who have to continue working for one reason or another. Alternative vocational skills training is provided to prepare them to shift to safer occupations. The children continue to work on the streets but the project staff try to convince them to sell in the market or at street corners, which are relatively safer. They sell hair ribbons, hats, juices or candies. This is seen as an initial transition measure. There are efforts to convince local ice-cream vendors or restaurants and shop owners to work with the children, but so far the project has not been successful because of the intense prejudice against them. The skills taught at the centre include food preparation (e.g. juice and jelly-making), candle and soap-making, making hats and hair ribbons, sewing, knitting, embroidery and patchwork.

Children in the third group are young children who work on the street but cannot yet be withdrawn because of the parents' objections. So far project staff have been able to encourage the children to visit the centre and play with the other children whenever they can. The centres are open twice a day, from 9-11 a.m. and from 1-3 p.m. The children beg or do other work at other times of the day. This is seen as a transition device so that at least for two hours a day the children can be out of the workplace and be engaged in normal childhood activities.

Project activities also include field visits to work sites, and certain days at the centre called "work-that-people-do days". These are designed to promote positive attitudes towards work, to teach children about other forms of work that are not dangerous and to encourage them to compare these with their current jobs. There are plans to organize part-time and short-term supervised work arrangements for older children to help them acquire positive attitudes towards work and explore future possibilities for themselves.

Box 4.13. Integral programme for children and teenagers at social risk – National Children's Patronage (PANI) and the Ministry of Public Education, Costa Rica

The programme focuses on street children who work in the informal sector in five cities in Costa Rica. They have no stable income and no fixed schedules. For example, in downtown Puntarenas, located on the Pacific coast, children working as vendors, shoe shiners, porters, garage helpers, market and factory helpers, and beggars are involved in the programme. Some belong to gangs organized according to their place of origin and are often involved in violent conflicts. Most of them are aggressive, some have substance abuse problems and some have been recruited into prostitution.

The programme aims to: (i) promote the active participation of children and their families in productive activities in the community; (ii) facilitate the integration of children, teenagers and their families in educational programmes; and (iii) increase their access to nutrition and health services, psychological interventions and other social services as needed. Recreation, sports, culture and arts, vocational training for work, assistance with establishing micro-enterprises and seeking jobs are among the activities. The programme is structured into five stages: approach, adjustment, re-education, follow-up and departure.

Street educators are the frontline workers who reach out to the children and their families. To establish the initial contact with the children, aged 11 to 16 years old, the street educators set up football teams, which are an essential motivating element in organizing the children. Then other activities are organized such as nutrition (a daily lunch), health (in coordination with the Ministry of Health), and education (with the Ministry of Public Education and PANI, which provides logistical support).

The educational activities are carried out within the facilities of formal schools with teachers of the formal education system, who receive a 30 per cent salary bonus. PANI is adapting the curriculum of the formal education system. Innovative, dynamic teaching techniques are used which do not rely on instruction only but emphasize participatory methods adjusted to the realities in which the children live.

Other activities in the project are making and repairing fishing nets, organization of a council for the protection of children, recreation and sports, and an "adapted school" which offers two-hour evening classes covering basic subjects and computer classes. Through these adapted classes children can take a test and qualify for progression to another grade level or cycle in the formal school system. In this way a child can finish sixth grade in three years. About 85 per cent of the children have been able to complete sixth grade.

Children of indigenous groups and other minorities

When providing education to children of indigenous groups and ethnic minorities, particular attention is required on the issue of language and the content of the curriculum, to ensure that the children's own culture and values are given due respect. Children who belong to ethnic groups need to be educated both in their own and in the national language, and they should be taught about their own culture from the point of view of their community and not from an outsider's point of view. It is clear that children learn best in their mother tongue, in particular when they start school. At the same time, they should learn to express themselves in the dominant language of their country to be able to fully function in society. The need to learn the dominant language – written and oral – has to be balanced with respect for the child's own language and culture. Adults in the community need to be actively involved as resources for the school in this respect. Several successful programmes have highlighted the importance of providing teachers who have the same socio-cultural and economic background as the children and of offering young people employment opportunities in their own communities.

In most countries, indigenous communities usually belong to the most disadvantaged groups and seldom have access to basic services such as education, health, housing and employment. That is why they often need integrated programmes that include adult literacy and income-earning components so that parents are educated alongside their children and are enabled to provide for their families' basic survival needs.

Box 4.14. The Don Bosco Educational Programme and Talita Kumi Programme – Don Bosco Salesian Association, Guatemala

In the K'ekchi ethnic community in Alto Verapaz, Guatemala, education for K'ekchies by K'ekchies is promoted. The Don Bosco Salesian Association developed programmes to provide bilingual education (K'ekchi-Spanish) at the primary and secondary levels to these indigenous groups, to encourage them to be actively involved in their own communities and to manage programmes for their community's benefit. From one education and training centre established in Raxruha, Chisec, in 1982, there are now 451 schools and educational centres in K'ekchi rural communities. Some of the centres provide literacy programmes for adults and teacher training in bilingual education. The teacher trainees study for six months at a teacher-training centre and then teach at the rural schools. They continue to receive training through distance education.

For children and young people up to 25 years of age the curriculum covers the same basic education content as the public schools, with the addition of K'ekchi. Vocational training in agriculture, cattle-raising, tailoring, carpentry and masonry is also offered. Among the important features of the programme is the emphasis on the active participation of students, teachers, parents and communities in the life of the schools and in managing the programmes. Parents were also involved in building the schools and making the furniture, and they provided food for the teachers.

The programme will be expanded as follows: (i) the teacher-training programme will be accredited by the Ministry of Education to enable the teachers to pursue a teacher's certificate or further studies in a tertiary education institution; and (ii) more schooling opportunities will be provided in the rural communities by setting up Basic Cycle schools with an appropriate curriculum. Thus, the programme contributes to the expansion of the human resources needed for the education of indigenous children by training local teachers to educate new generations of K'ekchi children.

The Talita Kumi Programme was established in San Pedro Carcha in 1991 to provide education and training to K'ekchi women. There is a similar emphasis on bilingual education, but the special focus is on women and their involvement in community development. The programme provides training on community action, health and nutrition, agriculture and animal husbandry, family life skills, literacy and post-literacy skills, self-management and entrepreneurial skills. Support is also given to enable the participants to manage community funds and centres for credit and health services, such as community pharmacies. By helping the women, usually mothers, to learn new skills both for household and community management, agricultural work and other marketable skills, the programme enables them to improve their income-generating capacity which will in turn benefit their children, their family and their own personal development.

The two programmes are a successful example of empowering an indigenous group. They have strengthened the cultural and linguistic identity of the K'ekchies and have enabled them to improve life in their communities.

4.3 EDUCATION PROGRAMMES AND INCOME OPPORTUNITIES FOR PARENTS

Families with child workers or at risk of resorting to child labour are often single-parent, headed by women or children, with many children, or are migrants, and are among the most vulnerable and disadvantaged groups.

Parents who were deprived of education are often only vaguely aware of its value and the risks to children of premature work. Since they are usually the ones who decide whether children will work full time, stay in school and work, or study full time, it is critical to invest in parent education about child labour. There are various forms of parent education programmes offered by governmental and non-governmental agencies as part of early childhood development, literacy or health programmes. The provision of information on child labour and on child rights, and the organization of workshops for extension workers from these programmes, can be ways of incorporating child labour concerns in these adult training programmes. Other forms of adult education through workers' organizations or trade unions and cooperatives which provide educational programmes for their members, and through other community-based structures or committees, should also be further utilized.

Women's literacy programmes that emphasize child development, family life, and children's and women's rights offer great potential for preventing and eliminating child labour and improving school enrolment. There is a tendency to look at women's and children's programmes separately or, at best, an incidental connection is made. However, women and children's rights are intimately linked. Thus, women's programmes should include components to promote children's rights and address child labour exploitation and – vice versa – programmes geared towards children should pay attention to the situation of mothers as women with their own needs and rights. In addition, more and better jobs and social protection are needed for adults through the provision of income-earning opportunities for the poor, employment creation and poverty alleviation schemes, small enterprise development, minimum wage systems, credit systems and social safety nets for the most needy.

Women's economic empowerment is an especially effective measure to strengthen vulnerable families. Programmes that enable them to learn skills (such as improved agricultural practices, entrepreneurship, specific crafts or food production), that provide them with resources to earn a stable income for the family, and manage households by using labour-saving devices, or increase their access to credit schemes, will go a long way in improving the life situation of children and their primary care givers.

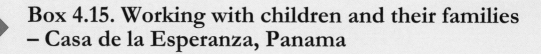

Box 4.15. Working with children and their families – Casa de la Esperanza, Panama

Casa de la Esperanza is an NGO working with street children through street-based, centre-based and community-based programmes in Panama City and Colon City. It implements an integrated programme for children and parents. It provides nutrition, first aid, primary health care and referral to other health services including volunteer doctors. In the field of education, it organizes early childhood education, financial assistance, follow-up with the teachers, tutorials, literacy and mathematics for those out of school, health and social education, handicrafts, dance and music, sports and recreation.

Casa de la Esperanza emphasizes an active, participatory approach. It uses non-formal and participatory teaching methods because it recognizes that "traditional" teaching is intimidating or not interesting for the children involved. It helps the children to reflect on their situation as workers and visits them in their own workplaces at the market or on street corners. Technical training is one of the most recent services introduced to enhance the capacity of adults to earn an income for their families and to assist adolescents by preparing them for jobs. They receive skills training in ceramics, woodcraft, or child-rearing and sewing. The NGO also facilitates referral to other vocational education programmes.

One of the significant features of Casa Esperanza's programmes is the family life education programme, which is intended to strengthen the working relationship between the families of the children and the staff of Casa Esperanza. This is seen as critical to its goal of removing the children from child labour and street life. It is aimed to improve the capacity of families, especially mothers, to take care of their children and maximize opportunities for growth in combination with training for income-generating activities and some economic support such as assistance towards the children's schooling.

Casa Esperanza works closely with government agencies such as the Welfare Bureau, the Juvenile Court, the Education Department, the Labour Bureau and the City Hall of Panama. At the same time, Casa Esperanza works with around 50 organizations which offer social services. This network enables it to facilitate the access of children and their families to integrated support services.

4.4 WORKPLACE AND COMMUNITY MONITORING

Systematic efforts to ensure that workplaces and communities remain child labour free mean first of all that awareness-raising activities should not be limited to the children and parents, but extended to all groups involved: employers, managers, and adult workers in workplaces, community leaders, service providers and enforcement agencies (see also Chapter 9). In a second stage, monitoring mechanisms need to be set up to ensure that the children withdrawn from work remain and complete school, and that new children do not enter work. This can be done in the schools or educational centres, in the workplaces and in the children's communities.

In any workplace monitoring programme, the active participation of the concerned employers, manufacturers, contractors and subcontractors is critical, as the commitment to free all manufacturing and production processes from child labour may call for a change in established and traditional manufacturing and production practices. The involvement of the concerned workers' representatives, and local community groups, as well as the concerned governmental agencies, is also critical (see also Chapters 6 and 7).

The involvement of children in the production and manufacture of goods for export has become a matter for international concern. Faced with outside pressure, some producers and manufacturers have turned to the ILO for advice on action to eliminate child labour from their particular industry. This has resulted in three instances in concrete prevention and monitoring programmes in the garment industry in Bangladesh, the football industry in Pakistan and its international counterparts, and the carpet industry, also in Pakistan. The result has been partnerships that span geographical and cultural boundaries, as well as positive changes in the attitudes and practices of the communities, in that the families have been willing to withdraw their children from work and send them to school.

The basic elements of the ILO-IPEC prevention and monitoring programmes are:

◆ ensuring cooperation and collaboration of employers/manufacturers, workers' organizations, district administration and other government departments;

◆ assessing child labour involvement in the particular sector or industry;

◆ assisting the participating employers/manufacturers in setting up their internal monitoring system;

◆ operating an external monitoring team involving ILO project staff;

◆ identifying and zoning monitoring area for visits;

◆ establishing a monitoring database to collect, analyse and synthesize data, to indicate schedules of surprise monitoring visits, and to prepare reports on progress; and

◆ establishing linkages with the social protection component of the programme.

Social protection programmes provide viable and practical alternatives to the children and their families affected by the prevention and monitoring programme. These programmes support the withdrawal of the children from workplaces and prevent them from working by sensitizing and mobilizing the communities. They also provide services to rehabilitate the children withdrawn so that they can be integrated into mainstream educational systems and other developmental activities. The basic elements of a social protection programme are:

- *awareness-raising, mobilization and counselling:* mobilizing families through one-to-one contact and group meetings to prevent child labour and to encourage them so that their children participate in the activities of the village education and action clusters set up under the project; communicating with the families on an ongoing basis;

- *group training* of adults to form the family clubs/committees for mothers and fathers to encourage them to play an active role in the programme;

- *non-formal education* to provide literacy, basic education and practical skills training to the children withdrawn and their younger siblings;

- *recreational activities* to foster social and physical development;

- *health services* through linkages with local health facilities;

- *mainstreaming* of younger children into formal schools;

- *training in income-generation activities (adults):* to follow up training in the credit/savings facility and training in various income-generation activities for the adults in the family;

- *provision of a credit/savings facility* to the adults in the family; and

- *mainstreaming* of children of employable age and adults into the labour market.

There is potential in local community watch systems to sustain action against child labour and to ensure that workplaces remain free from child labour. The establishment of local child welfare and vigilance committees is an effective tool which is increasingly being utilized in many countries. These committees can monitor, undertake action and even provide limited resources and services where necessary. Experience shows that programmes which stress a participatory approach and actively involve the children, their parents, community leaders and teachers are the most successful. Decentralization of authority to local governments and community structures also has a positive impact and results in effective community participation.

4.5 LESSONS FROM EXPERIENCE: PLANNING ACTION PROGRAMMES

Identifying priority target groups

There is a specific context for every direct action programme, and programme directions will depend upon the needs of specific groups of child workers in each country and the possibilities for practical measures.

As the child labour problem is so widespread, priorities have to be set based on the nature of the work and the risks involved for children. Given the socio-economic situation of some countries and the lack of adequate resources and infrastructure, the complete elimination of child labour will be a lengthy process. But there can be no excuse for ignoring flagrant cases of child abuse that are an outright breach of human rights and an affront to the dignity of children. Clearly the children who fall into this category are those engaged in activities that pose a serious danger to their health, or physical or moral integrity; those who work in slave-like conditions or are subjected to forced labour; and those caught up in illicit networks such as prostitution, drug trafficking and pornography (see Chapter 2, section 2.4). Some children are particularly vulnerable to this type of exploitation because of their age and sex, because they live and work on their own, or because they belong to socially excluded groups.

Appropriate measures need to be adopted urgently to rescue children from these worst forms of child labour. Prevention is crucial; but children must also be withdrawn from such activities and both they and their families provided with alternatives. Sometimes, especially if a country is only starting to address child labour problems, there is resistance to begin to combat some of the worst forms, because of political and social sensitivity. The existence of these types of child labour is even denied and very few partners come forward who can effectively address the problems. Nonetheless, at a minimum, the worst forms of child labour need to be tackled immediately.

Concerted action

In identifying the most strategically positioned programme partners or initiators, governments have the main responsibility to make action a top priority. They need to take the lead in designing national policies and programmes (see Chapter 1) and in allocating the necessary resources to enable implementation. When the policy framework is in place, care should be taken to translate it into feasible programmes and implementation guidelines, and to inform and enable all stakeholders to take the required action. Without such a commitment, countries will have great difficulties in overcoming the problem. However, the task is too enormous to be handled by governments alone.

A participatory approach and concerted action by all stakeholders is needed to eliminate child labour. Successful examples of effective cooperation between different sections of local government, NGOs, employers' and workers' organizations, and local communities are emerging. In other cases, effective programme delivery has taken place through proper coordination between government structures at the national and local levels. However, the implementation of multi-sectoral programmes by a range of different service providers is sometimes difficult. It has become clear that institutional mechanisms need to be set up to encourage joint planning and implementation for an effective convergence of services in countries where a start has been made in developing and implementing specific measures to combat child labour through education.

Participation should ideally begin at the planning stages. Often, the lack of consultative mechanisms at the various stages of programme implementation or the exclusion of stakeholders from the processes of planning, problem-solving and decision-making engenders a sense of remoteness and powerlessness of the participating groups in relation to the programme managers and leaders. This in turn pre-empts the development of any sense of ownership for the programme. Active participation – not just token participation – is a critical element to developing a sense of ownership for programmes.

Setting programme objectives

> *Direct action programmes usually have the following objectives:*
> - *prevention;*
> - *withdrawing children from hazardous work and providing them and their families with alternatives; and*
> - *awareness-raising of all concerned actors.*

◆ ISSUE:
Total or partial withdrawal of children from work

One of the main issues when starting a direct action programme is related to the partial or total withdrawal of children from work. But national goals must be defined in a clear, achievable and time-bound manner.

If either the partial or the total withdrawal from work is defined as an objective and made a precondition for the children's participation, the programme design and content must reflect this. For example, in programmes where children are totally withdrawn from their work in the commercial sex trade, there is a need to provide a complete residential facility for their rehabilitation. In other cases, stipends are provided for the children to participate and withdraw from work. For programmes which opt for partial withdrawal, the design either provides for a schedule which allows children to study and work part time or, alternatively, less hazardous income-generating opportunities are made available.

The ground rules are as follows:

◆ If children are involved in hazardous or exploitative forms of child labour, they need to be withdrawn completely. Child victims of human rights violations cannot be helped by the provision of support services while they continue to be in a slavery-like position. They must be rescued.

◆ If children are involved in work that harms them because of the working conditions or environment, a gradual phased approach may be used. The work hazards should be removed and children should gain access to education, but they can in a transitional phase continue to be involved in light work that is not dangerous.

In general, parents react positively to programmes where children work part time in light work and are involved in non-formal education. Even if this means a decrease in their income, it is more viable because of the continuing income. The parents also feel that the children are getting an education and learning practical skills which improve their employment opportunities for the future.

Another approach that can be seen as a step towards the ultimate goal of children's withdrawal from hazardous working conditions involves campaigns for making the workplace safer. Adult workers as well as owners of workplaces can be recruited as volunteers to participate in training workshops so that they can monitor safety.

◆ ISSUE:
Nutrition, health and other incentives

In many instances, improvements in education are not sufficient to attract and keep children from very poor families at school. Many families of child labourers live on the brink of survival and many millions of children in the world do not go to school because they are malnourished or frequently ill. Many more go to school hungry and are unable to pay attention, concentrate and learn. Numerous studies have shown a close link between school attendance, health and nutrition. A nutritious meal makes a tremendous difference to a child's health and ability to learn. The school is also an important entry point for providing essential health services such as immunization, detection of disabilities and childhood illnesses. Many organizations provide nutrition and health care to children through the education system and these have proved to be powerful incentives for parents to send their children to school.

Besides school-based food and health programmes, organizations have experimented with providing other economic incentives, such as school uniforms, books or transport. Cash payments, such as regular stipends or scholarships, have also been provided. Schiefelbein[2] has reviewed examples of such incentives in Latin American countries. These include cash payments for students, provision of school materials, and allocating additional funds to schools or municipalities which provide services for child labourers or children considered at risk of child labour to enable them to provide more responsive and flexible programmes. The various income-replacement strategies that have been tried in Latin America offer interesting examples of how effectively to provide for the needs of child labourers. Most require a combination of responsive local schools, and the political will of national and/or local governments, which provide the necessary policy support and resources to implement income-replacement measures.

An ILO survey[3] on economic incentives for children and families to eliminate or reduce child labour also aimed to identify whether income replacement and substitution activities offered viable options in the battle against child labour. Many of the incentives used by the NGOs which participated in the survey were directly related to schooling. Payments in kind were the most common form of benefits extended to children or their families. These included provisions for school uniforms or clothing, books, school bags and materials, school lunches or other food items, transport, or payment of school fees. Evidently, organizations which provide income-replacement services for child labourers, or for children who are at high risk of child labour, do so because the cost of schooling or the forgone income deters children from entering education. But Anker and Melkas also point out that there are many other factors that discourage children from attending school, and these are more directly related to the shortcomings of educational systems. Thus, they raise the question of whether replacing the lost income of children who attend school full time would in fact be adequate to keep them in school. Another important finding was that the provision of cash incentives could lead to abuse, and therefore many NGOs preferred to provide in-kind incentives rather than cash payments.

---

[2] E. Schiefelbein: *School-related economic incentives in Latin America: Reducing drop-out and repetition and combating child labour,* Innocenti Occasional Papers No. 12 (Florence, UNICEF, ICDC, 1997).

[3] A. Richard and H. Melkas: *Economic incentives for children and families to eliminate or reduce child labour* (Geneva, ILO, May 1996).

◆ **ISSUE:**
Incentives: How much is too much?

Support services are sometimes provided as incentives to attract parents and children to participate in action programmes. But it has been observed that some programmes offer too many incentives which make them more like welfare programmes. Among the disadvantages are: (i) high programme costs; (ii) the programme is not sustainable in the long term; (iii) child workers are perceived as privileged, because non-working while equally poor and disadvantaged children do not receive such benefits elsewhere; (iv) the practice may encourage more parents to remove children from school and send them to work in the hope of becoming eligible for similar benefits; and (v) parents of children who may not be part of the target group will insist on their children's participation, thus creating confusion and divisiveness in the community if they react negatively when their children are not admitted. The major disadvantage is the difficulty of sustaining and replicating the programme since the participation of parents and children will be heavily reliant on the availability of incentives; thus the motivation for participation is mainly external.

A careful balance must therefore be struck. One option is to encourage children's participation in running the programme. They can help prepare learning materials and contribute to cleaning and maintaining the centre and its equipment, repairing furniture and materials. They can also work with younger children as peer teachers and participate in home visits, especially to other children who have been absent for a while. After they complete their courses of study, they can also be asked to help with the programme activities and work as resource persons or volunteers with the other children. In this way they can serve as positive role models and share their own experiences.

Parents can be asked to work as volunteers for the programme, and the activities can depend upon their individual talents and skills. Whatever time and energy they can contribute should be discussed with them from the outset and also clarified so that they will not view incentives as a hand-out but feel that they have something meaningful to contribute. Parents who actively participate in the action programmes are also more likely to better appreciate the impact or the benefits of these programmes for their children, and ultimately their families.

It is important to assess whether direct action programmes should focus only on the objective of generating income for the children and their families, or should also serve as income-saving or expense-reduction measures for the family. If the children can use what they make, or if the family can eat what is produced through the programme, there may also be value added to encouraging such cost-saving measures towards self-reliance. The approach of helping children and their families opt for participation in courses that also involve the production of goods that meet the basic day-to-day needs of the children, and helping them to manage existing resources, may ultimately be more beneficial for the children. This approach will help them practice problem-solving and planning for very practical life needs, and at the same time help them achieve a sense of fulfilment in being able to meet their immediate requirements.

One of the more frequent reasons children drop out of programmes for their education and protection is the difficulty they have in delaying the gratification of their needs. Survival is a most compelling reason to work. Thus, the pressure of earning money or of securing the resources needed by the family can be overwhelming enough to forgo the opportunities of skills training and basic education.

Box 4.16. Innovative educational strategies for working children – Department of Education, Culture and Sports, Lapu-Lapu City, the Philippines

The administrators and teachers of the Public Schools Division of Lapu-Lapu City, in the Southern Province of Cebu, decided that they could not ignore the problems of child labourers from the elementary school classes in the public schools located in the poorest *barangays* (villages) of Suba-basbas, Babag and Sutunggan. These schools registered the highest drop-out rates for the province. Most of the children were in the fourth to sixth grade levels – usually 10 to 12 years old – and worked as stone cutters, vendors, helpers on tourist boats and in hotels, gardeners and dishwashers. A significant number were involved in fireworks production. The income of the children contributed significantly to their family incomes.

The school division administrators and teachers decided to conduct a household survey on the living and working conditions of the children to fully assess their needs and raise the parents' awareness about the children's problems. A series of community meetings was held by the school administrators and local government officials, including the Mayor and the city planning officer, social workers, health officers and parents. Plans for specific interventions were developed during these meetings, funding requirements were identified and government funds were allocated both from the national level and the local school board. The local school board also provided honoraria to teachers who did additional work for the programme.

Since it was clear that the families needed the income earned by the children, one of the programme activities consisted of providing time after classes on the school premises to enable the children to work under the supervision of teachers and NGO partners. For example, the children who worked as stone cutters were now involved in the production of fashion accessories made of indigenous materials like shells, fish scales, stones or paper. In this way, the children earned money through light work for a few hours per day. They did not drop out of school and were no longer late or absent from school.

For the children working in fireworks production, the immediate objective was to prevent them from continuing to work in the stages where gunpowder was involved. This is a hazardous form of employment in which children should not be involved but, since fireworks production was a legal cottage industry in the area, it was not viable to immediately remove children from the production process in their own homes. This would require longer-term interventions such as providing more lucrative economic alternatives, and continuing education and advocacy for the elimination of child labour among families and the business sector. As a means of addressing the immediate safety of the children and educating parents, a transitional measure was adopted which involved the supervision of children in schools as they worked on the initial stage of the production process – preparing the containers made out of paper – for a few hours per day.

In addition, community-based livelihood projects and literacy classes for the parents were organized through 30 schools in the Division. Parents responded positively to these programmes; they became conscious of the need to send their children to school regularly, and to assist them with homework. They also cooperated with school officials in a savings scheme where 20 per cent of the children's earnings from their participation in "school-based" income-generating activities were deposited in a savings account for the children. These savings would be important for their continuing education.

Another important issue in setting expense-reduction measures alongside income-generation or replacement is the possibility that children and their parents can be helped to learn to be more realistic about earning possibilities and about basic needs versus additional or emerging needs. In the case of children who have been involved in commercial sexual exploitation, the great difference between income through participation in an action programme and their previous earnings will be discouraging at the beginning. It is necessary to work closely with them and their parents, and clarify objectives with them at every step of the way.

◆ **ISSUE:**
Mainstreaming children into formal schools

It is important to determine whether the schools where the children are expected to enrol are actually receptive to the re-entry or the integration of working children. If they consider it as an imposition or a burden rather than as a responsibility, their attitude towards the children will be passive at best and negative at worst.

In relation to the mainstreaming of children into formal schools, some specific issues need to be considered:

◆ *1. The age of the children:* If children are older than the other children in the grade level for which they qualify, they usually feel uncomfortable, and often embarrassed, not only because they are older but because in most cases they also have difficulty in coping with the academic requirements. Former working children also find it difficult to adjust to the rigid structure and the regimen of formal schools. Despite the fact that their former work involved a lot of structure and a demanding pace, the routines of school life are not always easy for them to adjust to. If they had previous experience in a non-formal education programme, they would still need help to adjust to the formal school, especially in the nature of activities and the relationship with the teacher.

◆ *2. Parents' expectations and attitudes.* Parents may react negatively or may be impatient with apparently slow progress through formal school, especially when they are used to their children being economically productive. With the loss of income, any activity that replaces their child's work will be viewed badly if they have not yet fully accepted the fact that it is a better situation for their children, a worthwhile investment even from their family's economic viewpoint, and a responsibility that they should fulfil. Another problem that affects the parents' attitude is the burden of school-related expenses (e.g. uniforms, food to be brought to school, school supplies and materials, books, and travel expenses). If programmes cannot afford to cover the costs for some of these or find a way to subsidize them, the chances of children dropping out of school are increased.

◆ *3. Provision for follow-up and support programmes.* The need for follow-up support programmes, especially after the first year of re-entry into the formal schools, is evident in the trends of programme experiences. Action programmes in different countries show that many children tend to drop out after the first year, especially when assistance for meeting expenses is discontinued. Including activities that allow the programme implementors to follow up on the situation of children in formal schools is also important for monitoring programme impact and the achievement of objectives.

In addition, there are some questions to consider in connection with the issue of mainstreaming working children into regular schools.

Will parents of the participating children feel that the school curriculum responds to their conditions, needs and problems? Will they see schooling as useful for their children?

In developing countries where job opportunities are still limited and where a large number of youths with college or university degrees are unemployed, it is not surprising that many disadvantaged parents doubt whether their children can compete in the job market with a primary or secondary education certificate. Few parents expect their children to be able to proceed to tertiary levels of education. That is why they may appreciate vocational training because they consider it more realistic for work opportunities.

What access do the children have to supportive home environments or early childhood development programmes that will provide them with a foundation for learning and coping with the expectations of formal and non-formal education programmes? How will the programme address these factors that lead to children dropping out of the programme?

The experiences in education and child labour, and the strategy for maximizing education in the fight against child labour, clearly identify the expansion of early childhood development programmes as critical to meeting the needs of working children or those at high risk of recruitment in the near future. Research and case studies also show that disadvantaged children, who did not receive adequate health, nutrition and psychosocial cognitive and language stimulation in the early years of childhood, are highly likely to experience developmental and learning problems and will have difficulty catching up. A number of mainstreamed children have to drop out because they cannot compete with other, often younger, peers, and do not enjoy doing so. Thus, if the children concerned did not have the opportunity for such a foundation for school learning, it is necessary to provide them with additional support services. If there are younger siblings in the families of working children, they should be supported by facilitating their access to community-based early childhood development programmes and convincing parents that this is an important step to take for their children.

If mainstreaming into the formal school system will be the main approach, will children be provided with support so that they will be able to cope with the difficulties that they are likely to encounter? What programme activities will these be?

Box 4.17. Who are the groups to address and for what purposes?

◆ Parents are prime targets of awareness-raising. In addition to home visits and talking privately with parents, awareness-raising is also conducted through monthly meetings, educational workshops, organizing parents' committees, and involving them as volunteers and peer educators who can then work with other parents. In some action programmes, printed materials are used to promote awareness among parents and community members, but reportedly these are not always effective since many parents cannot read or have problems with their vision.

◆ Religious leaders, community leaders, and community members are secondary targets. In some ways they may be part of the problem, especially if they discriminate against child workers. But they may also be part of the solution and can contribute actively to withdrawing children from all forms of intolerable and hazardous labour by being firm and visible advocates. They can be active members of village-based child watch committees that monitor and take action against child labour problems in their own villages.

◆ Teachers, educational leaders and their organizations are potentially powerful and effective allies in the battle against child labour. Because they are in a position to teach children as well as parents about the risks involved in certain kinds of work, they will be able to help prevent child labour. In their daily and sustained contact with children, they can monitor patterns of attendance and investigate reasons for prolonged absences to determine if the child is involved in part-time or full-time work, or is being abused and exploited. If teachers are also aware about child labour issues, they will be more open to parents' and children's feedback about their expectations, especially about the quality of education. Linkages between schools and the non-formal education programmes allowing for the re-entry of working children into formal schools will not be possible without these awareness-raising efforts involving teachers and educational leaders.

◆ Another important target group is the business sector. Several action programmes have focused on involving the business sector in solving child labour problems. In Pakistan, for example, one action programme successfully involved loom holders, exporters and suppliers represented by the Pakistan Carpet Manufacturers and Exporters Association, in operating non-formal education centres for child carpet weavers. Eventually a number of centres were operated and funded entirely by the Association.

Tutorial sessions, materials and book-lending schemes, counselling and peer support through complementary non-formal education programmes will help children cope with life in the formal schools. They should be helped to work out the feelings that arise out of the difficulties encountered in the formal schools. Mainstreaming of former working children or children who continue to work part time is only viable if there are support services for them. Parents need support and information so that they will be able to support their children. Teachers need help to understand the perspective of former working children and the pressures of adjusting to formal schools. If these support services are not made available, re-entry into the formal schools may be a traumatic experience to be added to the already traumatic experiences of these children in the workplace. It is critical that, if a country programme chooses to adopt this as the primary approach to the education and social protection of working children, no omissions in support services will result because the impact on the children can be very negative.

◆ **ISSUE:**
Awareness-raising

Most action programmes include various forms of awareness-raising activities directed at parents, community members, local school authorities, the business sector, and policy-makers (see also Chapter 8). These have been included based on the realization that the understanding by these groups of child labour issues will be their basis for supporting the programme's objectives and activities. Ultimately, the programmes will also be the basis of their continued participation in concerted actions to prevent child labour, protect working children through community action, engage in needed policy reform and support effective law enforcement.

When awareness-raising efforts are not considered investments of the programme, there can be problems. For example, teachers in formal schools may not develop a positive attitude towards non-formal education programmes provided by these action programmes if they are not informed in any way, especially in the planning processes. They may refuse children entry into the formal schools. Apprenticeship programmes are unlikely to succeed without close coordination with the business sector. Individuals who own private businesses or their consumers may have certain attitudes towards working children and may not be open to working with them.

Checklist 4.1 Identifying target groups and selecting children

☐ Clearly identify target beneficiaries or programme participants.

   ✓ Are they at greatest risk?

   ✓ Are they accessible to those who will implement the programme?

   ✓ What are their ages?

   ✓ What kinds of programme components will respond to their specific needs given the:

      ◆ nature of their work;

      ◆ their ages (below 7; between 8 and 10; between 11 and 15); and

      ◆ their life conditions (e.g. living with or apart from families and original communities).

☐ Identify the stakeholders and the possible support systems for the children who have been identified as target groups to help ensure programme success.

   ✓ Will the "stakeholders" or those who benefit from the children's work (the children, their parents and siblings, employers) cooperate?

   ✓ Are there local government authorities who can help with monitoring or providing additional social services?

☐ Ensure that there will be no gender bias that will pre-empt the participation of girls or of boys who are involved in the same type of work.

☐ Are there provisions for programme elements to ensure equal access by children of both sexes:

   ✓ Is the centre or programme venue physically accessible?

   ✓ If the venue is not accessible, will transportation be provided?

   ✓ Are male and female programme staff and teachers to be recruited?

☐ If there are cultural reasons for working exclusively with boys or with girls, what are the alternative provisions for the group of children who are not as accessible?

☐ Can the programme work with existing schoolteachers, community and religious leaders who will be acceptable to the community?

☐ Define whether the programme will require additional criteria for children's participation.

☐ Are there certain age groups that the programme is more competent to work with?

☐ Are there certain minimum levels of functional literacy skills that are required for the children's participation?

☐ Will the degree of involvement and the nature of parents' cooperation be included as a precondition for participation?

☐ Are parents to be required to contribute fees, materials or time for their children to be eligible for participation?

☐ Can they afford these requirements?

☐ Will those who are most vulnerable and at greatest risk of exploitation be considered as priority groups:

✓ children who are separated from their families; and

✓ children who are rescued from the worst forms of child labour?

☐ Plan for a systematic and clear process for recruiting and selecting target children.

✓ Who will be responsible for recruiting and selecting the children?

♦ Programme staff only?

♦ A screening committee to be organized – with teachers, community leaders and workers, representatives of programme staff?

✓ Will there be public announcements in the community? Beyond the community?

✓ Will the children be interviewed in their homes or workplaces?

☐ Will aptitude tests be administered to determine their current level of functioning in terms of language, cognitive and other skills?

✓ Who will prepare the assessment instruments?

☐ How can the results be used in a way that will not exclude children or be prejudicial to their participation?

✓ Will the parents be required to bring their children to enrol in the programme?

✓ Can children apply to participate on their own?

✓ Are employers qualified to recommend children for participation?

✓ How will the children be informed that they will participate?

✓ What will be the policy if some children do not continue? Can they return?

✓ What is the timetable for recruitment, selection and admission?

✓ Will recruitment continue or be open to continue admitting children into the programme?

✓ Will there be cycles within a 12-month period when new participants will be admitted into the programme?

Checklist 4.2 Planning vocational skills training programmes

☐ Does the choice of content (topic, skills) and methods match the age of the children?

✓ Children aged 5 to 9 will need mainly pre-vocational skills and basic safety tips, and practice with using simple tools before they can safely and meaningfully participate in vocational training. Arts and crafts, simple woodwork, clay and pottery are excellent activities that provide these pre-vocational skills.

✓ Younger children can only pay attention for shorter periods – about one hour at a time. They need some respite or a change in activities or pace before resuming the same type of activity.

✓ The approach to teaching younger children requires more hands-on supervision and guidance. It is important to show and guide, rather than just talk and tell them what to do.

✓ Older children aged 10 to 15, with basic literacy skills, can benefit from vocational training. But it will still be important to include an assessment process to determine their current abilities and skills. Even if they can read or write, demonstration and guided practice are still the better approach to teaching vocational skills.

✓ The length of the course should be sufficient to allow children to complete a project gradually increasing in complexity. It is important to give them time to master basic skills and to work with simpler projects first to give them a positive feeling of success. This will be a motivating factor to continue with further training where they can learn to produce more high-quality goods. They will also learn to be more realistic and gradually develop confidence in their emerging skills and abilities.

☐ Does the choice of the topic and focus of the training match the children's present and possible work and labour market opportunities?

✓ Children who are migrants to urban communities and who may return to their rural communities may benefit from agri-based/related training. At the same time, this should include training in entrepreneurship (costing and pricing), management (accounting, negotiating and working with other people, credit and loans) and marketing (selling their products). Off-farm income-generating projects should also be part of the training because there are off-seasons in the agricultural cycle where the family will need income to tide them over.

✓ Children in urban communities may benefit from a multi-stage programme that prepares them for employment in industries, as well as for entrepreneurial/self-managed income-generating jobs. It is necessary to provide for both options.

✓ Children in rural and urban communities need to learn about planning for work options, applying for jobs, work ethics, the rights and responsibilities of workers, the advantages of being part of organized labour and of peasant organizations, and their responsibilities as members.

☐ What provisions are made to integrate basic education, pre-vocational skills and vocational skills?

✓ For older children aged 12 and above who have always been deprived of opportunities for basic education, this becomes even more compelling as they need to be able to make up for lost time. Limiting the programme to skills training that focuses on specific types of skills in preparation for work will not be truly responsive to their needs.

✓ Younger children, aged 9 and below, even if they are partially or fully withdrawn from the workplace and mainstreamed in regular schools, will still benefit from participating in complementary programmes which provide pre-vocational skills training, especially if the schools are focusing only on academic subjects.

☐ For children of all ages, what individual and group activities will the programme provide that are specifically designed for their psycho-social development, character-building and ability to cooperate with others, developing their problem-solving and conflict-resolution skills, work ethic, self-discipline and responsibility?

✓ Children should be provided with many opportunities to learn problem-solving, decision-making and conflict-resolution skills. In ensuring a balanced emphasis on social and emotional development alongside practical skills and the expansion of their knowledge base, the goals of better self-understanding and improved self-confidence, and hence a more positive sense of self worth will also be achieved. Special camps, recreational activities and study trips are among those that can complement other educational activities, whether in non-formal education programmes or formal schools.

☐ What provisions are made to ensure that children are taught basic safety rules and behaviour while engaged in skills training and supervised production activities?

✓ Safety gear – masks, gloves, aprons, footwear.

✓ Detailed instructions and close supervision when using tools that are sharp, or mechanical and electrical tools.

✓ Instructions on the use of raw materials that are toxic or dangerous to body parts, or that could react to heat or extreme changes in temperature.

☐ What provisions are made for including the following important parts of vocational training and education?

✓ Counselling about work options.

✓ Job placement assistance.

✓ Entrepreneurial skills and self-management: credit, costing, marketing or source raw materials, dealing with suppliers and buyers, selling products, quality control.

☐ What provisions are made for including supervised production activities which will allow children to learn confidently with the guidance of instructors and possibly earn at the same time?

✓ Supervised work contracts to produce items that are pre-ordered or to provide services for certain establishments.

Checklist 4.3 Measuring the impact of action programmes

☐ Summary of benefits to participating children:

✓ Removal from hazardous working conditions

✓ Safer working environments

✓ Reduced working hours thanks to participation in programme activities

✓ Education (literacy/numeracy/mathematical skills, non-formal/equivalency/remedial education)

✓ Vocational skills

✓ Non-formal education certificates necessary for access to formal education or employment at an appropriate age

✓ Better job prospects

✓ Better behaviour

✓ More discipline

✓ More rest and recreation

✓ Good communication skills

✓ Good concentration

✓ Better health, cleanliness

✓ More self-confidence and self-esteem

✓ Aspirations for the future

✓ Wider perspectives

☐ Impact on family:

✓ Parents learn literacy and/or vocational skills, benefit from counselling and medical check-ups

✓ Parents/family benefit from credit schemes by taking loans to establish small businesses

✓ Formation of parents' self-help groups

✓ Siblings benefit from attending programme activities with target children

☐ Impact on community and society:

✓ More awareness and understanding of child labour problems, the rights of the child, the value of education for children

✓ Village/community committees and vigilance groups working on child labour issues and prevention of child labour exploitation in the communities

✓ Policy adoption and replication of models of child labour interventions in schools, provincial plans and strategies on women's and child labour issues, and expansion of primary education.

Strategies to address child slavery

Michel Bonnet, Hirak Ghosh,
Victoria Rialp and Pin Boonpala

5

5.1   THE PROBLEM OF CHILD SLAVERY

Slavery is not dead. Societies are loath to admit it, but child slavery is alive and is the most extreme stage in the exploitation of child labour, one of the most reprehensible practices of our time and a blatant violation of national and international human rights.

This chapter gives an overview of the nature and extent of the problem of child slavery and the consequences for the victims. It describes the constraints that impede action against it and outlines relevant legal instruments. It highlights initiatives that are yielding encouraging results in preventing this scourge, as well as in rescuing and rehabilitating bonded children. It suggests ways to expand and accelerate these initiatives by linking them more directly with national programmes and international mechanisms specifically designed to combat child slavery. The chapter concludes by presenting strategies for comprehensive action against child bondage, child trafficking and the commercial sexual exploitation of children. A bibliography on child slavery is included.

The nature of the problem

All children in slavery are children who work, but not all children who work are slaves. Public opinion has a tendency to use the term "slavery" when speaking of particularly harsh and abhorrent work or working conditions of children. This dilutes the meaning of the word. In reality there exists a fundamental difference between labour and slavery: labour is an activity, slavery is a status. Labour is a visible activity, slavery is an invisible situation.

The ILO Committee of Experts on the Application of Conventions and Recommendations considers this question of **invisibility** as "a key issue in dealing with the problem of bonded labour".[1] There are two types of invisibility. One is related to the location where children are kept or where access to child slaves is difficult. They are usually hidden, locked away in small workshops, in remote quarries, on building sites and agricultural estates, in mobile enterprises, or in domestic work where entry is often prohibited because the workplace is private property. The other type concerns the status of the child workers in relation to their employers. Child slavery is built on violence. The children are the property of their employer and are subject to physical and psychological violence. Fearing repression, bonded child workers generally remain silent. Even in those cases where bonded children are freed, they are often unable to talk about their experiences for years and retain a deep distrust of adults in general.

To keep bonded children in their service, the proprietors also need the silence of the public. They therefore usually see to it that all contact between the workers and possible investigators is limited. Such children may be given supplementary surveillance, which is at the same time part of the machinery of recruitment and control of the slaves, namely the intermediaries. There are three categories of intermediaries: the recruiters, the transporters and the surveyors.

---

[1] ILO: *Report of the Committee of Experts on the Application of Conventions and Recommendations*, Report III, Part 1A, Geneva, 1996, p. 91.

Box 5.1. Sold in the Sudan

"My wife and four children were abducted during a raid in March 1994. Three of my children and my wife managed to escape, but my eight-year-old daughter remained behind. She is now kept in Maykata by a man who bought her from her captor. When I discovered where she was, I went north and tried to get her back by legal means. I opened a case against the man at the police station, and had to pay the police 20,000 Sudanese pounds (approximately US$250) to do this. A police officer... accompanied me to the home of the man. This man refused to give me my girl and demanded 50,000 Sudanese pounds for her release. The policeman said that as the man had bought the girl from her captor, she was his property and he could not insist on her release. I was forced to leave her there where she is badly mistreated by the man's wife.... I also lost the 20,000 pounds which the policeman refused to return to me. I had to return home empty handed".[2]

♦ **The recruiters**. They visit the most poverty-stricken villages or slums, especially in periods of financial difficulty. A loan may be proposed to the family by attracting them with the possibility of reimbursement through the labour of one of their children. The recruiters, acting, for example, on behalf of an enterprise active in mining or forest exploitation, may offer to pay the travel expenses to the place of work, to be reimbursed later. Sometimes the children are taken away without payment of any advance, merely with the promise of feeding them and letting them acquire some skills in a particular trade. In many cases, the recruiters do not operate clandestinely. They might even be well known to the families, sometimes to the extent that the parents consider them sympathetic and trustworthy.

Box 5.2. A bonded child worker in rural India

"I am 14 years old. I am a Kharia (tribe).... I am an orphan. I have five brothers and two sisters. I live in the house of my landlord, who owns 22 acres of land. I live in his house 24 hours a day. I work during the day in the fields. I scatter manure in the fields, fetch water from the well, graze cattle, give them fodder, bathe them in the pond, wash utensils, water the garden in the house of my landlord. I don't get paid any wage for this work. Only food. As food I get rice, dal and sometimes subzi (vegetables). Once a year, I get clothes on festivals. Two lungis (wraparounds), and sometimes old rejected clothes from the master's house. I have been working in this landlord's house for the past four years. My family has no land. My master doesn't allow me to leave. I tried last year, but he said no. My master doesn't beat me, but abuses me often. I would like to learn carpentry or tailoring or else I would like to do farming, if the government gave me land".[3]

---

[2] Testimony collected by Christian Solidarity International in May 1996 and presented by Anti-Slavery International to the United Nations Working Group on Contemporary Forms of Slavery, 21st Session, Geneva, June 1996.

[3] Excerpt from Bonded Labour Liberation Front: *Into that heaven of freedom?* (New Delhi, July 1989), p. 39.

◆ **The escorts.** The greater the distance between the family and the place of work, the more the children will have difficulty in fleeing or being rescued by their family.   Not all children in bondage are automatically taken hundreds of kilometres away from home. Many of them often live with their parents at the workplace. But, in many instances, bonded children live away from home. There are escorts who are charged with putting the children on a train or truck and ensuring that they arrive at the destination. In cases where inspections cannot be avoided, especially when national borders have to be crossed, escorts often pose as members of the family of the children in their charge.

◆ **The surveyors.** A child in bondage is an income asset and the proprietor usually requires the uninterrupted physical presence of the child at the workplace. The more child or adult workers there are in bondage on a site, the more the surveillance of the workers will be strict and organized. The surveyors' task is to prevent attempts to escape or communication with the outside world. In many cases, groups of private police, usually armed, watch over the workers.

Box 5.3. A *restavek* (domestic worker) in Haiti

Marie, who was about 7 years old, came from the countryside, although she did not know from where. She had no continuing contact with any of her original family. As a *restavek*, Marie rose at 5 a.m. Her first job was to fetch water from a nearby well. After returning to the house balancing the heavy jug on her head, she prepared breakfast and served it to the members of the household, including the boarders. She next walked the 5-year-old son of the employing family to school. While both of the employing family's children went to school, none of the *restaveks* did. Marie's next jobs were to buy food in the markets and run errands, such as collecting debts owed to her employer by various neighbours, who purchased from the employing family's store on credit. Marie was also responsible for starting and tending the charcoal fire behind the house, sweeping the yard, washing some of the clothes, washing dishes and cleaning the outside kitchen. At noon she would bring the boy home from school and help him change his clothes. She would then set the table, assist in preparing and serving lunch and accompany the boy back to school. She then returned to the house to be available for errands until it was time to prepare supper.

Marie was harshly treated by the employing family. The mother regularly beat her with a leather strap if she was thought slow to respond to a request or if she was considered disrespectful. While the mother occasionally hit her three children, the four *restaveks* were much more severely disciplined, and the discipline was designed to create and maintain a subservient attitude. For example, when one of the *restavek* girls ran away, she was pursued and found by the mother, and then severely beaten. It was the only time the child tried to run away. The *restaveks* performed all the physical labour in the household, at the direction of its various members, including the 5-year-old boy. The employing family seemed to view the *restavek* as a different species from themselves. Eventually the employing family moved to Montreal, Canada. The four *restaveks*, by then teenagers, were simply put out onto the street.[4]

---

[4] Testimony in Minnesota Lawyers International Human Rights Committee: *Restavek: Child domestic labor in Haiti* (Minneapolis, August 1990), p. 10.

The extent of the problem

It is difficult to assess the extent of child bondage because employers hide the illegal employment of children by physical restraints on their movement and other means of coercion. There are also problems of defining what constitutes bondage. Studies conducted in some countries, however, indicate the magnitude of the problem.

In India, the Gandhi Peace Foundation, in collaboration with the National Labour Institute, conducted a study in 1981 covering the agricultural sector in 10 out of 21 states in the country and arrived at a figure of 2.6 million bonded labourers. In the States of Orissa and Andhra Pradesh, one out of every five labourers was found to be bonded. The study concluded that bonded labourers constituted 8 per cent of labourers in India.

In Nepal, a survey conducted by the Ministry of Land Reforms and Management in February 1995 found that there were 15,152 *Kamaiya*[5] families comprising 83,375 persons. More than half (54 per cent) of the families were landless; 46 per cent were homeless and lived in the master's premises and 56 per cent were indebted to their masters. Another survey by a human rights organization found that 3.3 per cent of *Kamaiyas* had been working

Box 5.4. A carpet weaver in Pakistan

A carpet workshop in a village 24 miles from Lahore.... Of the 12 weavers, five were 11, two 14, and four were under 10 years old. The two youngest were brothers, aged 8 and 9. They had been bonded to the carpet master at the age of 5, and now worked six days a week at the shop. Their workday started at 6 a.m. and ended at 8 p.m., except, they said, when the master was behind on his quotas and forced them to work around the clock. They were small, thin, malnourished, their spines curved from lack of exercise and from squatting before the loom. Their hands were covered with calluses and scars, their fingers gnarled from repetitive work. Their breathing was laboured, suggestive of tuberculosis.

"The master screams at us all the time, and sometimes he beats us. He is less severe with the younger boys. We're slapped often. Once or twice he lashed us with a cane. I was beaten ten days ago, after I made many errors of colour in a carpet. He struck me with his fist quite hard on the face".

By way of corroborating this, the boy lifted a forelock, revealing a multicolour bruise on his right temple. Evidently the master did not consider the blow sufficient punishment:

"I was fined one thousand rupees and made to correct errors by working two days straight."

The fine was added to his debt, and would extend his "apprenticeship" by several months.[6]

---

[5] *Kamaiya*: a system of bonded agricultural labour in western Nepal.

[6] Excerpt from Jonathan Silvers: "Child labour in Pakistan", in *Atlantic Monthly*, Feb. 1996, p. 87.

Box 5.5. A sardine factory worker in the Philippines

Jacqueline started working as a domestic helper when she was 12 years old. She did all the household chores: scrubbing and sweeping the floor, washing clothes and dishes, running errands and countless other little tasks. When Jacqueline turned 14, she was promoted to work in a canning company, owned by her employer, which produces sardines. She worked for 12 hours a day starting at 3 a.m., during which time she filled as many as 3,000 small cans of sliced sardine. She frequently cut herself with the open cans and fish bones. Her hands and feet, constantly soaked in water laced with chemicals, are wrinkled and disfigured. For food, Jacqueline was served with noodles (the employer also owns a noodle factory) and leftovers from the employer's house. With six other child workers, she had to share a small bunkhouse which was locked to prevent them leaving. She was prohibited from talking with outsiders.

Jacqueline was recruited through an employment agency for which she was told she had incurred a debt of 16,000 pesos. The rule is that no one leaves the factory until the debt is paid. During her three years working there, Jacqueline received not one centavo of the 700 pesos a month she was promised. She could never pay off her debt as 25 pesos a day were deducted from her wages for food, 2 pesos more than she supposedly earned. Jacqueline thought of escaping, but she did not know where to go or how to find help and she was extremely afraid of the factory owners. She was finally released after a raid organized by the Kamalayan Development Foundation.[7]

in this way for four generations, 21.63 per cent for three generations and 28 per cent for two generations.

While trafficking in children within countries in South-East Asia has been a widespread phenomenon for some time, there is increasing evidence in recent years of children being trafficked across national borders because of the opening of frontiers and as a result of industrialization and globalization. Numerous previously remote areas are now exposed to rapid social changes. This has disrupted traditional ways of life, and made the population especially vulnerable to the problem of child trafficking. There exist a number of well-established trafficking routes in the Mekong sub-region. Thailand is the main receiving country where many victims are forced into prostitution and other exploitative forms of work. Most trafficking takes place over land, and there are well known gateways from each country. Cambodia and Yunnan province in China are, in addition to being sending countries, also on the receiving end. Vietnamese children are being trafficked to Cambodia for prostitution, and significant numbers of ethnic minorities from North Viet Nam and Myanmar are trafficked under the disguise of marriage to become domestic workers, often without pay.

---

[7] Excerpt from *Child Workers in Asia Bulletin* (Bangkok), Vol.11, No. 1, 1995, p. 18.

In South Asia, the most commonly known and most alarming situation is the trafficking of girls from Nepal into India. It is estimated that 5,000-7,000 Nepalese girls are sold to Indian brothels every year.[8] A considerable number of them had been either forcefully abducted or tricked into going to India and subsequently sold to brothels. In addition to the economic pressure, cultural practices among certain ethnic groups also contribute to the trafficking of girls in Nepal. In Bangladesh, the Government estimates that a few thousand women and children have been victims of trafficking for labour, including prostitution, and for other purposes in South Asian and Middle Eastern countries. Based on reports commissioned by IPEC, the problem also exists in other South Asian countries such as Pakistan and Sri Lanka.

Trading in children is a common practice in some African countries. There have been reports of boatloads of children being halted by authorities along coastlines on their way to Central Africa. Some of these children end up in households as unpaid child labour known as "house helps", while others end up in prostitution. Children also leave their homes and cross borders into other countries to work as domestic helpers and market traders.

Latin America is known for its large numbers of children working on the streets. There is a strong linkage between the street environment and commercial sexual exploitation. Children working on the streets become easy targets for the trafficking network which recruits them for prostitution. In Brazil, for example, young girls on the streets are lured by traffickers with the offer of better jobs in restaurants, but are forced to work in night clubs in faraway places in the Amazon, where they are kept captive like prisoners and moved from one region of the Amazon to another – from one mining community to the next.[9]

Box 5.6. Nepalese children enslaved in prostitution in Bombay

The High Court of Judicature in Bombay directed the Government of Maharashtra, India, in 1996 to take immediate steps to combat the problem of child prostitution in the state. The police, under the instructions of the Government, raided the red light areas in Bombay on 5 February 1996 and rescued 484 girls. The girls were produced before the Juvenile Welfare Board which remanded them to different homes. Almost half of the rescued girls were from Nepal. Through the joint effort of seven Nepalese and Bombay NGOs, 128 girls were brought back to Nepal.

---

[8] Ministry of Women and Social Welfare (MOWSW), Nepal, and ILO-IPEC: *National Plan of Action against Trafficking in Children and their Commercial Sexual Exploitation* (Kathmandu, 1998).

[9] NACLA (North American Congress on Latin America): *Report the Americas,* Vol XXVII, No. 6, May/June 1994.

Box 5.7. The account of Bina (aged 17)[10]

Bina is from Jhapa. Her father is a sharecropper. Her mother died long ago. She has an elder brother, two elder sisters (both married), a younger sister and a younger brother at school. Bina went to Kathmandu with her friends to work in a carpet factory. She stayed with a friend from Jhapa and worked in the factory for two years. The woman owner had promised her a wage of 300 rupees per month. She provided her with food and shelter and said that she would give her money when she went home. When Bina wanted to leave, she told her not to go and warned her about the danger of being trafficked to Bombay. Despite the warning, Bina and a friend ran away at night with two Nepalese men and a woman who had promised them a better job. The traffickers took them to an apartment and the next morning, they set out for India. Bina remembers passing through Gorakhpur where Bina and her friend were handed over to two Nepalese persons. When the original party disappeared, Bina asked about them but got no answer.

On arrival in Bombay, the traffickers put Bina and her friend on different buses. When Bina asked about her friend, she was told that she could meet her later. She was then taken to a brothel owner (a woman) in Bombay and was sold to her. She met 25 to 30 other women in the brothel, mostly Nepalese and some Indians and Bangladeshis, aged 20 to 25. There were five to six girls and women in a room divided by a curtain. Bina learned later that she had been sold for 50,000 Indian rupees.

After three days she was asked to serve an Indian client. When she tried to resist, she was beaten. Others told her that she would starve to death if she resisted. So she gave in. She served up to six or seven clients a day. She was told that she would receive money when she returned home, but she feared that day would never come.

After a year or so, the brothel was raided by the police, who took her and the other girls into custody. She was brought back to Nepal by the NGOs. She feels that she has been very lucky in having been able to return to Nepal. She is undergoing a six-month course in literacy and income-generating activities. She wants to find a job to support herself, and she wants to help other girls who are at risk. She said that she was not HIV positive.

5.2 INTERNATIONAL ACTION AGAINST CHILD SLAVERY

The international community has made the immediate suppression of child slavery one of its major priorities. The principal actors are the ILO, the United Nations and international NGOs.

---

[10] U. Acharya: *Trafficking in children and their exploitation in prostitution and other intolerable forms of child labour in Nepal,* Country Report for ILO-IPEC (Nepal, 1998).

International Labour Organization

International labour standards

One of the most widely ratified ILO Conventions is the **Forced Labour Convention,** 1930 (No. 29), which requires ratifying States to suppress the use of forced or compulsory labour. It defines the term as "work or service which is exacted from any person under the menace of any penalty and for which the said person has not offered himself voluntarily"– other than in certain excepted circumstances, for example, the performance of military service, and emergencies such as wars, fires, earthquakes and so on. It imposes an obligation on the ratifying State to punish the exaction of forced or compulsory labour as a penal offence and to ensure that penalties are strictly enforced.

Convention No. 29 is an important instrument to promote government action in countries where child bondage exists. Since it applies to everyone, whatever age, it

Box 5.8. Reports to the ILO Committee of Experts

The annual reports submitted by the Committee of Experts on the Application of Conventions and Recommendations to the International Labour Conference (ILC) contain information on those countries which have ratified ILO Convention No. 29 on forced labour and illustrate the range and diversity of the dimensions of bonded child labour that the Committee addresses. Excerpts are provided below, but the entire reports should be consulted for the complete context of the Committee's discussion and comments of the governments concerned.

Brazil:

"The Committee notes that in its report of 1995 on rural conflicts in 1994, the Pastoral Commission on Land (PCL) indicates that the figures relating to cases of slave labour in 1994 show a worsening situation. The number of victims rose from 19,940 in 1993 to 25,193 in 1994 which can be attributed to the cases of slave labour observed in various charcoal-producing plants in the region of Montes Claros in Minas Gerais, which involved 10,000 workers, and six municipalities of Mato Grosso do Sul, including 8,000 adults and 2,000 minors. The case of minors engaged in heavy labour in the countryside was, according to the PCL, the most significant and alarming in 1994." (Report, 1996, p.74)

India:

"In its previous comments the Committee referred to allegations brought before the United Nations Subcommission on Prevention of Discrimination and Protection of Minorities that children were in bondage in agriculture, brick kilns, stone quarries, carpet weaving, handlooms, matches and fireworks, glass bangles, diamond cutting and polishing; that child bondage and forced labour were connected with trafficking, kidnapping, repression, absence of freedom of movement, beating, sexual abuse, starvation, abnormal working hours and hazardous working conditions. The Committee noted the Government's indication that for the purpose of identification and rehabilitation by the machinery set up for this purpose no distinction is made between bonded child labour and bonded adult labour.

protects children from forced or compulsory labour and is applicable to children in bondage and their exploitation in prostitution and pornography. Indeed, the Committee of Experts and the Conference Committee on the Application of Standards have been dealing extensively with the problem of the forced or compulsory labour of children in relation to the application of the Convention by several member States. The Committee of Experts has stated on several occasions that the forced labour exploitation of children is one of the worst forms of forced labour, which must be fought energetically and punished severely.

Under the ILO's Constitution, ratifying Members must report to the ILO on measures taken to implement the Convention. Such information is often supplemented by reports from ILO constituents, which might forward reports from NGOs or others concerned. Moreover, reports to the United Nations Working Group on Contemporary Forms of Slavery are also considered by the Committee of Experts.

Given however the particular vulnerability of children and their specific needs, the Committee asked for information on any specific measures taken for identification, release and rehabilitation." (Report, 1996, pp.103-104)

Pakistan:

"The Committee recalls the observation on the application of the Convention made by the All Pakistan Federation of United Trade Unions in a communication dated 31 December 1993 (which was transmitted to the Government for comments and also remained without reply) that the feudals of the country had a strong hold over the administrative machinery, which was always used for the protection of the bonded labour system, and whenever any effort was made to eliminate this system, it was strongly resisted. The Committee further notes that in its communication of June 1996, the NZCTU (New Zealand Council of Trade Unions) had stressed the Workers' members' concern at the Conference Committee in June 1996 that the Government was putting more energy into attacking those, such as the BLLF (Bonded Labour Liberation Front), who seek to free bonded labourers, than into implementing the laws which purport to ban such labour.... It hopes that the Government will supply detailed observations on the allegations made, as well as indications on any action taken or envisaged...." (Report, 1997, p.92)

Thailand:

"In its previous comments the Committee referred to certain statistical data concerning the number of children exploited through prostitution (estimates from 86,000 to 800,000). The Committee notes the Government's indication to the Conference Committee that the latest estimates amount to some 20,000 to 30,000 children in prostitution. The Committee recalls that the Ministry of Health, Division of Venereal Diseases Control, reported in 1990 that child prostitutes numbered 86,000 and that data from the Police Department showed that around 160,000 prostitutes would be under 16. Given the number of children trafficked from the neighbouring countries, it is unlikely that these figures would have decreased since 1990. The Committee considers that swift and severe action is required to rescue these children trapped in prostitution." (Report, 1996, pp.114-115)

The new Worst Forms of Child Labour Convention, 1999 (No. 182), and its accompanying Recommendation (No. 190), provide additional and powerful weapons for the elimination of all forms of child slavery. Adopted by the International Labour Conference in 1999, the Convention applies to all children under the age of 18 and obliges member States to act immediately against the worst forms of child labour, which include slavery and practices similar to slavery – such as the sale and trafficking of children, debt bondage and serfdom – forced or compulsory labour – including forced recruitment for armed conflicts – and the use of children in prostitution, pornography and illicit activities, in particular the production and trafficking of drugs. The Convention also requires adequate penalties and encourages member States to assist one another through international cooperation or assistance to combat the worst forms of child labour.

Ratifying States are required to adopt programmes of action to eliminate the worst forms of child labour. These programmes are to include specific measures to prevent children from being exploited in forced labour and to rehabilitate and integrate them once they are removed from such exploitation. Thus, in addition to providing for a clear legal prohibition of child slavery, the new Convention is oriented towards immediate and effective action to assist the children concerned.

In 1998 the International Labour Conference adopted the ILO Declaration on Fundamental Principles and Rights at Work, which reaffirms the commitment of the ILO's Member States to promote fundamental labour rights, whether or not they have ratified the relevant Conventions. The elimination of all forms of forced or compulsory laboour and the abolition of child labour figure prominently among these rights.

International Programme on the Elimination of Child Labour (IPEC)

Consistent with the new Convention and the Declaration, IPEC gives top priority to action which will bring an end to the worst forms of child labour, such as slavery and similar practices, the exploitation of children in prostitution, pornography and for illicit purposes. In addition, IPEC gives special attention to children who are particularly vulnerable, those who are very young and girls. Examples of IPEC-supported action are given in section 5.4 on action at national level and strategies for action against child bondage, and in section 5.5 on trafficking of children and commercial sexual exploitation.

United Nations

International instruments

In 1926, the League of Nations adopted the **Slavery Convention** for the prevention and suppression of the slave trade and abolition of slavery. Slavery is defined as "the status or condition of a person over whom any or all of the powers attaching to the right of ownership are exercised" (Article 1). In 1956, a **Supplementary Convention on the Abolition of Slavery** applied in particular to debt bondage and serfdom. It defines debt bondage as "the status or condition arising from a pledge by a debtor of his personal services or those of a person under his control as security for a debt, if the value of those services as reasonably assessed is not applied towards the liquidation of the debt or the length and nature of those services are not respectively limited and defined" (Article 1(a)). It also calls for the abolition of any institution or practice "whereby a child or young person under the age of 18 years is delivered by either or both of his natural parents or by his guardian to another person, whether for reward or not, with a view to the exploitation of the child or young person or of his labour" (Article 1(d)).

The Supplementary Convention on the Abolition of Slavery (1956) was inspired by the **Universal Declaration of Human Rights,** adopted in 1948, which proclaimed that "no one shall be held in slavery or servitude; slavery and the slave trade shall be prohibited in all their forms". The **International Covenant of Civil and Political Rights**, adopted in 1966, echoes the assertion of the same rights. It states that "no one shall be held in slavery; slavery and the slave trade in all their forms shall be prohibited...", "no one shall be held in servitude"; and "no one shall be required to perform forced or compulsory labour".

The **United Nations Convention on the Rights of the Child**, adopted in 1989, contains specific provisions against various forms of child exploitation. Article 32 of the Convention provides for the protection of the child from economic exploitation and from performing any work which is likely to be hazardous or to interfere with the child's education, or to be harmful to the child's health or physical, mental, spiritual, moral or social development. Article 34 requires the State to protect the child from all forms of sexual exploitation and sexual abuse, and to take appropriate national, bilateral and multilateral measures. Article 35 imposes a similar obligation on the State concerning abduction, sale or trafficking in children. Article 36 provides for the protection of the child from all forms of exploitation prejudicial to any aspect of the child's welfare.

Box 5.9. International efforts to end child slavery

◆ International legal instruments of the ILO and the United Nations provide the legal framework for the abolition of all forms of child slavery and practices similar to slavery.

◆ International organizations cooperate to tackle the problem. For example, in 1992, the ILO, in collaboration with the United Nations Centre for Human Rights, organized the Asian Regional Seminar on Children in Bondage in Pakistan.

◆ The ILO Committee of Experts raises the issue of bonded labour – including child bondage – every year, and keeps the issue alive on the agenda of governments.

◆ The ILO's International Programme on the Elimination of Child Labour (IPEC) places a high priority on child bondage and supports action programmes to combat the practice in different countries.

◆ The United Nations Working Group on Contemporary Forms of Slavery, set up in 1974, reviews the reports and testimonies of NGOs on child bondage every year.

◆ International NGOs increasingly accord special attention to child labour and mobilize public opinion. Anti-Slavery International acts as coordinator for the NGO subgroup on child labour with the Committee on the Rights of the Child.

5.3 NATIONAL LEGISLATION AND ENFORCEMENT

Most countries in the world prohibit forced labour in their Constitution or in general labour legislation, but the problem of bonded child labour persists because of weaknesses in the laws and their implementation.

Legislation prohibiting forced and bonded labour

The constitutions of most countries contain provisions relating to fundamental rights which include injunctions that "no person shall be held in slavery or servitude" and "no person shall be required to perform forced or compulsory labour" or to the effect that no person shall be compelled to perform work or render personal services without his or her full consent and/or without fair compensation. Some constitutions deal with forced labour under general provisions on the right to work, stipulating that everyone has the right to freedom of labour and that involuntary labour is prohibited, or that work is an obligation for every citizen but that no one may be unlawfully forced into a specific occupation.

The Constitution of India prohibits a form of forced labour known as *Begar*, which is "labour or service exacted by government or a person in power, without remuneration". Honduras appears to be the only country in which the Constitution itself deals specifically with children in bondage: "Every child must be protected against every form of abandonment, cruelty and exploitation. No child shall be the object of any type of bondage." Penalties are provided for by law for those who violate the provision.

Many countries devote a section of their labour legislation to forced or compulsory labour. Definitions are often in conformity with the ILO's Forced Labour Convention, 1930 (No. 29). In about half the countries where the prohibition of forced labour is provided for in general labour legislation, there are specific penalties for the illegal exaction of work or any form of illegal constraint. In others, such provisions are found under general or penalty provisions of the labour legislation. Labour legislation typically declares that any person who imposes or permits the imposition of forced labour is guilty of an offence and liable to a fine of a certain amount of money and/or to imprisonment for some months or years. For example, in the Republic of Korea a person violating the provisions concerning employment of workers through violence, threats, illegal confinement or any other means of unjustifiable mental or physical restraint "shall be punished by imprisonment for not more than three years or suspension of civil rights for a period of not more than five years".

Two noteworthy examples of national legislation outlawing bonded labour are the Bonded Labour System (Abolition) Act, passed in India in 1976, and the Bonded Labour System (Abolition) Act, enacted in 1992 in Pakistan. These statutes represent a real advance in the conception of the problem because they do not only prohibit the bonded labour system, but provide for the rehabilitation of liberated workers and the establishment of broad-based vigilance committees with a mandate to advise and coordinate the implementation of the provisions concerning the identification and rehabilitation of the bonded labourers.

Problems in enforcement

All countries suppress slavery and different forms of forced labour by constitutional or legislative provisions. The legislation on slavery and bondage indicates their acceptance of the international standards and sets the goal in the national context. However, these practices persist in many parts of the world, because legislation by itself, even when sincere efforts are made for its implementation, cannot wholly eliminate them. On the other hand, the battle against slavery and bondage cannot be won without legislation.

Certain serious deficiencies persist in national legislation on slavery and bonded labour:

◆ While the constitution of a country may prohibit slavery and bondage, the punishment for contravention has to be provided by law. For example, the Constitution of Nepal states that "traffic in human beings, slavery, serfdom or forced labour in any form is prohibited. Any contravention of this provision shall be punishable by law". The most prevalent form of bondage in Nepal is the *Kamaiya* system. However, no law exists which identifies the system to be one of forced labour or which prescribes a punishment for imposing it on a person.

◆ Legal statutes do not always define bondage with sufficient precision. It is, therefore, often unclear whether a particular practice comes within its definition. For instance, article 149 of the Brazilian Penal Code condemns slavery, but does not define the term used, *plágio*, leaving it to the enforcement agency to interpret it. Anti-Slavery International reports a case in which police raided a plantation but made no arrests, nor did they liberate the bonded labourers because they did not find "any gunmen at the estate" and could not, therefore, characterize the case as falling under the provisions of the Code.[11]

◆ The lack of rules and instructions on the implementation of the statute often renders it a dead letter. For instance, in Pakistan the rules under the Bonded Labour System (Abolition) Act, 1992, were issued by the Federal Government in July 1995. Without these rules, it was not possible for the provincial governments to empower the district magistrates to release and rehabilitate bonded labourers. An important arm of enforcement of the law on the abolition of bonded labour in both India and Pakistan is the vigilance committee, but Reports of the ILO Committee of Experts over the past several years point out the delay in setting up these committees and the failure to monitor their functioning.

◆ The population, and in particular the social groups which are the most at risk, lack information because of insufficient diffusion of information, dissemination in a language which is not the ordinary language of the population, or dissemination only through the written press whilst the populations at risk are illiterate. This lack of information, and more generally the lack of education on human rights, is a crucial point for action, all the more since debt bondage, for example, is often profoundly anchored in the social customs of the populations concerned.

◆ The schemes for the identification, release and rehabilitation of bonded labour are designed with adult bonded labourers in mind.

---

[11] A. Sutton: *Slavery in Brazil,* (London, Anti-Slavery International, 1996), p. 19.

Box 5.10. National legislation on bonded labour in India and Pakistan

India

"The Act provides that the bonded labour system shall stand abolished and every bonded labourer shall stand free and discharged from any obligation to render any bonded labour. The law provides for the establishment of vigilance committees which include members of scheduled castes or scheduled tribes and social workers. The committees advise on proper implementation of the Act, provide for economic and social rehabilitation of the free labourers, co-ordinate the functions of rural banks and cooperative societies with a view to providing adequate credit to the freed labourers, and defend any suit instituted against a freed bonded labourer for the recovery of bonded debt. Under the Bonded Labour System (Abolition) Rules, 1976, the registers maintained by the vigilance committees must include the names and addresses of the freed bonded labourers and details of the benefits which they receive, including benefits in the form of land, inputs in agriculture, training in handicrafts and allied occupations, and loans. Under the Act's enforcement measures, 'compulsion to render bonded labour, advancement of bonded debt, enforcement of any custom, tradition, contract, agreement or other instrument requiring any service to be rendered under the bonded labour system are punishable with imprisonment for up to three years and a fine'."

Pakistan

"... In Pakistan, the Bonded Labour System (Abolition) Act, 1992, declares the abolition of the bonded labour system and states that every bonded labourer is to be freed and discharged from any obligation to render any bonded labour. No suit or other proceeding can lie in any civil court, tribunal or before any other authority for the recovery of any bonded debt or any part thereof. The Act provides for special enforcement measures, including the setting up of vigilance committees at district level. These committees comprise elected representatives of the area, representatives of the district administration, bar associations, press, recognized social services, and labour departments of federal and provincial governments. Their functions include advising the district administration on matters relating to the effective implementation of the law, helping in the rehabilitation of freed bonded labourers, monitoring application of the law, and providing bonded labourers with the necessary assistance to achieve the objectives of the law. The Bonded Labour System (Abolition) Rules, 1995, provide that provincial governments are to establish one or more authorities to deal with the restoration of the property of bonded labourers, and confer upon every district magistrate the power to inspect workplaces where a system of bonded labour is suspected to operate. Provincial governments are also to establish vigilance committees to enforce the Act, as well as a fund to finance programmes to assist bonded labourers. Compulsion to render bonded labour or extracting bonded labour under the bonded labour system is punishable with imprisonment from two to five years or with a fine of 50,000 rupees, or both." [12]

---

[12] ILO: *Child labour: Targeting the intolerable* (Geneva, 1996), p.65.

◆ The most serious deficiency in the legal system is the weakness in implementing the law. Although the general criminal law has an application in the case of bondage, it is seldom used to protect bonded workers. In fact, owing to close ties between the landlords and the police or the magistracy in some countries, the employers have been able to press charges of criminal breach of trust against the workers if they tried to escape before liquidating the loan.

Helping countries address the problem of bonded child labour has proved extremely difficult. Principal obstacles to freeing bonded child workers are the hidden character of the problem, and powerful vested interests to maintain the status quo. Local authorities are not keen or able to follow rules and regulations set at the national level, citing administrative apathy or complicated legal procedures. Such resistance prevails because servitude is deeply rooted in rural social and economic structure.

Reinforcing the lack of political will at the highest places of authority is the apathy engulfing both the victims of servitude, who are not aware of their rights, and the general public, who lack information on the human suffering taking place in their country.

The few NGOs who actively combat bonded child labour face serious resource limitations and other obstacles. In some countries, these NGOs are considered by the authorities to be engaged in subversive activities. The mistrust sometimes existing between government and NGOs involved with child rights and child labour prevents cooperation between them and hampers efforts by international organizations to support NGO activities in this field.

Enforcement of legislation against child bondage is a major problem. There are several reasons for this:

- *the informality and invisibility of bonded labour and the difficulty of reaching children in bondage;*

- *the long delay between identification, prosecution and release;*

- *the inadequacy of financial resources for inspection and enforcement, and the lack of capacity of organizations and lack of coordination among concerned agencies;*

- *the lack of cooperation from employers and, in some cases, the bonded child workers and parents themselves who, because the practice is illegal, may collaborate in concealing the problem; and*

- *apathy among the victims and the general public.*

Box 5.11. Prevention and elimination of bonded child labour

Pakistan

In Pakistan, a major pilot programme has been launched to prevent and eliminate child bonded labour. It is the first comprehensive programme to address child bonded labour in the country through concerted action by governmental and non-governmental organizations. The programme focuses on direct action with children and their families; strengthening government machinery responsible for law enforcement, social welfare and education at the local, provincial, and national levels; and strengthening capacities of NGOs. In addition, child bonded labour in the production of carpets will be targeted through future action programmes to eliminate child labour.

The programme's strategy is to mobilize a broad alliance of governmental and non-governmental agencies, communities, employers, parents and children in taking joint action against child bonded labour through a three-pronged approach:

◆ establishing 18 Community Education and Action (CEA) Centres for a selected number of children in specific economic sectors and occupations with a high incidence of child bonded labour; withdrawing a selected number of bonded children from exploitative and hazardous work, and preventing their younger siblings from entering such work; and mobilizing communities to prevent child bonded labour;

◆ strengthening the capacity of the Directorates of Labour and Welfare to monitor workplaces, to withdraw bonded children and to ensure that these workplaces become and remain free of child bonded labour; and

◆ institutional development of other key governmental agencies and selected NGOs to provide an integrated package of support services to ex-bonded child workers, their younger siblings and their families to prevent further child bonded labour through community mobilization.

5.4 ACTION AT THE NATIONAL LEVEL

The suppression of slavery must be achieved at the national and local levels for it requires not only measures which are within the jurisdiction of each government, but changes in social practices which are at times profoundly anchored in national history and culture. Such changes cannot be brought about without the committed engagement of local populations. In order to be effective, all policies and projects must be specifically targeted to slavery and bondage. Practical action should address three main target groups: society in general, the slave owners and the children in bondage.

Nepal

A broad-based National Task Force on Prevention of Trafficking in Children was set up under the Ministry of Women and Social Welfare in Nepal to provide guidance and policy advice for the implementation of action programmes against child trafficking. The Task Force consists of representatives of the concerned government ministries, representatives of the National Planning Commission, the police, and NGOs dealing with the issue. International organizations, such as the ILO and UNICEF, provide technical support to the Task Force.

The Ministry of Women and Social Welfare, in consultation with the National Task Force, has instructed the chairpersons of 19 District Development Committees (in areas where the problem of trafficking is endemic) to set up District Task Forces with themselves as the Chairpersons of the Task Forces, the Chief District Officers as the Vice-Chairpersons, and representatives from the police, social organizations, local NGOs, and District Child Welfare Boards as the members. The District Task Forces will be authorized to play an active role in coordinating district-level activities against trafficking in children and their commercial sexual exploitation; identifying the vulnerable Village Development Committees and communities in the district; and assisting in the implementation of suitable programmes in the affected areas.

A consultative workshop on the development of the National Plan of Action against Trafficking in Children and their Commercial Sexual Exploitation was held in Kathmandu from 22-24 April 1998. Sixty representatives from governmental and non-governmental organizations, employers' and workers' organizations, representatives of diplomatic missions and United Nations agencies, the police, NGOs and donor organizations participated and identified the following six areas of action to prevent trafficking:

(i) policy, research and institutional development;

(ii) legislation and enforcement;

(iii) awareness creation, advocacy, networking and social mobilization;

(iv) health and education;

(v) income and employment generation; and

(vi) rescue and reintegration.

Despite difficulties, communities and countries are making headway. Over the past decade or so, considerable experience in combating bonded child labour has been gained, and lessons learned from the efforts of communities, NGOs and governments.

Preventing child slavery

Priority must be given to prevention. This is the least costly action for society; it affects the greatest number of children, and its effects are long-term. Preventive action should take place in the legislative, economic, social protection, and educational and advocacy spheres.

Legislation

In countries where bonded child labour exists, legislation should be enacted to deal with the problem:

◆ in many cases, legislation needs to be revised and provide for precise definitions of the forms of slavery and bondage existing in the country. Slavery must appear as a crime;

◆ sanctions that are tough enough to be dissuasive should be provided for;

◆ the question of the liquidation of existing debts and other obligations must be answered unambiguously;

◆ regulations must be established to facilitate the implementation of the law, in particular to ensure rapid action from the judiciary;

◆ the law must envisage the possibility of special jurisdiction to be able to confront simultaneously a concentrated number of children in bondage at the same site and to safeguard the independence of the tribunals and institutions charged with executing the decisions taken;

◆ laws and regulations should also be transmitted swiftly with the appropriate instructions to the local institutions and authorities charged with enforcement;

◆ laws and regulations should be communicated to the victims, the offenders and society at large in a manner that is comprehensible to them, for example in local languages and over the radio, or through meetings if the concerned population groups are illiterate; and

◆ legal aid should be placed at the disposal of the child victims' parents to enable them to claim their rights, and special arrangements should be made, where required, to find the parents within a reasonable time-limit if the child is separated from them.

Poverty and social exclusion

Poverty and social exclusion should be addressed according to the needs of the concerned population groups. Agrarian reforms which provide access to land and incomes, as well as employment-promotion measures and social protection for disadvantaged families, can be effective in preventing bondage.

In most cases, the bondage of a child is the consequence of an urgent temporary financial need. Providing credit opportunities, other than via the employer and the region's dominant landlords, could break the vicious circle and provide an opening for the gradual lessening of dependence. Close to 10,000 institutions providing small loans have been listed in the world and many of them are modelled on the Grameen Bank approach. NGOs with the capacity to adapt appropriate micro-bank models to the local situation and introduce them to communities at risk might be one of the most promising ways of countering bonded labour.

Information, education and social mobilization

Government and other concerned groups should be encouraged to:

◆ launch research on bondage situations and facilitate analysis by organizing meetings between experts of complementary disciplines;

◆ diffuse information to all segments of society, provoke condemnation of bondage practices and mobilize the entire population;

◆ make known to the families at risk their rights and the ways in which they are able to have them respected;

◆ increase education on human rights, in particular children's rights;

◆ insert in administrative personnel training programmes an introduction to the problem of child slavery and bondage;

◆ launch sensitization programmes in employers' and workers' organizations;

◆ provide a specific component on child bondage in the training of labour inspectors and police officers; and

◆ set up effective protection for researchers, journalists, social workers and various activists who denounce practices of bondage.

Action against slave owners

Slave owners simply cannot be treated as employers of children who must be persuaded to cooperate with programmes of action. They are guilty of a crime. A policy of deterrence must be set up and the population informed of this policy. It could include the following elements:

◆ provision of sanctions strong enough to serve as both punishment and dissuasion;

◆ acceleration of judicial process in regard to bonded child labour; and

◆ punishment of all persons and institutions who actively participate in placing a child in bondage, not only the direct employer but equally the recruiters, escorts and surveyors.

Targeting children in bondage

The experience of direct action programmes concerning children in bondage, although limited, clearly presents two major lessons: firstly, without action directed towards society in general and slave owners in particular, activities targeting bonded children will have limited results and will not alone suppress the practice of bondage; secondly, support programmes must be organized taking into account that the child is in slavery and not simply at work under harsh conditions.

Direct action with bonded children involves three stages: identification, release and rehabilitation.

Identification

Identification means not only physically discovering a child in slavery-type situations, but having the child recognized as such. Slave owners often deny that a state of slavery exists. Possible counter-actions include:

◆ launching periodic appeals to the population to denounce known cases of slavery;

◆ having labour inspectors, police and social workers systematically verify whether children at work in slavery-prone areas are in bondage;

◆ informing and sensitizing parents so that they will testify about the slavery of their children; and

◆ setting up procedures permitting children to express themselves on their situation.

Release

The release of children is not an easy operation. Firstly, the children must be physically taken out of their slave environment. This requires the parents, the child or the workmates to overcome physical barriers and thwart the surveillance of the guards in order to escape, which is often difficult. Outside intervention is therefore usually necessary but cannot be organized by an individual who has no right of entry to private property. Specific solutions could include the creation of special police units and the granting of a legally recognized intervention power to certain special authorities.

Secondly, one must ensure that a child who has been freed from bondage is not recaptured by the employer. A very long period of time may elapse before the child is able to be returned to its parents. Often the child is distraught and traumatized by violence. The slave owners may take advantage of this to regain control of the child. Temporary reception centres must be set up. Because speed of operation is a key factor, emergency procedures must be elaborated enabling the identification and the release of the child to be effected simultaneously.

Thirdly, there is no real liberation until the debt which binds the child to the employer has been officially nullified. Such a decision in law assumes the participation of the two parties. As the parents of the child are often paralysed by fear of the employer and by lack of awareness of their rights, free legal aid should be put at their disposal.

Rehabilitation

Only by rehabilitation is the process of liberation completed. Rehabilitation means supporting the return of the child to a community. It must respond to two fundamental needs of the liberated child. Firstly, the child must be guaranteed the material needs for survival. It goes without saying that if the economic situation of the family remains unchanged and if the causes which had provoked the bondage persist, the provision of a temporary allowance, for example, would have little effect. Secondly, specialized treatment is needed to repair the psychological damage suffered by the child and to assist the child's reintegration in society.

Integrated action to address child slavery

Four examples are given below of effective action against child bondage and trafficking including rehabilitation and rescue centres, comprehensive services for parents and children in villages, and the organization of bonded labourers.

Box 5.12. Comprehensive rehabilitation of released bonded children in India

Amongst the existing release and rehabilitation programmes for children formerly in bondage, Mukti Ashram, linked to the South Asian Coalition against Child Servitude (SACCS), in a suburb of the Indian capital, New Delhi, merits particular attention. It was created in 1990 and has since rehabilitated close to 1,600 children. One of the successes of this approach is the increased number of children and youths who, after rehabilitation in their communities of origin, have become engaged in the fight against bondage.

Most of the children, between the ages of 6 or 7, were lured away or kidnapped from their native villages and taken to workplaces in industries, mines, construction sites and the agricultural sector, hundreds of miles away. The children, who often cannot understand or speak the local dialect, are confined to toil day in, day out, without any wages or cash remuneration. Fifteen to 18 hours of work without adequate or proper food, abuse, beatings, isolation, and humiliation are common. The children grow up and accept slavery as their destiny. They are not allowed to change the job or go back home to join their parents or relatives. Education, recreation, play, fun or even crying for their parents is beyond their imagination. The entire concept of Mukti Ashram has been designed to bring back their lost joy, hope and childhood.

When the children are freed they are traumatized, physically sick, and completely broken in heart and soul. They have no idea of good or bad education. It is very difficult to re-socialize them in families and villages. They are without any skill, initiative or enthusiasm. SACCS aims to ensure that these victims of slavery become their own liberators and leaders. This task is only possible by closely involving the children and adolescents in the programme.

The staff running the Ashram are freed bonded labourers and victims of exploitation, particularly those belonging to the lowest castes in India. They have been trained and educated to meet the requirements of the Ashram. Doctors, psychologists and extension workers are given special orientation to work with these children in a participatory manner. The management hierarchy is inverted to bring about a change in the enslaved attitude of the children. For example, the Chairperson and Director are required to clean the latrines, which is normally considered as the most degrading work and normally done by Untouchables. It gives a mental jolt to the children observing these unimaginable acts.

The Ashram reflects the environment of a village ambience. Learning, playing, physical exercises, cooking, eating, sleeping and all routine activities are done collectively. Special cultural events, religious and traditional festivals are celebrated in such a manner that they can learn the new interpretation of such events, the essence of norms and values and communal life. The need and advantage of democracy, the entitlement to vote and leadership aspects are taught through plays and songs. Folk culture and the use of local dialects are encouraged to give them a sense of belonging, and enable them to express themselves and gain self-confidence.

Basic literacy, social education and skills training are provided to the children for a period of three to six months. The children are stimulated to give feedback to the staff and others. Group training and its benefits, chanting slogans, argumentation and oratory skills, initiatives and risk-taking, wall-writing, poster making, effective communication, the handling of money and problem-solving skills are among the learning activities.

Box 5.13. Preventing and eliminating bonded child labour in the carpet belt of Uttar Pradesh, India

The Centre of Rural Education and Development Action (CREDA) has demonstrated positive results in what are now "child-labour-free" villages by implementing an integrated strategy of awareness-raising, community mobilization, and preventive and rehabilitation services for child victims and their families, primary education for children released from work and community services for the poor.[13]

CREDA works among child labourers in the Mirzapur-Bhadohi carpet manufacturing belt of Uttar Pradesh, many of whom are bonded. This and the surrounding areas contribute 80 per cent of India's total carpet production, most of which is exported. The majority of the target families belong to scheduled castes and tribes who are particularly vulnerable, and children's workplaces are scattered in remote villages.

The relocation of the carpet looms in villages inaccessible by road and far away from the district and block headquarters is apparently due, at least in part, to the vigilance of the Labour Department, especially since 1986, the year of enactment of the Child Labour (Prohibition and Regulation) Act. The newly found "havens" are villages which have a concentration of people from the socially weaker sections, such as the scheduled castes, scheduled tribes and backward castes, who are also economically vulnerable.

In the recent past, the demand for carpet weavers has risen because of the spurt in the export of carpets. This in turn led to a demand for higher wages. To overcome this new situation, the loom owners in collaboration with the middlemen started making overtures to poor families in far-away villages with the offer of attractive sums as "advances" for "mortgaging" their children to loom-owners. The offers are usually irresistible for the poor families, and the parents easily fall into the trap of loom-owners and their associates. Thus, for more than a decade, the practice of child labour has become more and more entrenched in the area. As no other source of regular employment is available for people in the villages in this belt, many non-weaving sections have taken up carpet weaving as their principal vocation.

The child worker goes through several "training stages" over two to four years. The entry age is between 8 and 10 years. Before formal induction as a worker, the child attends to light jobs, and is then taught to make simple knots. This goes on for more than a year, during which the child is paid nothing. During the second year, the child worker begins weaving carpets with simple designs. Most loom owners do not pay wages in the normal sense to child workers. Forty per cent of the children work to pay off advance payments to their parents and interest. The other 60 per cent work as apprentices at a very low fee for two to three years before becoming fully-fledged carpet weavers at the age of 13 or 14 years.

[13] Administrative Staff College of India (Child Labour Action and Support Project), *Eliminating child labour through community mobilization: A study on an NGO's efforts to eliminate child labour in the carpet industry in Mirzapur India* (New Delhi, ILO, 1996).

Prior to CREDA's intervention, child workers in the villages worked on carpet looms from 7 a.m. to 6 p.m. with a lunch interval of one hour and another hour for tea and rest. There was no sick leave, earned leave or even vacations during major festivals. A nine-hour work-day, seven days a week, was the routine followed at the looms.

CREDA started by opening health centres offering free medical check-ups, arranging vocational training, and organizing self-help groups through savings and credit. These helped it gain a firm foothold in the villages to mount a campaign of social awareness against the practice of child labour. The awareness campaign targeted the political leadership of the village, opinion leaders, parents, loom owners, manufacturers, adult weavers and the children themselves. At the same time, CREDA set up schools for children withdrawn from the looms, thrift and credit societies, skills training centres for adults, and pre-school centres for young children. In the first phase of the project, ten non-formal education centres were set up, where children were provided with locally relevant vocational training and recreational activities, a meal a day, basic health care and a stipend to help overcome the loss of income. In the second phase, 10,000 young children, at risk of being sent to work, were enrolled in regular schools and 1,000 child workers joined non-formal education. CREDA received wide support from the community.

The Mirzapur district administration came to accept CREDA as a professional and competent agency committed to the elimination of child labour in the carpet industry, and as a partner supplementing the efforts of the Government.

The programme spread to nine blocks in three districts reaching around 200 villages. A dialogue with carpet loom holders prompted many of them to release child labourers. CREDA also mounted a campaign to generate awareness about the ethical, economic and legal implications of child labour. It formed 140 village-level committees and set up two reporting centres in Mirzapur and Sonebhadra districts where information would be collected about bonded child workers. CREDA assisted needy families who were eligible for government schemes to become beneficiaries.

The work of CREDA in Mirzapur district has contributed significantly to the decline in the number of child labourers in carpet looms. One assessment of the number is that it has fallen from 50,000 in 1992-93 to 10-15,000 in 1996-97. CREDA has also been able to declare a number of villages child labour free. In addition, more pernicious forms of child bonded labour, which existed in the villages prior to CREDA's activities, where middlemen brought in migrant children who lived and worked with the employer, disappeared completely as a result of CREDA's work. However, these children were shifted to other areas where the communities were not sensitized on child bonded labour. This shows once again that action against child labour cannot be confined to one area, but must be addressed in a comprehensive manner in all areas where the problem occurs.

Box 5.14. Action against bondage among the *Kamaiyas* of Nepal

The *Kamaiya* system of bonded labour is prevalent in five districts of western Nepal. Under this system, a *Kamaiya* agrees to work for a landlord on the basis of an oral contract for one year, for a wage which is generally paid in kind. While the system has many variants, typically, a *Kamaiya* would get eight quintals of rice and 25 per cent of the produce of land cultivated by him and his family. Since the land is mono-cropped, *Kamaiyas* barely eke out a living in a normal year. Should the crop fail, or should they have to meet social obligations or medical or other emergency expenses, they are forced to take a loan (*sauki*) from the landlord. The family must then work for the landlord till the loan is repaid. The children of the *Kamaiyas* who are above 5 years of age serve the landlord as cowherds and do various other jobs. The family works in exchange for food. *Kamaiyas* are thus forced to borrow more for buying other necessities and are unable to free themselves from the vicious grip of debt. Indebtedness and bondage are transferred from one generation to the other. Although *Kamaiyas* are free to change master at the end of a year, a *Kamaiya* who has taken a loan can do so only if the new master pays off the loan.

Most of the *Kamaiyas* belong to an indigenous people in the Terai region of Nepal, called the Tharu. They had lived in relative isolation as the area was affected by virulent malaria (to which they had developed natural immunity) and originally owned most of the land. After the eradication of malaria in the 1960s, people from the hills migrated to the area and were able to gain ownership of the land from the Tharus through usury and mortgage. Fifty per cent of the Tharus now serve as *Kamaiyas* or live in a *Kamaiya* household. More than half of the *Kamaiyas* are indebted to the landlords and work as bonded labourers.

IPEC has supported NGOs to implement action programmes in three districts in western Nepal to raise awareness among the *Kamaiyas* about their rights, improve their living conditions, and ensure that their children are freed from work and receive education. Community meetings and street plays have been organized to raise awareness. The NGOs have provided over 500 *Kamaiya* children with non-formal education and have enrolled most of them in government schools. *Kamaiya* Support Committees have been established at the district level through community meetings. The *Kamaiyas* recently held a conference and established "the *Kamaiya* Liberation Forum", which is affiliated to a national trade union organization.

As the movement gathers strength, the *Kamaiyas* are beginning to escape from a state of passive resignation to their fate. An in-depth analysis will be carried out to identify the socio-economic factors contributing to the prevalence of the *Kamaiya* system. The results of this study will aid in the design of a comprehensive package of services to address the root causes of this problem.

Box 5.15. Rescue and rehabilitation of child victims of trafficking in Nepal

Maity Nepal, an NGO, has formed surveillance groups in the districts seriously affected by child trafficking and is carrying out campaigns against it with the help of college students and some victims of trafficking. It has set up a prevention-cum-interception camp at an important transit point. The camp provides shelter, basic education and vocational training for girls who are at risk of being sold into prostitution, as well as for those who have been rescued from trafficking. At the end of their training, the girls are helped in finding employment or setting up a small business. Another transit home is being set up at Kakkarvita, near the Nepal-India border, to provide shelter to girls who have been rescued from brothels in India and repatriated to Nepal.

Maity Nepal coordinates its activities with NGOs in India for the rescue and repatriation of victims, some of whom have been living in government-run homes for long periods of time. On the Nepalese side, it works with the police and other authorities for the rehabilitation of child victims and for the prosecution of the offenders. The victims are often in a state of trauma and many suffer from serious diseases, such as HIV/AIDS and tuberculosis, thus needing immediate medical attention and psychological counselling. The NGO plans to provide a wide range of rehabilitation services to help children regain their self-esteem and become self-reliant.

The United Nations Working Group on Contemporary Forms of Slavery

The Working Group on Contemporary Forms of Slavery was established as a permanent monitoring system of the application of the united Nations Conventions on slavery. It meets annually in Geneva and examines all forms of slavery throughout the world. It submits recommendations, some of which reach the United Nations General Assembly, for discussion. The Working Group encourages the widest participation possible in its work, inviting all organizations, including NGOs, to present documents, evidence or recommendations. Governments are attentive to the information presented to the Working Group, whose principal strength lies in its ability to bring to the recognition of the international community situations of slavery or violations of human rights existing in a specific place, and exert pressure on those responsible.

Local NGOs and community groups (such as vigilance committees) are often the best placed to be acquainted with child bondage situations. They can participate more actively in the Working Group by sending written evidence[14] directly or via the NGOs which usually participate in the work of the Group, or by going to Geneva to present the evidence themselves during the session of the Working Group.

[14] In English, French or Spanish, and not exceeding three pages (A4 format) to: Working Group on Contemporary Forms of Slavery, Human Rights Centre, Palais des Nations, Geneva, Switzerland.

The United Nations Voluntary Trust Fund on Contemporary Forms of Slavery

This body was created in 1992 and facilitates the participation of NGOs in the sessions of the Working Group on Contemporary Forms of Slavery by providing support (technical, humanitarian, legal or financial) to groups or persons victimized by slavery. For example, it supported the participation of a few local NGO representatives at the Working Group's session in June 1997.[15]

The United Nations Committee on the Rights of the Child

The United Nations Committee on the Rights of the Child is an internationally elected body of independent experts established to examine the progress made by States Parties in meeting the obligations of the Convention on the Rights of the Child. The Committee examines country reports prepared by the States on the status of their children and the measures taken by them to implement the Convention.

The Committee accords particular importance to child labour. To improve its assessment of the reports supplied by the governments, the Committee invites NGOs to submit comments on the country reports. In certain countries, NGO coalitions provide the Committee with a counter-report on children's rights, if they consider that the government report does not actually reflect reality. In other countries, governments have invited civil society, notably through NGOs, to participate in the elaboration of the report.

The NGO Group for the Convention on the Rights of the Child

The NGO Group for the Convention on the Rights of the Child facilitates contact between the non-governmental community and the Committee on the Rights of the Child. Defence for Children International serves as the Secretariat for the Group. The NGO meetings take place in Geneva, jointly with the Committee's sessions so as to take into account NGOs' views in analysing national reports. A subgroup has been established especially for child labour, for which coordination has been entrusted to Anti-Slavery International. All NGOs can send documentation directly to the United Nations Committee or through the NGO Group.

---

[15] NGOs can solicit support by addressing requests to the: Voluntary Trust Fund Against Slavery, Human Rights Centre, Palais des Nations, Geneva, Switzerland.

5.5 DEVELOPING COMPREHENSIVE PROGRAMMES OF ACTION

A few countries have placed forms of child slavery, such as the commercial sexual exploitation of children and child bondage, at the top of their agenda for action and have initiated concrete steps towards its elimination. Several other countries have addressed some aspects of the problem, for example in domestic service, in agriculture and in commercial sexual exploitation.

IPEC helps countries develop comprehensive responses to the problem by adopting a series of interventions at local, national, regional and international level. In a country where the practice has been identified, practical steps can be taken to start action programmes. At the regional and international level, awareness-raising and campaigns to mobilize support for action will be carried out in collaboration with relevant United Nations agencies and other international organizations.

IPEC's focus is on assisting partner organizations at the governmental and non-governmental level to effectively prevent the problem of child trafficking so that the practice will be totally eliminated. Prevention of the problem is the key solution. Once victimized, the children suffer extreme physical, psycho-social and emotional abuse which results in lifelong and often life-threatening consequences. Simultaneously, support is extended to partner organizations to rehabilitate the child victims, not only because they need urgent help, but also because demonstration projects for the victims are a powerful tool to mobilize societies against the worst forms of child labour.

Strategy for action against child bondage

A broad policy framework should include a comprehensive national policy and programme of action covering legislative reforms, effective systems to monitor the enforcement of decisions taken by the authorities, prevention, and rehabilitation and socio-economic reintegration programmes for victims through access to basic, relevant education, economic alternatives and awareness-raising among children and families. The following are examples of key components of a strategy for action against child bondage that can be carried out in different countries and regions, taking into account the context and needs in each country or region.

At national level

1. **Formulation of a national plan of action against the bonded labour system and child bondage**

   This includes:

   ◆ preparing national reports on bonded labour systems and the nature and extent of child bondage;

   ◆ organizing a national consultation on the forms of bondage, and the best ways of detecting, releasing and rehabilitating bonded labourers, including bonded children; and

◆ formulating a national plan of action for the eradication of the practice and rehabilitation of the victims.

2. Strengthening legislation and enforcement procedures with reference to the scope and application of international conventions

This includes:

◆ examining various forms of bondage relative to the existing legislation, identifying deficiencies in the coverage of legislation, reviewing the adequacy of measures in legislation for the release and rehabilitation of victims and prosecution of offenders, including the level of punishment prescribed for the offenders; and

◆ reviewing enforcement, including prosecution of offenders and the strength and effectiveness of the inspectorate.

3. Institutional capacity-building at national and local levels

This includes:

◆ establishing a national focal point to serve as a stimulus and to facilitate coordination among all partners;

◆ forming a broad based national task force which would advise on policy and programmes on bonded labour legislation and its enforcement (particularly concerning the remission/waiver of loans and release from bondage), as well as carry out surveys to identify bonded labourers and assess their indebtedness and socio-economic status with a view to their rehabilitation; awareness campaigns; orientation of governmental and non-governmental staff; and rehabilitation schemes; and

◆ forming vigilance committees to assist in identifying bonded labourers, provide legal education and oversee their release and rehabilitation.

4. Direct action programmes to prevent, rehabilitate and re-integrate bonded children

These include action programmes to:

◆ liberate children in bonded labour in specific geographical locations;

◆ implement rehabilitation and socio-economic reintegration programmes not only to receive the children once liberated but also to progressively guide them into a normal social life;

◆ set up a rehabilitation fund and the procedure for its operation;

◆ implement savings and credit schemes for poor families who are vulnerable to resorting to child bondage; and

◆ provide basic, relevant education to prevent child bondage.

5. Awareness-raising on the problem of bonded labourers and children in bondage among parents, employers, local communities, the general public and policy-makers

This includes:

◆ collecting and assessing information on a continuing basis on children in bondage and bonded labour systems, on the law and its enforcement, and on efforts made for prevention, debt repayment and rehabilitation;

◆ disseminating information and sensitizing parents, the community, schoolteachers who are in a position of leadership in rural communities and all sectors of civil society; and

◆ organizing public hearings and debates on child bondage, for example, in Parliament, and during specific human rights and children's rights related events.

6.   Measuring progress at local and national levels

◆ organize consultations among all key actors at local and national levels to review progress and problems and strengthen strategies for action.

At international level

◆ link action at the national level with the United Nations Working Group on Contemporary Forms of Slavery, the ILO Committee of Experts on the Application of Conventions and Recommendations and the United Nations Committee on the Rights of the Child;

◆ organize an international conference on child bondage; and

◆ conduct international campaigns against child bondage in collaboration with other international organizations and international NGOs.

Strategy for action against child trafficking and the commercial sexual exploitation of children

The programme focuses simultaneously on trafficking within countries as well as across borders. The following activities will be carried out in different countries and regions depending on the context and needs in each country or region.

1.   Appraisal of the problem and existing responses; identification of national, subregional and regional strategies for action:

◆ development of national policy and programmes of action by analysing the scope and current trends in trafficking of children, reviewing the existing responses to the problem (legislation, institutional mechanisms and types of intervention at the governmental and non-governmental level), and organizing consultative workshops at local and national levels;

◆ summarizing the main findings of national reports and compilation of subregional synthesis reports, leading to strategies for action at the national and subregional levels; and

◆ organization of subregional consultations to discuss and adopt bilateral, subregional and regional strategies for action.

2.   Implementation of comprehensive programmes against trafficking in children:

◆ intensive awareness-raising campaigns among the groups at risk, their environment and society at large;

◆ strengthening law enforcement, including the development or revision of legislation where necessary and the promotion of its application through the training of law enforcement personnel and the establishment of community "watch-dog" systems;

◆　undertaking investigation and rescue operations, bringing cases to prosecution and rehabilitating the victims; and

◆　mobilizing participation of and facilitating coordination among key actors, namely the police, non-governmental and community organizations, public prosecutors, and local and national governments.

The in-country programmes will be reinforced by action at the subregional or international level, because it is recognized that concerted action is needed in sending, receiving and transit countries to stop child trafficking. Therefore the aim is to develop inter-country mechanisms to prevent the problem and to provide protection and rehabilitation to the victims. This means that a series of social and legal measures will be proposed and agreed upon by countries in each region. As part of the process, subregional consultative and coordination meetings will be organized to review the nature of the problem, the application and enforcement of international labour standards, and the adequacy of national laws, regulations and enforcement practices against the trafficking of children, as well as to provide policy options and promote the implementation of concrete programmes.

Bibliography on child slavery

References

Acharya, U. 1998. *Trafficking in children and their exploitation in prostitution and other intolerable forms of child labour in Nepal,* Country report for ILO-IPEC (Kathmandu).

Administrative Staff College of India (Child Labour Action and Support Project). 1996. *Eliminating child labour through community mobilization: A study on an NGO's efforts to eliminate child labour in the carpet industry in Mirzapur, India* (New Delhi, ILO).

Anti-Slavery International. 1996. *This menace of bonded labour: Debt bondage in Pakistan* (London).

—. 1997. *Reporter.* Issue No. 3, Sep.

Blanchet, T. 1996. *Lost innocence, stolen childhoods* (Dhaka, University Press).

Boudhiba, 1982. *Exploitation of child labour,* Final report of the Special Rapporteur of the United Nations Sub-Commission on the Prevention of Discrimination and Protection of Minorities, Geneva, 1982.

Bonded Labour Liberation Front. 1989. Excerpt from *Into that heaven of freedom?* (New Delhi, July), p. 39.

Centre for the Protection of the Rights of the Child, Bangkok: A vivid portrayal of children in bondage is featured in a video called *"Paper cups"*.

Child Workers in Asia Bulletin (Bankok). 1995. Excerpt from Vol. 11, No. 1, p. 18.

Department of Women and Child Development, Government of India. 1994. *Child prostitution – In the twilight,* Report of the Central Advisory Committee on Child Prostitution, India.

Geffray, C. 1995. *Chronique de la servitude en Amazonie brésilienne* (Paris).

ILO. 1992. *Children in bondage: A call for action* (Geneva).

—. 1995, 1996. *Report of the Committee of Experts on the Application of Conventions and Recommendations to the International Labour Conference,* Report III, Part 1A (Geneva).

—. 1996. *Child labour: Targeting the intolerable* (Geneva).

Informal Sector Service Center (INSEC). 1992. *Bonded labour in Nepal under the Kamaiya system* (Kathmandu).

Ministry of Women and Social Welfare (MOWSW), Nepal; ILO-IPEC. 1998. *National Plan of Action against Trafficking in Children and their Commercial Sexual Exploitation* (Kathmandu).

Minnesota Lawyers International Human Rights Committee. 1990. *Testimony in restavek: Child domestic labour in Haiti* (Minnesota).

North American Congress on Latin America (NACLA). 1994. *Report of the Americas,* Vol. XXVII, No. 6, May/June.

Silvers, J. 1996. "Child labour in Pakistan" excerpt from *Atlantic Monthly,* p. 87.

Other publications

Anti-Slavery International. 1990. *Children in bondage. Slaves of the subcontinent* (London).

—. 1997. *Enslaved peoples in the 1990s: Indigenous peoples, debt bondage and human rights* (London).

Dingwaney, M. 1987. *Bonded labour in India* (New Delhi, Rural Labour Cell).

Effah, J. 1996. *Modernised slavery: Child trade in Nigeria* (Lagos, Constitutional Rights Project).

Human Rights Watch/Africa. 1995. *Children in Sudan: Slaves, street children and child soldiers* (New York).

Human Rights Watch/Asia. 1993. *A modern form of slavery: Trafficking of Burmese women and girls into brothels in Thailand* (New York).

—. 1995. *Contemporary forms of slavery in Pakistan* (New York).

Human Indian Social Institute. 1995. *Freedom from bondage*, Citizens Commission on Bonded and Child Labour, First National Convention (New Delhi).

Jain, M. 1997. *Bonded labour: Justice through judiciary* (New Delhi, Manak).

Lee-Wright, P. 1990. *Child slaves* (London, Earthscan).

Patnaik, U.; Dingwaney, M. 1985. *Chains of servitude: Bondage and slavery in India* (Madras, Sangam Books).

Sattaur, O. 1993. *Child labour in Nepal* (London, Anti-Slavery International).

Satyarthi, K. 1994. *Break the chains, save the childhood* (New Delhi, South Asian Coalition on Child Servitude).

Sawyer, R. 1988. *Children enslaved* (London, Routledge).

Schlemmer, B. 1996. *L'enfant exploité* (Paris, Karthala-Orstom).

Sutton, A. 1994. *Slavery in Brazil: A link in the chain of modernisation* (London, Anti-Slavery International).

United Nations ; Commission on Human Rights. *Report of the Working Group on Contemporary Forms of Slavery* (Geneva); annual reports, see especially 1985-97.

United States Department of Labor. 1995. *By the sweat and toil of children*, Vol. II, *The use of child labour in US agricultural imports and forced and bonded child labor* (Washington, DC).

—. 1996. *Forced labour: The prostitution of children* (Washington, DC).

Strategies for employers and their organizations

6

Amanda Tucker

INTRODUCTION

While child labour is widely agreed to be a consequence of poverty, it also perpetuates poverty: a working child often forgoes education and grows into an adult inevitably trapped into unskilled and poorly paid jobs. In fact, the poverty-child labour cycle results in scores of underskilled, unqualified workers. Employers are increasingly aware of the long-term negative impact that this detrimental cycle has on economic development and, as a result, are responding to the challenge of child labour and becoming partners in national efforts to combat it.

International attention is being focused on the issue of children's economic exploitation, with the media, consumers, investors, governments, and trade unions becoming ever more vocal. Individual enterprises have often responded either by dismissing child labourers or by coming up with new arrangements to prevent children's direct or indirect involvement in the manufacturing of their products.

Corporate initiatives to address child labour issues are in part also a reflection of growing regulatory pressures which employers face. For example, the European Commission operates a Generalized System of Preferences (GSP) to regulate trade relationships. In 1995, the European Commission approved a GSP provision stipulating that preferential treatment may be suspended if beneficiary countries are found to be using forced labour, child labour or prison labour in the production of goods for foreign markets. In 1998, the European Commission began offering special GSP incentives to countries able to provide proof that they have adopted and enforced the standards laid down in ILO Conventions concerning fundamental rights at work. There have been parallel efforts in the United States to introduce legislation to ban the imports of products from countries and industries where child labour is used. Discussions have been held in the World Trade Organization (WTO) on a "social clause" in trade agreements which would result in the imposition of trade sanctions in countries that do not observe core labour standards as defined by relevant ILO Conventions. The issue was raised by various trade unions and was supported by several governments from industrialized countries.

In the light of mounting international attention on child labour, employers and their organizations can play an important role in mobilizing civil society to develop sustainable strategies. Employers' organizations are well positioned to provide more specific information on the incidence of child labour in various sectors, including in the informal sector. Through their affiliates, these organizations are able to convey to large numbers of individual enterprises, employees, and their families, the importance of promoting children's education, protecting children against work hazards, and keeping children from premature employment. In addition, national employers' federations have a great potential for:

◆ influencing the development of national policies on child labour;

◆ assisting in the development of guidelines for sectoral industrial associations and small to medium-sized enterprises;

◆ working with NGOs and trade unions in the design of relevant vocational training programmes for working children; and

◆ influencing public perception on the rights of children and the relationship between skill upgrading and national socio-economic development.

6.1	# STRATEGIES FOR EMPLOYER ACTION

The International Organisation of Employers (IOE) has stated its commitment to the elimination of hazardous and exploitative child labour. Its action reflects the political will of its members as expressed in the Resolution on Child Labour adopted in 1996. This resolution calls on IOE members to raise awareness on the human, economic and social costs of child labour, and to develop policies and action plans to contribute to the international campaign for its elimination (see Appendix 6.1).

This chapter[1] illustrates some of the various actions which national employers' federations and sectoral business associations have already taken and provides information relating to:

◆　development of policies and programmes to combat child labour effectively;

◆　concrete action taken by national employers' organizations;

◆　corporate and sectoral initiatives to combat child labour; and

◆　various codes of conduct and labelling initiatives.

Planning for action at the national level

As a follow-up to its 1996 Resolution, the IOE sent out a questionnaire to assess the scope of its member federations' activities in the area of child labour.

The majority of the respondents indicated that child labour is not a major problem in their own countries and that national legislation prohibiting the employment of minors is respected. Among those identifying child labour as a national problem, the majority indicated that it primarily occurs in the informal sector. Most stressed that where child labour does exist, one must take into account the underlying social, economic and cultural causes, and that attempts to combat it must provide sustainable solutions for the children concerned and their families.

Respondents also indicated that the majority of employers' organizations are involved in the issue of child labour as part of regular consultations with their respective governments on the application of national legislation pertaining to the minimum age for employment or work. The majority indicated that they had engaged in informal consultations and information exchanges on the problem in their respective countries, usually motivated by the increasing international media attention on child labour, and their concern that child labour problems might be linked to international trading arrangements.

A number of employers' organizations have already implemented programmes on child labour within the framework of the ILO's International Programme on the Elimination of Child Labour (IPEC). They play a critical role on the National Steering Committees established in each IPEC participating country, and are well positioned to

---

[1] This chapter draws on material and case examples from the *Employers' handbook on child labour*, published by the International Organisation of Employers (IOE). Copies may be obtained from IOE, 26 chemin de Joinville, 1216 Cointrin, Geneva, Switzerland (tel: +4122 798 1616; fax: +4122 798 8862; E-Mail: ioe@ioe-emp.org). See p. 327 for more details.

become involved in the development of IPEC programmes on the ground to exert maximum influence over the national policy framework and the scope of activities envisaged.

Concrete actions by employers' organizations may take place at the *policy, programme* and *project* level. Although these components are closely linked, it is crucial to differentiate between the strategic progression of initiatives.

Policies, programmes and projects

An employer policy on child labour constitutes a public commitment to work towards the elimination of child labour. This policy must set clear objectives and priorities, and contain measures to ensure its effective implementation. The ILO's Minimum Age Convention, 1973 (No. 138), along with its companion Recommendation (No. 146), suggests two priorities:

> *Convention No. 138 stipulates that the basic minimum age for employment must not be less than the age of completion of compulsory schooling and, in any case, no less than 15 years or 14 years in developing countries, but sets a higher minimum age of 18 for hazardous work. Light work is allowed at age 12 or 13.*
>
> *The new ILO Convention (No. 182) concerning the prohibition and immediate action for the elimination of the worst forms of child labour establishes the priority for national and international action on these worst forms, which are outlined in Chapter 2.*

Thus, whatever the level of development of the country, the priority should be the identification and prohibition of hazardous work, and other worst forms of child labour, which – in addition to slavery-like practices, domestic service and much work in the informal sector – can also be found in agriculture and urban-based industries, where the direct impact of national employers' organizations could have a potentially large impact. Through advocacy work, employers' organizations can influence their governments to make a policy commitment to the long-term goal of eliminating child labour, coupled with short-term measures which protect working children.

Policies are the first step. They have to be implemented through concrete programmes and projects. Some of the areas where employers' organizations can make a unique and important contribution to national efforts to eliminate child labour are in:

◆ identifying child labour in economic sectors and occupations;

◆ designing basic education and vocational training programmes;

◆ developing human resource/skill development programmes;

◆ initiating enterprise-creation/income-generation activities; and

◆ devising schemes to improve the working conditions of children as a transitional measure.

Employer-initiated programmes generally target several sectors within a particular community with a high incidence of child labour or provide a framework for a sectoral approach involving many companies. In designing specific programmes on child labour, national employers' organizations build on their strong links with sectoral business associations and industry groups. They enlist other partners to assist in project implementation, such as experienced NGOs, workers' organizations, and various social ministries concerned with labour, education, health and welfare.

Projects are the building-blocks of employers' programmes on child labour. Employer projects on child labour have selected specific target groups in particular sectors, using one or a selected range of interventions over a set period of time. Section 6.2 highlights examples of child labour projects addressing a wide variety of concerns in specific economic sectors, such as tea, coffee and sisal estates in Africa; the manufacture of steel, footballs and carpets in Asia; and the footwear and citrus fruit industries in Latin America.

Projects vary in objectives and types of output and activity. Two of the most promising examples of employer projects at the workplace or community level are those concerned with expanding the access of working children to education and training, and those whose primary objective is the provision of protected work and income-earning opportunities.

Building alliances

There are no "quick fixes" to the complex problem of child labour, which is closely related to the level of economic and social development in a country. Economic disparities between countries make it unrealistic to expect developing countries to afford the same facilities for their children as industrialized ones. Similarly, employers' organizations in developing countries are constrained in terms of available resources and institutional capacity. Nevertheless, employers' organizations have unique strengths on which they can capitalize, particularly in the areas of advocacy, awareness-raising, and policy development, and by forging alliances with other concerned stakeholders who have a proven track record in combating child labour and who share the same objectives (see Chapter 9). Many NGOs, for example, have been innovative and dynamic in the struggle against child labour and more employers are working closely with NGOs and trade unions as part of the civil society response to child labour.

The key initial goal should be to raise the problem of child labour – its characteristics, causes and consequences – before the board or management of the national and sectoral employers' organizations in each country, making it clear that this is an issue with wide ramifications on national economic, social and human resource development.

In countries which are starting to address their child labour problems, employers' organizations can take several steps. An employers' organization interested in joining national efforts to combat child labour can identify a member of its staff to serve as a "child labour focal point". This person can play an active role on the National Steering Committee on child labour and in national networks for the elimination of child labour. Initial activities may be modest and aimed primarily at information gathering and at increasing the awareness of the problem among its own members, other sectoral business groups, and society at large. Initially, employers' organizations can work alongside and support other groups active in the area of child labour, rather than embarking on a major programme alone. In this respect, linkages with IPEC national programmes are important in ensuring coordination.

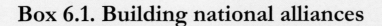

Box 6.1. Building national alliances

Who are potential local or regional partners for employers' organizations in combating child labour?

- ◆ National and local governments
- ◆ Chambers of commerce
- ◆ Individual companies
- ◆ NGOs advocating for children's welfare and rights
- ◆ Schools and other educational institutions
- ◆ Trade unions
- ◆ Consumer associations

Key issues in project design

Designing projects consistent with the mandate of employers' organizations to improve the national business environment involves the following steps:

- ◆ identifying and assessing the problem (situation analysis);
- ◆ designing the project;
- ◆ implementing the project; and
- ◆ evaluating and monitoring progress.

Prior to any action, employers' organizations must identify and assess the problem, as well as the existing framework in which it can be addressed (see also Chapter 1 and Appendix 1.4).

The major elements of problem identification are:

- ◆ the definition and description of the problem (see Chapter 3). This requires an accurate assessment of the magnitude and scope of the child labour problem in a given area, such as the geographic distribution, the age, sex, class and ethnic distribution of child workers, the family and social context, and the wider social and economic context;
- ◆ an assessment of actions which have been taken in the past; and
- ◆ an evaluation of what remains to be done and what can be done better in the future.

This requires time and structured research, but is essential in avoiding duplication of action which other groups might have taken. The information required includes statistics or studies identifying the number of working children between the ages of 5 and 14, and 14 and 18, and their main problems and needs, as well as local school enrolment figures and drop-out rates. This information may be available from official government sources and local NGOs. The checklist below may be useful for problem assessment.

Box 6.2. Resource checklist

◆ **What statistics or studies are available?**

◆ **How reliable are they?**

◆ **What action is already being taken?**

◆ **Who is involved?**

◆ **What are the economic sectors or occupations which might pose the most serious problem?**

◆ **What action can employers' organizations take on their own?**

◆ **What action can employers' organizations take as partners in a coalition?**

◆ **Does the country concerned participate in ILO-IPEC?**

The next step is the design and implementation of a project with clear indications of effective strategies to reach working children. If a project is intended to provide non-formal basic or vocational education to child workers, the views of these children and their families should be taken into account. Project implementation may involve either the provision of direct support to working children, or indirect institutional support to other partners (e.g. community groups and local NGOs) who themselves work with the children concerned and their families.

Once the project has been clearly drawn up and the roles of each partner defined, a budget should be carefully and realistically determined. Budget details should be made available so that all parties concerned can understand the specific allocations for project support.

Long-term sustainability of action on child labour requires national employers' organizations to give institutional support to these programmes and to integrate them into the broad range of action programmes in other areas. The child labour focal points (i.e. groups of employers who highlight the issue of child labour in their respective areas) in each employers' organization may find it useful to plan regular team meetings with colleagues within the organization and with the cooperating partners. Stock-taking should take place at regular intervals to evaluate achievement, success, and failures. Any necessary modifications to project implementation should ideally be made during the course of the project. It will also be useful for employers' organizations to evaluate and assess their projects during their final stage. This information is valuable in identifying "best practices" to guide employers who are embarking on new programmes.

Ten steps to enhance employer action on child labour

Ten steps are suggested to improve the participation of employers and their organizations in the campaign against child labour. They provide a logical framework for action, although many of the activities described can and should be carried out simultaneously.

(1)   *Institutional development*: Designate officials in national employers' organizations and sectoral business organizations to serve as child labour focal points.

(2)   *Investigation*: Collect detailed and reliable country-level data about the exact magnitude, nature or effects of child labour in specific sectors or industries.

(3)   *Awareness-raising*: Conduct awareness-raising events aimed at particular sectors and the sensitization of society at large.

(4)   *Policy development*: Develop policy recommendations on child labour to which employers' organizations and their members can subscribe.

(5)   *Coalition building*: Form partnerships to carry out direct action in cooperation with NGOs and, where appropriate, trade unions.

(6)   *Prioritizing action*: Based upon the information collected, select particular industries in which comprehensive programmes on the elimination of child labour can be launched. Action should be guided by a focus on the most exploitative forms.

(7)   *Direct support to working children*: In partnership with coalition members, develop the role of employers' organizations in broad-based efforts to provide alternatives, such as apprenticeships, education, and training.

(8)   *Monitoring and evaluation*: Establish systematic processes to work with focal points in specific industries to measure progress in progressively eliminating child labour.

(9)   *Compiling information on "best practice"*: Compile positive initiatives undertaken by local enterprises and business organizations.

(10) *Communications policy*: Develop a systematic approach to publicizing positive action taken by employers (e.g. newsletters, media campaigns, public merit awards).

> *Employers and their organizations can take proactive and innovative steps to respond to the challenge which child labour presents. While concern about the use of child labour on the part of importers in industrialized countries is valid in view of mounting consumer pressure, instant dismissal of children may go against the "best interests" of the child if no alternatives are in place. This has been a key problem with initiatives focusing solely on the export sector, which is only a small part of the worldwide problem. Children should be removed from the workplace in a planned and phased manner to prevent them from simply being thrown unaided into a situation far worse than that which they left. Governments, employers' and workers' organizations, and other concerned stakeholders are beginning to work together towards responsible ways of transferring children from work into education, training and other activities which promote their welfare and development.*

6.2 EMPLOYER "BEST PRACTICES" ON CHILD LABOUR

The range of actions on child labour taken by employers and their organizations to date can be broken down into the following categories:

◆ general awareness-raising and policy development initiatives;

◆ prevention of child labour in specific sectors;

◆ direct support for initiatives aimed at the removal and rehabilitation of child workers;

◆ certification schemes for specific goods; and

◆ corporate and industry codes of conduct.

Awareness-raising and policy development initiatives

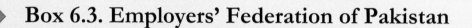

Three examples of such initiatives are provided below.

Box 6.3. Employers' Federation of Pakistan

The Employers' Federation of Pakistan (EFP) has been actively contributing to national efforts to eliminate child labour. The EFP started by raising awareness of the characteristics, causes and consequences of child labour among its own members, beginning with the translation of international instruments and national legislation on child labour into local languages. It then created a network of local employers for the protection of working children. This network is supported by a child labour unit at the EFP secretariat in Karachi and comprises 20 focal points nationwide. The EFP regularly publishes information on the activities of this network in its quarterly newsletter.

The EFP is also involved in the employer-led Skills Development Council (SDC), which aims to promote the development of vocational training programmes which are flexible, demand oriented and cost-effective, with the maximum participation of employers. The SDC also registers school leavers, uneducated youth, child trainees and industrial workers, in order to identify training needs which will ensure the availability of trained personnel and provide better employment opportunities to trainees. Through the SDC, the EFP has been involved in awareness-raising and in exhorting local employers to improve the working conditions of children. The EFP has proposed that its office-bearers, the members of its managing committees, and the leaders of local chambers and national business associations establish systems to ensure that their own companies and those to whom they subcontract do not employ child labour.

Box 6.4. Employers' Confederation of the Philippines

In April 1997, the Employers' Confederation of the Philippines (ECOP) initiated awareness-raising activities among its own members and affiliated business groups. Its objectives were to obtain a better understanding of the attitudes and concerns of member companies on the issue of child labour; formulate an employers' policy statement to reflect the commitment of Filipino employers to the elimination of all forms of child labour; raise awareness and develop advocacy positions for leading business organizations; and develop capacity within ECOP to offer services to local enterprises in the area of child labour.

To accomplish these goals, ECOP committed itself to:

◆ surveying member companies to document prevailing corporate policies, programmes and activities that may directly or indirectly affect working children. This includes a special survey examining the linkages between the formal employment sectors and child labour, primarily in the form of blind procurement and subcontracting policies;

◆ documenting "best practices" which can serve as models for other companies;

◆ conducting awareness-raising and advocacy programmes for industry associations, and affiliated organizations and members of ECOP; and

◆ establishing a "child labour focal point" at ECOP to:

  ❖ raise employers' awareness and sensitivity to the needs of working children;

  ❖ advise enterprises on options available on how best to approach and pursue child labour initiatives;

  ❖ design a system whereby employers could share access to data, information and services on strategies to eliminate child labour; and

  ❖ provide employers with a platform to participate in national policy development and implementation on child labour.

A child focal point is responsible for training activities in support of these objectives and for monitoring the progress of employer action to eliminate child labour.

Box 6.5. National Association of Colombia Industrialists

A number of employers' organizations have adopted policies in the area of child labour. One example is a resolution adopted by the National Association of Colombia Industrialists (ANDI) in December 1996. Such statements serve the dual purpose of bringing greater attention to the issue of child labour and of providing policy guidance to individual companies.

Resolution on Child Labour by the Board of Directors of the National Association of Colombia Industrialists

Considering:

(a) That it is the Association's duty to foster the application and respect of ethical values among the employer community and society as a whole;

(b) That in every work relationship respect for individual dignity must prevail;

(c) That the rights of children and young people must be upheld, so that they are protected against economic exploitation and against performing any work which may be dangerous or which interferes with their education, their leisure, or their physical, mental, spiritual, moral or social development in general;

(d) That the lack of education and technical training among children and young people prevents them from enjoying better working and social conditions in a world which requires people to be increasingly qualified; and

(e) That, despite the difficulties in evaluating the extent of the problem, recent studies indicate that at least 2,447,000 youngsters between the ages of 9 and 17 work in our country – that is, almost 90 per cent of the children and young people in that age group, who are suffering from poverty and misery, are performing some kind of work.

Resolves:

(1) That its members will not engage for work any individual of less than 18 years of age.

(2) To invite its members to check whether those people with whom they have contracts – such as contractors, clients, distributors, agents, subcontractors, etc. – do not employ any persons of less than 18 years of age.

(3) To request that, when they have dealings with community or cooperative type enterprises, whose activities encompass work which involves family groups, including youngsters of less than 18 years of age, enterprises ensure that the rights of those children and young people are not violated and that their working time allows for education and recreation.

(4) To request the Executive President of the Association to continue supporting efforts to abolish the employment of children and young people in other sectors of Colombia's economy, and to assist in the design and implementation of rehabilitation, training and recreation programmes for displaced children and youngsters.

Employer action to combat child labour in specific sectors

Once an employers' organization has established a general policy framework on child labour, it is possible to follow up with more focused activities in particular sectors (including the informal sector) where child labour may pose a particular challenge. Such action is preceded by an information-gathering stage in which sectors and representative business associations are identified as partners in the design of direct programmes to prevent child labour.

Five examples of such actions are described below.

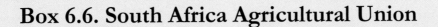

Box 6.6. South Africa Agricultural Union

The South Africa Agricultural Union (SAAU), a member of Business South Africa (BSA), participated in outreach programmes with the ILO, UNICEF, and the Departments of Labour, Education, and Health, to examine the working conditions of minors in the agricultural sector.

It developed a policy on child labour which sets out the following conditions under which children may engage in light work:

◆ with the full consent of the child and its parents, preferably in writing;

◆ no forms of bonded child labour should be allowed or tolerated;

◆ the work to be performed by children should contribute to their social and possible career development;

◆ the mental and physical ability of children must be taken into consideration in deciding whether or not to employ them and in determining what tasks they should perform;

◆ the working hours should be limited to no more than ten per week (two per day) during school terms and 25 per week (five per day) during holidays; and

◆ a working child should be paid a market-related wage.

The SAAU policy also stipulates that compulsory education should be supplemented by an effective schooling infrastructure to enable children in rural areas to attend school within reach of their homes.

Box 6.7. All-Indian Organization of Employers

The All-Indian Organization of Employers (AIOE), the national employers' organization in India, has taken a multi-pronged approach involving employers and their organizations, trade unions and workers, parents of working children, and opinion leaders. The project is being implemented in five cities/areas (Hyderabad, Pune, District Sagar, Chennai-Madras, and Ferozabad) with the help of the regional Chambers of Commerce. It seeks first to improve the working conditions of children while devising plans of action for the replacement of child workers with adult workers. The AIOE has appointed a senior staff member to serve as the focal point for child labour activities and to coordinate this work.

The chief objective of the project is the sensitization and modernization of industries where there is a prevalence of child labour. The sectors selected to take part in this activity were the bangle industry, the stainless steel industry, the *bidi* (cigarette) industry, the hotel industry, and small automobile garages and workshops. The AIOE collaborated directly with the Stainless Steel Manufacturers Association in October 1996, starting with a survey of working children, the parents of working children, employers of the children, and trade unions. The AIOE persuaded steel manufacturers that the use of child labour in their industry would result in the rejection of exports by developed countries. The members of the Association agreed not to hire additional child labourers and to start an educational fund for working children. Social workers helped to familiarize individual employers and the families of working children with the implications of the recent Indian Supreme Court directives against child labour. Employers began to support the gradual phasing-out approach, and to create better working conditions, on the proviso that they continue to receive encouragement and assistance from the Government.

The local Chamber of Commerce affiliated with this project – the Southern India Chamber of Commerce and Industry (Madras) – has in turn developed its own action plan to combat child labour. It involves the following components:

- focused removal of child labourers in selected manufacturing units;
- creation of a permanent fund for rehabilitation of child labourers with contributions from industry, chambers of commerce, employers of child labour and other organizations;
- psychological analysis of child labourers and the impact of child labour on society;
- educating parents of child labourers through adult education programmes;
- charting an alternate income-generating programme;
- monitoring establishments employing child labour; and
- freezing further recruitment of child labour.

In early 1997, the AIOE organized a regional seminar in Chennai-Madras on the elimination of child labour in collaboration with IPEC and the Southern India Chamber of Commerce and Industry (SICCI). As a follow-up to this seminar, SICCI supported the creation of a permanent fund – financed by industry, chambers of commerce, employers of child workers, and other organizations – to maintain rehabilitation programmes for children. This fund is managed by a combined group of trustees drawn from each of the above groups. The SICCI is now monitoring other sectors in the region where child labour occurs, and continues to impress upon its members the need to freeze further child employment in their units, to devise plans for the gradual phasing out of existing child labour, and to establish strategies for the rehabilitation of these children, including flexible and relevant education.

Box 6.8. Federation of Kenya Employers

The Federation of Kenya Employers (FKE), during the initial phases of its programme, convened regional awareness-raising workshops in which it formulated and disseminated employer guidelines on child labour.

The target group of the FKE's current programme includes selected member companies, such as the Kenya Tea Growers Association, Sasini Tea and Coffee, Mumias Sugar Co., Chemelil Sugar Co., Aheroi Rice Scheme, West Kno Rice Scheme, Hotel Keepers Association, Sisal Growers Association, and Kensalt Ltd. The aims of this programme are as follows:

◆ assisting selected companies in formulating and implementing policies and an action plan on child labour;

◆ providing technical advice and support to the selected companies willing to initiate measures to combat child labour;

◆ identifying feasible measures and activities for selected employers in the fight against child labour; and

◆ collaborating with the Government, trade unions, NGOs, and other interested parties in fighting child labour.

The main activities which have been carried out under this programme include:

◆ conducting field visits to selected companies to evaluate the working conditions and hazards faced by working children;

◆ holding discussions with the management and workers of selected companies to draw up a policy and plan of action;

◆ preparing action plans at the sectoral level to guide effective employer interventions to combat child labour;

◆ establishing a Working Children's Welfare Committee within each selected company to oversee the implementation of the above action plan;

◆ formulating guidelines for the Welfare Committee established in each company;

◆ preparing a comprehensive report at the end of the programme; and

◆ conducting follow-up visits to the selected companies.

A child labour unit has been established by the FKE under its Research and Information Department. A column on child labour has also been incorporated into the FKE quarterly newsletter. Employer guidelines on child labour have been issued, which focus on:

◆ adopting more aggressive methods of recruiting adult workers in labour surplus areas;

◆ establishing working norms for various activities in the plantation sector and other areas of work for children that are appropriate to their ages;

◆ providing longer and more frequent rest periods;

◆ providing regular medical check-ups;

◆ providing protective clothing and devices, field shelters and subsidized midday meals, where applicable, as well as safe and comfortable transport to and from work.

The FKE monitors application of these guidelines and assists its members in formulating internal company policies and action plans on child labour which take their individual situations into account.

Box 6.9. Association of Tanzania Employers

The Association of Tanzania Employers (ATE) started with raising awareness of the extent of child labour on sisal estates in 1995. An initial workshop gave estate owners and managers the opportunity to discuss child labour and the improvement of general working conditions, for example, through the development of piecework tasks organized according to the capacity of child labourers. One outcome of the workshop was an agreement by the participating employers to exclude working children from tasks which are dangerous and hazardous, provide protective gear, set up a cooperation arrangement with teachers and parents to curb child labour, and improve school enrolment and education standards in primary schools located on the estates.

The workshop also defined short- and long-term goals for sisal estate owners and managers. Long-term goals included action to improve labour inspection by providing inspectors with transport, and establishing credit facilities to provide opportunities for workers in the informal sector to generate income. Another was the establishment of secondary day school and vocational training centres, along with the establishment of dispensaries, welfare, and day-care centres. Short-term action identified by the employers included the provision of protective gear, introducing payment-by-results schemes to improve the earnings of adult employees, and prohibiting child labour in hazardous tasks. To ensure effective implementation of this programme, the ATE recommended that committees be established to oversee follow-up on the action programmes. These committees were recommended to be made up of the sisal estate owner, the regional labour and education offices, trade unions, and community leaders.

The ATE is currently working to assist its members in the tea and coffee plantations in Tanga, Mbeya and Arusha regions, where children below 15 years of age, including primary school drop-outs and others not yet enrolled in school, engage in harvesting. The ATE organized sensitization seminars for the owners and managers of six tea plantations with a high incidence of child labour in the Arusha region during which the ATE assisted its members in formulating action plans for the prevention of child labour and the protection of child workers.

Box 6.10. Turkish Confederation of Employer Associations

In 1993-94, the Turkish Confederation of Employer Associations (TISK) conducted four seminars in Ankara, Adana, Bursa and Istanbul in which local employers assessed the causes of child labour. They determined the primary factors to be rapid population growth, an inadequate education system, and the economic and social structure of families. These seminars presented the situations of children working in both the formal and informal sectors and in large industries, while academics presented information on children's social security rights and benefits.

In a second phase, TISK focused on the small and medium-sized employers in the metal industry. This particular target industry was selected because the results of a survey carried out by the Ministry of Labour and Social Security's Labour Inspectors revealed that children working in this sector are at particularly high risk. Three industrial sites in Istanbul were selected to implement the programme. In each of these sites, 100 small-scale enterprises – a total of 300 employers – were reached.

In the course of field studies, information on the formal apprenticeship system was supplied to small-scale industry employers to increase their awareness of child labour issues. Surveys were carried out by the teaching staff of the Apprenticeship Training Centres to provide the best information on the system to employers. TISK encouraged employers to register the children participating in apprenticeship programmes of the Apprenticeship Training Centres of the Ministry of Education.

At the recommendation of the Turkish Ministry of Labour, TISK also focused on improving the working conditions of the children employed in the metal sector. Seminars were held in 1997 to identify appropriate measures, for example through the control of dangerous gases, improved ventilation of the workplaces, and the modification of ergonomic conditions. Several workshops were held for the purpose of outlining, with the cooperation of national experts and TISK member associations, the content and design of a booklet entitled *The risks of child labour and the measures to be taken in the metal sector*. This book was published by TISK in July 1997.

TISK has also published a book entitled *Child labour in Turkey*, which describes the activities carried out to date on child labour. It summarizes statistics compiled by the State Institute of Statistics, including information on the age of the working children and their economic activity, and gives an overview of child labour legislation in the country, as well as TISK's views on the child labour problem and strategies to combat it in Turkey.

Direct support for the removal and rehabilitation of child workers

Employers' organizations and their members have also undertaken direct action programmes to remove and rehabilitate children working in a particular industry. Because these types of intervention are generally complex, significant resources and broad social mobilization are required to ensure that the best interests of the children are safeguarded.

Examples of direct support are found below.

Box 6.11. The garment industry in Bangladesh

The garment industry in Bangladesh is an example of the dangers of precipitate action. In 1992, the threat of possible trade sanctions under proposed legislation in the United States, its major market, created panic in the industry. There is evidence that employers dismissed children in an effort to forestall possible trade sanctions. This led to a transfer of child workers largely to the informal sector, which posed even more dangers to the children because of the unregulated nature of this work.

In response, a positive initiative was undertaken by a broad social alliance. On 4 July 1995, the Bangladesh Garment Manufacturers and Export Association (BGMEA) signed a Memorandum of Understanding (MOU) with the ILO and UNICEF aimed at the elimination of child labour in the garment industry and the provision of credible alternatives.

ILO-IPEC led in setting up the monitoring and verification system, and the compensation system, while UNICEF concentrated on establishing educational facilities available near the children's homes. A project known as the Verification and Monitoring System for the Elimination and Prevention of Child Labour in BGMEA Factories and the Placement of Child Workers in School Programmes was launched, the core elements of which are as follows:

◆ conducting, during 1995, a survey to identify the children working in the garment industry;

◆ developing and implementing an experimental monitoring and verification system to remove child workers under the age of 14 from garment factories and to prevent other children from entering employment in such factories;

◆ withdrawing over 10,000 children under the age of 14 from work in garment factories and enrolling them in special education programmes; and

◆ paying partial compensation to the children and their families for the loss of income and to enable the children to participate in the education programmes.

The BGMEA collaborated with ILO-IPEC on a monitoring and verification system to ensure that BGMEA factories and their subcontractors did not employ children younger than 14.

Prevention and monitoring

IPEC has set up an external and internal workplace monitoring system to identify the occurrence of child labour in the football-making industry in Sialkot and to ensure its phase-out. The monitoring team collaborates with the participating manufacturers, who are responsible for internal monitoring. The monitoring system for the Sialkot football industry is based on the principles and concepts of the monitoring system developed by the ILO for the garment industry in Bangladesh.

The ILO's external monitoring programme started on 1 October 1997, with the recruitment of 15 monitors and one national team leader. The monitoring team is supervised by an ILO international expert on the subject. The initial period was spent in thoroughly training the monitors, drawing up zones and doing test field runs. Sialkot district was divided into seven zones and each zone was assigned a team of two monitors, with a defined frequency of surprise visits each month.

Twenty-eight child labour monitors were trained and were responsible for inspecting factory sites in Dhaka and Chittagong, and for monitoring school attendance. Close collaboration has been forged between the ILO, BGMEA and the Government.

Out of 1,314 factories inspected between January and April 1997, 12 per cent were found to employ children, a significant drop from 1995 and 1996, when, respectively, 43 per cent and 34 per cent of the factories surveyed were found to employ children. In the event of an infraction of the agreement, the name of the violating manufacturer is reported to BGMEA for further action. The penalty for an infraction can either be a fine of US$1,000 or, in the case of a repeat violation, a temporary withdrawal of the manufacturer's export licence.

In collaboration with the Social Investment Bank Ltd. (SIBL) Bangladesh, a system has been set up for the disbursement of an allowance to compensate the families of the ex-working children for loss of income. SIBL is in charge of disbursing the allowance, which is contingent on the regular school attendance of the children. As of 31 January 1997, 8,031 former garment child workers had been enrolled in 316 schools. Four schools have introduced skills training programmes, which are gradually to be extended to other schools.

To enhance the support base, UNICEF has been involved in the design and support of non-formal education programmes, which are operating through close collaboration with respected local NGOs such as the Bangladesh Rural Advancement Committee (BRAC).

The vocational career-oriented curricula envisaged for the second phase of the project is to include para-skills training (short-term and low-cost light vocational courses), pre-vocational education (introduction to occupations), and career counselling. In addition, the scope for entrepreneurship training and mainstreaming to established vocational training schools will be explored through a working partnership with established vocational institutions in Bangladesh. The project will also aim to enhance the capacity of local institutions and agencies to implement vocational training schemes.

Box 6.12. The sporting goods industry in Pakistan

Another industry-based employer initiative aims to eliminate child labour in the manufacture of footballs in Sialkot, Pakistan. The Partners' Agreement was signed in 1997 by the Sialkot Chamber of Commerce and Industry, the ILO and UNICEF. The Agreement marks the first time that local manufacturers and exporters, as well as their international counterparts in an entire industry, have cooperated closely with the ILO to phase out child labour and to ensure that viable alternatives are provided.

The Agreement led to a joint project aimed at eliminating child labour in the manufacture of footballs through voluntary participation of manufacturers. The project is implemented jointly by the ILO, UNICEF, the Sialkot Chamber of Commerce and Industry (SCCI), Save the Children – United Kingdom, Pakistan Bait-ul-Mal (Government Welfare Fund Department) and Bunyad Literacy Community Council, a local NGO.

The aim of internal monitoring is to provide data which is cross-checked by the external monitoring system. Participating manufacturers have each appointed a senior manager to supervise the company's internal monitoring. The internal monitors are responsible for collecting and providing the following data on a regular basis to the external monitors:

◆ the names and contact information of all stitching centres;

◆ the names, addresses and ages of all stitchers working in the stitching centres run by the manufacturers;

◆ the names and addresses of the stitching centres run by the subcontractors;

◆ the names, addresses and ages of all stitchers working for the subcontractors; and

◆ the estimated number of stitchers necessary to reach target production.

The participating manufacturers are to set up stitching centres within a given time frame as follows:

◆ within six months of joining the programme, the registered stitching centres should represent at least 25 per cent of the yearly target production;

◆ within 12 months of joining the programme, the registered stitching centres should represent at least 50 per cent of the yearly target production; and

◆ within 18 months of joining the programme, the registered stitching centres should represent 100 per cent of the yearly target production.

All stitchers younger than 14 are to be placed in the social protection programme, and a qualified member of the family is to be offered to take the place of the child worker.

Social protection

The children withdrawn from football stitching and others affected by the monitoring programme are not left to wander off to other work situations. The IPEC social protection programme provides these children and their families with alternatives, including non-formal education. The programme works closely with the families and the communities. The focal point for the social protection services in the communities of varying size and nature are the Village Education and Action (VEA) Centres, or *Umang Taleemi Centres* (UTCs), as they are known locally. These form a network of activity centres in the football stitching communities in Sialkot district. By the end of the first six-month period about 3,000 children and their families, of the 5,400 to 7,000 targeted, were already in the social protection programme, through some 90 Village Education and Action Centres. Prior to joining the social protection programme, about half of these children were stitching footballs full time, and most of the others were helping their families with football-related work.

Getting working children to accept educational programmes and services requires considerable mobilization and awareness-raising with the children and their families, particularly if the children are earning well. The children are offered no stipends or family allowances on joining the programme.

A local partner NGO and IPEC have developed assessment and review instruments to measure progress and enable the sound monitoring of social protection components of such child labour programmes and projects. The success and impact of this project has encouraged the carpet manufacturers in Pakistan to develop a similar Prevention and Monitoring Programme in the carpet industry, which was launched in 1999.

Box 6.13. A tripartite campaign in Italy

Employers' organizations in developed countries have provided assistance for child labourers in developing countries. One example is the campaign in Italy by the ILO's tripartite constituents – Italian trade unions, the Confederation of Italian Industry (CONFINDUSTRIA), and the Italian government – and the national committee for UNICEF. A protocol was signed on 29 February 1996 committing workers to donate one hour or one day of their wages to benefit working children in developing countries. The participating employers agreed to match these contributions. A Conference entitled "Italian Working World Against Child Labour" was held in Rome, where a contribution of over US$ 1.66 million was raised for IPEC and UNICEF activities to combat child labour in Bangladesh, Nepal and Pakistan.

The Italian financial contribution stipulates that its supported projects must have a strong element of involvement of the workers' and employers' organizations in 44 countries. The project's immediate objectives are to strengthen the capacity of trade unions and employers' organizations in the designated countries to fight against child labour at both the national level (policy formulation, public awareness campaigns) and at the community and workplace level (direct assistance to working children). The programmes supported by the Italian fund are targeted at the garment industry in Bangladesh, children in bonded labour in Nepal, and surgical instrument manufacturing in Pakistan.

Box 6.14. The informal sector in Bolivia

Employers' organizations have been involved in efforts to provide rehabilitation to former child labourers in the informal sector. For example, the *Confederación de Empresarios Privados de Bolivia* (CEPB), the central employers' organization in Bolivia, has a private foundation called the National Training and Skill Development Foundation, which it established for the purpose of training manual labourers. Branch training centres are located in each of the major cities in Bolivia. With the support of IPEC, the CEPB established a pilot training centre in Santa Cruz to upgrade the technical skills of adolescents between the ages of 12 and 16. This programme – "A Beginning, A Future" – is designed for street children. During late 1995 and early 1996, the CEPB, with the assistance of local NGOs, recruited 430 children who were working on the streets of Santa Cruz (selling cigarettes, newspapers, flowers, or as shoeshiners, etc). These young people were enrolled in a skills development programme run by the CEPB, which is carried out in four cycles of ten weeks each in the following subjects:

◆ metal mechanics;

◆ automotive mechanics;

◆ embroidery and sewing;

◆ basic electronics; and

◆ toy craftsmanship.

Daily transportation for the young people to and from various locations in Santa Cruz and the training centre is provided by the CEPB. The courses are held five days per week, for two hours each day, with breaks for a snack provided by the CEPB. The course work is 30 per cent theory and 70 per cent practical training, and is overseen by a social worker/teacher hired by the CEPB. Although this is an experimental project, the success thus far has been impressive. Despite the fact that course attendance is not compulsory, only 4 per cent of those children who have entered the programme to date have dropped out. Those working with the programme have already identified the positive impact on the young people, including a marked improvement in their attention spans, discipline, overall hygiene, and motivation for work and learning. In addition to the technical training courses, leisure activities are organized for the young people, including football matches, folklore music sessions, dance evenings, and Christmas craft bazaars where their products are sold.

The broad goal of the CEPB programme is to build up the children's self-esteem. The aim of the project's second phase is to integrate the children who have completed the training into specific industry branches. Agreements have been signed for this purpose between the CEPB and the sectoral associations and enterprises with which it is affiliated, especially in forestry, tourism, and commercial industries. Many corporations (including multinationals such as Coca-Cola) are also actively supporting this programme. The CEPB is motivating other branches of the private sector to initiate similar measures to upgrade the skills of children who are working in the informal sector, and plans were underway to expand the number of training centres to ten. The CEPB also envisages the creation of a scholarship programme for children who lack sufficient resources to attend school, and is working towards the development of micro-enterprises (such as gardening and bakeries) where these adolescents can work after completion of their study course.

With a view to sharing their experiences with other employers' organizations in the subregion, the CEPB hosted the first Ibero-American Employers' Subregional Seminar on the Elimination of Child Labour in 1998.

6.3   CORPORATE INITIATIVES ON CHILD LABOUR

Labelling or certification schemes

A labelling or certification scheme aimed at the elimination of child labour, often referred to as "voluntary social labelling", involves affixing a ticket or label on goods to certify that they have not been manufactured by children. Labelling and certification schemes have been developed by many retailers and manufacturers who have come under criticism from civil and human rights groups for outsourcing to suppliers in developing countries where child labour is a problem. Some employers' associations in developing and developed countries have initiated certification and labelling schemes to prevent the boycott of their goods. The primary objective of these schemes is to inform consumers about the social conditions of production, and to assure them that the item they purchased was produced under fair and equitable working conditions, without the use of child labour.

According to an ILO study[2] most voluntary social labelling initiatives share the following features:

◆ the physical labelling of certain products, or of the retail outlets which sell specific products, by using either a descriptive label or a logo that has specific social meaning for its sponsors. The label or logo implies that certain social standards have been met in production;

◆ an outreach to consumers to inform them of the importance and social implications of purchasing the labelled products rather than any others;

◆ monitoring to ensure that the standards which the label promises to uphold are being maintained in the countries of production; and

◆ the collection of a levy from the retailers or importers to improve working conditions in the country of production.

Despite a number of common features, labelling schemes may vary widely in their objectives, target groups and means of operation. Problems most often associated with labelling include the limited extent of monitoring and inspection, the frequent lack of transparency for consumers and the unsure fate of the children working in industries targeted by labelling initiatives.

The ILO study suggests that labelling may offer prospects for helping some working children but must be used as part of a series of activities within a broader policy and strategy. This should include appropriate labour market legislation and oversight; the availability of educational and other alternatives for children; and awareness-raising among parents, employers' and workers' organizations, and the public at large. The study concludes that, within this larger picture, social labelling may establish a long-term place for itself as one way of helping children. However, the ILO is currently carrying out more in-depth research to assess the effectiveness and impact of social labelling on child labour.

---

[2] J. Hilowitz: *Labelling child labour products, A preliminary study* (Geneva, ILO, 1997).

Corporate codes of conduct

Codes of conduct are commitments made by industry groups or individual companies to uphold certain labour standards in their own direct operations and in those of their subcontractors. Such codes (also frequently known as "codes of ethics") are principally aimed at international trading arrangements in which products for the developed world are produced in whole or in part in developing nations. Companies sometimes develop these codes in response to consumers who manifest their concern that companies based in developed countries may be producing goods in developing countries where inferior working conditions exist.

Some corporate codes of conduct are general in nature and cover issues of basic business ethics. These codes often do not discuss specific issues, nor do they include methods of enforcement (80 per cent of codes of conduct fall into this category). Certain companies have gone beyond statements of general ethics and developed codes of conduct which specify the standards to be achieved and the methods of enforcement. Codes can either be limited to directly controlled activities, or be applied to contractors or subcontractors who do business with the company. Companies generally develop a name to identify their codes of conduct – such as "Global Sourcing Guidelines" (Levi Strauss), "Code of Business Practices" (International Council of Toy Industries) or "Statement of Responsibility" (American Apparel Manufacturers Association). These agreements, which are entered into on a voluntary basis by the company or industry, are often important to the company or industry image.

Industry codes of conduct

In an effort to ensure a harmonized standard and coordinated action within a specific industry, several industry associations in both developing and developed countries have adopted codes of conduct to which companies within the industry may subscribe.

Selected examples are given below.

IOE views on voluntary codes of conduct and labelling

Although the IOE does not object to truly voluntary codes of conduct and labelling schemes, it has made clear its opposition to officially sponsored, endorsed or promoted "voluntary" schemes which border on official boycotts. This is based on the belief that such measures risk trade distortion, and violate the spirit and possibly the letter of the rules of an open trading system. The IOE is opposed to the imposition of monitoring by an outside party of individual company compliance with a voluntary code of conduct, except where a firm or organization is voluntarily retained by a company or group of companies for the purpose of helping attain the goals or benchmarks of the code.

While the IOE believes that the intention of voluntary codes of conduct is laudable, it views such initiatives as often limited in their ability to address the root causes of child labour. This is due not only to their very general nature, but also to the difficulties encountered in their implementation and in the monitoring of their provisions. Corporate codes of conduct, whether they be broad codes of ethics or issue-specific codes focusing on

Box 6.15. Charles Veillon S.A.

Veillon is a major Swiss mail-order fashion apparel and home furnishings catalogue company. In March 1994, a television documentary on child labour alleged that a major home furnishing retailer had unwittingly sold hand-knotted carpets produced by children working under dangerous conditions. At the time of the documentary, this company was one of the largest home furnishing companies in Switzerland, and Switzerland was one of the top ten importers of hand-knotted carpets in the world.

This incident prompted Veillon to accept a proposal by the Swiss-based *Association François-Xavier Bagnoud* (AFXB) to develop a supplier code of conduct and independent monitoring programme. The proposal called for a transparent standard on forced child labour and an independent monitoring system to verify suppliers' adherence to the new standard.

The policy developed by Veillon set two major goals: the elimination of child labour and the creation of conditions enabling children to acquire a basic education. In the initial stages of the project, Veillon discussed the policy with its buyers to ensure its implementation in a spirit of cooperation and partnership. In the second phase, the independent experts responsible for monitoring met with each of the partners to explain the monitoring techniques to be followed. It was also stipulated that the monitors would provide advice where appropriate on solutions to the individual challenges which each supplier faces in eliminating child labour.

Veillon explained to its partners that the monitoring system would involve ongoing cooperation with an NGO able to guide and advise companies in the area of child labour. Veillon obliged any partner wishing to consolidate its commercial relationship on a durable basis to respect the code of conduct and to agree to the monitoring of compliance with the code. In practical terms, Veillon stipulated that the independent experts responsible for monitoring must be able to:

◆ freely visit, with no restrictions whatsoever, all the premises considered necessary in the exercise of their mandate;

◆ hold an in-depth dialogue with the person or persons responsible for the company, so as to obtain the information needed for monitoring working conditions;

◆ speak freely to the persons of their own choice employed in the workshops, in the absence of any third parties, and with no pressure or subsequent retaliatory action against such persons;

◆ ensure that workers leave the production premises at the end of the day and that, if work continues at night, no children are employed during the night hours; and

◆ ascertain whether any adolescents who are employed receive a basic education.

In 1996, Veillon's executive council agreed to make a contribution of 35,000 Swiss Francs to AFXB to support its ongoing child welfare programmes, which included the implementation of the pilot monitoring programme of Veillon's principal suppliers in India. Prior to this, AFXB had received no compensation from Veillon. The executive council also approved AFXB's recommendation to support MALA, a non-profit foundation which had developed an innovative project for working children in the carpet-weaving region of India, providing basic education to the children, along with hot meals and basic health care.

Box 6.16. The World Federation of the Sporting Goods Industry

The World Federation of the Sporting Goods Industry (WFSGI) has made it a priority over the last few years to address child labour concerns. In August 1997, the WFSGI unveiled a model code of conduct which was developed by its Internal Committee on Ethics and Fair Trade. The provisions of this code include the following:

◆ member companies and the companies to which they subcontract should operate under full compliance with national and local laws, rules, and regulations relevant to their business operations;

◆ member companies should follow minimum labour standards regardless of the national legal framework, particularly in the areas of forced and child labour, non-discrimination in employment, freedom of association and collective bargaining;

◆ workers should be paid at least the minimum legal wage or a wage that is consistent with local industry standards, whichever is the greater. Wages should be paid directly to the worker in cash or an equivalent. Information relating to wages should be available to workers in an easily comprehensible form, and wage rates for overtime should be higher than the rates for regular hours of work. Employers should not require a work-week in excess of 60 hours, including overtime, on a regular basis. Workers should have at least 24 consecutive hours rest per week on a regular basis, and should benefit from annual paid leave; and

◆ member companies should take measures to ensure that no children are employed under 15 years of age (or 14 in countries with insufficiently developed economies and educational facilities), or children who are younger than the age for completing compulsory education if that age is higher than 15. No children should be involved in any employment which jeopardizes their educational, social or cultural development.

The WFSGI also encouraged its members to draw up their own specific codes of ethical conduct, building upon the industry-wide framework.

child labour, generally do not reach children who are working in the informal sector in the most hazardous conditions.

The IOE takes the view that employers can be more effective in making a positive contribution towards international efforts to eliminate child labour by joining forces with broad national-based coalitions to raise awareness and to provide long-term solutions for working children and their families. The IOE has stated that it will continue to work closely with the ILO's Bureau for Employers' Activities and IPEC to identify best practices of employers in the area of child labour and to provide technical assistance for effective employer action programmes which attack the problem at its roots.

Box 6.17. The Brazilian citrus fruit industry

In 1990, the Brazilian toy manufacturers established the Abrinq Foundation in collaboration with UNICEF to "ensure respect for the rights of the child in compliance with national and international standards". The Foundation aims to promote business involvement in proposals for addressing the commercial exploitation of children through political action in defence of children's rights and through the dissemination of exemplary business actions. As part of the strategy to combat child labour, Abrinq developed a "Child Friendly Corporation Seal" which is awarded to companies who do not employ children under the age of 14.

The Abrinq Foundation approached potential partners at the national level, among which was the Citrus Fruit Exporters (ABECITRUS). Following initial contact, ABECITRUS called for a meeting of its members to discuss with the Abrinq Working Group for Children and Adolescents the development of a campaign for the eradication of child labourers in the citrus fruit industry.

On 28 May 1996, ABECITRUS signed a "Terms of Commitment" document with Abrinq and the State Government to collaborate with them in their campaign to eradicate child labour in rural activities and in their actions to provide schooling for all children and adolescents under the age of 14. In this agreement ABECITRUS and Abrinq agreed to:

◆ recommend to its associates that they require all suppliers and other components of the production network not to employ children in the production chain;

◆ initiate action to keep children at school;

◆ collaborate in the development of action to promote professional training for adolescents with a view to their integration into the formal job market; and

◆ lend support to the initiatives of the State Government, municipal councils and non-governmental entities for joint participation in actions foreseen under the present commitment.

The Terms of Commitment indicated that failure to comply with these stipulations would result in the termination of business and service contracts.

ABECITRUS organized the First Mobilization Seminar for the Municipal Councils of Children and Adolescents' Rights – "Children Should be at School" – together with UNICEF, the ILO, the Abrinq Foundation, the Brazilian Municipal Administration Institute (IBAM) and the Municipal Council of the City of Araraquara in June 1996. The Araraquara Pact was signed on this occasion by 18 cities to support a programme for the progressive elimination of child labour in the citrus fruit-producing region of the State of São Paulo. This Pact, and the accompanying Plan for the Eradication of Child Labour in the Citrus Fruit Producing Region of the State of São Paulo, seeks to return children to school and to devise means to maintain them there, including complementary school programmes, family guidance programmes, and income-generation schemes.

For employers' organizations which become involved in the process of developing codes, the IOE suggests that they could usefully take the following steps:

◆ carry out a survey of what other codes on child labour exist in the country;

◆ prepare a study of existing codes in order to standardize industry strategies;

◆ provide assistance in the drafting of model voluntary codes;

◆ provide assistance with the implementation of verification procedures; and

◆ organize training courses for concerned parties in the implementation of these codes.

6.4   KEY LESSONS FOR FUTURE ACTION

The examples in this report show that where employers' organizations are active players in local and national initiatives to combat child labour, they can be instrumental in raising society's awareness of the problem and can make valuable contributions to broad social alliances to provide long-term solutions. Over the long term, their actions can make a positive difference for the children toiling today in hazardous and exploitative working conditions in both the formal and the informal sectors. Several key lessons have been reported by employers taking action against child labour.[3]

The first key lesson is that it makes better financial and business sense for employers and their organizations to **be involved in the issue of child labour proactively rather than reactively.** While programmes which aim at the removal and rehabilitation of child labourers are often crucial – particularly in situations where children are working in hazardous and exploitative situations – they are at the same time extremely costly and complex, and tend to attack the symptoms of the problem rather than its roots. For this reason, employers and their organizations should not wait until they are pressured by outside groups to assess the child labour situation in their own industries. Instead, they should identify and enlist the support of other partners – governments, international and national organizations – with whom they can work together to identify how best to collaborate and to prevent child labour problems. In this respect, through their central employers' organizations, companies and sectoral organizations can directly approach IPEC for assistance in the area of policy development and action implementation.

A second key lesson concerns the importance of **building effective alliances.** No concerned member of civil society can hope to fulfil alone all the possible functions necessary to effectively curb and progressively eliminate child labour on a global scale. Because of their influential contacts in society, many employers' organizations have a comparative advantage in the areas of public advocacy and policy development. NGOs, which are generally issue specific, have a comparative advantage in designing social support programmes. For their part, most trade unions have a comparative advantage in raising social awareness of the issue. The examples of successful employer initiatives presented above were implemented through a broad coalition of actors working together. It is recommended therefore that companies and employers'

---

[3] *Employers' handbook on child labour*, op. cit.

organizations involve other like-minded partners in the design and implementation of any action to combat child labour.

The third key lesson is the importance of **prioritizing action**. There is now a much greater awareness of the scope and magnitude of child labour than ever before. The total eradication of this problem will demand significant resources and concentrated action over the foreseeable future. This, however, should not be used as an excuse for apathy. The role of employers and their organizations is crucial in identifying industries and/or sectors that pose the greatest risks to working children. Employers can begin by playing an active role in promoting the ratification of Convention No. 182 and the implementation of measures also suggested in Recommendation No. 190. These instruments will serve as the cornerstone of international efforts to eliminate child labour, beginning with its most intolerable forms. They place the immediate suppression of extreme forms of child labour as the main priority for national and international action for the abolition of child labour.

Appendix 6.1   IOE General Council Resolution on Child Labour

The General Council of the International Organisation of Employers,

Having met in Geneva on 3 June 1996 for its 73rd ordinary session,

Considering that one of the most disturbing aspects of poverty is the necessity for poor families to rely on the labour of their children,

Considering that, although the problem is complex and requires long-term action for its prevention and progressive elimination, its most intolerable aspects - namely the employment of children in slave-like and bonded conditions and in dangerous work - must be abolished immediately and unconditionally,

Concerned that children without education are denied opportunities to develop their full potential and can constrain the social and economic development of their countries,

Aware that the long-term solution to the problem lies in sustained economic growth leading to social progress, in particular poverty alleviation and universal education,

Noting that, although the solution to the problem requires the active and coordinated involvement of society as a whole, with government playing a critical role through its development plans and special education programmes, the business community has a significant contribution to make,

Noting that, while enterprises and business organizations, along with other groups in society, are concerned about child labour and have adopted policies and taken action to improve the situation of working children, further concerted action is required,

Recognizing that the positive actions taken by employers have not been adequately acknowledged and in some cases employers have been subject to unfair accusations,

Noting that simplistic solutions, which can merely throw children out of work without providing alternative means of livelihood for them and their families, often put the children concerned in a worse situation,

Further concerned that attempts to link the issue of working children with international trade and to use it to impose trade sanctions on countries where the problem of child labour exists are counterproductive and jeopardize the welfare of children,

Resolves this 3rd day of June 1996 to:

Raise awareness of the human cost of child labour as well as its negative economic and social consequences.

Put an immediate end to slave-like, bonded and dangerous forms of child labour while developing formal policies with a view to its eventual elimination in all sectors.

Translate child labour policies into action plans at the international, national, industry and enterprise levels.

Implement the plans, taking care to ensure that the situation of the children and their families is improved as a result.

Support activities targeted at working children and their families, such as the establishment of day care centres, schools and training facilities, including training of teachers, and initiate such activities wherever possible.

Encourage and work with local and national government authorities to develop and implement effective policies designed to eliminate child labour.

Promote access to basic education and primary health care, which are crucial to the success of any effort to eliminate child labour.

Calls on the IOE Executive Committee to:

a.   Create a database on companies and organizations active in combating child labour.

b.   Develop and distribute an Employer Handbook addressing child labour developments.

c.   Receive periodic reports from the IOE membership on their initiatives and other developments in the area of child labour.

d.   Report to the General Council on an annual basis as to work being done in combating child labour.

Trade unions against child labour

7

Satoru Tabusa

INTRODUCTION

This chapter provides examples of action by workers and their organizations towards the elimination of child labour. The information is based on surveys, reports, journal articles and booklets produced by trade unionists who are engaged in the fight against child labour, as well as in activities under the ILO's International Programme on the Elimination of Child Labour (IPEC) and the ILO Bureau for Workers' Activities (ACTRAV). It is designed for trade union officials at the branch and local chapter level who are considering or planning to start concrete activities to promote the elimination of child labour.

Section 7.1 establishes why child labour is a trade union issue. Section 7.2 describes action already being taken in a range of industries and regions to fight child labour, and joint initiatives with other organizations. Section 7.3 focuses on the opportunities for trade unions to take action in their own industry or locality. These range from raising awareness among fellow workers, to specifying conditions in collective bargaining agreements or codes of conduct, and to lobbying for relevant legislation. They are presented in a ten-point action guide.

7.1 WHY CHILD LABOUR IS A TRADE UNION ISSUE

The history and role of trade union involvement

From the start, trade unions have worked for the prevention of child labour and the removal of children from the workplace, and for their placement in schools. The first International Workers' Congress in 1866 called for an international campaign against child labour and, with the establishment of the ILO in 1919, the first Convention on minimum age for admission to industry was adopted. The fight against child labour has been part of the core mandate of the ILO since its inception and the labour movement has been identified as one of the key pressure groups for limiting child labour in the twentieth century.

The ILO's position is founded upon a range of international labour standards, the most important of which are the Minimum Age Convention, 1973 (No.138), and the Worst Forms of Child Labour Convention, 199 (No. 182). Convention No. 138 obliges ratifying States to undertake a national policy to ensure the abolition of child labour and to progressively raise the minimum age for admission to employment or work. It consolidates earlier instruments, and applies to all sectors of economic activity, whether or not the children are employed for wages. To complement the provisions of Convention No. 138 and to encourage the immediate suppression of the worst forms of child labour, the ILO member States adopted Convention No. 182 at the 1999 session of the International Labour Conference (see Chapter 2).

The development of protective legislation in the form of minimum age statutes, and the gradual introduction of compulsory education helped to reduce child labour in

Box 7.1. Health and safety statistics from South Africa

"In 1991 in agriculture, 381 children under 16 were killed or injured at work, 50 per cent were temporarily disabled, 7 per cent were totally disabled and 1 per cent received fatal injury. Out of 13,730 children injured in the 16-20 age group, 3 per cent were permanently disabled and 0.4 per cent were killed. Children are more liable to suffer occupational injuries due to fatigue, poor judgement, insufficient knowledge of work processes and the fact that machinery and equipment are designed for adults."

(Department of Manpower, South Africa, Annual Report 1991)

the now industrialized countries. Universal education was seen as a major factor in the development of a modern nation, and trade unions played an important part in lobbying for the transfer of children from the workplace to the classroom.

Involvement in action against child labour can also bring additional benefit to trade union organizations. Many unions have seen an increase in membership, and hitherto inactive or even dormant branches have been revitalized through these activities. Activities against child labour also bring trade unions into contact with workers in the sectors where they need better protection through unionization. For example, the All India Trade Union Congress (AITUC) found that the campaign against child labour in the slate-mining industry helped develop a new approach to trade union activity, by reaching the workers through their children. A worker commented that the image and credibility of the union had "shot up" and that the enthusiasm generated by the campaign was shared with other trade unions.

Trade unions can contribute directly and indirectly to the elimination of child labour in a number of ways. Evidence shows that there is little child labour in organized industries, and this demonstrates to other parties the benefit of trade union organization in the workplace. In addition, trade unions:

◆ are well placed to undertake information-gathering and to participate in national surveys;

◆ are often strong players in child labour campaigns;

◆ can negotiate collective bargaining agreements and codes of conduct to protect workers and children; and

◆ are able to monitor ongoing workplace practices and ensure that agreements are not abused.

Trade unions have a history of campaigning, and considerable experience of appropriate strategies to raise awareness and bring about change. International trade union organizations can assist trade unionists at national level and support their organizations and campaigns.

Trade unions can also work in partnership with other unions, NGOs and employers' organizations (see Chapters 6 and 9). At the same time, such joint action assists understanding of the specific role the trade union movement is playing in the eradication of child labour.

While trade union action against child labour is fast growing, it is also important to acknowledge the difficulties some trade unions face.

In some countries it is difficult for trade unions to be a major contributor to activities, as awareness-raising is only just beginning, and the members are not necessarily sympathetic to the need to eradicate child labour. In other cases, where there are strict regulations on organizing workers, many unions have a range of other problems to face.

In order to understand the relatively slow start of trade union action against child labour in Indonesia, Thailand, and Viet Nam, and to explore strategies to remove existing obstacles, 300 trade union leaders were surveyed. Sixty-four per cent indicated that the most relevant role for trade unions was to raise awareness, and 15 per cent felt that there should be a focus on lobbying. While all respondents agreed that child labour should be the concern of every trade unionist, technical and financial resources were not thought to be adequate to begin campaigns or take action. In each of these countries, the fast growth in the informal sector has also made it increasingly difficult for workers' organizations to organize along traditional patterns. Fundamental workers' rights to organize and to establish collective bargaining agreements have been restricted in free trade zones, and there has been an increase in subcontracting, homeworking, and piece-rate work.

Similar constraints are found in other countries. However, campaigning against child labour can help trade unions address these issues through effective liaison with and education of non-governmental organizations (NGOs), employers' organizations and governments. There is evidence that where strong trade unions exist, the occurrence of child labour is less likely.

The examples in the next section illustrate the growing activities of trade unions and how they can contribute to the elimination of child labour, even given the constraints they often face.

Box 7.2. Gold mining in Peru

"In Peru, action is limited since there is no national mine union, only a small union in the north east which does not have full-time representatives, so it is difficult for them to participate in meetings in the capital. It is also difficult to conduct surveys and take action due to the geographical conditions. There is very little union organization, more and more children are going down the goldmines, there are almost no teachers in these areas and therefore few children have the opportunity to go to school."

(Anne Brown, International Federation of Chemical, Energy, Mine and General Workers' Unions (ICEM))

7.2 HOW TRADE UNIONS ARE FIGHTING CHILD LABOUR

Trade unions are involved in the fight against child labour, working as individual unions, with national trade union centres and international trade secretariats, or with the support of international confederations. Trade unions are also closely involved in inter-agency cooperation. They are among the key players in every country where ILO-IPEC supports activities to eradicate child labour. Each IPEC participating country has a National Steering Committee on child labour in which workers' organizations are represented. A distinct contribution of trade unions is their quick dissemination of ideas within a country, through the extensive networks that they have established. Trade unions are involved at strategic and practical levels of operation by strengthening trade union organizations in combating child labour, carrying out surveys on child labour, raising awareness and taking direct action to prevent child labour and withdraw children from work in workplaces and communities.

Trade unions strengthen their capacity to address child labour issues

Institutional development is aimed at strengthening the capacity of workers' organizations to address child labour problems. This enables trade unions to develop the necessary infrastructure, skills and relevant programmes to combat child labour.

Trade unions support children, their families and communities

In many countries, trade unions ensure that children are not employed in hazardous labour, and, in partnership with other organizations, provide them with welfare services and relevant education. In this way, trade unions are able to improve conditions in their industrial sector and help children move into education or vocational training.

Trade unions raise awareness on child labour issues

Trade unions are raising awareness among their members, via publicity and poster campaigns, workshops, and other educational events. Trade unions also raise awareness within the community, with children and their families, and increasingly cooperate with other partners such as employers' organizations and NGOs in conducting anti-child labour campaigns. In addition, trade unions have raised awareness in export markets by targeting consumers (see also Chapter 8).

Box 7.3. Brazilian trade unions against child labour

Between 1992 and 1995, the *Central Unica dos Trabalhadores* (CUT) carried out a programme in 25 out of the 27 states in the country to train trade unionists on child labour issues in industries, in the informal sector and in agriculture; to provide assistance to union leaders concerning support for implementation of the laws related to children's rights; and to raise awareness on child labour among the general public.

CUT launched a national campaign with the slogan – "A child's place is in school. Say NO to child labour!". In the footwear industry and in the orange-picking sector, CUT drew attention to the use of child labour in these export-oriented industries. It also became instrumental in enforcing protective legislation for working children.

Another central trade union organization, the General Confederation of Workers (CGT), trained 120 trade union leaders and raised awareness on child labour. CGT organized meetings in five federal states where children work in the building industry, on sugarcane plantations, in textile factories, in markets, and in rural activities. The CGT focused on the hazardous conditions under which children work and the legal aspects of employing children.

The National Confederation of Workers in Agriculture (CONTAG), with over 50,000 affiliated trade union branches, organized a massive awareness-raising programme for trade unionists, workers, and the general public in 88 municipalities in eight federal states. The main objectives of the action programme were to produce and disseminate information concerning the rights of rural working children and to train trade unionists and monitors to improve collective agreement clauses. The project produced 10,000 copies of a booklet on the rights of rural working children, provided five training courses for trade union leaders and monitors, and produced a highly successful radio programme aimed at awareness-raising using a network of 200 local radio stations.

CONTAG activists were trained to support law enforcement of children's rights, to negotiate the prohibition of child labour with employers, and to participate in policy-making in municipal and state councils to protect child labourers. Recently, activities have focused on child labour in charcoal yards, sugar plantations and gold digging.

For several years, CONTAG served as the secretariat of the National Forum for the Prevention and Elimination of Child Labour. The Forum, established in 1994 and coordinated by the Ministry of Labour, includes the participation of governmental agencies concerned with child labour, employers' and workers' organizations and NGOs. It sets priorities for preventing and eliminating child labour and supports the implementation of Integrated Action Programmes by government and civil society in the fields of social assistance, education, health, law enforcement and social mobilization. CONTAG and the Forum are also involved in developing inspection and monitoring of child labour with the national government and NGOs.

Trade unions gather and disseminate data on child labour

Within trade unions and other organizations there has been an increasing recognition that basic data is scarce, and that local circumstances need to be considered in project planning. Therefore, trade unions work alongside other partners in the collection of data and the monitoring of child labour. This is an area that is becoming increasingly important, and it is likely that trade unions will expand their involvement in this field in the future. Situational analyses and needs assessments, evaluations, and information exchanges among partner organizations are essential for sound programme development. Sometimes trade union organizations have conducted surveys in particular sectors. In other instances, the research is undertaken by other agents such as universities (see also Chapter 3).

Box 7.4. Direct action by trade unions

The programme of the Bangladesh Building and Woodworkers' Federation (BBWWF) attends to children working in informal construction industries in two locations. It provides 300 working children with access to government-sponsored schools and a "food for education" programme. It also raises awareness among adult construction workers, trade union leaders and parents of working children about the hazards of child labour and the advantages of education.

The Metal Workers' Union of Bangladesh is involved in a programme to remove child labourers from hazardous conditions in automobile, welding and engineering workshops. It has provided non-formal education and technical training to 60 children, who were also given food and stipends after they were withdrawn from work. After completing this training activity, older children found work, and younger ones continued their training with an NGO.

The Trade Union Congress of the Philippines assisted three NGOs which help abused child workers. When the telephone help line identified a serious problem among child domestic helpers, trade union lawyers assisted in removing the children from their employers' homes. Despite considerable difficulties and obstruction from the employers, who had paid a cash sum for the children, the children were eventually removed to a safe place.

The Rural Workers' Union of Petrolina in Brazil organized a project for child agricultural labourers who were working long hours and handling hazardous agrochemicals. These children were removed from work and given complementary education, as well as help with formal education. They were introduced to horticultural skills, together with their parents and communities. This project will now expand to another area and will provide training in raising birds, handicrafts and marketing.

Box 7.5. Mobilizing trade unions against child labour

In Nepal, the trade unions were somewhat ambivalent about the issue of child labour until 1995, when the national-level trade unions asked IPEC to organize a workshop on child labour. During the workshop trade unions identified how they could help combat child labour in tea plantations, carpet manufacturing and construction industries, and also among the street sweepers of Kathmandu. Since then unions have been a strong force in the nationwide campaign against child labour. Workers' and employers' organizations and NGOs are currently working together to implement a programme to eliminate child bonded labour.

In India, the All India Trades Union Council (AITUC) mobilized their members against child labour in slate mining in Markapur, Andhra Pradesh:

"The slate mines in Markapur were 50 feet deep and the children working in them were mostly under 12. Women and children in the slate mines were getting the same wages. Labour laws were flouted and safety measures were non-existent. We were horrified by the scenes in Markapur, especially the sight of little ones climbing down deep mines with trembling feet. A visit to Markapur sensitized our workers more than all our workshops."

(Armajeet Kaur, All India Secretary of the AITUC)

Trade unions include child labour concerns in collective bargaining agreements

The National Federation of Workers in Agriculture (CONTAG), in Brazil, conducted training courses for trade union leaders on how to incorporate and improve clauses on children's rights, including child labour, in their collective bargaining agreements. An analysis of existing agreements was undertaken to see how child labour clauses could be incorporated into bargaining agreements. This has been a successful strategy, and other trade unions have followed their example.

The clauses relating to child labour focus on prohibiting the employment of children under 14 years of age. They also state that the employment of minors over 14 years is subject to national legislation which offers protection and restriction in relation to the employment of children and adolescents in Brazil.

Other clauses, as in the coffee plantation agreement, state that there shall be equal remuneration for men, women and minor workers above 14 years. Other agreements include educational provision for the children of workers. The collective agreement for cane plantation workers in Pernambuco provides that employers engaging more than 50 workers must guarantee free primary schooling for the children of their workers, unless there is a school within 1 kilometre of the workplace.

Box 7.6. Data collection and dissemination by trade unions

Although the gathering of data in these examples does not always directly involve trade unions at the initial stage, trade unions are none the less critical in the dissemination of information in the fight against child labour.

The economic implications of replacing child labour with adult labour were examined in the carpet and glass industries by the Centre for Organizational Research and Training, Baroda, India, in cooperation with the ILO's Employment Department. The results were presented at a workshop for the Government, trade unions, employers' organizations and NGOs. The data showed that the cost of replacing child labour with adult labour was not very great, and that some successful carpet manufacturers were able to run their businesses without child labour. Information from the major markets such as the United States indicated that the small increase in production costs would not impact on sales. The workshop also addressed other issues that encourage the employment of children, such as children's greater docility and acceptance of longer working hours. The findings also broke the myth that the nimble fingers of children are necessary for carpet making, because adult strength is needed to make high-quality carpets. This information was confirmed in an ICFTU (International Confederation of Free Trade Unions) study on child labour in 1994 which reported:

> *"In our interviews with managers of carpet weaving workshops, we asked in particular whether children's small hands were a necessary prerequisite to rapidly produce quality work. The answer was negative.... As regards quality, measured in terms of knots per square centimeter, it is in fact the adult weavers, whose strength helps them to ... produce the best-quality carpets."* [1]

The same finding was made in the gemstone industry in India, where children work under hazardous conditions. Again, children produce goods of medium quality and adults are needed for the best work.

In Moradabad, Uttar Pradesh, trade unions undertook a study on child labour in brassware production:

> *"Our survey found that in and around Moradabad, there are 22,000 children under 14 who work from the age of 5 or 6. Many of the poor parents earnestly wish to send their children to school but poverty and a general lack of schools prevents them from doing so. Trade unions have come forward to combat child labour. I know our limitations in fighting this serious problem. We are trying to help set up non-formal schools for working children."*
>
> *(Z.M. Naqvi, lawyer and local AITUC leader in Moradabad)*

The General Federation of Nepalese Trade Unions undertook a survey in the tea plantations in Nepal, to examine the nature and extent of child labour and provide the information needed to develop an action programme for the elimination of child labour in tea plantations. The results of the survey were published as a booklet entitled *LIFE – Inside Dhurmas*.

[1] Quoted in Institute for Applied Social Science and Norwegian Institute of International Affairs: *Child labour and international trade policy* (Oslo).

Box 7.7. An agreement in Uganda

The Memorandum of Understanding signed between the National Union of Plantation and Agricultural Workers (NUPAW) and the Uganda Tea Association (UTA) includes a clause on child labour, which reads:

"UTA and NUPAW agree that employment of children under the age of 18 years is not condoned and therefore the management shall not directly employ or allow the employees to bring their children in the Estates to work their task."

Trade unions advocate for codes of conduct

Codes of conduct were originally proposed in relation to the activities of multinational companies in the 1970s. In the past five or six years there has been an increasing interest in unilaterally adopted codes of conduct concerning labour practices by various companies (see Chapter 6, section 6.3.).

With the global sourcing of products, codes are becoming increasingly important. On the one hand, codes of conduct can be a company's response to consumer demand. On the other, their adoption is negotiated by trade unions to support basic trade union rights, including that of collective bargaining.

When negotiating a code of conduct, trade unions emphasize that codes need not be limited to cover child labour only, but should try to cover all aspects of core international labour standards. Codes should also include a provision for monitoring.

Codes of conduct, such as the two described below, are to be distinguished from corporate codes of conduct which are formulated by enterprises without negotiating with trade unions and which often do not cover all areas of core standards. Trade unions aim at achieving negotiated codes of conduct.

Trade unions work in partnership with NGOs, employers' organizations and governments

Over the past years collaboration between agencies has been increasing worldwide as more experience is being gained in carrying out successful measures against child labour and, as a result, trust develops between partners. The bringing together of employers' organizations (see also Chapter 6), NGOs, governments and trade unions creates a powerful tool to identify child labour abuses and eradicate them. There is a growing recognition that the complex social, cultural and economic issues underlying child labour present dilemmas to all those working in the field and that it is essential to share experience, and carefully consider, plan and implement strategies. Trade unions are well placed as a pressure group towards both employers and governments, and at the same time local trade union branches increasingly cooperate in community-based activities with a wide range of NGOs (see also Chapter 9).

Box 7.8. Code of Labor Practice for

PRODUCTION OF GOODS LICENSED
by the
SYDNEY ORGANISING COMMITTEE FOR THE OLYMPIC GAMES
and the
SYDNEY PARALYMPIC ORGANISING COMMITTEE

Agreed between the Sydney Organising Committee for the Olympic Games (SOCOG), the Sydney Paralympic Organising Committee (SPOC), the Australian Council of Trade Unions (ACTU) and the Labor Council of New South Wales. Having concurred on the necessity for effective monitoring to ensure that the Code is respected at all levels, the above organisations are continuing discussions on practical measures to achieve these objectives.

PREAMBLE

In accordance with the goal of the Olympic Movement to contribute to building a peaceful and better world by educating youth through sport practised without discrimination of any kind and in the Olympic spirit, which requires mutual understanding with a spirit of friendship, solidarity and fair play, SOCOG/SPOC recognises its responsibilities to consumers for the quality of products produced under its licensing arrangements, and workers involved in the making of SOCOG/SPOC licensed products and the conditions under which these products are made.

Each licensee awarded the right to use the SOCOG/SPOC name or logo in the manufacture and/or supply of licensed product to SOCOG/SPOC has been audited to ensure that they have appropriate standards of operation and has, as a condition of license agreement, confirmed in writing that employee work conditions meet the relevant industrial regulations.

Licensees further agree to ensure that these conditions and standards are observed by each contractor and subcontractor in the production and distribution of SOCOG/SPOC licensed products. Licensees should, prior to placing orders with suppliers or engaging contractors and subcontractors, assess whether the provisions of this Code can be met.

Each SOCOG/SPOC licensee, and each contractor and subcontractor engaged by the licensee, shall compulsorily implement and respect the following principles in the production and/or distribution of products bearing the SOCOG/SPOC name and/or SOCOG/SPOC authorised marks. Furthermore, each licensee shall warrant that these principles shall be equally imposed upon all those employed or delegated by such licensee.

EMPLOYMENT IS FREELY CHOSEN

There shall be no use of forced or bonded labour (ILO Conventions 29 and 105).

THERE IS NO DISCRIMINATION IN EMPLOYMENT

Equality of opportunity and treatment regardless of race, colour, sex, religion, political opinion, nationality, social origin or other distinguishing characteristics shall be provided (ILO Conventions 100 and 111).

FREEDOM OF ASSOCIATION AND THE RIGHT TO COLLECTIVE BARGAINING ARE RESPECTED

The right of workers to form and join trade unions and to bargain collectively shall be recognized and respected (ILO Conventions 87 and 98).

FAIR WAGES ARE PAID

Wages and benefits paid shall meet at least legal or industry minimum standards and should be sufficient to meet basic needs and provide some discretionary income.

HOURS OF WORK ARE NOT EXCESSIVE

Hours of work shall comply with applicable laws and industry standards.

WORKING CONDITIONS ARE DECENT

A safe and hygienic working environment shall be provided, and best occupational health and safety practice shall be promoted, bearing in mind the knowledge of the industry and of any specific hazards held by licensees, contractors and subcontractors.

THE EMPLOYMENT RELATIONSHIP IS ESTABLISHED AND TRAINING PROVIDED

Employers should endeavour to provide regular and secure employment. Appropriate training should be available for all employees.

IMPLEMENTATION AND MONITORING

Licensees, their contractors and subcontractors shall undertake to support and cooperate in the implementation and monitoring of this Code by:

◆ Prior to engagement, the licensee shall provide SOCOG/SPOC with written confirmation that the licensee, as a minimum, adheres to relevant international labor force standards; providing SOCOG/SPOC or its agent with relevant information concerning their operations; permitting inspection at any time of their workplaces and operations by approved SOCOG/SPOC personnel; maintaining records of the name, age, hours worked and wages paid for each worker and making these available to approved inspectors on request; refraining from disciplinary action, dismissal or otherwise discriminating against any worker for providing information concerning observance of this Code.

Any licensee, contractor or subcontractor found to be in breach of one or more terms of this Code of Labor Practice shall be subject to a range of sanctions up to and including withdrawal of the right to produce or organise production of SOCOG licensed goods as per the contractual provisions. Furthermore, licensees who fail to ensure that their contractors or subcontractors abide by the Code of Labor Practice shall be subject to the same range of sanctions.

A joint Committee comprising Representatives of the ACTU; Labor Council of NSW; SOCOG staff and the SOCOG Board shall meet as required to review reported breaches of this code and make recommendations to the SOCOG Board for action as appropriate.

Box 7.9. Code of conduct by the International Federation of Football Associations (FIFA)

"One of the trail-blazing codes of conduct... was that agreed between FIFA and the international trade union movement... it grew out of the exposure of stories... about the widespread employment of children in the stitching of footballs, mainly in Pakistan but also in India."

(Neil Kearney, General Secretary of the International Textile, Garment and Leather Workers' Federation (ITGLWF))

The Code of Labour Practice negotiated with FIFA provides that FIFA authorized marks cannot be given to footballs produced with child labour. The code includes provision for effective monitoring and consideration is being given to the provision of education and training for child labourers displaced by the implementation of the code.

The code includes a preamble stating FIFA's commitment to fair play and ethical conduct. The preamble also recognizes responsibility to customers for the quality of the product, and to workers involved in the production of FIFA licensed products. The key features of the code include:

- employment is freely chosen (no forced or bonded labour);

- no discrimination in employment (equality of opportunity and treatment);

- child labour is not used;

- freedom of association and the right to collective bargaining are respected;

- fair wages are paid;

- hours of work are not excessive (hours of work shall not generally exceed 48);

- working conditions are decent (safe and hygienic);

- the employment relationship is established (regular and secure employment);

- no excessive use of temporary or casual labour, no labour-only subcontracting;

- no abuse of apprenticeship schemes, and education and training for younger workers;

- implementation and monitoring (including licensees, their contractors and sub-contractors);

- monitoring to include:

  - relevant information concerning operations;

  - inspection at any time;

  - maintaining records of workers – age, hours worked;

  - wages paid for each worker – for inspection;

  - informing workers about the code; and

  - no disciplinary action to be taken against any worker who gives information relating to observation of the code;

- severe penalties for breach of the code; and

- interpretations of meaning of the code's provisions to be resolved by the Memorandum of Understanding on the Code of Labour Practice between FIFA and the ICFTU (International Confederation of Free Trade Unions)/ITGLWF (International Textile, Garment and Leather Workers' Federation)/FIET (International Federation of Commercial, Clerical, Professional and Technical Employees).

The international trade union movement plays a major role

The international trade union movement plays a key role in consumer and public awareness, and is committed to continue to advance the issue of child labour. Major initiatives have helped shape the way in which child labour campaigns are carried out, and support and resources have increased for projects in many countries.

The International Confederation of Free Trade Unions (ICFTU) has played a major role in the campaign, as have the International Federation of Commercial, Clerical, Professional and Technical Employees (FIET), the International Federation of Building and Wood Workers (IFBWW), the International Textile, Garment and Leather Workers' Federation (ITGLWF) and the International Union of Food, Agricultural, Hotel, Restaurant, Catering, Tobacco and Allied Workers Associations (IUF).

International trade union organizations have been able to compare experiences within countries and industrial sectors. They have up-to-date information from various sectors and have access to national networks to disseminate information. They are also well placed to advise on standards and to monitor patterns of industrial activity. International workers' organizations also play a critical role in developing codes of conduct and model collective bargaining agreements.

Box 7.10. Cooperation between trade unions, NGOs and employers' organizations

In India, the Hind Mazdoor Sabha (HMS), a national confederation, has a long history of working with NGOs to set up non-formal education centres to help combat child labour. In Rajasthan, an NGO has been able to continue its support for a school for former child workers from the gem and marble industries with help from the state branch of the All India Trade Union Congress (AITUC). The South India Chamber of Commerce and Industry in India has worked with trade unions to reduce child labour in the stainless steel industry. This is also helping to develop trade unions and improve the conditions for all workers.

In the Philippines, a strategy for trade unions and NGOs to jointly mobilize within communities in several pilot projects has resulted in the formation of 100 volunteers known as the Trade Union Anti-Child Labour Advocates (TUCLAS), who monitor and report incidences of child worker abuse in their respective workplaces and communities. The Federation of Free Workers (FFW) formed a child labour action network in three farming and fishing communities. The members of the network include local government officials, NGOs, community organizations and local trade unions.

In Kenya, the Federation of Kenya Employers (FKE) and the Central Organization of Trade Unions (COTU) have each set up child labour sections to research and raise awareness with employers and to introduce child labour issues into educational programmes and collective bargaining discussions.

Box 7.11. Gemstone production in India

In the gemstone industry in India, the employers are powerful and trade union representation is very limited. Nevertheless, the ICFTU, the Universal Alliance of Diamond Workers (UADW) and FIET have campaigned to raise awareness of child labour abuses in gemstone workshops.

"Workplaces are normally congested, poorly lit, and poorly ventilated.... These conditions, combined with long and irregular hours, cramped working positions, continuous stress and strain, are all sources of workplace sickness and injuries.

The learning process takes five to seven years. During the first two years the child does not receive any wage except for occasional remuneration, and works for ten hours a day. After two years, the children are paid Rs. 50 a month, when they actually do work worth Rs. 250-300 a month, at the very least. By the time the children are 14 or 15 years old and have acquired the skill of gem polishing, they would be earning Rs. 150-200 a month whereas adults would get Rs.500-600 for the same job." (Chandra Korgaokar, Indian Coordinator, UADW)

Owners avoid the law by managing a range of small, adjacent premises, but the international campaign has raised awareness within India, and in export markets. The campaign stresses that child labour is often a consequence of low wages paid to adult workers in a family, and that exploitation of all workers is a serious problem.

7.3 WHAT A TRADE UNION CAN DO

Many trade unions wish to start or further develop their policies, practices and strategies toward eliminating child labour. To guide them to develop a new programme, or to strengthen current programmes, this section outlines a ten-point action guide.[2]

Ten-point action guide

❶ Investigation

Gathering data on child labour is an essential contribution to its eradication. Data can be gathered formally or informally, and, if necessary, under disguise. For example, in India, trade unionists posed as tourists to gather evidence, through photographs and stories, to expose the abuse of child labour in slate mines in Markapur.

---

[2] A. Fyfe and M. Jankanish: *Trade unions and child labour: A guide to action* (Geneva, ILO, 1997).

Box 7.12. Sialkot football campaign

The IPEC programme in Sialkot, Pakistan, for the elimination of child labour in the manufacturing of footballs was started in December 1997. The programme is the result of a chain of events which was begun by an international campaign launched by the trade union movement more than a year earlier.

In early 1996, the ICFTU started an international campaign highlighting the use of child labour in the production of footballs bearing the emblems "FIFA-approved" and "Euro 96" (marking the European football championship being held that year). The campaign drew media attention to child labour in football production, particularly in Sialkot, and FIFA agreed to investigate.

Later that year, FIFA agreed to discuss with the ICFTU, ITGLWF, and FIET a code of labour practice. The code was agreed in September 1996 (see box 7.9).

In November 1996, the World Federation of Sporting Goods Industry (WFSGI) organized a special conference on child labour in London and the FIFA code of labour practice was discussed. The WFSGI, together with the Soccer Industry Council of America, which represent more than 50 sporting goods brands, launched an initiative to eliminate child labour from the production of footballs in Pakistan.

Following this initiative a Partners' Agreement was signed by the ILO, UNICEF and the Sialkot Chamber of Commerce and Industry, in Atlanta, United States, in February 1997, for the purpose of implementing a joint project to eliminate child labour in football production in Sialkot. Project activities started in December 1997.

The trade union campaign against child labour in football production is an example in which an international campaign has encouraged and made it possible for concrete action to be taken at national and local levels.

Trade unions can:

◆ gather stories, pictures and other evidence from children engaged in labour, and their families;

◆ assess the working environment in which children are working;

◆ record where child labour is being used;

◆ take part in national or industry-wide surveys;

◆ work with others to help examine child labour in the informal sector; and

◆ disseminate the information gathered.

② Institutional development

Trade unions need to establish an effective infrastructure to coordinate anti-child labour activities, and to raise awareness among members. This process can enhance trade union membership and provide a useful focus for solidarity. Most international trade union organizations have established child labour units, and are building child labour issues into their other technical assistance programmes.

Institutional development can include efforts to:

◆ form study circles on child labour as part of training and membership development;

◆ set up child labour committees and/or a child labour unit within unions;

◆ develop child labour liaison groups;

◆ include the issue of child labour in ongoing training programmes;

◆ design and develop materials for trade union courses;

◆ liaise with national trade union organizations; and

◆ attend and organize local, national or international seminars on the subject.

❸ Policy development

Policies should be used in everyday practice, and should not be a "paper tiger" with no impact in the real world. Policies should be judged by the benefits that accrue when they are implemented in workplaces or communities. Policy statements should arise out of a process of information-sharing and consultation, so that the "ownership" of the commitment to the policy is felt by a large number of people. Only then will action follow.

Policy statements can be used to:

◆ put child labour on the agenda of meetings for discussion and action;

◆ communicate and disseminate via newsletters, displays, radio, etc.;

◆ organize and attend workshops, seminars and conferences; and

◆ liaise with other child labour activists and youth organizations.

❹ Monitoring

Trade unions are well placed to observe and monitor the use of child labour, and to bring to the forefront of public attention breaches of collective agreements and codes of conduct. Monitoring requires continuous overview, not simply reporting violations. This allows trade unions to keep track of how bargaining agreements and codes are being implemented, and any gains and losses which result.

Through monitoring activities, trade unions can :

◆ bring child labour cases to light;

◆ report violations to authorities;

◆ lobby national authorities in relation to national and international standards; and

◆ track compliance under these agreements and standards.

❺ Awareness-raising

Trade unions can engage in awareness-raising activities on various trade union issues through education and training programmes at the workplace. Child labour issues can be incorporated into ongoing workers' education programmes. Alternatively, specific workshops can be used to focus attention on child labour.

Box 7.13. How to start raising awareness

Awareness-raising is personal and political. Trade unions need to consider the context in which they are working, and begin to work accordingly. If a trade union does not have experience of local or national campaigning, it can consult with those who have been active to develop an appropriate strategy.

For those at the very beginning of campaigning, this checklist might be useful:

◆ seek the support of your trade union;

◆ consult with others who have experience in other unions or national organizations, or others working in your community;

◆ seek to build alliances with others who share your commitment locally and nationally;

◆ work in a small group and keep in touch with a bigger network;

◆ find out what is happening in your area (where and how children are employed, what support is available for them and their families), and gather other relevant information to discuss with your trade union;

◆ avoid problems: work alongside others when necessary and appropriate. Long-term sustainable solutions are necessary and short-term "fixes" can cause more harm than good;

◆ plan activities such as seminars and discussion groups;

◆ publicize issues appropriately and sensitively;

◆ have a strategy for response, e.g. if local media contact your union; and

◆ use publicity materials where appropriate.

It is useful to remember that:

◆ cultural and social issues can prevent change or make it difficult;

◆ economic incentives are sometimes necessary, e.g. payment-in-kind, free schooling or food;

◆ short-term benefits alone will not change behaviour without long-term planning; and

◆ raising awareness is not always visible.

What about the media?

Trade unions have had considerable success in campaigning through the media at the local level, particularly through local language radio, and at the national and international levels through newspapers, television, radio and other electronic means. Involving the media needs to be part of a carefully coordinated campaign, and is not likely to be a first step for any trade union.

Some early campaigns have used publicity to expose the employment of children. However, this direct approach can cause problems for the children and their families, and it is now usual to carefully plan, manage and coordinate campaigns.

What if we do not have child labour in our industry?

Trade unions, even if they find little or no child labour in the sector that they organize, can still take action. For example, bank workers in Thailand were able to come to an agreement with employers that the banks would not make loans to businesses in which child labour was being used. If you want to contribute to a national or international campaign in your sector, contact your national organization for advice. Your trade union could support their work, and help with networking, gathering data or other strategies.

What if employers refuse to let unionists campaign?

Contact your national organization for advice and guidance.

Raising awareness needs to be done in a way which is appropriate to the target groups and takes into account existing levels of consciousness. Trade unions can organize seminars for their members, working children, employers, specific communities, youth organizations, NGOs and the general public.

Raising awareness and social mobilization can include efforts to:

◆ develop child labour modules in ongoing education programmes;

◆ organize seminars, conferences and workshops on child labour;

◆ use trade union media and the mass media;

◆ work alongside other organizations such as women's and youth organizations;

◆ work with employers' organizations and NGOs;

◆ work with families of child labourers; and

◆ work with teachers and social workers.

⑥ Campaigning

Trade union campaigns can:

◆ mobilize membership through awareness-raising, and work towards policy commitment;

◆ mobilize unorganized workers, marginal workforces or workers within a local community, including families of child labourers;

◆ lobby local authorities over enforcement of regulations and standards, and for appropriate educational provisions and/or reform;

◆ support the implementation of standards; and

◆ take part in industry- or sector-specific national and global campaigns, e.g. to promote codes of conduct and labour standards.

⑦ Collective bargaining

Collective bargaining agreements that have clauses excluding the employment of children directly benefit the eradication programme. These clauses also make it possible for the trade unions to work with employers' organizations to develop or implement relevant codes of conduct. Where codes of conduct have been agreed, trade unions can use these to back up collective bargaining agreements that prohibit child labour.

In relation to the eradication of child labour, collective bargaining can include measures to:

◆ build the prohibition of child labour into agreements;

◆ bargain for reform of task/piece-work systems pending their abolition;

◆ develop model agreements with employers on an industry-wide basis; and

◆ use and adapt model agreements and codes of conduct developed by international and national trade union organizations.

⑧ Direct support to children

Trade unions can:

◆ work to remove children from high risk and hazardous conditions;

◆ rehabilitate child labourers with non-formal education and training or relocation to appropriate work, or reduction of working hours;

◆ develop apprenticeship systems;

◆ support programmes to replace child workers with adult workers from the same family on an industry basis; and

◆ support development programmes in fields such as literacy, women's equality, and family income-generating activities.

⑨ Mobilization

Mobilization can include:

◆ networking with others in the labour movement;

◆ linking with NGOs and employers' organizations;

◆ establishing contacts with political organizations and the media; and

◆ participating in national anti-child labour coalitions.

⑩ Using international instruments

International labour standards can be used to support campaigns and to lobby local and national political organizations. These standards themselves are developed and strengthened when trade unions receive feedback and information on the situation on the ground.

Making use of international instruments can include:

◆ fact-gathering for national reporting and complaints;

◆ contributing to national reports; and

◆ supporting national affiliates to use the ILO and/or other United Nations supervisory structures and machinery.

Bibliography on trade union action

Anker, R.; Melkas, H. 1996. *Economic incentives for children and families to eliminate or reduce child labour* (Geneva, ILO).

Fyfe, A. 1997. *Child labour: A guide to project design* (Geneva, ILO).

—; Jankanish, M. 1997. *Trade unions and child labour: A guide to action* (Geneva, ILO).

Grimsrud, B.; Melchior, A. 1997. *Child labour and international trade policy* (Oslo, FAFO/NUPI).

International Federation of Free Trade Unions (ICFTU) Briefing. 1996. *Children in the sports goods industry in Pakistan* (Brussels, Sep.).

International Federation of Building and Wood Workers (IFBWW). 1995. *12 hours a day, every day: Child labour in the brick kilns in India*, Survey and South Asian workshop results (Geneva).

International Labour Office (ILO). 1995. *IPEC implementation report*, review of IPEC experience, 1992-95 (Geneva).

—. 1996. *Child labour: Targeting the intolerable*, International Labour Conference, Report VI, 86th Session, 1998 (Geneva).

—. Bureau for Workers' Activities. 1997. *Report of the Seminar for International Trade Secretariats on Developing National and International Trade Union Strategies to Combat Child Labour, Geneva, 7-8 April 1997.*

—. 1997. *Protecting children in the world of work*, Labour Education, 1997/3, No. 108.

—. 1997. *Showing the way: Trade unions against child labour in India* (New Delhi).

International Textile, Garment and Leather Workers' Federation (ITGLWF). 1996. *Human and trade union rights: Codes of labour practice*, paper presented to the ITGLWF Praesidium Meeting, 3-4 November 1996.

Awareness-raising

Sherin Khan

8

INTRODUCTION

> *"Child labour touches on the livelihood and survival of many millions of families and communities, as well as the comfort and prosperity of others. It inspires conflicting feelings and reactions and these are best resolved if regulatory action is complemented by dialogue, education, and information-sharing among all concerned. Hence the importance of public awareness-raising efforts in the prevention and elimination of child labour. If society as a whole recognizes that child labour is a problem, the stage has been set to stigmatize and then eradicate its most abusive manifestations. Government policy, especially the enforcement of national laws, requires public backing."*
>
> ILO: *Child Labour: Targeting the intolerable* (Geneva, 1996)

Given that child labour problems are ingrained in the socio-cultural and economic structure of society, the process to solve them effectively is complex and diverse. That is why the ILO aims at simultaneously facilitating both policy reforms and a change in attitudes within countries, among those directly concerned with the problem – children, parents and employers – and in society as a whole. These two aims are closely related. Extensive awareness-raising and social mobilization lead to a shift in attitudes about child labour in society, which in turn creates public demand for policy reforms, and thus to changes in legislation, programmes, budgets and institutional structures.

This chapter illustrates positive experiences in awareness-raising and advocacy on child labour issues emerging from recent initiatives around the world, many of them with support from the ILO and its International Programme on the Elimination of Child Labour (IPEC). It highlights important messages that can be used to overcome misconceptions and constraints posed by established socio-cultural patterns which lead to or perpetuate apathy, resistance or inaction. It focuses primarily on the communication process in the fight against child labour.

Aspects of communication

Creating awareness about child labour to bring about positive changes within society starts with awakening the minds of individuals – and consequently of the social structures within societies – by, in the first place, identifying it as a problem and then as an unacceptable state that has to be changed. To achieve this requires effective use of communication processes. Communication that aims to restructure or redefine the mindset of individuals does not generally yield immediately observable results for reasons that include resistance to change. In fact, in some cases, the initial response can very well be negative. For example, a good number of individuals from different walks of life, when first exposed to the simple but stark message that child labour is "bad", quickly respond by defending child labour on at least half a dozen premises. To bring about a change in the mindset, reinforcement of the message is generally necessary.

This reinforcement does not have to be a repetition of the same message. It can address different aspects of the issue and be relayed in different forms. Once minds have been changed and the message grasped, the redefinition of child labour as being not only unnatural but unacceptable will follow. Experience has shown that this is a precondition for action.

To have *impact*, each message passes through several stages. These can be identified as:

◆ the **initial stage** of awareness-raising;

◆ the **intermediate stage** of information dissemination, which includes some response; and

◆ the **impact stage**, resulting from adoption of the message and bringing about a change of mind.

A message can focus on any one of these stages.

Process of communication

The communication process is a "whole" and not a set of isolated features or events. The various aspects of the process are:

◆ content – **what** is communicated;

◆ sender – **who** is communicating;

◆ audience – for **whom** the communication is intended; and

◆ channels – **how** the message is transmitted.

8.1 THE MESSAGE

The message is the core of the communication process. It is sent by an individual or an organization to increase knowledge or awareness and lead to change. To bring about action for the elimination of child labour, messages have to be put out in various forms, by different sources, to numerous recipients and through a variety of channels. There are a range of messages: separating myth from reality, giving accurate information, showing the effects of child labour, throwing light on the nation's obligations under national and international legal instruments, and showing the inadequacies of the law enforcement, education, health and social welfare systems. Messages can also be aimed at providing guidance on what alternatives are available and creating alliances among and between senders and receivers.

The messages can be simple, direct and forceful, such as "stop child labour", and can use simple channels, such as posters. They can also involve entire campaigns that use multiple channels, such as the campaign in Brazil against child sexual exploitation, discussed below.

"Action against child labour can be taken now"

The conclusion is often drawn that child labour and poverty are inseparable and that an end to child labour will remain unrealistic until world poverty is ended. However, while poverty is the most important reason why children work, it cannot be said that poverty necessarily causes child labour. The picture varies, and in many poor households at least some children are singled out to attend school. Similarly, there are regions in poor countries where child labour is extensively practised, while in other equally poor regions it is not. In addition, when a child is engaged in hazardous labour, someone – an employer, a customer or a parent – benefits from that labour. This element of exploitation is often overlooked by those who see child labour as inseparable from poverty. It is also becoming more widely recognized that child labour actually perpetuates poverty, as a working child grows into an adult trapped in unskilled and badly paid jobs.

In recent years, more governments have begun to fulfil their national and international commitments, such as those under the United Nations Convention on the Rights of the Child and the ILO Minimum Age Convention, 1973 (No. 138). There has also been an active interest in the new ILO Convention (No. 182), which calls for the prohibition and elimination of the worst forms of child labour as a matter of urgency. The premise of Convention No. 182 is that some forms of child labour are so intolerable that they must be eliminated no matter what the level of development. Further, their elimination cannot wait for long-term education and poverty-alleviation strategies to be effective. At the local and international levels, governments, employers' and workers' organizations, NGOs and activists' groups are exploring ways to remove children from dangerous work situations and provide alternatives to them and their families. ILO experience, including that of IPEC, demonstrates that immediate action is feasible. The message is clear: while neither poverty nor child labour can be eliminated overnight, action can be taken now.

"Prioritize the most harmful, often invisible, forms of child labour"

Export industries are a highly visible sector in which children work. Footballs made by children in Pakistan for children in industrialized countries and adults in World Cup matches may be a compelling symbol. But in fact, only a very small percentage of child workers are employed in export-sector industries – probably less than 5 per cent – and tens of millions of children around the world work in non-export areas, often in hazardous or exploitative work or working conditions.

A study in Bangladesh, for example, revealed that children were active in more than 300 economic activities. These ranged from household work to brick-making, from stone-breaking to selling in shops and on streets, from bicycle-repair to garbage-collecting and rag-picking, and jobs in the informal sector. This assessment took into account only jobs done in cities. A total of 39 occupations were rated as hazardous for children.[1] Such a range of work by children is found in many countries.

---

[1] W. Rahman: *Hazardous child labour in Bangladesh* (Dhaka, Government of Bangladesh, 1996), pp. 2, 3.

The message needs to get through to the media that, worldwide, the overall majority of children work on farms and plantations or in private homes, far from the reach of labour inspectors and media scrutiny. Many children labour in virtual invisibility, doing dangerous work.

"Positive action and international cooperation are needed"

Having recognized and acknowledged that child labour problems exist, governments concerned have also realized that eliminating child labour requires the cooperation of other governments and organizations, and that the problems cannot be resolved overnight. Some believe that the only way to make headway against child labour is for consumers and governments to apply pressure through sanctions and boycotts. International means of pressure can be important, but sanctions affect only export industries, which, as noted above, use a relatively small percentage of child labourers. Sanctions may also have long-term unforeseen and harmful consequences and leave children worse off. Indications are that positive incentives and international commitments and cooperation will lead to much more promising and sustainable solutions. Comprehensive action through ILO-IPEC is an important demonstration of worldwide concern and a multi-pronged approach to addressing the problem of child labour. Partnerships and action are created to ensure that children removed from work have viable alternatives.

"Tradition cannot justify the exploitation of children"

It is becoming almost universally accepted that if children are to develop normally and healthily, they must not be involved in premature work and labour. Understanding the various cultural factors that lead children into work is essential. But deference to tradition is often cited as a reason for not acting against child labour. The harder and more hazardous the jobs become, the more likely they are to be considered traditionally the province of the poor and disadvantaged, the lower classes and ethnic minorities.

"Prevention is better than cure"

Rescuing and rehabilitating child victims is an expensive and difficult task. For some, the damage and trauma are so severe that it might be impossible for them to rejoin their communities or to become modern citizens. Thus prevention is not only desirable from a cost point of view, but also a humanitarian necessity. Preventing children from engaging in work is the most cost-effective measure because sustainable and long-term results in the fight against child labour will be achieved only when new generations of children are effectively prevented from entering work. The results of preventive measures are in many cases not immediately visible, which can make them less attractive in political terms. Moreover, to be more than superficial they must deal with the root causes of the problem. This may require scrutiny of the social fabric of society and an exposure of inequalities and vested interests.

Given that many countries do not have the infrastructure and resources to immediately undertake large-scale rescue and rehabilitation programmes for all child labourers and to enhance income generation for parents, the priority should be on the immediate prevention and removal of children from the worst forms of child labour and a step-by-step time-bound national programme of action to progressively eliminate all child labour.

8.2 THE AUDIENCE

For a message to have maximum impact it needs to be tailored and channelled for a specific target group. For example, it is easier and more effective to group labour inspectors and government officials as one target group and parents and children as another. Even within the overall target group of government there are different important target groups, such as policy makers and legislators, bureaucrats, implementors and so on. There will, of course, be general messages that have a more general target group. Examples are advertisements aimed at the public on special occasions such as Labour Day or Universal Children's Day. Such general messages might only repeat a government's commitment or policy, and thus might not be designed to change attitudes or inspire action on the part of any specific target group. Other campaigns for general audiences can be designed, however, to change societal views towards child labour.

The target groups can be both direct and indirect receivers of the message. The indirect message is important because in many cases it may be reinforcing a direct message. An example of an indirect message is an employer or a primary school teacher who reads a newspaper report (indirect) about a training session (direct) for labour inspectors.

An important target group for information campaigns is children; well-informed children are often their own best advocates. Children need information about the exploitative realities of child labour – especially children from areas and groups most likely to feed the child labour market. Most of them simply do not know what they are getting into when they first enter the labour market, or how ignorant they are of the dangers they face. They need concrete information, put into a form and language they can understand, that will warn them of at least the main dangers they may well encounter in going to work.[2]

To make an impact it may be necessary to tailor the same message and direct it through different channels to different receivers within an overall target group. Box 8.1 gives an example of how this has been done at the community level in India.

---

[2] A. Bequele and W. Myers: *First things first in child labour* (Geneva, ILO, 1995), p. 59.

Box 8.1. A programme in the carpet region of Mirzapur, India

The Centre for Rural Education and Development Action (CREDA) started its campaign against the employment of child labour in Manda and Hallia blocks of Allahabad and Mirzapur districts respectively in 1982. These two blocks were identified as having a high concentration of child labour. CREDA started working in 15 villages by providing facilities for free medical check-ups of the working children. This was followed by non-formal education classes after working hours. Then, an extensive awareness campaign was initiated through discussions, posters and other means of communication in four contact centres established for this purpose.

CREDA created awareness about children's rights and against the practice of child labour among the numerous community groups. Villagers in small groups, including the parents and loom owners, were brought to the contact centres to be familiarized with the legal aspects of child labour. Additionally, issues such as the negative effects of child labour on the health and development of children, the responsibility of parents and the community towards a better future for the children, the creation of a "child labour free" carpet industry, the rights of the child in the United Nations and ILO Conventions, and the idea of becoming a model village in the district, were discussed in small group meetings. Later, CREDA contacted the parents of working children through the mail, and organized rallies of the children demanding educational facilities, food and proper shelter.

CREDA worked out a strategy to involve all stakeholders of the carpet industry including the loom owners, carpet manufacturers and local government in its campaign against the employment of children. The most important aspect of the strategy was community mobilization through face-to-face interaction with individuals and groups. Through this interaction, awareness was created about the negative effects of making children work on carpet looms. CREDA identified activists and leaders in each village who were keen to contribute, and they were brought into all CREDA activities at the village level. Although many loom owners resented the villagers working for CREDA, they were unable to do anything about it because CREDA had gained credibility in the communities.

Receivers of the CREDA message included the following target groups:

Parents of working children. This group is the most important and central to the issue of child labour from CREDA's point of view. Convincing parents who want their children to earn and supplement the family income was the most difficult job. Apart from face-to-face discussions to educate parents about the legal provisions against child labour and the ill effects of sending children to work, the parents were also given assurances of protection by the state administrative machinery in case the loom owners threatened them for withdrawing their children from work.

Child workers. Members of the CREDA team met the child workers whenever they found an opportunity after working hours and informed them about the ill effects that carpet weaving could have on their health and their future, and about the special provisions made for their education and recreation in special schools. These efforts were aimed at encouraging them to join the special schools, where non-formal education and skills training were provided.

Schoolchildren. CREDA team members interacted with schoolchildren in the village and persuaded them to wean their friends away from work on the carpet looms. The children were briefed to provide details of the education they were getting, and to demonstrate the skills gained at school. Exhibitions on various aspects of child welfare and development were held in the contact centres for the children.

Neighbours. CREDA activists visited every family in the village and pleaded with them to discourage their neighbours from sending their children to work on the looms. This was part of the campaign to build community opinion against child labour.

Adult weavers. CREDA involved adult weavers in its campaign against child labour. They were urged to canvass quietly among their junior co-workers against working on looms, informing them that their work kept otherwise able-bodied adult workers out of employment.

Loom owners. CREDA teams visited the loom owners to familiarize them with the legal prohibition against employing children and the extent of the penalties prescribed for violating the law. Other effects of employing children, such as the possible loss of business and the loss of revenue to the loom owners, were highlighted in face-to-face discussions.

The village community and the panchayat: CREDA organized village-level meetings and involved the village community, particularly the *panchayat* (administrative) functionaries to collectively discuss the need to eliminate child labour and to put children into school. The role of the village community in implementing the law on child labour was emphasized in the meetings and the village *panchayat* members and opinion makers in the village were co-opted in the CREDA campaign.

Carpet manufacturers. Since the loom owners depend on carpet manufacturers for business orders, the role of the manufacturers became crucial in the campaign. Hence, CREDA also involved the manufacturers in raising general awareness against child labour and persuaded a large number of manufacturers to discourage the loom owners from employing children.

8.3 MEANS OF COMMUNICATION

Any message communicated from the sender to the receiver goes through one or more channels of communication. Some more traditional channels have been replaced by television, radio, newspapers, magazines and books.

But the traditional channels, such as the family, story-telling, folklore and theatre are still effective for delivering the message. An example from the United Republic of Tanzania (box 8.2) shows that drama is an interesting and powerful channel for conveying the message. Other countries, such as Pakistan, have used street theatre by children and puppet shows by professional groups to get the message across to the masses. The family is a useful channel for passing on ideas, attitudes and beliefs. On many issues such as child labour, the ideas can flow in either direction: from the parents to the children or vice versa.

In addition, there are other channels which can reach large audiences. Among these are billboard displays, specialty items (T-shirts, pens, bags, and many others), special walks, rallies and marches. A recent example of the latter was the Global March, culminating in Geneva in June 1998 at the time of the International Labour Conference (see box 9.5). The Internet is another new channel reaching world audiences.

Channels that do not reach a large audience, but that are useful because of their specialized nature, are seminars, meetings and workshops which have a very specific message and audience. These include meetings on thematic issues, such as national policies and plans of action on the elimination of child labour, bonded labour, and the role of employers, workers and NGOs in eliminating child labour. They are also an effective channel for orienting and training specific target groups, such as labour inspectors, programme implementors and so on.

Among the more innovative and more appealing channels are comic books depicting the plight of children caught in exploitative working situations and stories about working children.

8.4 THE NEED FOR A COMMUNICATION STRATEGY

The process of communication is central to the achievement of the ultimate goal of eliminating child labour. All programmes and activities to this end should include communication strategies that make it possible to create or enhance awareness, mobilize the target groups, address notions and myths about the issue, clarify misconceptions and contribute to clear and precise knowledge of the issue. Although the problems and solutions are complex, the message has to be clear, precise and simple.

Guidelines for the effective use of communication strategies for the elimination of child labour require that:

◆ all programmes should have a communication component;

♦ communication opportunities should be identified at the programme design stage;

♦ special communication campaigns, using single or multi-media channels, should be considered;

♦ both traditional and modern channels of communication should be explored;

♦ the message should be simplified by repackaging technical information or legal documents before communicating it, or by translating documentation into local languages;

♦ the perspectives and perceptions of the working children and their families should be reflected;

♦ media attention should be encouraged on related issues such as education and health, poverty alleviation, adult employment opportunities; and

♦ communication processes within a programme and communication about a programme should be differentiated: both are important to different target groups.

Box 8.2. Traditional theatre

The commercial agriculture and plantation sector in the United Republic of Tanzania has been associated with a generally high incidence of child labour. Various interventions by IPEC partner agencies in recent years have, however, significantly changed the scenario on tea, coffee, sisal and tobacco plantations across the country, with children being withdrawn from work and reintegrated in schools. Trade unions as well as employers are taking decisive measures to prevent child labour on plantations and rural communities are campaigning against it.

The many and varied programme activities implemented by agencies include public awareness-raising on child labour, using drama groups with the assistance of the Tanzania chapter of the African Network for the Prevention and Protection Against Child Abuse and Neglect (ANPPCAN). Targeting three tea and tobacco plantation districts in Iringa region, ANPPCAN has involved schoolteachers and cultural officers to organize and train 26 drama groups, involving 795 primary school children, with a view to sensitizing rural communities on child labour to reduce and eventually prevent child labour on plantations. The organization of the drama groups drew upon the experiences of the traditional rural media in which cultural groups give performances in the form of songs, dances and plays, with specific messages pointing out and decrying practices and behaviour that are unbecoming or inconsistent with the norms and values of the community.

There has been a 25 to 30 per cent reduction in the incidence of child labour on the plantations in the three districts, while school enrolment and attendance have improved. Village governments have made land-lease arrangements for landless peasants to enable them to earn incomes and withdraw their children from plantations, and have instituted by-laws against child labour in the three districts.

Box 8.3. Comic strips : Samroeng goes to work

Child Workers in Asia, an NGO collecting and distributing information about child labour abuse, demonstrates what can be done in reaching children. It produces comic books that portray the hard life of many working children. These are distributed to schools and other places where they are likely to be seen and read by children. Each country in the region has its own comic book, which draws from material collected there. For example, the book for Thailand reports the tragic case of a real boy, Samroeng.

Source: Center for Protection of Children's Rights, Bangkok

Box 8.4. Beware! Brazil is watching you

The above slogan is the lead message of a nationwide campaign in Brazil against the commercial sexual exploitation of children, initiated by EMBRATUR (the Brazilian Tourist Agency). The campaign uses various communication channels to build a national and international information network about the hazards to children in sex tourism, and the links between Brazilian and foreign groups which organize sex tours to Brazil. The awareness-raising campaign is funded by the Ministry of Justice and implemented through NGOs working in child abuse prevention programmes and tourism-related activities.

Brazil had long promoted tourism, with promises of beautiful women alongside the samba, carnival and football stereotypes. To counter this sexual come-on, the Ministry of Justice is advising media and advertising groups to refrain from using images and expressions highlighting the physical attributes of young Brazilian women in newspapers and television, and particularly in tourism promotional materials. More importantly, it is building up a network among INTERPOL, local and international NGOs, and governments concerned with the exploitation of children in sex tourism.

Media professionals from EMBRATUR's marketing group have designed a strategy to:

◆ raise public awareness about the criminal character under Brazilian law of child sexual exploitation;

◆ encourage citizens to report violations and incidences of child sexual exploitation by local and foreign tourists; and

◆ push for the prosecution of identified offenders in Brazil or in their home countries.

Brazilian embassies and consulates, especially in Western countries, now issue visas with an accompanying pamphlet warning tourists that they will be prosecuted for any sexual contact with minors. Tour agencies have been advised to similarly warn their clients.

Large-scale media support is a critical ingredient in the campaign. Local, national and international newspapers, television and radio disseminate information on the problems of children in sex tourism, on the lures and mechanisms of the child sex industry and agencies, and on the efforts of government and NGOs to curb the victimization of children. International media involvement has been particularly directed to countries where organized charter tours tend to originate, such as Germany, Italy, France and Switzerland.

Various awareness-raising materials have been produced and disseminated around the campaign's logo and the slogan, "Fight Child Sex Tourism". These include T-shirts, billboards, airline tickets, passport inserts, and hotel doorknob cards. A warning stamp bearing the message is distributed in tourist areas and placed inside hotel rooms.

Positive results are evident, particularly in terms of citizens reporting observed violations through telephone hotlines and prompting investigations, as well as the closing down of a number of bars and nightclubs after proven violations within their premises.

Appendix 8.1 | Informing the public

Excerpt from BGMEA–ILO and UNICEF Agreement: A quick reference for managers and owners, October 1996 (ILO-Dhaka)

◆ **Questions and answers about the Memorandum of Understanding (MOU)**

WHAT IS THE MOU?

It is an agreement to remove children under 14 from BGMEA (Bangladesh Garment Manufacturers and Exporters Association) garment factories (including their subcontractors) and place them in education programmes.

WHY DID THE MOU BECOME NECESSARY?

Under the perceived threat of proposed legislation in the United States (the Harkin Bill to ban the import into the US of items produced by children) and actions by many consumers and buyers to boycott products made by children, several factory owners – in an attempt to get rid of children in their establishments – dismissed them overnight and pushed them into less favourable conditions. In light of the resulting backlash, many concerned parties sought a way for a more humane approach which would both protect the best interests of the child and those of the garment factory owners, their workforce and the country as a whole.

At the request of BGMEA and the Government of Bangladesh, the ILO and UNICEF at that time supported BGMEA's initiative to gradually phase out child labour under controlled conditions.

WHAT WAS AGREED TO?

It was agreed in the MOU signed on 4 July 1995: (a) that no child under the age of 14 would be recruited to work in garment factories, and (b) that children – who were already working – would not be terminated by the factory owners before they were placed in a school programme.

WHO AGREED?

BGMEA, together with the ILO and UNICEF, signed the MOU with the support of the Government of Bangladesh and the US Embassy.

HOW IS THE MOU BEING IMPLEMENTED?

(a) First of all a joint survey (by BGMEA, the ILO and UNICEF) was conducted to count exactly how many children were employed in the garment factories. Over 10,000 children were identified.

(b) UNICEF, based on the actual locations of the children surveyed, began to map out where and how many schools should be established.

(c) The ILO is devising a monitoring and verification system with an expanded contribution to its IPEC programme from the US Department of Labor.

(d) BGMEA has agreed to the monitoring and to the placing of children in the school programme.

Appendix 8.2 Popular theatre as an effective communications tool

Excerpt from a theatre production prepared by the African Network for the Prevention and Protection Against Child Abuse (ANPPCAN).

TITLE OF PLAY: BORN TO SUFFER

Cast

Mr. Mutuku – father   Wanjiku – mother   Bob, Mutavi, Musa – sons
Grace, Mwikali – daughters   Mutua – farmer   Njoki, Nduta – girls
Kimau, James – boys   Rose – teacher   Joshua – pastor
Two other characters

Summary

◆ **Scene One**

Poverty strikes Mr. Mutuku's home. The children have been sent home for school fees and uniforms, but there is no money and nothing to eat. Mutuku decides to engage the family in odd jobs to help them survive.

◆ **Scene Two**

The following morning at Mukutu's home, the children wake up early, excited about their jobs.
(*Dialogue not included in this excerpt*)

◆ **Scene Three**

Mr. Mutua at his farm is seen harassing children employed to attend to his flowers.

◆ **Scene Four**

By coincidence, the children meet at the river bank and discuss the ordeal of their jobs and curse the unfairness of life.

◆ **Scene Five**

At the marketplace, Mr. Mutua, Mutuku, Rose (teacher) and Joshua (the village pastor) meet and discuss the fate of the children and child labour.

SCENE ONE
(In the evening at Mutuku's home)

Wanjiku: (*shouting*) Children! Children, do you hear me?

Children: (*in unison*) – Yes, mother!

Wanjiku: Come in and have your supper.

Mwikali: (*puzzled*) But where is supper, mother?

Musa: (*pointing at the mugs on the table*) I can only see mugs of porridge.

Wanjiku: Sorry children, that's all we have.

Bob: I do understand mother, thanks.

(Together they sit down and take their porridge; a knock at the door)

Grace:	*(Loudly)* Come in!
Wanjiku:	*(Excusing herself)* Let me open the door .....(after opening) Oh! My husband, you look tired. Come in.
Mutuku:	Thank you, my wife.
Children:	Good evening, father!
Mukutu:	Good evening, my children, but it is not so good.
Children:	*(Surprised)* Ahhh!
Wanjiku:	What happened? Were you hurt or ill?
Mutuku:	Not at all *(Pause)*. It's only that I didn't get any money today.
Bob:	*(Worried)* Dad, does it mean we won't go back to school?
Grace:	Leave Dad alone. Don't you see he is tired and hungry?
Mwikali:	*(Asking her mother)* What will Papa eat?
Mutuku:	Please don't bother. I'm fine, children.
Wanjiku:	What can we do, my husband? The children have been sent home for fees and uniforms and here there's nothing to eat.
Mutuku:	*(Thoughtfully)* I know. *(Nodding his head)* We have no choice but for all of us to work, and hard.
Mutavi:	*(Surprised)* Work! But we are too young to work!
Bob:	But not too young to eat and go to school!
Wanjiku:	Listen! Let us plan how we will work.
Mutuku:	Yes! Mutavi and Bob will collect sand, for now. They are strong enough for that.
Wanjiku:	Grace and I will work at Mr. Mutua's coffee farm.
Mutuku:	*(Pointing at Musa)* Musa, my son, you can do well with fishing. You will sell some of your catch and some you bring home for our meal.
Mwikali:	What of me, mother?
Wanjiku:	Oh, my last born! You will take care of our home: clean up, draw water, etc.
Grace:	*(Standing)* I feel tired and sleepy. Let me go to sleep.

(Others also excuse themselves and leave the stage)

SCENE TWO
(Not included)

SCENE THREE
(At Mutua's farm)

Mutua:	*(Shouting)* Njoki! Njoki!
Njoki:	*(Fearfully)* Y-yyes, boss?
Mutua:	*(Pointing at her)* I told you that I don't want nonsense.

Njoki:	But what have I done?
Mutua:	As if you don't know.
Njoki:	Sure boss, believe me I don't know.
Mutua:	*(Annoyed)* Listen child! I'm not a fool or your mother and I don't intend to be your teacher.
Njoki:	*(Worried)* Y-yyes boss.
Mutua:	I told you to tell your friends that these flowers are to be picked today so that you can start weeding.
Njoki:	B-but this farm is big.
Mutua:	*(Shouting)* I pay you to work not to complain! Am I right?
Njoki:	Y-yyes please.
Mutua:	*(Loudly)* YES SIR!
Njoki:	YES SIR!
Mutua:	Good! Those are orders and orders must be obeyed or children die. *(Shouting)* You hear me all of you?
ALL:	Yes sir!
Mutua:	Quick, Quick! These flowers must be finished today. *(Leaves and the children shake their heads).*

SCENE FOUR – Excerpt
(At the river bank)

Kimau:	We are toiling for men and women who are supposed to be our guardians, our protectors, our parents.
Njoki:	But they turn against us, to betray us, and enslave us.
Kimau:	Yes, *(Nodding his head)* We are insulted as children, denied our only future. We are a hopeless generation.
Bob:	It is bitter. *(Shaking his head)* We are insulted as children, denied our only future. We are a hopeless generation.
Mutavi:	Look at the flower farms – children.
James:	What of the river banks? Children.
Musa:	We are the cow and donkey boys.
Nduta:	To be fished out of school to nothing.
Grace:	The whole world watching as the voiceless society erodes.
Nduta:	Why can't they help us finish our education?
Kimay:	And be grown-ups, both strong, wise men and women.
Njoki:	I think that is when we will work for ourselves.
Bob:	Sure! This is unfair. What have we done? The rate of school drop-outs is alarming.
Mutavi:	At the hands of child labour.

Grace:	*(Looking up and sobbing)* Why were we born to suffer? Please, we need an answer. *(She sobs loudly and leaves the stage).*
Njoki:	*(Following Grace)* Grace! Please don't cry. They have heard.
Nduta:	*(Also going)* I hope they will do something this time.
Musa:	*(Leaving)* The time is now or never.
Mutavi:	*(Collecting his shovel)* Why are we born to suffer? *(Shaking his head and the rest do the same while leaving the stage).*

SCENE FIVE
(At the market)

Mutuku:	*(Meeting Mutua and shaking hands)* Hello my friend, Mr. Mutua. You seem to be doing fine.
Mutua:	*(Boasting)* Of course, of course, Mutuku. I'm doing perfectly fine.
Mutuku:	How are your farms doing?
Mutua:	Splendid! With all the village children working for me.
Rose:	*(Interrupting)* How are you gentlemen?
Mutua and Mutuku:	Fine, madam.
Mutua:	What about your school, madam?
Rose:	Not so fine.
Mutuku:	Yes! I knew there is a big problem at school.
Mutua:	You mean you are also a teacher?
Rose:	You don't have to be a teacher to know if there's a problem at school.
Mukutu:	A minute ago my friend you told me that you have employed all the village children, now tell me who is going to school?
Mutua:	*(Stammering)* We-ll-well! you know...
Joshua:	*(Cutting him short)* Good day folks, I'm happy to see you. *(Shaking hands).*
Rose:	*(Serious)* Pastor! there is a problem at school, the rate of school drop-out is increasing.
Joshua:	Yes! at last people are seeing how crucial child labour is.
Mutuku:	What a waste of children – though some parents are unable, like myself, but we should be helped.
Mutua:	My friend, how do you want to be helped?
Joshua:	*(Ignoring his question)* Mutua, I would say your farms have a lot of children employed.
Rose:	*(To Mutua)* If you think you are rich and in need of employing, please employ grown-ups.
Joshua:	People like Mutuku, your friend, have no job and are suffering; his children have been sent home from school.
Rose:	What a friend you are! If you employ his children instead and abuse them.
Mutuku:	*(Interrupting)* Folks! Let's think twice... What of tomorrow?

Joshua:	True! It is time for we adults to reason and commit ourselves for the wellbeing of these children.
Rose:	Bring back the children to school! They need education. Besides, we can't teach empty classrooms.
Mutua:	I'm sorry, I think I have been too greedy thinking of myself individually instead of the welfare of my community.
Mutuku:	If only one can help a single child, remember you have saved a future.
Joshua:	*(Loudly)* Child labour must be stopped! Look at our farms and everywhere – Children! Are they donkeys or slaves?
Rose:	What a pity how we as parents have betrayed our own children and waste them instead.
Mutuku:	But, how can we confine these children to school, without being sent home for fees and uniforms?
Joshua:	*(Nodding his head)* That is an issue we should address ourselves to.
Rose:	I think if we can start an income-generating project at school, it will help to sustain the children's education.
Mutua:	*(Excited)* Yes! I do think that's a better idea, and I offer to donate and commit myself on such a project.
Mutuku:	I also do agree with the idea, but the sooner the better.
Joshua:	First let's inform our community about this by holding a meeting at the school for parents and village elders.
Rose:	*(Excited)* That's great! I have to arrange for that immediately.
Mutua:	Children should not be born to suffer *(shaking his head)*.
Joshua:	Let us campaign on this, and with that, God bless *(waving his hands while leaving)*.
Mutuku:	I can't wait till I tell my family of what we are planning, bye! *(hurrying off)*.

Rose and Mutua also say goodbye and go their separate ways.

THE END

Action by community groups and NGOs

9

Pin Boonpala

9.1 CIVIL SOCIETY ORGANIZATIONS AND CHILD LABOUR

> *The active involvement of civil society organizations – in particular of non-governmental and community-based organizations – is an essential element in the fight against child labour.*
>
> *In many countries, initiatives against child labour have been launched first by non-governmental organizations (NGOs) and community-based organizations (CBOs).*

In the child rights movement, NGOs and CBOs have assumed proactive roles. Whether as advocates within the community, as direct service providers, or as resource persons for capacity building in research and training, they have made significant contributions at the national and international levels.

NGOs and CBOs play a crucial role in discovering and publicizing concrete cases of child labour. They are well placed to document areas, activities and workplaces that put working children at serious risk. They are able to point out the shortcomings in public sector action, in particular failure to enforce relevant laws and regulations.

They can influence family and community concerns and values that determine whether and where children work. They can stimulate the required changes in popular culture.

More importantly, NGOs and CBOs are able to devise and implement action programmes on behalf of children already working. They are close to the children concerned, know their special needs, and generally enjoy the trust of the local communities in which these children live. They are therefore well placed to mobilize the human and material resources available in the community.

In many countries, they have been able to demonstrate the impact of innovative, relatively low-cost interventions. Many of their initiatives have proved especially relevant to child workers because they were developed and implemented with the active participation of children and their parents. Most of their programmes are community-based and are implemented in the workplaces of children or close to the places where children converge. This proximity allows for an understanding of the children's reality as well as a more sympathetic attitude, and sets the stage for open, participatory approaches.

In the past decade, NGOs and CBOs have become more visible and have been recognized for their work with children and families in difficult living and working conditions. Governments, intergovernmental organizations and donors have shown increasing interest in their work against child labour. There is widening support for and linkages with NGO activities by governments and donors in the search for effective and innovative strategies and responses. This chapter highlights selected practical experiences of NGOs and advocacy against child labour.

Box 9.1. NGOs and CBOs

Non-governmental organizations (NGOs) are non-profit oriented legal organizations composed mostly of socially concerned and committed professionals who are often involved on a full-time basis in the welfare, human rights promotion and development of marginalized sectors and communities. Their services are usually in the form of resources, capacity building, issue advocacy, information, legal and moral support, and other support services. Since the ultimate judges of the effectiveness and success of their operations are the communities or sectors they serve, NGOs are considered to be primarily accountable to them. NGOs may have their own independent offices or may be based within church institutions or universities. If based within the latter, they have separate legal identities, charters and boards, and perform activities that are developmental in nature.

People's organizations or community-based organizations (CBOs) are associations of communities or sectors, formed mainly to protect and promote the welfare and interests of their members. The scope of their membership and activities may be focused on a neighbourhood or community, or may expand up to the municipal, provincial and national levels, and even to the international level.

In start-up activities in most countries participating in the ILO's International Programme on the Elimination of Child Labour (IPEC), NGOs have taken on the role of discovering and denouncing child labour abuses, lobbying and advocating for children's rights and policy reform, and providing direct services for working children and their families.

Much of the earlier NGO involvement covering child labour was stereotyped as relief and welfare action, and sometimes as part of community development approaches. Often, actions of various NGOs were neither coordinated nor designed to deal with child workers and child labour in a comprehensive way. NGOs are progressively facing the newer challenges of (a) addressing the structural roots of the problem, and (b) systematically eliciting the support of all sectors of society, including those with whom they have sometimes had an adversarial relationship, such as government and the private sector, to successfully eliminate child labour.

Many NGOs and CBOs have increased their collaboration with the ILO's social partners, and their project areas have been important laboratories for sensitization and orientation on child labour issues. Successful projects are adopted and replicated on a larger scale, and incorporated into mainstream programmes. For example, agencies responsible for large-scale programmes, especially for (ex-) child workers, have involved NGOs and CBOs through one or more stages from planning and design to implementation, monitoring and evaluation. This has enabled governments to benefit from the insights and experiences of NGOs and CBOs, and in turn, has allowed NGOs and CBOs to obtain a broader perspective on the challenges of implementing large-scale programmes.

Box 9.2. Strengths of NGOs and CBOs

◆ campaigning for the rights of children and the elimination of child labour, initiating media campaigns, providing documentation;

◆ conducting action research into issues related to child labour;

◆ providing direct services to children at risk and their families;

◆ providing technical support to other NGOs; and

◆ training (of welfare officers and legal professionals, for example), and building partnerships with other actors.

9.2 PRACTICAL EXPERIENCE OF NGOs IN COMBATING CHILD LABOUR

Types of NGO action

Local NGOs are in a good position to remain in close contact with working children and their families, to stay attuned to their needs, perspectives and viewpoints, to facilitate their active participation in identifying and solving their problems and assuming control over their lives. Some NGOs excel in developing and implementing projects that can serve as models to address child labour problems. Much of their experience can be adapted and expanded through public programmes. In addition, NGOs, through cooperation at the national, regional and international levels, engage in advocacy and mobilize for action against child labour.

NGOs with differing levels of operational experience can also document and share knowledge, pool resources and know-how with other public and private entities at local, national and international levels, and act as collective "child watchers" or vigilance groups, so that abuses or violations of child rights can be prevented or monitored, reported and sanctioned.

NGOs also participate and contribute to ILO action against child labour. For example, national-level NGOs have been active partners in the implementation of IPEC in a number of ways. First, NGOs are actively involved in the process of setting policy and a framework for implementation of IPEC country programmes. When a country joins IPEC, the government is assisted in the preparation of a national plan of action against child labour, which is carried out through broad-based consultation among government agencies, workers' and employers' organizations, and NGOs (see Chapter 1). At the implementation stage, the government is required to set up a National Steering Committee (NSC), which is composed of representatives of key government agencies, workers' and employers' organizations, and experienced national NGOs. The NSC sets priorities for the implementation of programmes in line with the national policy on child labour. The NSC also selects and endorses action programmes to be supported financially and technically by IPEC.

NGOs in most countries are supported by IPEC to implement action programmes for the prevention of child labour, through, for example, awareness raising and assisting families and children at risk to find alternatives to child labour. In some countries, NGOs play a crucial role in the process of withdrawing children from hazardous work, and providing them with appropriate options and rehabilitation programmes, through non-formal education, counselling, health care and income-generation activities for the affected families.

IPEC has also supported activities of international NGOs in advocacy and research, such as the Global March against Child Labour (box 9.5), a survey of NGO views on the new ILO Convention (No. 182) on the worst forms of child labour, and the preparation of a handbook for research and action on child domestic workers by Anti-Slavery International.

NGOs also let their views be known on international standards that affect child labour; for example, in implementing the United Nations Convention on the Rights of the Child, NGOs comment on government reports to the Committee on the Rights of the Child. NGOs have also disseminated information and advocated for provisions in Convention No. 182, holding workshops and addressing the delegates in the Committee on Child Labour during the International Labour Conference.

Examples of NGOs in action

Box 9.3. Community action against child trafficking

In *Nepal*, IPEC has been supporting direct action by an NGO at community level. The NGO, Maity Nepal, has formed surveillance groups in the districts seriously affected by child trafficking and is carrying out campaigns with the help of college students and victims of trafficking. It has set up a prevention-cum-interception camp at an important transit point. The camp provides shelter, basic education and vocational training for girls who are at risk of being sold into prostitution, as well as for those who have been rescued. At the end of their training, the girls are helped in finding employment or setting up a small business. Another transit home is being set up at Kakkarvita, near the Nepal-India border, to provide shelter to girls who have been rescued from brothels in India and repatriated to Nepal.

Maity Nepal coordinates its activities with NGOs in India for the rescue and repatriation of victims, some of whom have been living in government-run homes for long periods of time. On the Nepalese side, it works with the police and other authorities for the rehabilitation of child victims and the prosecution of the offenders. The victims are often traumatized and many suffer from serious diseases, such as HIV/AIDS and tuberculosis, needing immediate medical attention and psychological counselling. The NGO plans to provide a wide range of rehabilitation services to help children regain their self-esteem and become self-reliant.

In *Thailand*, since 1992, IPEC has supported an NGO called Development and Education Programme for Daughters and Communities Center (DEPDC). DEPDC aims to prevent child prostitution and child labour by providing alternative education to girls at high risk of exploitation. These include children from families in extreme poverty, often with debts, children of tribal communities, children from broken homes and children of drug-addicted parents. Alternative education provided by DEPDC is a combination of formal and non-formal education and basic skills training. In addition, it has been raising awareness among parents and the community concerning the sexual exploitation of children, child labour and potential options that DEPDC and other organizations can provide to parents and children.

DEPDC has learned that, owing to the lack of education and abject poverty among rural and tribal communities, young girls in the North are easy targets for the trafficking movement. Through intervention by DEPDC and others, many of them are prevented from becoming victims of trafficking. While the DEPDC experience is very valuable, the problem is too complex for DEPDC to solve alone. The mobilization of other actors in the field is therefore one crucial action strategy to protect and prevent such children from entering the sex trade.

Box 9.4. Targeting child domestic workers

In *the Philippines*, a particularly successful project is being carried out by an NGO known as Visayan Forum. Because it is virtually impossible to make contact with child domestic workers, "Luneta Outreach Activities" was organized at Luneta Park, in Manila on Sundays, where child domestic workers gather. It has proved to be an effective way of organizing and providing direct services to child domestics. Launched with IPEC support in 1995, the project has achieved the following results:

◆ Children have been assisted to leave their abusive working conditions and reunited with their families or relatives.

◆ Basic needs of child domestic workers, such as temporary shelter, medical care, legal assistance, counselling, and schooling expenses, have been provided on a regular basis.

◆ Children have been enabled to support their peers and negotiate better working conditions.

◆ Many children have gained leadership skills and have been able to take part actively in advocacy and awareness- raising programmes, resulting in improved practice by employers, and a greater understanding of the situation by society and policy makers.

During the last two years, Visayan Forum has been able to consolidate and provide direct services to 1,500 child domestic workers and has also been successful in expanding operations in three more cities, tracing about 2,000 more.

The Forum has organized various consultations with the domestics themselves, human rights groups/institutions and legal practitioners to map out a common strategy to lobby for the adoption of the proposed House Helper Act.

In the *United Republic of Tanzania*, a Tanzanian association of women journalists and lawyers (TAMWA) took the lead in the child domestic workers prevention campaign, in response to concern over the growing number of girls under 14 recruited from rural areas to work as domestics in the cities of Dar-es-Salaam, Arusha and Mwanya. Over 4,500 girls in six urban centres have been reached by TAMWA. Girl domestics are paired with women domestic workers who offer them individual support and guidance.

The TAMWA centres are located at major crossroads where the girls are recruited. TAMWA contacts the girls upon their arrival in cities and provides them with basic assistance. The programme is also raising awareness among parents and institutions responsible for the welfare of children, religious bodies and women's groups. A multi-media awareness campaign was launched which included broadcasting the problem through radio programmes, producing and distributing pamphlets and cartoon booklets, and developing a video and a play for community theatre. Village-based seminars for parents and community leaders have exposed the harsh realities that can face girl domestics in towns and have contributed to a sharp decline in recruitment of young girls from rural areas.

Box 9.5. The Global March against child labour

To promote worldwide action against child labour, a Global March was initiated by NGOs, in collaboration with workers' organizations, between December 1997 and June 1998. This global campaign involved an alliance of 350 organizations in 82 countries. It aimed to mobilize worldwide efforts to protect the rights of all children, especially their rights to receive free, meaningful education, to be protected from economic exploitation, and to be freed from performing any work that is likely to be damaging to their physical, mental, spiritual, moral or social development.

Global March campaigns were organized at national and international levels in different continents starting in Asia in January 1998 and continuing in Latin America, Africa, North America and Europe. The March converged on Geneva at the time of the International Labour Conference (ILC) in June 1998.

Core marchers were joined by other marchers in the participating countries. Activities in these regions included thousands of people demonstrating against child labour, cultural events, such as theatre performances and concerts, and core marchers meeting with local officials. In Geneva, there were community activities and the March delivered its message to the delegates of the ILC and expressed support for the ILO's proposed new Convention on the worst forms of child labour (adopted in June 1999).

The Global March was received at ILO Headquarters by the ILO Director- General, and by ILO delegates. A Global March sculpture depicting child labour and children's rights to education was unveiled in the ILO grounds.

A round table meeting was organized, attended by marchers, ILC delegates and representatives of NGOs. A press conference was also organized.

Again in 1999, Global March activities took place in Geneva before and after the ILC in June. These included an international workshop in which former working children and their families discussed the reality of the worst forms of child labour, and their views on effective measures which had been or could be implemented. They presented the conclusions of the workshop to Ruth Dreifuss, President of the Swiss Confederation, Juan Somavia, Director-General of the ILO and Mary Robinson, United Nations High Commissioner for Human Rights. The Global March children also presented a dramatic interpretation of their plight to Conference delegates through mime. An exhibition graphically illustrated the lives of children in the worst forms of child labour.

9.3 LESSONS LEARNED

The role and participation of NGOs in action against child labour in different countries varies depending on political culture and tradition. The quality of NGO involvement also depends on their experience and maturity. In some countries, NGOs have been criticized for inadequate administrative and management capability, leading to non-sustainability of operations. Their insufficient resource base means that they can only continue their programmes as long as there is internal or external support. However, mature and well-established NGOs survive changes in political systems, continue to receive public support and have effectively worked towards the elimination of child labour. Some of the lessons learned from NGO action against child labour are:

◆ NGOs, particularly those implementing their activities at community level, are able to mobilize community awareness and action against child labour. Strong community participation can lead to prevention of the problem and long-term sustainability of action.

◆ Many NGOs have practical experience in creating alternatives for families at risk and disadvantaged groups in society, such as income-generating activities, setting up of cooperatives and community-based savings groups, literacy programmes for adults and children, provision of legal aid, family counselling, and so on. This experience is relevant and can be applied in direct action against child labour. Indeed, NGOs in many countries are doing so.

◆ Awareness-raising and advocacy are important strategies and NGOs often have experience and skills in conducting awareness-raising campaigns.

◆ Capacity building through, for instance, training programmes on various aspects of development and implementation of action against child labour, is required to assist the effective operation of NGOs.

◆ For greater effect, NGOs also coordinate and network their activities with others, including government bodies, workers' and employers' organizations, media, universities, the judiciary system, parliamentarians, and so on.

Resources on child labour

10

INTRODUCTION

This chapter provides selected reference sources on printed and audiovisual media to assist governments, employers' and workers' organizations, non-governmental organizations and other interested parties, in the design of programmes to address the problem of child labour. It includes primarily ILO and UNICEF publications. These are studies, technical reports, books, periodical publications (monographs, articles), audiovisual material and conference proceedings, especially those produced since 1995. The publications are grouped under two main headings: general publications on child labour; and thematic publications. They are classified alphabetically by author. Each bibliographical entry indicates: author, title, publisher, year of publication, and number of pages. Whenever relevant, geographical references are added. Language versions are indicated after each abstract, as well as ISBN numbers where appropriate.

The selected publications and material cover the context, causes and consequences of child labour; legislation, policies and programmes; the working conditions and occupational safety and health hazards to which working children are exposed; economic implications and incentives; workers' and employers' participation; education and training; labour inspection; advocacy and awareness-raising and other measures which can effectively contribute to the fight against child labour.

ILO publications can be obtained through major booksellers and ILO local offices in many countries, or can be ordered from ILO Publications, International Labour Office, CH-1211 Geneva 22, Switzerland (website: www.ilo.org/public/english/180publn/index.htm). A free catalogue of child labour publications is available from this address or website.

There are many publications on the ILO's child labour website (http://www.ilo.org/childlabour). IPEC country and regional-level studies have also been produced. IPEC places all its materials on its website. Working papers will be available for downloading.

10.1 GENERAL PUBLICATIONS ON CHILD LABOUR

ILO reports for the International Labour Conference (ILC) and Governing Body (GB)

ILO: Reports IV (2A) and (2B), International Labour Conference 87th Session, 1999, fourth item on the agenda

CHILD LABOUR

Geneva, 1999.

Report IV (2A) summarizes comments from ILO member States, including separate replies from employers' and workers' organizations, on the proposed Convention and Recommendation concerning the prohibition and immediate elimination of the worst forms of child labour. The texts of the proposed Convention and Recommendation are published in Report IV (2B), which will be the basis for discussion by the International Labour Conference in June 1999.

Language of the text: English, French, Spanish

Report IV (2A) ISBN 92-2-110811-2 (English)
Report IV (2B) ISBN 92-2-010812-7 (English)

ILO: GB, 271st Session, GB 271/TC/2, 1998

OPERATIONAL ASPECTS OF THE INTERNATIONAL PROGRAMME ON THE ELIMINATION OF CHILD LABOUR (IPEC)

Geneva, February 1998, 27p.

The paper gives an overview of IPEC's scope, performance and strategies, and illustrates the distinctive characteristics of IPEC's work. It reviews critical issues for sustaining the programme's momentum.

Language of the text: English, French, Spanish

ILO: Report IV (1), International Labour Conference, 87th Session, 1999, fourth item on the agenda

CHILD LABOUR

Geneva, 1998, 14p.

This report contains the texts of a proposed Convention and Recommendation concerning the prohibition and immediate elimination of the worst forms of child labour. These texts are based on the Conclusions adopted by the International Labour Conference following the first discussion at its 86th Session in June 1998.

This report was circulated to ILO member States for comment or suggested amendment to the text. In addition, the Office invited comments on several proposed formulations to clarify the text. The Office also invited comments on several questions related to issues that the Committee indicated would be particular subjects for the second discussion in June 1999. Comments are summarized and commented on in Report IV(2A), above.

Language of the text: English, French, Spanish

ISBN 92-2-110810-4 (English)

ILO: Report VI (2), International Labour Conference, 86th Session, 1998, sixth item on the agenda

CHILD LABOUR

Geneva, 1998, 177p.

The Governing Body of the ILO, at its 265th Session in March 1996, decided to place the question of child labour on the agenda of the 86th Session (1998) of the International Labour Conference. The question is dealt with by the double-discussion procedure, meaning a first discussion in June 1998 followed by a second one in June 1999, with a view to final adoption. A first report (*Child Labour: Targeting the intolerable*, Report VI (1), International Labour Conference, 86th Session, Geneva, 1998) in which the law and practice on the subject were examined in various countries, was sent, together with a questionnaire, to the Governments of the member States of the ILO.

The report contains the replies to the questionnaire by governments, and employers' and workers' organizations on the possible content of new ILO standards on child labour and commentaries by the ILO identifying the main issues for discussion. Proposed Conclusions were prepared on the basis of the replies and are found at the end of the report. These served as the basis for the first discussion.

Language of the text: English, French, Spanish

ISBN 92-2-110660-8 (English)

ILO: Report VI (1). ILC, 86th Session, 1998, sixth item on the agenda

CHILD LABOUR: TARGETING THE INTOLERABLE

Geneva, November 1996, 80p.

Drawing on the experience of the ILO, this report surveys international and national law and practice, and points the way towards effective action. Submitted to the 174 member States as a discussion document for new standard setting on child labour, it is a timely report, invaluable to all those working to bring to a halt such abusive conditions as bonded labour, child prostitution, and the exposure of children to dangerous chemicals, machinery and other hazards.

Language of the text: English, French, Spanish, German, Russian, Chinese, Arabic, Italian

ISBN 92-2-110328-5 (English)

ILO: Document for discussion at the Informal Tripartite Meeting at the Ministerial level, ITM/1/1996, Volume 1

CHILD LABOUR: WHAT IS TO BE DONE ?

Geneva, 12 June 1996, 37p.

The document describes the current child labour problem in the world. Based on the lessons learned from IPEC action since 1992, the report examines basic elements of a possible national strategy and strongly recommends setting up and/or improving a data collection system; designing a national plan of action; and raising awareness on the dangerous effects of child labour. The report presents the ILO action, and proposes future directions and priorities.

Language of the text: English, French, Spanish

ISBN 92-2-2110270-X

ILO: GB doc. GB.264/ESP/1, 264th Session, Geneva, November 1995. Document prepared as a contribution to the discussion on child labour in the Committee on Employment and Social Policy. First item on the agenda

CHILD LABOUR

Geneva, November 1995, 31p.

The document is in three parts. The first describes the problem of child labour in the world. The second part discusses what can be done at the country level, and examines the possible contents of a national policy in this area, based largely on the conclusions drawn by the ILO from the action carried out worldwide under IPEC. The third part describes ILO action and makes suggestions on how it could best be pursued.

Language of the text: English, French, Spanish

ILO: Report of the Director-General, International Labour Conference, 69th Session 1983

REPORT OF THE DIRECTOR-GENERAL: Part I: Child labour

Geneva, 1983

The text analyses the magnitude of child labour, its major forms and sectoral distribution; examines causes, conditions and consequences; and focuses on legislation as well as on economic and social measures. The elimination of child labour as an objective, coupled with a commitment to improve the condition of working children, are the two planks of ILO policy and programmes which aim at:

◆ attacking the basic causes of child labour through employment-generating and poverty-eradicating policies;

◆ providing education, vocational education and training opportunities for children and young persons;

◆ restricting child labour by promoting the ratification and application of international labour standards and by encouraging member States to promote labour inspection; and

◆ protecting children at work by introducing measures for their immediate protection from adverse working conditions and for the improvement of their working and living conditions.

The report sets out a strategy for action in the light of the standards adopted in previous years and for subsequent action both by the ILO and member States.

Language of the text: English, French, Spanish

ISBN 92-2-103121-7

Reports of the International Programme on the Elimination of Child Labour (IPEC)

ILO-IPEC

ILO-IPEC HIGHLIGHTS OF 1998

Geneva, October 1998, 28p. plus tables

In addition to providing an overview of IPEC action in 1998, this report also features an update on IPEC partners and an overview of recent evaluation initiatives. The tables detail financial contributions from IPEC donors.

Language of the text: English, French, Spanish

ISBN 92-2-111467-8

ILO-IPEC

ACTION AGAINST CHILD LABOUR, LESSONS AND STRATEGIC PRIORITIES FOR THE FUTURE: A SYNTHESIS REPORT

Geneva, October 1997, 47p.

The report outlines IPEC highlights for 1996-97, summarizing the main lessons learned and strategies for the future. It includes an overview of the problem, an explanation of the IPEC response, its main achievements, core strategies for promoting the application of international instruments and direct action, and future strategic priorities. The report also delineates action at national level, especially multi-sectoral strategies, the role of programme partners and the implications of mainstreaming child labour concerns in future programme development.

Language of the text: English

ILO-IPEC

PROFILES OF IPEC PROGRAMMES 1992-97

Geneva, October 1997

The purpose is to provide an overview of the IPEC programmes implemented during the period 1992-97, under the following main categories: type of objectives; IPEC priority target groups; IPEC partner organizations; geographic and sectoral dimensions; main programme areas and type of interventions; and media production.

Language of the text: English

ISBN 92-2-111005-2

ILO-IPEC

ILO-IPEC HIGHLIGHTS OF 1996-97 AND GUIDELINES FOR FUTURE ACTION

Geneva, October 1996, 37p.

This report sets out the main directions and priorities for the future: emphasis on in-country ownership and sustainable action; the prevention and abolition of the most intolerable forms of child labour; the creation of a broad alliance of partners; and the use of multi-sectoral integrated interventions. Information on partners, status of IPEC objectives, selected IPEC highlights in 1996-97, and donor contributions to IPEC is also provided.

Language of the text : English

ISBN 92-2-110434-6

ILO-IPEC

IMPLEMENTATION REPORT: REVIEW OF IPEC EXPERIENCE 1992-95

Geneva, October 1995, 139p.

The report is divided into two parts: the first sets out IPEC strategy and summarizes the overall lessons for future development, drawn from experience between 1992 and 1995. The second part describes the activities conducted at regional, national and international levels, assesses the progress made, and identifies potential challenges for the future.

Language of the text: English

ISBN 92-2-110024-3

ILO-IPEC

IMPLEMENTATION REPORT 1992-1993

Geneva, 1993, 39p.

The report is divided into two parts: the first part sets out the general activities conducted from the beginning of IPEC work to 1993, detailing, for example, preparatory work that ILO member States had to carry out before starting in-country programmes, coordinating work with other organizations, and the worldwide movement promoted against child labour. The second part provides information on national programmes in IPEC participating countries such as Brazil, India, Indonesia, Kenya, Thailand and Turkey.

Language of the text : English

Policy studies

Assafa BEQUELE & Jo BOYDEN
ILO

COMBATING CHILD LABOUR

Geneva, March 1995, second impression with modifications, 226p.

This major study of child labour in Africa, Asia and Latin America vividly describes the harsh reality of children's work in various industries and occupations, and gives an account of the striking evolution that is taking place in public policy and programmes in dealing with the problems.

The book offers a wealth of information on child labour and a wide-ranging analysis of policies and programmes which are being implemented in a variety of industrial socio-economic and political contexts. It provides a glimpse of innovative developments in the campaign against child labour and the defence of the rights of children. Includes 16 pages of photographs.

Language of the text: English, Spanish

ISBN 92-2-106389-5
ISBN 92-2-306389-2 for Spanish

Assafa BEQUELE & William MYERS
ILO (Child Labour Collection)-UNICEF

FIRST THINGS FIRST IN CHILD LABOUR: Eliminating work detrimental to children

Geneva, July 1995, 163p.

The limited resources available to fight child labour should be concentrated in the first instance on abolishing the hazardous work of children. The difficulty of defining work which is hazardous to children, and the various preventive and rehabilitative approaches are discussed, using examples taken from Brazil, India, the Philippines, Sri Lanka, the United Republic of Tanzania, Thailand and Zimbabwe. The book also explains the levels of intervention for mobilization and the importance of establishing child labour legislation and enforcement through both a national policy and international agreements. The authors present an action-oriented overview which, as well as being of interest to the general public, can also provide policy makers with useful material drawn from personal experience. This is particularly valuable an area where documentary data are scarce. Such experiential data necessarily rely on the use of numerous case examples, which have been chosen for their discussion value. The book has been designed so that it can also serve as background material for training courses.

Language of the text : English

ISBN 92-2-109-197-X

Jo BOYDEN, Birgitta LING & William MYERS
UNICEF-Rädda Barnen

WHAT WORKS FOR WORKING CHILDREN

Florence, Italy, 1998, 364p.

This book examines recent information and thinking about children's work in relation to child health and development, education, child protection laws, the market economy, children's role in society, and other issues of importance for policy makers, programme planners and children's advocates. It reviews and summarizes recent research and experience regarding child work and the processes of child development as they relate to work, and proposes alternative concepts and approaches.

Jo BOYDEN & William MYERS
ILO-UNICEF International Child Development Centre, Innocenti Occasional Papers: Child Rights Series No. 8

EXPLORING ALTERNATIVE APPROACHES TO COMBATING CHILD LABOUR: CASE STUDIES FROM DEVELOPING COUNTRIES

Florence, Italy, February 1995, VI, 45p.

This paper focuses on four different strategies to combat child labour, presenting them within specific country contexts:

1. public-sector initiative through child labour legislation and the establishment of universal, compulsory basic education;

2. community mobilization and NGOs' initiatives with government support;

3. planned shared responsibility between government and civil society within a legal framework that sets national child protection standards but devolves implementing power and initiative to the local level; and

4. cross-national and private-sector initiatives against child labour.

Language of the text: English

ISSN 1014-7837

Hugh CUNNINGHAM
ILO

CHILD LABOUR AND INDUSTRIALIZATION

Geneva, 1995, 15p.

The author refers to publications on the relationship between industrialization and child labour in the Western world, from the 18th to the early 20th centuries. In particular he focuses on five factors which led to the decline in child labour in the process of industrialization: labour power, preventing adults from being replaced by child labour; family strategies, preferring education to child work; technology, demanding capability to operate more complex machinery; legislation against child labour; and ideology which has progressively considered respect for the rights of children.

Language of the text : English

ISBN 92-2-109754-4

ILO
Janet HILOWITZ

LABELLING CHILD LABOUR PRODUCTS – A PRELIMINARY STUDY

Geneva, 1997, 98p.

This study contains a general discussion of what social labelling is; descriptions of six specific labelling initiatives attempting to improve the lives of working children; and a more detailed discussion of the issues involved in social labelling as a way of combating child labour. It points to the inherent problems of monitoring and inspection, the frequent lack of transparency for consumers, and the unsure fate of the children working in industries targeted by labelling initiatives. It also emphasizes the need for a more in-depth examination of the issue which could identify the factors that can bring about success and accountability.

Language of the text: English

ISBN 92-2-11-0589-X

International Conference on Child Labour, Oslo, 27-30 October 1997

FINAL REPORT OF THE CONFERENCE AND AGENDA FOR ACTION

The report highlights some of the most important aspects and outcomes of the debate of the Conference, focusing on child labour as a human right as well as a development issue by addressing the problem from the bottom up, through broad-based development, poverty eradication and social mobilization, and from the top down, by establishing political priorities and appropriate frameworks. The document contains the opening statements, the report from the technical and the political sessions, the statements by the ministers and heads of delegations, the adoption of the Agenda for Action and the closing statements. Three annexes are also included: the programme, the list of ministers/heads of delegations and the Agenda for Action.

Language of the text: English

ISBN 92-2- 109584-3

Mark LANSKY
ILO-IPEC, extract from the *International Labour Review*

CHILD LABOUR: HOW THE CHALLENGE IS BEING MET

Geneva, 1997, 28p.

The author examines the evolution of long-term initiatives aimed at abolishing child labour and classifies them under law, direct interventions and market-based schemes. IPEC strategies and priorities are illustrated, including SIMPOC, the Statistical Information and Monitoring Programme on Child Labour.

Language of the text: English

Offprint also distributed by IPEC

Ministry of Social Affairs and Employment, the Netherlands.

COMBATING THE MOST INTOLERABLE FORMS OF CHILD LABOUR: A GLOBAL CHALLENGE. REPORT

Geneva, 1997, 111p.

The Amsterdam Child Labour Conference was organized in February 1997 by the Government of the Netherlands in close collaboration with the ILO.

The aim was to stimulate global discussion on measures to put an end to the most intolerable forms of child labour without delay, i.e. slavery, forced or compulsory labour, the use of children in prostitution, pornography and the drugs trade, and the employment of children in any type of work that is dangerous, harmful or hazardous or that interferes with their education.

This report reflects on the discussions that took place during the Conference and includes ILO background papers on:

◆ meeting the challenge: national and international action;

◆ international and regional cooperation on child labour;

◆ globalization, liberalization and child labour; and

◆ proposed ILO standards on child labour.

Government representatives, mostly at ministerial level, from 33 countries in Asia, Africa, the Americas and Europe, representatives of workers' and employers' organizations and NGOs, representatives of working children and other parties actively participated in the discussion.

The Conference urged all countries to launch a time-bound programme of action to eliminate child labour and to immediately put an end to its most intolerable forms.

Language of the text: English

Translation available in French, Spanish

UNICEF

THE STATE OF THE WORLD'S CHILDREN 1997

New York, 1997, 107p.

The report discusses the role of the Convention on the Rights of the Child and explores some of the implications for children, with a particular focus on child labour. It calls for the immediate end to hazardous child labour and proposes strategies to help eliminate and prevent it including: access to education; wider legal protection; birth registration for all children; collection of information; and mobilization of the widest possible coalition of partners among governments, communities, NGOs, employers and trade unions. Economic and social statistics on the nations of the world, with particular reference to children's well-being, cover basic indicators such as health, nutrition, education, demographics, economic progress and the situation of women.

Language of the text: English, French, Spanish

ISBN 0-19-262871-2

Information kits, training manuals and guidelines

Alec FYFE
ILO: Child Labour Collection

CHILD LABOUR: A GUIDE TO PROJECT DESIGN

Geneva, February 1993, 99p.

This manual was written to assist policy-makers and practitioners in designing practical and targeted projects by applying the techniques of project design to the complex problem of child labour. The text, through a logical sequence of the steps, provides guidance necessary for effective project design and the drafting of coherent project documents. These are complemented by guidelines on international labour standards, situation analysis and interviewing techniques.

Language of the text: English

ISBN 92-2-108005-6

Rachel HODGKIN and Peter NEWELL
UNICEF, Regional Office for Europe

IMPLEMENTATION HANDBOOK FOR THE CONVENTION ON THE RIGHTS OF THE CHILD

Geneva, January 1998, 681p.

The handbook provides a detailed reference for the implementation of law, policy and practice to promote and protect the rights of children. It brings together under each article of the Convention an analysis of the interpretation by the Committee on the Rights of the Child during its first six years and its examination of the 68 Initial Reports of States Parties. It places these in context of key comments, decisions and reports of other treaties bodies and relevant United Nations bodies.

The handbook also provides a concise description of the role, powers and procedures, and developing activities of the Committee. Appendices include a guide to United Nations bodies and the text of key international instruments.

Language of the text: English

ISBN 92-806-3337-6

ILO-IPEC

CHILD LABOUR: AN INFORMATION KIT FOR TEACHERS, EDUCATORS AND THEIR ORGANIZATIONS

Geneva, 1998

The kit provides information about child labour for teachers, educators and their organizations to help them carry out actions and campaigns against child labour, particularly in developing countries. It contains facts and figures on child labour and presents a collection of successful initiatives from 13 countries. It also illustrates the role of education in the elimination of child labour and shows how various groups have worked to solve child labour problems through educational programmes.

The kit also contains posters, pedagogical tools, and a film on child labour which highlights health hazards, law and rights of children, the roles of educators and teachers, and networking with other actors in the field.

Language of the text: English, French, Spanish

ISBN 92-2-111040-0

ILO-IPEC

DESIGN, MANAGEMENT AND EVALUATION OF ACTION PROGRAMMES ON CHILD LABOUR

Geneva, 1994

This information kit and training package is the result of a collaborative effort between IPEC and the ILO's International Training Centre, Turin. Its objective is to help ILO constituents and NGOs design, implement and evaluate action programmes. The information kit consists of:

◆ an information booklet on action for the elimination of child labour: "Overview of the problem and response";

◆ the IPEC Strategy Paper: "Strategy into action – A guide to planning action programmes under IPEC 1994-95";

◆ a video programme: "ILO's action for the elimination of child labour"; and

◆ a poster.

The training package on "Design, management and evaluation of action programmes on child labour", is made up of the following modules:

◆ Module 1:   Situation analysis: Finding out about child labour

◆ Module 2:   Design of action programmes

◆ Module 3:   Starting and managing IPEC action programmes

◆ Module 4:   Monitoring and evaluation of IPEC action programmes.

Each module has been further subdivided into a series of training units supported by appropriate training elements (exercises, case studies and transparencies to help the trainer).

Language of the text: English

ISBN 92-2-109620-3

Michele JANKANISH
ILO-Working Conditions and Environment Department

ABOLISHING EXTREME FORMS OF CHILD LABOUR

Geneva, 1998, 23p. plus 24 loose-leaf p.

The briefing kit contains key information on proposed ILO standards on child labour, extreme forms of child labour and examples of action taken against them. It includes a 23-page article plus 24 coloured loose-leaf pages, each on a different specific theme, including children in hazardous work, slavery and prostitution. The text of proposed conclusions which served as a basis for discussions by the International Labour Conference during its 86th Session in 1998 is also included. The main article describes the major issues that were likely to be debated during the Conference.

Language of the text: English, French, Spanish

ISBN 92-2-111112-1
ISBN 92-2-109584-3

ILO-IPEC

TARGETING THE INTOLERABLE: A NEW INTERNATIONAL CONVENTION TO ELIMINATE THE WORST FORMS OF CHILD LABOUR

Geneva, 1999; press kit

This press kit consists of a series of leaflets on Convention No. 182 and Recommendation No. 190 concerning the prohibition and immediate elimination of the worst forms of child labour, adopted by the International Labour Conference in 1999. It contains details of these new instruments, as well as facts and figures on child labour as a whole, and on its worst forms, in different sectors and industries. It also covers the activities of the ILO's International Programme on the Elimination of Child Labour (IPEC), national action and action by employers, and the Global March on Child Labour.

Language of the text: English

ISBN 92-2-111669-7

Audiovisual materials

ILO

CHILD LABOUR IN SIALKOT, PAKISTAN

Geneva, 1998, 8:30 minutes

This videotape reveals the nature of the hand-stitched football production line. Four out of every five footballs are produced in Sialkot, where whole families, including children, huddle together on the floor of their one-room homes. It is a craft that has been practised and perfected for over a century.

The video documents efforts to eliminate child labour and provide children with educational programmes. To make sure that no child labour is used in the making of footballs, large suppliers decided to take control of the entire assembly process. They eliminated the subcontractor who acts as middleman between the supplier and the stitcher. The Sialkot Chamber of Commerce, together with the ILO and other agencies, persuaded smaller manufacturers to set up centres where the stitching of footballs could take place and workers could be monitored.

Available in English and French

ILO

UN IN ACTION. FEATURETTES ON CHILD LABOUR

Geneva, 1998 (3-4 minutes)

The features portray child labour situations around the world and show – either at a political, technical or field level – action to eradicate child exploitation. Main themes covered are: child labour in mines, domestic service, and agriculture; sexual exploitation of children; and street children. Designed for television broadcast, the featurettes also serve as a helpful "curtain raiser" for seminars, round tables and meetings. This audiovisual material is available in VHS format, in PAL and NTSC versions.

Available in English. International version without narration also available.

Miguel SCHAPIRA (director)
ILO-IPEC

CHILD LABOUR: THE DESPAIR AND THE HOPE

Geneva, 1998, 8 min

This videotape not only presents footage of children working in hazardous and degrading jobs, but also illustrates the work of the ILO to eliminate child labour. It highlights the aims of the International Programme on the Elimination of Child Labour (IPEC) and shows IPEC in action in several countries, including Kenya, Thailand, Bangladesh and Pakistan.

Available in English, French, Spanish, German, Japanese and Italian.

VHS PAL:	ISBN 92-2-110373-0
VHS NTSC:	ISBN 92-2-110374-9

Miguel SCHAPIRA (director)
ILO

I AM A CHILD!

Geneva, 1996, 52 min.

In this videotape, working children speak of their plight. Examples from around the world are shown of the hazardous conditions in which children labour. Government officials explain how the situation is being fought in their country.

Through compelling images and moving personal stories, the viewer discovers children working in Kenya in fields and plantations, as domestic servants and on the street; in agriculture, workshops and charcoal production in Brazil; and in sweatshops and brothels in Thailand. The videotape also shows the work of IPEC in preventing and eliminating such child labour and in helping the children involved to a better life.

A short version – seven minutes – prepared for the International Labour Conference in June 1998, is also available in English, French and Spanish.

Available in English, French, Spanish, German, Japanese and Italian.

English	VHS PAL:	ISBN 92-2-110373-0
	VHS NTSC:	ISBN 92-2-110374-9
French	VHS SECAM:	ISBN 92-2-210373-4
Spanish	VHS PAL:	ISBN 92-2-313073-8
	VHS NTSC:	ISBN 92-2-310374-6
German	VHS PAL:	ISBN 92-2-710373-2
Japanese	VHS NTSC:	ISBN 92-2-810373-6

UNICEF

THE STATE OF THE WORLD'S CHILDREN 1997: CHILD LABOUR

New York, 1997, 28:30 minutes

The half-hour programme features testimonials from working children – bonded child labourers in India's cigarette industry, street beggars in Senegal, and under-age garment workers in Bangladesh. Stories illustrate the appalling conditions faced by millions of children around the world each day. Designed for television broadcast and educational screenings, the programme serves as a companion piece to *The State of the World's Children 1997* report on child labour, published by UNICEF.

Address requests to: UNICEF House, 3 United Nations Plaza, New York, NY 10017, United States. Tel: (212) 326 7290, Fax: (212) 326 7731.

Available in English, French and Spanish.

UNICEF/ILO, (International Conference on Child Labour, Oslo, October 1997)

VIDEOTAPE FOOTAGE

The footage is in three parts:

1. Images of hazardous child labour around the world

2. Four feature stories on child labour:
    1. Bangladesh: Beauty's story
    2. Kenya: A day in the life of Christine
    3. Colombia: Rescued from the coal mines
    4. Thailand: Girls warned against sex trade

3. Interview excerpts:

    Carol Bellamy, Executive Director, UNICEF
    Ali Taqi, Assistant Director-General, ILO

Address requests to: UNICEF House, 3 United Nations Plaza, New York, NY 10017, United States. Tel: (212) 326 7290, Fax: (212) 326 7731.

10.2   SPECIAL THEMES

Richard ANKER & Helina MELKAS
ILO-Labour Market Policies Branch

ECONOMIC INCENTIVES FOR CHILDREN AND FAMILIES TO ELIMINATE OR REDUCE CHILD LABOUR

Geneva, 1996, ILO, 60p.

The task of eliminating child labour is not simple in low-income countries, where poverty often makes child labour necessary for families. This report helps to fill a gap in the knowledge in this area by investigating the effectiveness of policies and programmes that rely on economic incentives to eliminate child labour. It is based on an experimental survey, which collected information from those now implementing economic incentive programmes (mostly, but not exclusively, specialist NGOs).

Language of the text: English

ISBN 92-2-110285-8

Kritaya ARCHAVANITKUL
Institute for Population and Social Research, Mahidol University/ILO-IPEC

TRAFFICKING IN CHILDREN FOR LABOUR EXPLOITATION INCLUDING CHILD PROSTITUTION IN THE MEKONG SUB-REGION

Thailand, July 1998, 97p.

This subregional report provides an overview and synthesis of the problem of trafficking in children in the Mekong subregion, which covers Yunnan province in China, Myanmar (or Burma), Lao People's Democratic Republic (Lao PDR), Thailand, Cambodia, and Viet Nam. Four research teams were involved: one team each to cover Viet Nam, Yunnan (China), and Cambodia; the Thailand team also covered Lao PDR and Myanmar. The report presents a synthesis of the findings. Separate country reports are available, and summaries of the Cambodia, Viet Nam and Yunnan studies can be found in the appendices.

The research was not confined to trafficked children only, but also involved victims who were trafficked when they were younger. Practices related to trafficking in young women were also explored. In addition, information was obtained from key informants such as children's parents, children's employers, and government and NGO staff dealing with child trafficking.

Language of the text: English

Kebebew ASHAGRIE
ILO

IMPROVING THE KNOWLEDGE BASE ON CHILD LABOUR

Geneva, February 1998, 25p. & four appendices

This report has two objectives: first, to describe briefly the lack of meaningful statistical data on child labour at the individual country level, the reasons for this deficiency, and the efforts made recently by the ILO to develop, through field experiments in a number of countries, methodologies, concepts, definitions, classifications, etc., which assist in quantifying the child labour phenomenon in all its facets. Second, it provides detailed descriptions on the more suitable methodological approaches, as well as technical guidelines for determining the extent, character, causes and consequences of child labour by means of surveys and other inquiries at the national level.

Language of the text: English

Kebebew ASHAGRIE

ILO-METHODOLOGICAL CHILD LABOUR SURVEY AND STATISTICS: ILO'S RECENT WORK IN BRIEF

Geneva, June 1997, 19p. & three appendices

The report provides descriptions of the ILO methodological surveys experimented in four countries, the survey instruments and the variables used, the lessons learned from the exercise, the effectiveness of the different methodological approaches, concepts and definitions tested. It contains the conclusions and recommendations made by the ILO inter-regional seminar of child labour specialists who met for a week and examined critically the findings of the experiments. It also outlines the statistical work to be undertaken by the ILO in the near future, including national surveys in some 40 countries over a five-year period. The appendices provide some of the highlights of the overall findings of the experimental surveys in the four countries.

Language of the text: English

Kebebew ASHAGRIE

ILO-STATISTICS ON WORKING CHILDREN AND HAZARDOUS CHILD LABOUR IN BRIEF

Geneva, April 1998, 15p.

This report presents the statistical data assembled to date by the ILO concerning child labour at the global level and regionally, with total figures broken down by sex. It describes briefly, and depicts graphically, the overall picture of the child labour situation in regions, rural and urban areas, and in major industry divisions and occupational groups. It provides information on the working conditions of working children by analysing hours worked and earnings. It contains more detailed descriptions of hazardous child labour – again in words and graphically – by industry, occupation and sex, thereby identifying the types and severity of injuries and illnesses suffered by children. It also contains a fact sheet showing some indicators of the extent of child labour in the countries where national surveys have been conducted recently using the newly developed ILO methodologies.

Language of the text: English

Kebebew ASHAGRIE
ILO-*Bulletin of Labour Statistics*

STATISTICS ON CHILD LABOUR: A BRIEF REPORT

Geneva, 1993, No. 3, p.11-24

This article is a brief evaluation of the data assembled to date relating to child labour. It describes the concepts, definitions and methods used for collecting and cross-classifying the relevant statistics, including analyses of regional and subregional response patterns and data quality. It also provides an outline of the activities being pursued for improving and expanding the data.

Language of the text: English, French, Spanish

ISSN 0007-4950

Saeed A. AWAN
Directorate of Labour Welfare, Punjab (Pakistan)/ILO-IPEC

CHILD LABOUR IN THE FOOTBALL MANUFACTURING INDUSTRY

December 1996, 78p.

This study was undertaken by the Directorate of Labour Welfare Punjab, to assess the magnitude and dimensions of child labour in the football industry. It is intended to: (i) provide comprehensive data on the problem, with an emphasis on the working conditions of the child workers; their wages and working hours; habits, hopes, fears and aspirations; and the views of the parents and employers, and (ii) formulate an action-orientated approach to the elimination of child labour in this sector of the economy.

Language of the text: English

Saeed A. AWAN
Directorate of Labour Welfare, Punjab (Pakistan)/ILO-IPEC

CHILD LABOUR IN THE SURGICAL INSTRUMENTS MANUFACTURING INDUSTRY

December 1996, 81p.

This study was carried out to provide vital data to policy makers, individuals and organizations interested in the welfare of working children. It is an example of cooperation between government and international organizations in assessing the dimensions and finding solutions to the complex social problems related to child labour.

Language of the text: English

Maggie BLACK
ANTI-SLAVERY INTERNATIONAL

CHILD DOMESTIC WORKERS.
A HANDBOOK FOR RESEARCH AND ACTION

London, 1996

This study stemmed not only from a deep concern about exploitative child labour in general, but from the terms of employment, the ways in which children are placed in exploitative work in the informal sector and in particular the way in which children typically enter domestic work. Child domestic labour contractual and practical characteristics have features akin to slavery. A child employed in a private household may be unpaid; be expected to work around the clock without set hours or time off; and be virtually imprisoned and treated as the chattel of the employer.

In January 1996, at the invitation of ASI and with IPEC support, a seminar was convened for researchers from all over the world. The purpose was to gain insights for the development of the research guidelines contained in this handbook. The handbook, therefore, offers a practical approach to research that will inspire other child labour NGOs to enter the field, along with workers' and employers' organizations and relevant government departments.

Language of the text: English

ISBN 0900918-411

Maggie BLACK
ILO-Child Labour Collection

IN THE TWILIGHT ZONE: CHILD WORKERS IN THE HOTEL, TOURISM AND CATERING INDUSTRY

Geneva, 1995, 92p.

This report challenges a number of assumptions about the involvement of children in the tourist industry. It is based on four studies carried out by the ILO in Kenya, Mexico, the Philippines and Sri Lanka, which investigated the conditions of child work in hotels, clubs and restaurants, the relevant laws and their enforcement, and programmatic and project action. It also highlights the problems of inadequate data and the distorting effect of sensationalist reporting on the subject of child sex. Many of the girls usually described as child prostitutes by journalists are actually working in the twilight zone of the tourist industry rather than in brothels. The tourist industry, as a sector characterized by low pay, irregularity of work and lack of skills, favours the employment of under-age workers.

The author argues that a better understanding is needed of the dynamics surrounding the employment and career paths of these young people, especially of girls.

Language of the text: English

ISBN 92-2-109194-5

Catherine BOIDIN
ILO-Labour Administration Branch Document No. 42

LABOUR INSPECTION AND THE ADOPTION OF A POLICY ON CHILD LABOUR. The working child: psycho-sociological approach

Geneva, 1995, 102p.

The document emphasizes risk factors in the psychological and social well-being of working children and the different forms of violence exerted on them; it proposes a training method to interview working children. It is designed for trainers responsible for the training of labour inspectors and others in order to elaborate a coherent policy. As part of ILO action for the training of labour inspectors, it constitutes the second part of a series which began with a training guide, first published in 1994.

Language of the text: English, French, Spanish

ISBN 92-2-209539-1

Regeringskansliets Offsetcentral

REPORT OF THE WORLD CONGRESS AGAINST COMMERCIAL SEXUAL EXPLOITATION OF CHILDREN

Stockholm 1996, two volumes, Part I: 267p.; Part II: 255 p.

The Congress was held in Stockholm in August 1996. Part I consists of a chapter on the adoption of the Declaration and Agenda for Action (which is described in detail), as well as chapters on the organization and running of the Congress. Annexes list participants and reprint the keynote speeches by co-organizer ECPAT (End Child Prostitution in Asian Tourism) and other NGOs and United Nations agencies, reports from panels and workshops, and concluding remarks by the Rapporteur. Part II consists entirely of statements by Heads of State.

In the Declaration and Agenda for Action, the Congress called on all States to criminalize, among others, the commercial exploitation of children, to enforce laws, and to promote action with society to prevent children from entering the sex trade.

There were 1,300 participants from more than 130 countries, including youth from eight countries.

Language of the text: English

Panudda BOONPALA
ILO-IPEC

STRATEGY AND ACTION AGAINST THE COMMERCIAL SEXUAL EXPLOITATION OF CHILDREN

Stockholm, Sweden, 1996, 15p.

This report was prepared for the World Congress against the Commercial Sexual Exploitation of Children, held in Stockholm to generate discussion and to encourage partner organizations to develop action programmes.

It gives an overview of the problem and analyses the causes of child prostitution and trafficking, with the consequences and effects; it also provides an outline of international labour and human rights standards, an update on developments in international labour legislation and the IPEC action, including new initiatives carried out in various countries. The annex contains a resolution concerning the elimination of child labour, which was submitted to the Congress.

Language of the text: English

Jo BOYDEN
UNICEF ICDC. Innocenti Occasional Paper, Child Rights Series 9

THE RELATIONSHIP BETWEEN EDUCATION AND CHILD WORK

Florence, 1994, 52p.

This paper argues that making education compulsory cannot alone remove all the social and economic obstacles that keep children out of work and at school. Education, however, will have an important impact on full-time work, although children will continue to combine work and school. It points out that while work can cause children to drop out from school, school also causes them to work in order to pay for tuition, books and uniforms. It also notes the poor quality of schools, which limits enrolment. Gender differences in level of work and educational participation are significant, with girls working longer hours and attending schools less. Genuine reform will come only as governments increase resource allocations to primary education and support school reform measures such as greater flexibility of scheduling, and curricula and teaching methods better suited to low-income children and their families. Education is only part of the answer, and multi-sectoral governmental interventions to relieve the economic and social burden of poor families are also required.

Language of text: English

ISSN 1014-7837

Jean-Maurice DERRIEN
ILO-Labour Administration Branch

LABOUR INSPECTION AND THE ADOPTION OF A POLICY ON CHILD LABOUR. Training guide

Geneva, 1994, Document No.36, 182p.

The guide is designed for training labour inspectors and other persons concerned with the problems of child labour, and for formulating a coherent and concerted national policy on child labour. There are three modules comprising a progressive training programme of methods for resolving problems related to child labour: identification of the problem (Module 1: Watching and listening); evaluation of its gravity (Module 2: Evaluating and understanding); and the determination of the most adequate solutions for an efficient action programme (Module 3: Taking action and educating). A bibliography of documents published by the ILO and other organizations is included.

Language of the text : English, French, Spanish

ISBN 92-2-209145-0 (English)

Judith ENNEW
UNICEF ICDC

LEARNING OR LABOURING? A compilation of key texts on child work and basic education

Florence, 1995, 152p.

This is a compilation of extracts from essential reference works on child labour and basic education, divided into four main areas: ideas, debates, evidence and case studies. It includes a discussion of the nature of childhood, work, exploitation and education; the relationship between compulsory education and elimination of child labour; descriptions of child labour in Ghana, Nigeria, Peru, India, the United States and Colombia; the relationship between school and work; and case studies on education and experimental approaches.

Language of the text: English

ISBN 88-85401-20-1

Valentina FORASTIERI
ILO-Occupational Safety and Health Branch

CHILDREN AT WORK. HEALTH AND SAFETY RISKS

Geneva, 1997, 138p.

In order to fill the gap in information on the health of working children, this report provides an assessment of available information and discusses existing legislation, statistics, case studies on children's actual working conditions in selected occupations and their impact on children's health. A possible approach to a national policy for the elimination of child labour is also discussed. In this context, the development of a programme on occupational safety and health is proposed to address working children. Insights are provided into technical instruments and their application to the evaluation of the damage caused to the physical and mental health of children in various jobs. Methodological tools on occupational safety and primary health care, which could be adapted to address the health status of working children for preventive and control purposes, are examined in the annexes.

Language of the text: English

ISBN 92-2-109520-7

Alec FYFE
ILO-Bureau of Workers' Activities

BITTER HARVEST. CHILD LABOUR IN AGRICULTURE

Geneva, 1996, 24p.

Informative and action oriented, the booklet conveys a clear and comprehensive message to raise awareness on the risks working children in agriculture face. The central question, "What can rural workers and their organizations do?", finds guidance and support in the substantial richness of information and suggestions.

Alec FYFE & Michele JANKANISH
ILO-Child Labour Collection

TRADE UNIONS AND CHILD LABOUR: A GUIDE TO ACTION

Geneva, 1997, 108p.

The authors explore the numerous possibilities for trade union action against child labour at local, national and international levels. The guide also illustrates what can be achieved by presenting a variety of innovative approaches currently taken by workers' organizations. To assist trade unions in their policy and action to combat child labour, the guide also sets out and elaborates upon a ten-step framework of action for trade unions, consisting of investigation; institutional development; policy development; monitoring; awareness-raising; compaigning; collective bargaining; direct support to working children; mobilization; and utilizing the supervisory machinery of international instruments.

Language of the text: English

ISBN 92-2-109514-2

S. GOONESEKERE
ILO-Child Labour Collection

CHILD LABOUR IN SRI LANKA: LEARNING FROM THE PAST

Geneva, 1993, 77p.

This report focuses on government measures to eliminate the employment of children in Sri Lanka, where child labour is frequently exploitative in nature, characterized by poor wages and dangerous working conditions, and occurs in workplaces completely lacking in workers' rights and labour organization. The author analyses past experiences and existing legislative provisions to seek to demonstrate how collaborative efforts on the part of the Government, non-governmental organizations and international agencies could lead to innovative approaches to the problem. The author argues that absolute prohibition of the employment of children should be the ultimate goal of such policy measures.

Language of the text: English

ISBN 92-2-106473-5

S. GUNN and Z. OSTOS
ILO-*International Labour Review*, Vol. 131, No. 6

DILEMMAS IN TACKLING CHILD LABOUR: THE CASE OF SCAVENGER CHILDREN IN THE PHILIPPINES

Geneva, 1992, 18p.

This report of a pilot ILO child labour project describes an example of child labour in the informal sector – child scavengers. It reviews various policy and programme dilemmas encountered in addressing the problem at the enormous Philippine garbage dump known as Smokey Mountain. It shows that a multi-pronged approach beginning with highly targeted research is crucial and provides an example of how this can be done. It concludes with an assessment of the lessons learned from the project and suggests components for future effective urban child labour programmes.

Language of the text: English, French and Spanish

English	ISSN 0020-7780
French	ISSN 0378-5599
Spanish	ISSN 0378-5548

Het Spinhuis Publications, Amsterdam

CHILD HEALTH AND CHILD LABOUR: FROM INFORMATION TO INTERVENTION

Amsterdam, 1999, 63p.

The Netherlands Foundation for International Child Health (NFICH) and the Amsterdam Foundation for International Research on the Exploitation of Working Children (IREWOC) initiated in 1997 a meeting of international experts from different disciplines to elaborate on possible interventions to improve the health situation of working children. This book is the result of this two-day international seminar attended by representatives from a number of organizations, including the ILO, WHO, UNICEF, NOVIB, Terre des Hommes, Anti-Slavery International and SCF. New ways of intervention and regulation are pointed out, and the need for a participatory community-based approach is highlighted.

Language of the text: English

ISBN 90-5589-117-7

ILO

ATTACKING CHILD LABOUR IN THE PHILIPPINES. AN INDICATIVE FRAMEWORK FOR PHILIPPINE-ILO ACTION

Geneva, 1994, 28p.

This report reflects the outcome of the National Planning Workshop on Child Labour, held in Manila in July 1994. The workshop brought together representatives of a wide range of government institutions and NGOs, local government officials and academics from Manila and the provinces. It is meant to be used in developing policies, programmes and strategies, and contains information regarding children who are victims of trafficking; children employed in mining and quarrying; children in home-based industries, especially under subcontracting arrangements; and children trapped in prostitution.

The report also indicates the partners active in the struggle against child labour, as well as the priority areas for action.

Language of the text: English

ILO-*Conditions of Work Digest*

CHILD LABOUR: LAW AND PRACTICE

Geneva, 1991, Volume 10, No. 1, 225p.

This issue of the *Conditions of Work Digest* provides a factual and analytical review of the law and practice on child labour throughout the world. It contains a fact sheet summarizing legal provisions on minimum ages for work, including light and hazardous work, and selected provisions of the relevant international labour standards and other instruments on children. It also includes analytical chapters on national policies and legislation, and enforcement and implementation of international labour Conventions on child labour.

Language of the text : English

ISBN 92-2-107751-9

ILO (ILO-GB.267/WP/SDL/2)

REPORT OF THE ORGANIZATION FOR ECONOMIC COOPERATION AND DEVELOPMENT (OECD) ON TRADE, EMPLOYMENT AND LABOUR STANDARDS

Geneva, November 1996, 22p.

This report to the ILO Governing Body gives a summary of an OECD study of trade and labour standards, finalized in May 1996 and submitted to the Ministers of the OECD at their meeting in the same month. It covers three majors themes and identifies a small set of labour standards, which it describes as core standards, including the elimination of child labour and the prohibition of forced labour.

The report reviews the links between certain core labour standards, trade, investment and economic development. In the final part, it discusses the effectiveness of a number of mechanisms that are either already operational or could be introduced to promote respect for these core standards.

Language of the text: English, French, Spanish

International Organisation of Employers (IOE) in collaboration with ILO/IPEC

EMPLOYERS' HANDBOOK ON CHILD LABOUR: A GUIDE FOR TAKING ACTION

Geneva, 1998, 65p.

The purpose of the handbook is to guide national employers' federations in the formulation of policies and programmes to actively join national and international coalitions against child labour. It offers guidance in the design of employer programmes on child labour, and illustrates some of the various actions which national employers' federations and sectoral business associations have already taken. Practical information is included on the following subjects:

◆ content of international standards;

◆ explanation of existing international programmes;

◆ examples of concrete action taken by national employers' organizations;

◆ examples of corporate and sectoral initiatives;

◆ description of various codes of conduct and labelling initiatives; and

◆ guidance in the development of policies and programmes.

For more information, contact the International Organisation of Employers: 26 chemin de Joinville, Case Postale 68, CH-1216 Cointrin/Geneva. Telephone: +41 22 798 1616, Fax: : +41 22 798 8862

Text available in English, French, Spanish.

ILO

INTERNATIONAL LABOUR STANDARDS A WORKERS' EDUCATION MANUAL

Fourth edition (revised)

Geneva, 1998, 148 p.

This book provides a brief but thorough introduction to the formulation, adoption and application of internationally agreed standards of good practice in labour matters – international labour Conventions and Recommendations – and has been updated to cover developments up to mid-1997. By 1997, the ILO had adopted 181 international labour Conventions and 188 Recommendations on all aspects of the world of work. The most comprehensive child labour Convention is the Minimum Age Convention, 1973 (No. 138) How are these standards elaborated and how is their application ensured ?

The manual is intended for trade unionists, students and the general reader interested in labour matters, social issues and human rights. It is designed for use in workers' education courses as well as for individual study.

Language of the text: English and French

ISBN 92-2-110330-7

ILO-IPEC

N. HASPELS, F. DE LOS ANGELES-BAUTISTA, P. BOONPALA, and C. BOSE

ACTION AGAINST CHILD LABOUR: STRATEGIES IN EDUCATION. COUNTRY EXPERIENCES IN THE MOBILIZATION OF TEACHERS, EDUCATORS AND THEIR ORGANIZATIONS IN COMBATING CHILD LABOUR

Geneva, forthcoming, 118p.

In 1995, IPEC launched a project, "Mobilizing Teachers, Educators and their Organizations in Combating Child Labour", in cooperation with UNICEF, UNESCO and Education International, the international organization representing trade unions and professional associations of teachers and educational personnel, with the financial support of the Norwegian Government. The objectives were to identify "best practices" worldwide on how to promote education as a major strategy in the elimination of child labour and on how to further mobilize teachers, educators and their organizations in the fight against it. This synthesis report summarizes the outcome of action research in 13 countries in Africa, Asia and Latin America which identified how educational initiatives have been instrumental in combating child labour at local and national levels. Consensus on the research findings and recommendations was reached during a Round Table Meeting on Education and Child Labour held in May 1997.

The report aims to provide guidance and models for future action to teachers, educators, their organizations and policy-makers on how to combat child labour more effectively through education. It analyses where, why and how education has been successful in keeping children in school and out of the workplace, and in meeting the needs of children who are still working. It also identifies strategies for further addressing child labour concerns in educational policies and programmes.

Language of the text: English

ILO-IPEC

ALTERNATIVES TO CHILD LABOUR: A REVIEW OF ACTION PROGRAMMES WITH A SKILLS TRAINING COMPONENT IN ASIA

Bangkok, 1998, 43p.

This report reflects the results of a thematic evaluation of action programmes with a skills training component in Asia. The evaluation reviewed 19 action programmes in Bangladesh, India, Indonesia, Pakistan and Thailand.

Language of the text: English

ILO-IPEC. Technical Workshop on Child Labour

CHILD LABOUR IN COMMERCIAL AGRICULTURE IN AFRICA

Geneva, 1997, 58p.

The report reviews the Technical Workshop on Child Labour in Commercial Agriculture, held in Dar-es-Salaam, United Republic of Tanzania, in August 1996, organized by the ILO-IPEC. The objectives were to elaborate a programme of action on practical and feasible priority measures to remove children from hazardous and exploitative tasks, improve working conditions of children in commercial agriculture in African countries, and ultimately eliminate such forms of employment.

The report summarizes the six working papers which were prepared for the workshop, and contains the Programme of Action adopted by the participants. The annexes include the proceedings of the workshop, the list of participants and the programme of the workshop, the opening speeches and the closing statements.

Language of the text: English

ISBN 92-2 110485-0

ILO-IPEC

CHILD LABOUR SURVEYS. Results of methodological experiments in four countries 1992-93

Geneva, Bureau of Statistics, 1996, 83p.

In 1993, in an effort to improve the production of quantitative and qualitative data on child labour, which were lacking in the majority of the countries concerned by this problem, IPEC, in collaboration with the respective national statistical institutions, carried out experimental surveys in Ghana, India, Indonesia, and Senegal. The aim was to test a specially designed methodology measuring children's activities as schooling and out-of-school work affecting the 5-14 age groups. The surveys were administered at household and enterprise level and among street children (in Ghana), in both urban and rural areas.

The publication is aimed at assisting each country in the collection of reliable detailed data on child labour, necessary for planning national action. It provides survey instruments and findings, the problems the surveys encounter, references and recommended survey approaches (in an annex).

Language of the text : English

ISBN 92-2-110106-1

ILO-*Labour Education*. Bureau for Workers' Activities

PROTECTING CHILDREN IN THE WORLD OF WORK

Geneva 1997, No. 108, 59p.

The ILO Bureau for Workers' Activities devoted this edition of its quarterly publication to child labour on the eve of the Oslo International Conference on Child Labour, held in October 1997. It was specifically addressed to trade union organizations with the aim of contributing to a fruitful exchange of ideas among workers and their counterparts attending the Conference, and at the same time was meant to inspire awareness and action to combat child labour both at a national and international level.

Language of the text: English, French, Spanish, Italian

ISSN 0378-5467

ILO-*Labour Education*. Bureau for Workers' Activities

TRADE UNIONS AND CHILD LABOUR

Geneva, 1996, No. 102, 57p.

This issue of *Labour Education* aims to contribute to promoting awareness among trade unions on the problem of child labour as part of the general effort the ILO is undertaking to eliminate this social evil.

It is divided in two parts: the editorial, comprising eight articles, which gives an indication of the actual extent of the problem; and the appendices, composed of texts of the major ILO Conventions and Recommendations, as well as non-ILO treaties relevant to child labour.

Language of the text: English, French, Spanish

ISSN 0378-5467

ILO

ILOLEX on CD-ROM. A database of international labour standards
1998 edition

ILOLEX is a full-text trilingual database (English/French/Spanish) on international labour standards, including those on child labour, with sophisticated search and retrieval functions. A single CD-ROM contains all three language versions.

Each language version includes, among others, the ILO Constitution; all ILO Conventions and Recommendations; comments of the Committee of Experts on the Application of Conventions and Recommendations and reports of the Conference Committee on the Application of Standards, from 1987; and ratification lists by Convention and by country.

The whole database can be searched by subject classification, country, particular Convention, or free text query using words or expressions.

DOS version ISBN 92-2-010608-6

Windows version ISBN 92-2-010604-3

ILO-UNITED NATIONS CENTRE FOR HUMAN RIGHTS

CHILDREN IN BONDAGE. A CALL FOR ACTION

Geneva, 1992, 66p.

The publication provides an overview of the problem of child bondage and suggests measures which can be carried out to combat it. It is based on the proceedings of the Asian Regional Seminar on Children in Bondage held in Islamabad, Pakistan, organized by ILO-IPEC in collaboration with the Ministry of Labour, Manpower and Overseas Pakistanis and the United Nations Centre for Human Rights. The Programme of Action against Child Bondage formulated and adopted by the participants was intended to encourage and assist governments, workers' and employers' organizations, lawyers and judges, and NGOs to take concrete and concerted action.

Language of the text : English

ISBN 92-2-108724-7

D. LEVISON, R. ANKER, S. ASHRAF & S. BARGE
ILO-Employment Department. Labour Market Papers 15

IS CHILD LABOUR REALLY NECESSARY IN INDIA'S CARPET INDUSTRY ?

Geneva, 1996, 33p.

The study – which surveys 362 carpet-weaving enterprises in India – differs from previous studies of child labour by considering child activities from the perspective of the industry (labour demand) rather than from the perspective of the child and his or her family (labour supply). It describes how children work in the "Carpet Belt" of the northern state of Uttar Pradesh and examines how indispensable children are in this industry because of the relative cost advantage of using child labour. It also dismisses as entirely fallacious the "nimble finger" argument to justify child labour in the industry, as it finds that children are not more likely than adults to make the finest knots. The sample survey of enterprises is supplemented with in-depth case studies of employers, exporters, and American importers.

The report contains a thorough bibliography, two appendices – one on measures of carpet quality and working conditions, and the other on the United States case study of carpet importers and retailers – and economic data tables.

Language of the text: English

ISBN 92-2-110205-X

ISSN 1020-2633

Ministry of Women and Social Welfare (MOWSW), Nepal and ILO-IPEC

NATIONAL PLAN OF ACTION AGAINST TRAFFICKING OF CHILDREN AND THEIR COMMERCIAL SEXUAL EXPLOITATION

Nepal 1998, 19 p.

The document describes the outcome of the National Consultative Workshop, held in Kathmandu in April 1998. After detailing the National Plan and the commitment of His Majesty's Government in action against trafficking, the paper details the initiatives already taken to confront the problem, including the formation of the Council for Women and Children's Development in 1995. Subsequent chapters address policy, research and institutional development; legislation and law enforcement; awareness creation, advocacy, networking, and social mobilization; health and education; income and employment generation; and, finally, rescue and reintegration. Each chapter has its objective, priority, programme activities and actors summarized in tabular form in an appendix.

Language of the text: English

National Commission on Women's Affairs, Office of the Prime Minister, Thailand

NATIONAL POLICY AND PLAN OF ACTION FOR THE PREVENTION AND ERADICATION OF THE COMMERCIAL SEXUAL EXPLOITATION OF CHILDREN

Thailand. 1996, 37p.

The Government of Thailand, through the Office of the National Commission on Women's Affairs (ONCWA), has prepared a Master Plan of Action to deal with the issues raised by the commercial sexual exploitation of children. Many were involved in the preparation of this plan, including representatives from NGOs, planning and policy bodies, academics and researchers, officers from concerned government departments, representatives from UNICEF and other international organizations. The key strategy is built on five structural pillars: prevention; law enforcement; assistance and protection; rehabilitation and adjustment to normal life; and establishment of structures, mechanisms and systems for supervision, control, follow-up and speeding up of the implementation.

Language of the text: English

David PARKER
UNICEF, Innocenti Occasional Papers, Child Rights Series, Number 6

RESOURCES AND CHILD RIGHTS: AN ECONOMIC PERSPECTIVE

Florence, April 1994, 28p.

Several key measures are identified for increasing the availability of resources for the implementation of child rights: budgets can be restructured; non-traditional human and organizational resources can be mobilized; technologies and processes can be made more efficient; critical input can be made available; and targeting can be improved to increase equity. The paper concludes with a discussion of the changing economic and political roles of the different actors for the fulfilment of child rights, considering the responsibility for the financing of actions, the provision of services, and the management of social sectors.

Language of the text: English

ISSN 1014-7837

Loïc PICARD
ILO

COMBATING CHILD LABOUR: THE LEGAL FRAMEWORK

Geneva, 1995, 7p.

The author discusses a national policy against child labour and proposes guidelines for its operation. He also reviews provisions in international Conventions on child labour under the following categories: a minimum age for admission to employment or work; the regulation of child labour conditions; different sectors of economic activity; and jobs and work considered as hazardous.

Language of the text: English, French, Spanish

S. PARDOEN with R. ADI and H. PRASADJA
ILO-IPEC in cooperation with Atma Jaya Research Centre

CHILDREN IN HAZARDOUS WORK IN THE INFORMAL SECTOR IN INDONESIA

Geneva, 1996, 103p.

This book describes the working conditions of children who are employed in hazardous work in the informal sector in Indonesia. The study focuses in particular on children involved in *jermal* (fish-trapping) operations in North Sumatra, petty trading on the congested streets and intersections of Jakarta, scavenging at the major dump-sites in Bekasi, sea-fishing in Central Java, and deep-sea pearl diving in South-east Maluku. The study concludes with a list of recommendations regarding action that can and should be taken to address the problem of child labour in the informal sector in Indonesia.

There are photographs and health data tables throughout the text, and two appendices – a sample questionnaire for child workers and a model clinical examination scheme for child workers.

Language of the text: English

ISBN 979-8827-04-X

V. RIALP
ILO-Child Labour Collection

CHILDREN AND HAZARDOUS WORK IN THE PHILIPPINES

Geneva, 1993, 72p.

This report focuses on hazardous child labour in the Philippines, paying particular attention to efforts to eliminate child involvement in prostitution and deep-sea fishing. The historical change in emphasis in the Philippines from intervention through legislation to direct action at the local level is well documented. The study also highlights the important role of advocacy, public awareness-raising and community mobilization in the fight against child labour. The author argues that the complexity of the problem requires collaboration between different agencies, interest groups and the Government for effectively tackling the problem of child labour and instigating social change.

Language of the text: English

ISBN 92-2-106474-3

V. MUNTARBHORN
UNICEF

EXTRATERRITORIAL CRIMINAL LAWS AGAINST CHILD SEXUAL EXPLOITATION

Geneva, 1998, 126p.

Extraterritorial criminal laws on the sexual exploitation of children are increasingly important in an era when sex tourists and paedophiles can so easily travel to countries other than their own to abuse children. This study provides an analysis of the state of extraterritorial laws and their application. Through extensive research in a number of countries, the author analyses the practicability of such laws. The key findings are that extraterritorial criminal laws should be seen as a complement to rather than a substitute for the laws, policies and enforcement of the destination country; that at present there is no uniformity of extraterritorial criminal laws between countries; and that the presence of extraterritorial criminal laws is inadequate unless there is close cooperation between the countries of origin and the destination countries of the sex exploiters.

Language of the text: English

ISBN 92-806-3394-5

Christian ROOTAERT & Ravi KANBUR
ILO-*International Labour Review*

CHILD LABOUR: AN ECONOMIC PERSPECTIVE

Geneva, 1995, Volume 134, No. 2, p.187-203

Starting with the questions "what is a child ?" and "what is work ?", the authors review data on child labour. Focusing on its determinants, they examine supply factors at household level, including family size, education, wages and risk of income loss, and factors affecting demand, including technology. They argue that given the established link between poverty and child labour there are certain advantages in interventions to improve the lot of employed children even if these induce an increase in the supply of child workers. Economic incentives and legislation are the two pillars on which efforts to help working children should be based.

Language of the text: English, French, Spanish

ISSN 0020-7780

M.C. SALAZAR and W.A. GLASINOVICH (eds.)
UNICEF

CHILD WORK AND EDUCATION: FIVE CASE STUDIES FROM LATIN AMERICA

Ashgate Publishing Ltd, Aldershot, England, 1998, 162p.

This edited collection addresses the relationship between child work and education, through five case studies in Brazil, Colombia, Ecuador, Guatemala and Peru. The authors argue that child labour occurs not only as a result of economic need or exploitation, but as children drop out of school in favour of work due to the poor quality of schooling. The authors argue therefore that what is required when attempting to combat child labour is a major reform of the educational system, in particular improvements in coverage, quality and affordability of schooling. They also suggest that, in cases of severe hardship, subsidies and scholarships may need to be considered as incentives to children and their parents.

Language of the text: English

ISBN 1-80414-926-4

University Press, Amsterdam

HEALTH ASPECTS OF CHILD LABOUR – REPORT OF A WORKSHOP AND SYMPOSIUM

Kuala Lumpur, 1996

The Netherlands Foundation for International Child Health (NFICH) and the Foundation for International Research on the Exploitation of Working Children (IREWOC) joined in the initiative for a pre-congress Workshop on the Health Aspects of Child Labour at the 4th International Conference of Topical Priorities in Kuala Lumpur, Malaysia. Representatives from ILO, WHO and UNICEF were present.

The purpose was to present the available knowledge by experienced professionals and to invite improved cooperation between the parties involved.

Language of the text: English

ISBN 90-5383-531-8